History Maker

To Dad
Happy Christmas 2024
Love Simon

History Maker

Essays in honour of Brian Smith

Edited by Mark Smith and Ian Tait

The Shetland Times Ltd
Lerwick
2024

History Maker

First published by The Shetland Times, 2024.

ISBN 978-1-910997-59-8

Copyright © Mark Smith, Ian Tait and individual authors.

Mark Smith and Ian Tait have asserted their right under the Copyright, Designs and Patents Act 1988, to be identified as Author of this work.

All rights reserved. No part of this publication may be reproduced, stored in a retrieval system or transmitted, in any form, by any means, electronic, mechanical, photocopying, recording or otherwise without the prior written consent of the publishers.

A catalogue record for this book is available from the British Library.
British Library Cataloguing-in-Publication Data

Printed and Published by
The Shetland Times Ltd.,
Gremista, Lerwick,
Shetland ZE1 0PX.

Contents

Introduction
 by Angus Johnson ... vii

Proud towers to swift destruction doomed – some unresolved questions about brochs
 by Noel Fojut ... 1

Shetland: A Norse country between earls and kings
 by Steinar Imsen ... 14

Kebister – an ordinary and remarkable place
 by Olwyn Owen ... 28

Revisiting -staðir place-names in Shetland
 by Peder Gammeltoft ... 38

The Shetland verses in Orkneyinga Saga ch. 85
 by Judith Jesch ... 60

A parallel naming voyage through a familiar seascape
 by Andrew Jennings and Arne Kruse ... 70

Baliasta and Stembelshoull – two thing sites in the island of Unst
 by Alexandra Sanmark ... 88

Shetland's foreign trade before 1500
 by Mark Gardiner and Natascha Mehler ... 97

Earl Patrick's domra of Shetland in the name of the old law
 by Jørn Øyrehagen Sunde ... 107

Research into the destruction of the 17th century Broo township, Shetland Islands, through burial in aeolian sand: an update
 by Gerald F. Bigelow ... 116

The phonology of Shetland Norn – preaspiration and vowel length in Jakobsen's Etymological Dictionary
 by Remco Knooihuizen ... 138

Peer Gynt meets the Trow of Windhouse
 by Terry Gunnell ... 151

Genetic genealogy of Fair Isle – an extreme Northern Isles microcosm
 by James Flett Wilson 161

A Shetland witchcraft case: historical documents and oral tradition
 by Liv Helene Willumsen 174

James Loutit and Shetland Methodism
 by David Bebbington 183

'Is du da man?' – male violence and ritual in Shetland
 by Lynn Abrams and Callum G. Brown 194

Appendix: Works by Brian Smith (to date) 203

Index 213

Introduction

Angus Johnson
(Shetland Archives)

'What I am getting at is that I don't think that modern Shetland is a pale version of its glorious past. I don't believe that Shetlanders died spiritually when they decided to speak Scots or English, and I shall even argue that they made a rational and humane decision when they gave up caain whales.'

Brian Smith, 'Whale Driving in Shetland the Faroes',
Shetland Sea Mammal Report 2003.

I think I first heard of Brian Smith when I was at school. I'm sure we'd entered the new world of the Anderson High School extension, making it late 1977 or so. Brian had been appointed as County Archivist earlier, in 1976. A copy of the *The Shetland Times* prompted things on Friday – Brian was in the paper and a teacher remarked on it. I can't quote the remark precisely but it was to the effect that Brian was on the left, and would "stir things up." I'm not sure our class really knew much about archives at all though.

Since it was Friday I went home for the weekend. My father had seen *da paper* and wondered if Brian was the son of Bertie Smith. He was, and both Bertie and he had shared the same employer after the war, an ill-starred handloom weaving enterprise. My occasional discussions with Brian on weaving centre round short-time work and, frankly, poverty. At that time I thought all this was incidental, as I was on the university trajectory, going sooth and likely to stay there.

I didn't get away that easily. At Aberdeen University I met Dr J.R. Coull, a long-term Shetland fishery researcher, who used the archives for many years. He'd issued a reading list, including Brian's essay 'Lairds and Improvement in Shetland in the seventeenth and eighteenth centuries'. I'd read it with interest and pleasure. "He's a bit radical," remarked Dr Coull. In Shetland terms he certainly was. I hadn't seen a reference to Shetland historical studies having theories before, with one group of thinkers described as "anti-Scottish". I hadn't noticed that among all the background noise of the time. Shetland was a more interesting subject after reading Brian's essay. I'm certain I'm not the only person who's felt that after reading a piece by Brian.

I didn't have any occasion to use the archives during university. I read Brian in the *New Shetlander* magazine, or heard him on the radio. Radio Shetland and the archives are of roughly the same vintage, and once operated side by side in Brentham Place. These were new facilities in a Shetland changing before its inhabitants' eyes. Brian understood that people wouldn't always respond to the printed word, but often would to the spoken one. So he did talks, took part in discussion programmes, or appeared on the *Good Evening Shetland* broadcasts, with news from the archives, or an appeal for information. It still works for us. The station once ran *Da Week Dat's Awa*, five minutes of someone talking about what happened in their past week. Brian was a go-to person, who could be relied on having something to say. Often what was important to Brian was politics, so he spoke about it. Somebody once wrote to Radio Shetland's feedback spot, asking for someone who lived a more "normal life." Perhaps they missed the point – Brian's political goal was that everyone should have the chance of a normal, and decent life.

Brian opposed the Thatcherite politics of the 1980s, a time that had a kind of brutality for the youth, trying to score that elusive job. After a spell of post-graduate unemployment I met Brian and he gave me a job – a one year contract on an oral history project, funded by the Manpower Services Commission and the Shetland Amenity Trust. It was a good year. By that time the Archives had settled down in a former navigation classroom off King Harald Street. I didn't get to explore the Archives deeply but was aware it was a place where interesting people turned up, among them Dr T.M.Y. Manson, and the late Douglas Sinclair. They were encouraging and knowledgeable, and so was Brian.

It was a good time in the Archives, the project often contacting the victims of the last great depression in the 1930s, who also had to struggle through the difficult times of post-war Shetland. There was no doubt that the archives were run by someone who opposed the rightward lurches of our rulers. Brian's letters to the *Shetland Times* of that time, sometimes pungent and often provocative, would make an interesting little volume. People entering Brian's office would see placards in support of the Labour Party set by, evidence of support for CND, and obvious signs of trade union activism for the then public sector union NALGO. Brian has long been a very effective union representative. The encounters there merit another exploration entirely. It could come down to the person with the best knowledge of the law not being the person who graduated from a law faculty.

Margaret Thatcher spoke in favour of what she thought were Victorian values. The Archives collections thicken measurably through Victoria's reign, and the Poor Law documents are a treasure. Brian had a look in there, and wrote an essay about a pauper, Kirsty Caddell. Kirsty lived a precarious existence, and fell foul of a poor law inspector with a good twist in him. Denied relief, she died of hypothermia on the Lerwick Tollbooth stairs, her children present to boot. Kirsty was in the lowest strata of society, her fate decided by a comfortably-off middle class man, who did what he liked not what he was employed to do.

She got a death sentence; he got off with what he did, and continued to live in comfort.

Kirsty's story is a story of class, and how a human being can be ground beneath it. She made limited attempts at resistance, and getting above herself sealed her fate. Brian told her story grippingly and skillfully, a riposte to Thatcherite notions, complete with references to Charles Dickens' tale of Victorian hypocrisy and cant, *Hard Times*. It remains an affecting piece of work and Kirsty's story grew. People created art about it, a play with Shetland actress Sandra Voe, and a novel by poet Sheenagh Pugh. More information came to light, and Brian was able to produce an extended version of Kirsty's story in the *The Shetland Times* during the Covid lockdown.

We outgrew our accommodation in the early 2000s, despite a small extension. Brian's office became cramped as he vanished behind piles of paper and books. He's always been a person who had more to do and read than there was time for, despite prodigious efforts. Not simply academic or Shetland books, detective novels have always had a place on his desk. The works of Stephen Jay Gould (1941-2002) were a shared pleasure in the Archives. A paleantologist's work can echo archival problems, with lessons about how to deal with evidence. Revisiting original evidence (document or specimen) can yield new conclusions. Then there are all the tantalising gaps. Brian's introduction to *Shetland Documents* Vol. 2 tells the story of the information we will never have, the documents lost to fire and disposal. Extinction events, you might say.

1977 is a long way away now, and a great deal has changed, and the Archives has expanded vastly beyond what was expected when Brian was first allocated a room. If we go back to the quotation at the beginning, it reads like a kind of mission statement about how Brian has proceeded in his work. Shetland history is very much history from below, and there isn't much glory to recover. He had the good sense to realise that many important things have happened after 1469, and collecting archives could allow people to study and explain them. He never neglected the pre-1469 era either, as many a published paper shows. There's a possible fork in the road here – another archivist might have believed that Shetland was a *pale imitation of its glorious past*. We're lucky we avoided such a dismal creature.

Brian has never been an anonymous archivist, and he has had a tireless engagement with the society the Archives serves. More than once he's been stopped in the street by people who wanted to make a donation. A famous one is a document with photographs of Shetland Home Guard members. As time passed and the Archives and its reputation grew, people and institutions from further afield came to appreciate the service Brian could offer. Brian is a few years short of five decades of work now, and people can still walk into the searchroom and meet the archives founder. He has a remarkable record of work, not only in his own considerable output of essays and articles (see the appendix to this volume), but in the help he has offered to others. I could remark on the many things that are required for a person to serve so long, the level of dedication, and fortitude. Our former colleague Joanne Wishart got it best, when she wrote a history of the Shetland Archives and said Brian was seen as the soul of the Shetland Archives. She was so right.

1

Proud towers to swift destruction doomed[1] – some unresolved questions about brochs

Noel Fojut
(formerly of Historic Scotland)

Brian Smith (left) and Noel Fojut discussing brochs at Clickhimin, May 2019. Photograph reproduced with kind permission of Gordon Johnston.

I think my first contact with Brian Smith was over the Society of Antiquaries of Scotland's Shetland conference in May 1980, papers from which he edited and published as *Shetland Archaeology* (Smith, 1985). As a young researcher, I had contributed on the significance of sites other than brochs to understanding Shetland's Iron Age.

More than forty years on, Brian's growing interest in brochs, combined with his attentive listening and considered questioning, did much to extend

---

1 The line is from Milton's *Paradise Lost,* book v.

my engagement with the topic. As I reach the end of my career, broch studies – or 'brochology', as I prefer it – still fascinates.

What follows is a review of some of the unanswered questions about brochs. It takes account of some important recent publications and reflects on what may be knowable and what may not. It is written from a Shetland perspective, with as little technical jargon as possible. I offer it to Brian in recognition of years of support and intellectual stimulation, and in the expectation that he will disagree with at least half of it.

The nature of broch studies

My research into Shetland's Iron Age brochs began in 1976 with a simple thesis: that the setting of these structures in the landscape could be interrogated to shed light upon some of the 'problems of the brochs' without the need for costly excavation. At that time, circumstances suggested that there might not be many more major excavations on brochs, and that we would have to make the best of what information we already held.

Fortunately, circumstances change. In the event, a great deal of excavation has taken place over the last half-century, much of it in Shetland, including some projects of impressive scale. Over the same period, copious ink has been expended on papers and books, ranging from the minutiae of individual brochs to grand theories about the nature of the Iron Age society in which they arose. Brochs have a fair claim to being the most-studied and most-discussed category of prehistoric sites in Scotland. Yet many questions about brochs remain as intractable as ever, and some always will.

Archaeology can tell us much, especially with new scientific and analytical techniques, but such knowledge is always specific to the sites and situations we have examined. We cannot know what lies beyond the tips of our trowels or beyond the field of our microscopes. However, the patient accumulation of site-specific information does lead steadily to a richer understanding: by generalising, we can imagine an ever-clearer picture of the realities of daily life and toil. But an understanding of the underlying nature of Iron Age society, in which that daily life proceeded and out of which the brochs arose, cannot be achieved by excavation and generalisation alone. It requires the exercise of a different type of imagination.

Much of broch studies consist of developing, challenging and refining theories about how Iron Age society operated in the second half of the first millennium B.C. In this, brochs are a given, a fact whose existence must be accommodated: brochs in general and specific brochs in specific locations. In the critical exploration of such theories, it is essential that all the observed facts are fully integrated. Theories which work for most brochs, but not for all, are of no more use than a car which starts most mornings.

In presenting our work to wider audiences, we often fail to separate observed facts (the locations, surviving structures and excavated evidence) from inferred facts (such as wooden fitments or the purpose of specific construction features), and both from social and (pre)historical theories. Worst of all, we distract ourselves over matters of definition. Despite the enduring fascination of brochs, discussions about their precise typology surely represent some of the most sterile debates in the last century of archaeology.

What are brochs?

So, where better to start this short survey than with definitions?

The word 'broch' is not ancient. It was invented by 19th century antiquarian writers, based on sites with 'burgh' or 'broch' names in Orkney and Caithness: it is a classic example of specialist jargon. We do not know what the broch builders called these structures.

In 1977, the late Raymond Lamb, for many years Orkney's Archaeologist, heard that I was taking an interest in brochs. He cautioned me to remember that 'all brochs are not brochs in an archaeological sense.' He had in mind sites with 'brough' placenames such as the Brough of Birsay and the Brough of Deerness, both in Orkney. But I was soon to learn that there was no agreement, even in 'an archaeological sense,' on exactly what constitutes a broch. More energy has been spent on this topic over the past 50 years than seems credible.

Many subtly different definitions of a broch have been proposed, but for present purposes the key features are: drystone construction, a near-circular ground plan, a single entrance, a thick wall (at its base occupying up to 25 percent of the overall diameter) with evidence that the wall was double-skinned above the lowest few metres, with narrow, horizontally-floored, spaces located within the inner and outer skins. Other commonly observed features are a stair rising within the wall thickness, hollow chambers or galleries in the basal part of the wall, and a horizontal ledge or 'scarcement' built into the inner wall face. Taken together, these features define what John Barber has called the 'canonical' broch – a structure whose broad principles became widely understood in Iron Age times and which, for reasons which may never conclusively be elucidated, became the dominant building form of northern Scottish Iron Age society for a period of several centuries from 500 B.C. (Barber, 2018).

As Barber points out, any definition should rest on what is observable: it must not make assumptions about 'lost' elements, such as supposed wooden fitments, floors or roofs – matters which continue to generate much debate and will be discussed below. Nonetheless, it is hard to escape the conclusion that brochs were engineered for height. We cannot know how tall each of Scotland's 500-plus supposed brochs once stood,[2] there can be little doubt

---

2   Until recently, any definition of brochs would have added that they are unique to Scotland. However, a case has been made for the former existence of a broch in Berwick-upon-Tweed, just a few miles inside England (Kent, 2019). The evidence is circumstantial and the site lies deep below later deposits, though certainly worth investigation should an opportunity ever appear. Of course, medieval concepts such as Scotland and England did not exist back in the Iron Age.

that most of what are now little more than mounds of rubble were once *capable* of having once stood tall enough to be described as towers, some at least as tall as Mousa (Fojut, 1982b). How many actually did so, we may probably never know.

What was the ancestry of the broch concept?

Barber has suggested that the broch was invented, and did not arise from random experimentation. He notes that stone structures do not 'evolve' in a Darwinian sense, despite the widespread use of this term in relation to their structural origins. His view is that the idea at the core of the broch 'concept' is simple: a tall, vertical, inner wall-face. All other detailed features of broch engineering, he suggests, are necessary corollaries of this: the hollow-wall construction and corbelled cells merely ingenious ancillary inventions necessary to enable the primary objective of building circular and building tall (Barber, 2008 etc).

Accepting that argument – one of the few recent contributions to broch studies which seems hard to oppose – then the brilliant 'inventor' of the broch was a skilled structural engineer, used to working in drystone and well-versed in the various types of structure which were already being built in the north around 500 B.C. By implication, that inventor was almost certainly local, though to which part of the north and west we do not know, and we never will.

Massive, near-circular structures are widespread across northern Scotland from the Bronze Age onwards, though only a small number have provided radiocarbon dating evidence which could make them plausible 'ancestors' of the broch: the best-known are the sites of Bu and Howe (both in Orkney). There are others, undated, not least the indeterminate structure into which the broch at Clickhimin appears to have been built.

Sites such as the promontory 'forts' at Ness of Burgi and Scatness North, the 'blockhouse' and ring-wall at Clickhimin, and the double-skinned arc of walling at Rubh an Dunain (Skye) all contain features which would be perfectly at home in a broch, such as corbelled cells and broch-like door passages. However, none of these sites has been closely dated, which means that such features may be later borrowings from broch architecture rather than ancestral forms.

This is particularly frustrating in the case of Shetland, which possesses a wider range of broch-like features in non-broch structures than any other region. If all were proven to be early in date, this might further strengthen a case for Shetland as the birthplace of the broch concept. In one of his last papers Euan MacKie, the pre-eminent broch scholar of the second half of the 20th century, declared himself prepared to abandon his lifelong advocacy of the west coast origin of brochs (MacKie, 2008). Shetland may be where it all began – though we may never be able to prove it!

When were the first brochs built?

We remain short of secure dates for the first construction of brochs: Old Scatness,[3] Channerwick,[4] Thrumster (Caithness), Howe (Orkney), Dun Vulan (South Uist) and most recently Clachtoll (Sutherland) are the key examples. However, each site seems to tell a somewhat different story. At Old Scatness and Dun Vulan a broch seems to have been built on a cleared site at some date in the century from 400 B.C. At Thrumster, a substantial roundhouse was erected at about the same date: soon afterwards its walls were thickened up to broch proportions. At Howe, a relatively thin-walled roundhouse which had been built into the mound of a Neolithic tomb was similarly thickened up, sometime after 400 B.C., and rebuilt again around 200 B.C. At Clachtoll, an early broch seems to have been almost completely rebuilt at a date two centuries or more later.

Construction dates are scarce for good reasons. The interiors of brochs seem, at least initially, to have been kept clean, so we lack 'original' floor deposits. This means that our best hope for a date lies beneath the thick walls. Few excavators have had the opportunity or the courage to look there, at the cost of great labour and the partial destruction of the broch itself. Old Scatness has so far produced the only construction date for a broch wall which seems totally secure. The "ghost" of the robbed-out broch at Channerwick (Shetland) recently offered a rare chance to examine the same situation: the evidence suggests this was possibly built as early as Old Scatness. The location and the elaborate well at Channerwick bear close comparison with the broch at Jarlshof, which was dug long before radiocarbon dating was available – was Jarlshof also an early example?

We will never answer the question of where the 'prototype' broch was built. Even if we could locate, excavate and date every surviving broch, the remains of that first example may have been destroyed long ago. However, as more sites are dated, we may expect early dates to begin to converge, giving a fair degree of probability about when brochs began to appear.

Current evidence is converging on the first brochs being erected soon after 400 B.C. But this needs to be treated with caution. As a profession, we have a distinct tendency to look to the earlier end of radiocarbon date brackets – every excavator wants their broch to be as early as possible. Thus, we look at Old Scatness's construction date of 390 to 200 BC and say 'soon after 400 BC' rather than 'sometime before 200 B.C.'.

Nonetheless, our limited evidence supports an idea, periodically advanced by researchers such as Horace Fairhurst in the late 1970s, that 'tower' or 'canonical' brochs were constructed over quite a short period of time. Barber and collaborators have recently resurrected this idea of a broch-building 'craze' or 'mania' which swept northern Iron Age society in the 4th and/or 3rd centuries B.C.

---

3 Sites named below are in Shetland unless otherwise specified on their first mention.
4 I am grateful to Dr Joanna Hambly of SCAPE (University of St Andrews) for sharing information about Channerwick in advance of publication.

Interestingly, the earliest date which we might accept today is one of about 500 B.C. from Crosskirk (Caithness), which Fairhurst, the excavator, dismissed as 'too early'. At the time of the excavations there, in the 1970s, brochs were thought to be linked in some way to the expansion of the Roman Empire. One of the very few things we know for certain about brochs, and which we did not know fifty years ago, is that their origin long precedes Roman expansionist activities. Intriguingly however, the last few brochs to be built may indeed have been contemporary with the Roman army's presence in Scotland.

How long did broch-building last?

We think the first brochs were built around 400 B.C., with early examples being erected in several different areas.

But we also have solid evidence that other brochs were constructed much later, even within the northern 'homeland' of the brochs. Later examples include Upper Scalloway, constructed in the final century B.C., a date also suggested for the Cairns, South Ronaldsay (Orkney). Substantial rebuilding at Thrumster, the Howe and Clachtoll may also fall into this later phase of activity.

We do not (and may never) know if all brochs were constructed over a relatively short period, perhaps only a generation or so, if their numbers gradually built up over a much longer time-span, or if there were distinct 'pulses' of building. The evidence we currently have might support an early pulse, followed, perhaps two centuries later, by a second pulse in the north, in which new brochs were built and existing roundhouses were adapted to look more broch-like. These were perhaps followed by a final 'pulse' in which the small group of brochs in central and southern Scotland may have been erected in the first or even second century A.D. The possibility and extent of interaction between the builders of this final, outlying scatter of brochs and the Roman army continues to fascinate researchers.

One emerging idea is that some brochs may only to have stood as towers for relatively short periods of time: Clachtoll and Thrumster may fall into this category. Others appear to have stood as towers for much longer before being subsumed into later constructions: the Cairns for perhaps three centuries. It has been suggested, based partly on recent work in Caithness, that many 'brochs' marked on the map may never have been towers at all, but were roundhouses adapted to look like former towers. (Cavers, Heald and Barber, 2021). Others of course, most definitely stood tall for much longer: a few still do.

Orkney and Caithness have the most evidence for existing structures being adapted into brochs, while the Western Isles, the western Highlands and southern Scotland seem to be areas where brochs were usually built from scratch. In Shetland, most brochs were probably built on relatively clean sites, were definitely towers, and continued visually to dominate their sites for centuries. But the possible counter-example of Jarlshof must be kept in mind. John Hamilton, who partially excavated the site and wrote the definitive report believed that the broch tower there was deliberately reduced in height when the wheelhouses began to be built. This has not been disproved, while Old Scatness was later to produce evidence of a broch being deliberately reduced in Iron Age rather than in later times.

Although we know the Iron Age names of not a single broch site, it is possible that place-names offer some light. The preponderance of 'howe' names attached to Orkney broch sites, in contrast with more frequent 'burgh/brough' names in Shetland, has been cited as evidence that the Norse settlers found what were recognisably ruined towers in Shetland, whereas in Orkney they found mainly nondescript mounds.

Looking across the whole of Scotland, there is little disagreement that a sizeable number of brochs once stood as towers. Some, of course, managed to survive as tall structures into modern times. It is, however, becoming increasingly apparent that, despite the similarity of the features deployed in their construction, individual brochs may have experienced radically different 'biographies' of construction, use and modification. Despite this, it seems clear that the idea of 'broch-ness' acquired and maintained significance over five centuries or more.

What purpose – or purposes – did brochs have?

Brochs would have dominated their surrounding landscapes. This suggests that those who built them, or caused them to be built, were the dominant actors in local Iron Age society.

The forbidding appearance of brochs, especially Mousa, led early antiquaries to the assumption that they were intended as defences. Over the latter part of the 20th century, alternative views developed, first to regard brochs as defensible but primarily as elite residences, and then to see them as high-status farmsteads, relegating their impressive architecture to the role of signifier of social status.

Much has been written in recent years about brochs as indicators of social status, with a tendency to downplay defensibility as if it were a contrary purpose. But surely these functions are not antithetical? A willingness to defend would be entirely consistent with a desire to maintain social ascendancy.

It may be worth bearing in mind the fact that Norse settlers saw the still recognisable broch towers as defences – hence *borg/burgh/brough* names, and that in Gaelic speaking areas they have the label of *dún*, which also indicates a fortified place. These names were given at dates around 1,200 years after the first brochs were built – approximately halfway between their construction and modern times.

Such hypothesising might be more productive if we had any useful evidence to help determine what function(s) brochs were intended to perform when first constructed. To date, every broch which has been excavated to natural ground level has produced evidence only for its use in subsequent periods, not at the time immediately after its first construction. It appears that, when new, the interiors of brochs were kept scrupulously clean and tidy. Either that, or else at some later date the interiors of each broch were emptied out so thoroughly that the term 'sterilisation' might be appropriate. Only later was the rubbish of daily life was allowed to begin the slow process of filling up the central space. As a result, we lack any significant artefactual or environmental evidence for the first use of brochs.

Thus, while all the evidence we have is that excavated brochs were used as dwelling places for most of their later existence, it remains entirely possible that their primary purpose was not residential at all. Possible uses might include preparation for some anticipated invasion, as watch-towers, signal stations or strong points. There is also an emerging idea that at least a few brochs may have been built around pre-existing wells or other underground chambers: this seems to be proven at the Cairns (Orkney) and might also be the case at Gurness (Orkney), Jarlshof and Channerwick. Such places may have had what archaeologists call 'ritual' uses – for ceremonial, worship, initiations or suchlike. An unroofed broch, by contrast, might be an ideal place to conduct auguries by watching the movements of stars, clouds or the passage of birds.

But these ideas may be no more than flights of fancy: brochs may have been habitations from the very beginning, but kept immaculately clean and tidy by the first generation(s) of house-proud dwellers – perhaps these people were so special that their very rubbish was 'tabu', to be carefully removed and ritually disposed of? If that was indeed the case, then some significant change took place in the history of brochs, after which began a gradual build-up of refuse as each ceased to be kept clean.

The truism that 'absence of evidence' is not 'evidence of absence' applies here: once built, brochs surely did not stand pristine, empty and unused until it belatedly occurred to people to live inside them. We can reasonably assume that, having built them at the cost of huge labour input, those who had the power within contemporary society to build brochs had some important and perhaps urgent use in mind.

Although the individual 'biographies' of excavated brochs show that they were used and modified in a variety of ways in their later existences, it seems more likely than not (at least to this writer) that their intended original purpose was the same. The alternative seems less likely: a society in which there existed a range of different purposes, each requiring an elaborate stone building, to which the builder's response, regardless of purpose, was the universal one-size-fits-all broch.

[As a hopefully relevant digression, consider the example of domestic garages. I used to live in a street of suburban houses, all built in the 1950s and each provided with a garage capable of sheltering a small to medium car. Yet by the 1990s, my garage was the only one in the street which still housed a car: others housed accommodation for guests, surplus furniture, garden equipment, home gymnasia, home offices and even a small-scale wine supply business. Even if archaeologists of the future did not know about motor-vehicles, they would be correct in concluding that all of these similar-shaped and -sized buildings, in similar relationships to larger buildings (the homes), had been *intended* to serve an identical purpose, regardless of any remains they found amongst their ruins. But the surviving evidence of whether that purpose had ever been fulfilled might be extremely slight and hard to interpret – perhaps no more than the occasional oil-stain.]

Can we deduce anything from the location of brochs in the landscape?

If brochs were intended as residences, perhaps elite residences, from their first construction, then it seems reasonable to regard them as 'estate centres,' controlling and exploiting available resources within a distinct 'territory'. The exact balance of resources would have varied greatly from site to site: land with arable and pastoral value (which would contain the legacy of earlier settlers' efforts), access to wild resources both terrestrial and marine, and mineral resources including peat for fuel. An ideal location for such a centre of operations might be where the arable land meets the pastoral land and with good access to the sea, in so far as we understand where the Iron Age shoreline would have lain. There is no doubt that the majority of Shetland's brochs are on sites which broadly meet these criteria.

However, a small number of brochs do not fit this template: the Loch of Houlland, set just back from the cliffs of Eshaness; the broch on a desperately exposed promontory on the isle of Balta; that on a hilltop at Tumblin near Bixter or the several on tiny offshore islets. These do not look like natural choices for a broch which is intended to function as the centre of a farming and fishing estate. It is possible to explain away such awkward cases one by one: perhaps Loch of Houlland 'controlled' the rich seabird nesting cliffs nearby, for example, or the islet sites represent communities who made their main livelihood from the sea. But to do so using an economic rationale requires the assumption of a sophisticated and integrated local economy based on exchange. But even then, there are a few brochs whose location simply does not make sense in such terms.

Which returns us to the point that we do not know for certain the primary intended function of brochs. Either they did indeed have a range of different primary functions or they all had the same function, one which could be carried out just as effectively on a site without significant natural resources as on one which was better-endowed.

One persistent idea, though nowadays a minority view, imagines that the 'need' arose to build a network of about a hundred brochs in Shetland as a series of lookout stations, capable of keeping watch on the coast and communicating all around the islands. Unless these were being imposed upon the will of the local population, it seems logical that they would be sited, wherever possible, within existing areas of settlement, whose populace would provide the necessary labour and presumably benefit from the completion of the project. But there would inevitably be some gaps, where there was no pre-existing settlement conveniently situated to complete the chain, and no area with good farming potential in the gap, where such a community might be 'planted' and required to build a broch. While we might still puzzle over how brochs in such extreme locations came to be constructed and operated, this theory does at least offer a logical reason for all locations. But it fails to explain why brochs in unhandy places were constructed on just the same generous scale as brochs in locations with better natural endowments and which were almost certainly home to sizeable communities.

How important is the time dimension in all of these questions?

In a word: vital. Most researchers into brochs and their physical and social landscapes have tended to assume not only that brochs were all built around the same time, but also that they carried on in more or less continuous use for extended periods. It appears, from recent work at Clachtoll and elsewhere, that neither assumption might be correct (Barber, Cavers and Heald, 2021). It has even been suggested that brochs may have been invented more than once, though this seems a little unnecessary (MacKie, 2008).

This matters hugely, because the settled landscape would have looked, and functioned, very differently depending on the answer. If all of Shetland's brochs – perhaps once around 100 in number – were built and in use at the same time, then suggestions of deliberately placed chains of inter-visibility and communication could indeed be valid. But if these brochs were built over four centuries or more, and/or were not in use for extended periods thereafter, with only a few in use in any one generation, such ideas would be much less tenable.

The concept of each broch having a 'territory' has been used to try to explore questions about broch-period economics (Fojut, 1982; Armit, 2005). This model would be critically impacted by how many brochs were 'active' at any time. Might Shetland once have been carved up into a hundred small territories, at the time the brochs were built, but then over time seen these merge into, say, twenty much larger territories, as one broch site continued to prosper while others were gradually demoted to secondary status or entirely abandoned? This ought to be something which we could investigate with existing archaeological techniques, given the resources and energy.

Perhaps most important of all, the time dimension matters because of the implications for the structure of society in the mid-first millennium B.C.

Constructing one hundred towers in Shetland over a small number of years surely implies either that the building was mandated by a strong centralised authority or, conversely and just as possibly, was the outcome of some 'mania' in a fragmented but highly competitive society. It seems beyond doubt that 'brochs were the answer': unfortunately, we do not know 'what was the question?' What motives might drive such an extraordinary effort? Perhaps brochs do, after all, represent an organised defence against a threat perceived as imminent? Or might they equally well represent the exact opposite, the establishment of a new social order after a major social or military takeover? Or might the 'mania' have been religious?

On the other hand, if brochs were built over a more extended period of time, each falling out of use after a period, an entirely different picture might emerge: each broch might mark the presence of a family which, for a period, had risen to the top of the local social pyramid. This model, of the rise and fall of individual groups over an extended timespan, has recently been proposed for Caithness, and might well have worked in Orkney too. If all brochs were in use at the same time, then each cannot have housed anything like a 'royal' family. But a 'rise and fall' model allows for some form of local competition over paramountcy within what might loosely be called a chiefly society.

Was 'broch society' the same everywhere?

Recent writing increasingly focusses on the idea that brochs may have served different purposes, both over time and over space. It may also be that differences and changes in function may not have been synchronous across the whole of the north and west. The idea of a unified 'broch province' may be something invented by recent scholars.

Might the first wave of these impressive towers have been entirely non-residential, but lookout points or markers of territorial possession, or perhaps even religious in function? Could the broch form subsequently have come to represent something else, more to do with social status, so that retro-fitting one's roundhouse to be more broch-like was 'simply' what a 'good' family did once it had 'arrived' at the top of the social heap? Once built, the inconvenience of such a building for daily life would surely have become ever more apparent.

What may also have been true is that those tower brochs which survived as landmarks may have acquired after-lives as markers of ancient ancestry – relics of auld decency – which accorded special status to those who possessed and lived around them. In short, there may have been social capital in what is nowadays termed heritage conservation, even two millennia ago. There may even have been social capital in converting one's perfectly ordinary roundhouse so that it looked as though it had once, long ago, been a tower broch.

The wooden bits – more absences of evidence

Brochs which survive to the requisite height, about three metres, have a ledge in the stonework of the inside-facing wall, known as a 'scarcement'. This feature only seems to be capable of explanation as the outer edge of some vanished internal feature, either a raised floor or a roof, which sat within the tower and was presumably made of wood. This interpretation has been given support by the discovery in a few excavations of rings of post-holes in the floor of the broch interior.

Although there has long been a persistent minority view that brochs may never have been fully roofed, recent writers have imagined ever more elaborate wooden internal fittings and roof structures, culminating in the classic cut-away 'reconstruction' drawing by Alan Braby (reproduced in Fojut, 2005). By the time of the 2000 'Tall Stories' conference in Shetland, this was already coming to be looked at with a degree of scepticism. One contribution there pushed the idea of elaborate timber fittings for Shetland's brochs to its logical endpoints in terms of logistics and politics, to prompt consideration: have we properly considered the consequences of kitting out a hundred Shetland brochs with timber of the scale, quality and character envisaged? (Fojut, 2005).

Picking up on such doubts, some recent researchers have pursued the idea of much simpler fittings, such as circular mezzanines and partial or lightweight roofs using smaller-dimension timber, and have re-emphasised the scanty nature of the evidence for massive timber fittings (Romankiewicz, 2021). Ideas about brochs sometimes appear to go round in circles: perhaps Brian Smith's suggestion that Mousa may not have been roofed will one day be seen as orthodoxy (Smith, 2016).

The question of roofs might, just possibly, be capable of resolution if luck was with us. Imagine that, one day, some startled excavator should come upon a scale model of a roofed broch. After all, clay models of the *nuraghi* of Sardinia have been found, and these Bronze Age towers are considerably older than brochs (though not, we think, ancestral to them). Those familiar with archaeologists will not be surprised to learn, however, that debate continues about how exactly accurate these nuraghic models may be. Our imagined lucky broch digger could expect the mouth of his gift horse to be very closely examined!

The persistence of brochs, and of questions about brochs

A roofed, inhabited broch would have been perceived in landscape terms entirely differently from a broch which was unroofed and did not routinely contain people, either because it had never done so, or because its day had passed. Current thinking is that the former presence of a broch, even a ruined one, was a matter of social significance for later Iron Age communities. But at some point, in the case of Shetland perhaps after the Norse settlement, this ceased, with brochs from then on being fair game for stone-quarrying (Tait, 2005), with only out-of-the-way brochs surviving, in ever-diminishing numbers, eventually to find yet more new purposes as the objects of study and as tourism resources.

It seems fitting to close by reflecting upon the extraordinary timescales involved in the broch phenomenon. First constructed 2,400 or more years ago. Still being built, or being built again after a pause, four hundred years later. Retaining social significance for over a thousand years. Offering a resource of building stone over more recent centuries. Now finding a new value as tourism destinations. Not to mention underpinning the careers of innumerable archaeologists....

Perhaps it is hardly surprising that we still have so many questions.

Bibliography

(NOTE: References to individual broch excavations have been omitted. Reports can be found easily online.)

Armit, I. (2005) 'Land-holding and inheritance in the Atlantic Scottish Iron Age', in V. Turner *et al.* (eds.) *Tall Stories? 2 millennia of brochs*. Shetland Amenity Trust: Lerwick, pp.129-143.

Barber, J. (2018) References are to the Society of Antiquaries of Scotland's Rhind Lecture series: 'Drystone technologies: Neolithic tensions and Iron Age compressions'. Available at: https://www.socantscot.org/uncategorised/2018-rhind-lectures-now-online/ (Accessed: 27 January 2023).

Barber, J., Cavers, G., Heald A. and Theodossopoulos D. (2021) 'Memory in practice and the practice of memory in Caithness, northeast Scotland, and in Sardinia', in Stoddart, S., Aines, E.D. and Malone C. (eds.) (2021) *Gardening Time: Monuments and landscape from Sardinia, Scotland and Central Europe in the very long Iron Age*. Cambridge: Macdonald Institute Conversations. Available at: https://www.arch.cam.ac.uk/mcdonald-institute-monographs/mcdonald-institute-monographs-archive-2021-2025 (Accessed 15 February 2023), pp.7-15.

Cavers, G., Heald A. and Barber, J. (2021) 'Monuments and memory in the Iron Age of Caithness', in Stoddart, S., Aines, E.D. and Malone C. (eds.) (2021) *Gardening Time: Monuments and landscape from Sardinia, Scotland and Central Europe in the very long Iron Age*. Cambridge: Macdonald Institute Conversations. Available at: https://www.arch.cam.ac.uk/mcdonald-institute-monographs/mcdonald-institute-monographs-archive-2021-2025 (Accessed 15 February 2023), pp.17-27.

Fojut, N. (1982a) 'Towards a Geography of Shetland Brochs', *Glasgow Archaeological Journal* 9, pp.38-59. [Reprinted in V. Turner *et al.* (2005) Turner V.E., Nicholson R.A., Dockrill S.J. and Bond J.M. (eds.) (2005) *Tall Stories? 2 millennia of brochs*. Lerwick: Shetland Amenity Trust, pp.144-165.].

Fojut, N. (1982b) 'Is Mousa a broch?', *Proceedings of the Society of Antiquaries of Scotland* 111, pp.220-228.

Fojut, N. (2005) 'Brochs and Timber Supply – A Necessity Born of Invention?', in Turner V.E., Nicholson R.A., Dockrill S.J. and Bond J.M. (eds.) (2005) *Tall Stories? 2 millennia of brochs*. Lerwick: Shetland Amenity Trust, pp.190-201.

Kent, C. (2019) 'La Roundele, Berwick-upon-Tweed: a lost southern broch?', *Proceedings of the Society of Antiquaries of Scotland* 149, pp.131-144.

MacKie, E.W. (2008) 'The broch cultures of Atlantic Scotland: origins, high noon and decline. Part 1: early Iron Age beginnings c.700-200 BC', *Oxford Journal of Archaeology* 27 (3), pp.261-279.

Romankiewicz, T. and Ralston, I. (2021) 'Revisiting Glenelg a century after Alexander O. Curle: reconstructing brochs in treeless landscapes' in Stoddart, S., Aines, E.D. and Malone C. (eds.) *Gardening Time: Monuments and landscape from Sardinia, Scotland and Central Europe in the very long Iron Age*. Cambridge: Macdonald Institute Conversations. Available at: https://www.arch.cam.ac.uk/mcdonald-institute-monographs/mcdonald-institute-monographs-archive-2021-2025 (Accessed 15 February 2023), pp.65-74.

Smith, B. (ed.) (1985) *Shetland Archaeology*. Lerwick: The Shetland Times Ltd.

Smith, B. (2016) 'Did the broch of Mousa have a roof? - and why not!', *The New Shetlander* 276, pp.4-17.

Stoddart, S., Aines, E.D. and Malone C. (2021) *Gardening Time: Monuments and landscape from Sardinia, Scotland and Central Europe in the very long Iron Age*. Cambridge: Macdonald Institute Conversations. Available at: https://www.arch.cam.ac.uk/mcdonald-institute-monographs/mcdonald-institute-monographs-archive-2021-2025 (Accessed 15 February 2023).

Tait, I. (2005) *What use are brochs?*, in Turner V.E., Nicholson R. A., Dockrill S.J. and Bond J.M. (eds) *Tall Stories? 2 Millennia of brochs*, Shetland Amenity Trust, Lerwick.

Turner V.E., Nicholson R.A., Dockrill S.J. and Bond J.M. (eds.) (2005) *Tall Stories? 2 millennia of brochs*. Lerwick: Shetland Amenity Trust.

2

Shetland: A Norse country between earls and kings

Steinar Imsen
(Norwegian University of Science and Technology)

'Shetland had an economy, and a local government and other local institutions of her own. To suggest that Shetland society in 1300 or 1700 was a replica of Norwegian or Scottish society at the same time is nonsense.' (Smith, 1990, p. 25)

The first country in the Solund Sea

Shetland was probably settled from western Norway at the end of the eighth century (Cant, 1984, p.175). Almost a hundred years later a Norse earldom was established in Orkney. The Icelandic *Earls' Saga* (*Orkneyinga Saga*) from the early thirteenth century tells us that King Harald of Norway, during an expedition west over sea to punish Vikings, subdued Shetland, Orkney, and the Hebrides. To compensate Earl Ragnvald Øysteinsson Mørejarl (died c.900 A.D.) for the loss of his son Ivar in battle, King Harald gave him Shetland and Orkney. Ragnvald, however, passed both countries on to his brother Sigurd, and before King Harald sailed westwards, he bestowed the title of earl upon him. Sigurd ruled over Orkney and Shetland until his death, but when his son Guttorm died without heirs, the earldom was returned to Ragnvald, who gave it to his youngest son Einar. Meanwhile Orkney had become a Viking nest, and Einar had to ask the Shetlanders for military aid to overcome his enemies. Einar would become progenitor of the Norse dynasty of earls in Orkney. Although this is the story given in the saga, very few people believe this version today (Krag, 2003, p.302; Woolf, 2007, pp.277-89).

The Latin *Historia Norwegie* (c. 1160-70) gives a more trustworthy account, saying that 'certain Vikings descended from the stock of that sturdiest of men, Earl Ragnvald, crossing the Solund Sea with a large fleet, totally destroyed those peoples [the Picts] after stripping them of their long-established dwellings and made the islands subject to themselves.' After having built winter quarters, they used the islands as a base to ravage England, Scotland,

and Ireland, and they 'established their realm (*suum regnum*) in Orkney, which in fact remain up to this moment under the lordship of their descendants, with the provision that they are bound to pay tribute to the Norwegian kings' (Ekrem and Mortensen, 2003, pp.65-69; Koht, 1949).

When *Historia Norwegie* was written, Shetland belonged to the earldom of Orkney, however, it does not seem to have been reckoned among the islands which Earl Ragnvald's descendants conquered. According to *Historia Norwegie* the original name of Orkney was *Petland*, which was the reason the strait between the archipelago and Scotland was called *Petlandicum Mare*. True enough there were Picts in Shetland too when the settlers from western Norway arrived there, but according to *Historia Norwegie* the islands which Earl Ragnvald's descendants occupied at the end of the ninth century were at the opposite side of the Pentland Firth and close to the Scottish mainland. Shetland was far away, almost midway between Scotland and Norway. We should add that *Historia Norwegie* mentions Shetland explicitly only once. When telling about King Olav Tryggvason's conversion of the pagan population along the seaboard of Norway at the end of the tenth century, the author lists Shetland, Orkney, Faroe, and Iceland, as separate countries.[1] The list does not mention any earldom, nor is there any hint of Shetland being subordinate to earls. The oldest Icelandic laws refer to 'Ejum [the Isles, i.e. Faroe, Orkney, the Hebrides], Grænlandi, Hjaltland', and name their inhabitants as 'norræn (Norwegian), hjaltlendskur, orkneyskur, færeyskur, katneskur' (Karlsson 2001, p.53, 479, 107).

In her book *Scandinavian Scotland*, Barbara E. Crawford writes of Shetland that '[t]hese islands had formed pirate lairs since the late eighth century, and until the establishing of control by the earls must have been subject to different Viking chieftains for half a century or more' (Crawford, 1987, p.56). And when it comes to Shetland's relations with the earldom of Orkney during the reign of Torfinn the Mighty (died 1065) she says: 'The extension of Torfinn's power over Shetland seems to have been regarded as a matter of conquest. Throughout *Earls' Saga* Shetland is usually referred to as a port of call *en route* between Orkney and Norway with little mention of any political control exercised there by earls' (Crawford, 1987, p.75). And she ends: 'A contemporary poem about King Olav the Saint, by Ottar the Black, says specifically that the Shetlanders were subject to him' (Crawford, 1987, p.75). Crawford therefore suggests that Shetland might have been King Olav's country, which he enfeoffed to Earl Ragnvald Brusesson (1987, p.56; cf. Cant 1984, p.173).

On the contrary, Brian Smith in 1988, even though he is sceptical of the account of King Harald's gift to Earl Ragnvald, takes it for granted that 'the Earldom of Orkney included Shetland from the outset' (Smith, 1988, p.22).

---

1 '...within five years he [King Olav] made all the tributary territories, that is, Shetland, Orkney, Faeroe, and Iceland, remarkable in their devotion, joyous in their expectations and glowing in their affection for Christ.' (Ekrem and Mortensen, 2003, p.95).

Crawford has recently considered Smith's opinion, writing that the first earls of Orkney 'would claim Shetland as part of their earldom, for Shetland was a vital maritime base for earls whose estate in Norway was in Møre...' and that 'Shetland formed an integral part of the early Orkney earldom' (Crawford, 2014, p.145). Which estates in Møre she is hinting at is unknown, and neither do we know anything about the relationship between the earls of Orkney and their kin in Møre after the conquest.

In fact, we do not know anything certain about Shetland's relations with either Orkney earls or Norwegian kings before the time of Earl Sigurd the Stout (c.991-1014) and his sons Bruse, Sumarlide, Einar, and Torfinn. Since Shetland was Bruse Sigurdsson's share of the heritage after his father, Shetland was probably regarded as part of the earldom of Orkney since the end of the tenth century (Smith 1988, pp.25-26). Until then it is likely that Shetland was a Norse country of its own with close ties to western Norway, and probably a Viking nest dominated by local chiefs. There is nothing like an earl's residence in Shetland or any other material relics that can support the presence of, or relationship to, a superior lord of the country. The longhouse in the ruin-complex at Jarlshof in Sumburgh may have been the seat of a local magnate, but it is modest in size compared to many Norwegian longhouses from the same period; the largest of these is the excavated and now reconstructed longhouse at Borg in the Lofoten archipelago, which covers 700m². According to Anna Ritchie 'Jarlshof [was] never more than a farm, although it grew more substantial as the years went by and the family increased in size (Ritchie, 1993, p.65).

To understand Shetland's history prior to the pledge in 1469 we must consider the geographical position of the isles in the Norse world. Judith Jesch has baptised this period *The Viking Diaspora*, and in her book of the same name she writes: 'Shetland was often the first port of call for travellers going west, *especially* to Faroe and Iceland' (Jesch, 2015, p.26). Barbara E. Crawford also points at Shetland's connections with Iceland (Crawford, 2014, p.149). In a sense Shetland was a crossroads between the way to the Irish Sea and the sailing route to Faroe, Iceland, and Greenland. The connection northward, especially to Faroe, was still important in the late Middle Ages.

King Harald did not conquer all of Norway, and Shetland was probably not made part of any earldom of Orkney in his lifetime. All through the Viking Age the Norse world was a melting pot of changeable and temporary polities. Adam of Bremen, who in c.1070 wrote the *History of the archbishopric of Hamburg-Bremen and the Nordic countries and peoples*, conceived the land of the Northmen (*Nortmannia*) as an almost endless periphery stretching from Norway westward to the Irish Sea and northward to Greenland and Vinland, different from the compact territories of Sweden and Denmark (Imsen, 2015, pp.39-41). A hundred years later the Norse polities west over sea had become tributary countries under the king of Norway, and Norway was territorially united and about to become some sort of state. Another hundred years later Norway was a monarchical state with well-defined borders between its neighbours in Scandinavia and Britain. Meanwhile, the king of Norway had annexed Shetland, and the earldom of

Orkney had become a border county in the realm of the Norwegian king (Imsen, 2009a). The question is how to define the changing political status of Shetland from the turn of the millennium until the second half of the fifteenth century.

The age of earls

Historia Norwegie reports that the Norse countries along the coast of Norway converted to Christianity on Olav Tryggvason's command; Shetland is listed separately. Some years later Olav Haraldsson (1015-30) forced Bruse (died c.1035) and Torfinn (died c.1065), sons of Sigurd the Stout (c. 991-1014), to become his liegemen and hold their land as a feudal grant (Smith, 1988, p.25). Then once again, when in 1066 Olav's half-brother Harald Sigurdsson landed in Orkney on his expedition to conquer England, the earls Paul and Erlend (c.1065-1098), Torfinn Sigurdsson's sons, were forced to accept the Norwegian king as their lord. But none of the Norwegian kings established any feudal overlordship on a regular basis until the turn of the century. Before Harald arrived in 1066, Torfinn Sigurdsson had extended his power to parts of mainland Scotland and the Western Isles and had established a Norse-Scottish principality of his own.

The earls' subordination under a Norwegian king only became permanent during the reign of Magnus Olavsson Bareleg and his successors. On his first expedition to the Western Isles (1098), Man, and Ireland, Magnus took Paul and Erlend as hostages, sent them to Norway and installed his own son Sigurd as ruler over the Northern Isles. It was the same Sigurd, who in time appointed the Norwegian Kale Kolsson as earl of Orkney: Kale was appointed twice, the next time being by Sigurd's Irish half-brother Harald Gille (Gilchrist). Then Kale took the name Ragnvald. Like Bruse Sigurdsson, Kale Kolsson had a special relationship to Shetland. From then until 1468, the earls of Orkney were royal liegemen, and as a token of their submission to the king of Norway they had to render a tribute (*skatt*).

Like in Norway, we can observe a nascent state-formation process in the earldom of Orkney in the twelfth century. As a parallel to St. Olav (Olav Haraldsson) in Norway, the earldom got its own patron saint, St. Magnus (the former Earl Magnus Erlendsson 1106-1117). Magnus was Ragnvald Kale Kolsson's uncle. Ragnvald too was considered a holy man, and most of the miracles connected to him are reported from Shetland. However, Ragnvald was never officially accepted as a saint. The portrait of Ragnvald in the *Earls' Saga* resembles that of a *rex justus*, the ideal prince in ecclesiastical political ideology (Mundal, 2018).

Taxation based on the value of land was introduced too. Like Orkney, Shetland was divided into assessment-units called ounceland (ON *eyrislǫnd*) and pennyland (ON *penninglǫnd*). This system of taxation was probably borrowed from the Gaelic-Norse principalities in the Irish Sea and at the western seaboard of Scotland (Oram, 2011). However, we do not know when ouncelands and pennylands were introduced in the Northern Isles. Some scholars have claimed an ancient origin for the system, which is not likely. It might have been introduced during the reign of Torfinn the Mighty, who made the Western Isles part of his realm. The Norwegian historian Per Sveaas Andersen, however, has argued that taxation based on land was introduced only at the end of the twelfth or beginning of the thirteenth century. Since ouncelands and pennylands still existed in Shetland at the end of the thirteenth century, it must have been introduced prior to 1195, when King Sverre confiscated the country. That means either under Harald Maddadson or Ragnvald Kale Kolsson. I like to imagine Ragnvald as the 'moderniser' of the fiscal system, since the *Earls' Saga* reports relatively frequent talks between him and the countrymen on financial matters (Andersen, 1991; cf. Imsen, 2000).

In addition to tax, the Shetlanders also rendered *veizla*, i.e. foodstuffs for the earl and his household and retainers. Such contributions had been customary in Norway since the Viking Age, and still were in the Middle Ages when kings travelled across the country. According to the *Earls' Saga* Ragnvald collected veizla when he first landed in Shetland on his way to Orkney to claim his right as earl. The saga also tells that in Kirkwall he ordered his men to collect veizla in the countryside for Christmas. The earl collected viezla in Caithness too. Later, veizla was converted into an annual due, called *wattle* (*wesel*) in both Shetland and Orkney (Ballantyne and Smith, 1999, no.18; cf. Thomson, 1996). Moreover, the earls had manors around the earldom run by stewards, and like the Norwegian kings they were itinerant. The earls also had *hirð*, i.e. a body of armed retainers who had sworn allegiance to their lord. Some of them had attained the status of *skutilsveinar* serving at the earl's table. They probably enjoyed the highest rank in the earl's hirð. In Norway, the skutilsveinar were promoted to the rank of knights after 1277. We also meet *kertisveinar* in the earl's hall. In Norway they were pages at the royal court and recruited from among the best families in the country.

We must assume that, like their overlords in Norway, the earls contributed to the formation of an earldom aristocracy in the twelfth century. In his article 'On the nature of tings: Shetland's law courts from the middle ages until 1611', Brian Smith writes about local potentates situated at central church – and thing-locations (Smith, 2009, p.41; cf. Smith, 1988, p.32). I suspect that their ancestors may have belonged to a former earldom-aristocracy in Shetland, and it is tempting, when in 1299 we meet a group of royal *hirðmen* at the Shetland lawthing, to think that they might well have been rooted in an old country elite.

There was no central authority or power covering the whole earldom. Torfinn Sigurdsson's position as single ruler over the Northern Isles, Caithness, and the Western Isles was exceptional. Orkney was a joint earldom until the 1230s. and how the earls shared power, land and income varied. Shetland seems to have been treated as a land of its own. Regarding local organisation, Brian Smith says: 'Trying to understand the organisation of justice in Shetland before Magnus the Lawmender's time is a near hopeless task.' Nevertheless, he draws up a convincing picture out of the scanty remains of the past: 'Shetland might have had an althing, a general assembly of free men, during the centuries after the Scandinavian settlement of the islands, if so, it met at Tingwall' he says, and continues: 'sometime in the ancient period Shetland was divided into administrative units called quarters and eighths, but also into much smaller ones called *heraðs*, which may have had their own tings' (Smith, 2009, p.43; cf. Sanmark et al., 2022, p.205). All this corresponds to the *fjorðungr*, *áttungr*, and *herað* which we know from western Norway and the law province of Gulating. Smith also draws a parallel to Faroe and Iceland, saying that all these countries must have been influenced by the law of Gulating, which is likely as well (Helle, 1994).

As already mentioned, Christianity was forced upon the pagan Orcadians, Shetlanders, Faroese, Icelanders, and Greenlanders by Norwegian kings. Real conversion was certainly a much more complicated and drawn-out process. Until the 1070s, the Northern Isles were part of the archbishopric of Hamburg-Bremen. From then on, the archbishops of York claimed obedience from the Northern Isles, even after the newly erected archbishopric of Lund (in Denmark) in 1103 took over Scandinavia, including the Isles. In the second half of the century the Lund province was parted in three, Lund (Denmark), Nidaros (Norway and the Norse countries 1152/53) and Uppsala (Sweden 1164). Until 1472 the diocese of Orkney belonged to the Nidaros Church.

We do not know for certain when a joint bishopric for Orkney and Shetland was established on a permanent basis. Earl Torfinn the Mighty made his residence at Birsay in Orkney a bishop's seat as well, and the bishop's authority probably extended to Shetland. However, this might have been a temporary situation. Much is unclear with regard to the ecclesiastical situation in the Northern Isles in the decades after Torfinn's death in 1065 and King Harald Sigurdsson's occupation of Orkney in 1066 (Kolsrud, 1913, p.295ff, Crawford, 2003, p.144). At the same time Norway was finally divided into dioceses. Thus, in 1070, King Olav Haraldsson Kyrre (1066-93), who had accompanied his father on the expedition to England, saw to it that a bishop's see was established at the island of Selje outside Stadt. The diocese corresponded to the law-province of Gulating, i.e. western Norway (except Møre and Romsdal) and Faroe. Selje was St. Sunniva's island, and Sunniva was the patron saint of western Norway. King Olav was also the founder of Bergen, which was to become the commercial and administrative centre for western Norway and the Norse countries overseas. In fact the bishops mostly resided in Bergen, even though the bishop's see was only formally transferred to the city in 1170.

There are some indications that Shetland too may have been part of the west-Norwegian diocese in the late eleventh and early twelfth century. The prominent Norwegian historian Edvard Bull argues that an annual fee called *sunnivamel*, which the Shetlanders still in the fourteenth century paid to the shrine of Sunniva in Bergen cathedral, must have been introduced before Shetland became a part of the diocese of Orkney (Bull, 1931, p.134; cf. Hamre, 1964, col.664). Moreover, Eldbjørg Haug (2009, p.478) refers to ecclesiastical connections between Shetland and Southwestern-Norway in the early 1100s (Haug, 2014, p.120). Until the establishment of a bishop's see in Stavanger (1125), southwestern Norway was also part of the Bergen bishopric. We may add that the oldest local church organisation in Shetland according to Ronald G. Cant (1984, p.178) resembled the Norwegian communally-based parish system, and not the Orcadian, which was marked by the authority of earls and bishops.

I suspect that a joint Orkney-Shetland bishopric was established during the episcopacy of Bishop William the Old (1112-68), probably when Ragnvald Kale Kolsson ruled the country. Ragnvald built the Magnus Cathedral, and in 1137 he transferred the bishop's see from Birsay to Kirkwall. At almost the same time, Faroe became a bishopric of its own, but still with strong ties to Bergen (Imsen, 2021, pp.64-65). We should add that from the beginning of the twelfth until the middle of the thirteenth century, Norwegian kings played a central role in the appointments of almost all bishops in Orkney.

The age of kings

In 1195 Earl Harald Maddadson was forced to cede Shetland to King Sverre, with all taxes and dues. Harald also committed himself to share all penal fines from Orkney with the king, who claimed rent as well from land belonging to those who had taken part in the Battle of Florvåg outside of Bergen (1194) and the attempt to overthrow him. Sverre then sent Arne Lørja to Orkney to see to that the settlement was kept. Arne's position was that of a *sysselman*, and as such he was an officer and not a royal liegeman. The *Earls' Saga* also reports that Earl Harald, some time before the 1195 settlement, had been forced to share the tax of Caithness with the king of Scots. By and large, the earls of Orkney had their wings clipped and their earldom curtailed at the turn of the century. With that, the northern flank of the earldom became more Norwegian while the southern flank turned more Scottish.

When in 1202 King Sverre died, Harald Maddadson had Arne Lørja murdered, and according to the *Bagler Sagas* he took back Shetland. It was still civil war in Norway, and Harald's sons David and Jon kept the isles after their father's death (1206) until 1210, when they were called to King Inge Bårdsson in Norway and forced to surrender on extremely hard conditions (Gundersen and Hødnebø, 1979, p.338). After that, the Orkney earls never claimed Shetland back. However, in 1267 Earl Magnus Gilbertson was forced to confirm the 1195 settlement.

The annexation of Shetland did not mean that the islands were incorporated in Norway as an ordinary Norwegian *sysle*, i.e. the administrative unit of a *sysselmann*. From then on Shetland was a separate tributary country, and the sysselmen who were sent to Shetland were more like royal governors than ordinary sysselmen. We know only three of them by name, and two belonged to the inner circle of the royal house. Gregorius Kik, who in 1223 represented Shetland together with the archdeacon Nikolas at a nation-wide assembly in Bergen, was married to King Sverre's daughter Cecilia (Munch, 1857, p.653 note 3). Torvald Toresson, who was Håkon Magnusson's representative in the country, was married into the royal family as well. He stayed in office until the 1330s, probably serving for almost 40 years (Helle, 2002). His daughter Herdis left a huge inheritance that was split among a lot of Norwegian descendants

(Smith, 2011). These absentee proprietors, called Lords of Norway, were among the richest landowners in Shetland for centuries. In Orkney, on the other hand, there were hardly any Norwegian landowners (Thomson, 2001, pp.149). Erling Vidkunsson, the regent of Norway during Magnus Eriksson's minority (1323-1331/32), sold his estate in Orkney to Katarina, the widow of Earl Magnus V, in 1329. Erling had inherited this land from his deceased Orcadian wife, and that was it (Gunnes and Kjellberg, 1979, nos. 660, 661, 664).

Malise Sperra was sysselman in Shetland in the 1380s. He was a Scot and grandchild of the late Earl of Orkney, Malise of Strathearn, who died in 1353. Malise Sperra's cousin, Henry Sinclair, had been appointed earl of Orkney in 1379, and both Henry and Malise attended the meeting in 1389 where Erik the Pomeranian was received as hereditary king of Norway (Taranger, 1912, p.14). Being a knight and a member of the council of the realm Malise ranked among the most prominent men at the royal court, even though he was a foreigner by birth. We have no information about Malise in his capacity of royal officer, but in a letter issued by the king's steward Ogmund Finnson, dated 8 October 1386, we learn that Malise had been engaged in a struggle with Herdis Torvaldsdotter's Norwegian heirs about landed property in Shetland, among whom was Håkon Jonsson, former governor in Orkney (Ballantyne and Smith, 1999, no.13). In 1391 Henry Sinclair had Malise killed, although we do not know why (Wærdahl, 2011, p. 246).

In a royal letter from Lund, dated 15 April 1412, we are told that Alexander of Clapham, King Erik's 'troo þiænare ok man' had been granted royal income from Northmavine, such as 'skatt', 'landskyld', and 'veizla'; 'tegngjeld' and 'fridkaup' were excluded (Ballantyne and Smith, 1999, no.18). 'Tegngjeld' and 'fridkaup' were penal fines for manslaughter, and an important source of income for the crown, which is well documented from all over the vast realm of the king of Norway (Imsen, 2009; and Imsen, 2014, pp.64-69, 78-94). The letter also reveals that the king had officers in the islands called *fouds* ('fogder'), which in late medieval administrative terminology was equivalent to ON sysselman. Alexander's grant was not contingent on any administrative service in Shetland.

In 1418 King Erik the Pomeranian enfeoffed Shetland to John Sinclair, son of the former Earl of Orkney, Henry Sinclair I. This was a feudal grant, and hereafter Shetland is referred to as a lordship in English texts. The term lordship is not easily translated into Norwegian. In contemporary Danish and Norwegian John might have been called a royal 'lensmann'. John was granted the fief for his lifetime, with authority to rule the country on behalf of the king and enjoy all royal income. However, it was stated that 'the land of Hietland shall revert to the king and his successors and to the crown and kingdom of Norway, as he received it, without impediment or delay, by heirs, successors, or any others' (Ballantyne and Smith, 1999, no. 20). John Sinclair's position in Shetland was unique, but it did not last long.

We do not know who succeeded John as the king's governor in Shetland. A letter issued in Kalbakk on 28 June 1431 was sealed by Thomas Håkonsson, 'syslumaðr in Meginlandi [Mainland] i Hetlandi' (Ballantyne and Smith, 1999, no.21). There might, therefore, have been more than one sysselman (or foud) in Shetland in the 1430s, and this resembles the situation in Faroe. I suspect that after John Sinclair, there was no superior royal officer in the isles, and that Shetland was governed from Bergen. Thus, in the 1440s, Olav Nilsson, royal 'lensmann' and 'høvedsmann' at Bergenhus castle, ruled Iceland by controlling a body of native Icelanders, called sysselmen. In any case, all royal officers in the tributary countries were accountable to the royal treasurer in Bergen and had been so since the end of the thirteenth century.

Communitas Hietlandia

Besides the appointment of a sysselman or governor, we do not know anything about the royal regime in Shetland until the 1290s when Duke Håkon Magnusson ruled the country. In 1273 Magnus Håkonsson the Lawmender decided that his eldest son Eirik should succeed him as king, while his younger son Håkon should have the title of duke and his own dukedom, though subordinated to the king. Håkon's part of the realm comprised the Oslo area, southwestern Norway, Shetland, and Faroe. The arrangement was dynastically motivated. However, strategic motives cannot be left out. Thus Ronald G. Cant says: 'In the thirteenth century, indeed, Shetland tended to be grouped with Faroe in the pattern of Norwegian imperial administration as a kind of deliberate buffer-zone between the Earldom of Orkney to the south and the Commonwealth of Iceland to the north.' And he adds: 'Here local autonomy might be tolerated, and even encouraged, because it ensured social and economic stability and held no threat to the supremacy of the Norwegian crown' (Cant, 1984, p.178). We may add that King Sverre, who annexed Shetland in 1195, was himself Faroese.

The orientation northward to Faroe, which the construction of Håkon Magnusson's dukedom implied, was strengthened in the late Middle Ages, when in 1350 King Magnus Eriksson of Sweden and Norway (1319-1374) decided that his eldest son Erik should take over his Swedish kingdom in due course, while Håkon as hereditary king of Norway was to take over the throne when he reached his full age. For himself, Magnus kept all the tributary countries, except Orkney. Håkon VI, who ruled Norway from 1358, took over the tributary countries only at his father's death in 1374. Diplomas from Faroe in the fifteenth century confirm an enduring contact between these islands and Shetland (Jakobsen, 1907, pp.18-43, 45-47).

In 1298 Duke Håkon commissioned Sigurd, lawman of Shetland, and Erlend, bishop of Faroe, to consult the Faroese about the part of their laws that concerned fishing, whale-hunting, and farming. These consultations were probably part of a process to adjust Faroese laws to the new law code of the kingdom, Magnus the Lawmender's Landlaw, and we get to know about it in a comprehensive *retterbot* (amendment) published in the name of Duke Håkon on 28 June that year (Keyser and Munch, 1849, pp.33-39). The office of lawman was in itself a consequence of the legal reforms carried through in Norway

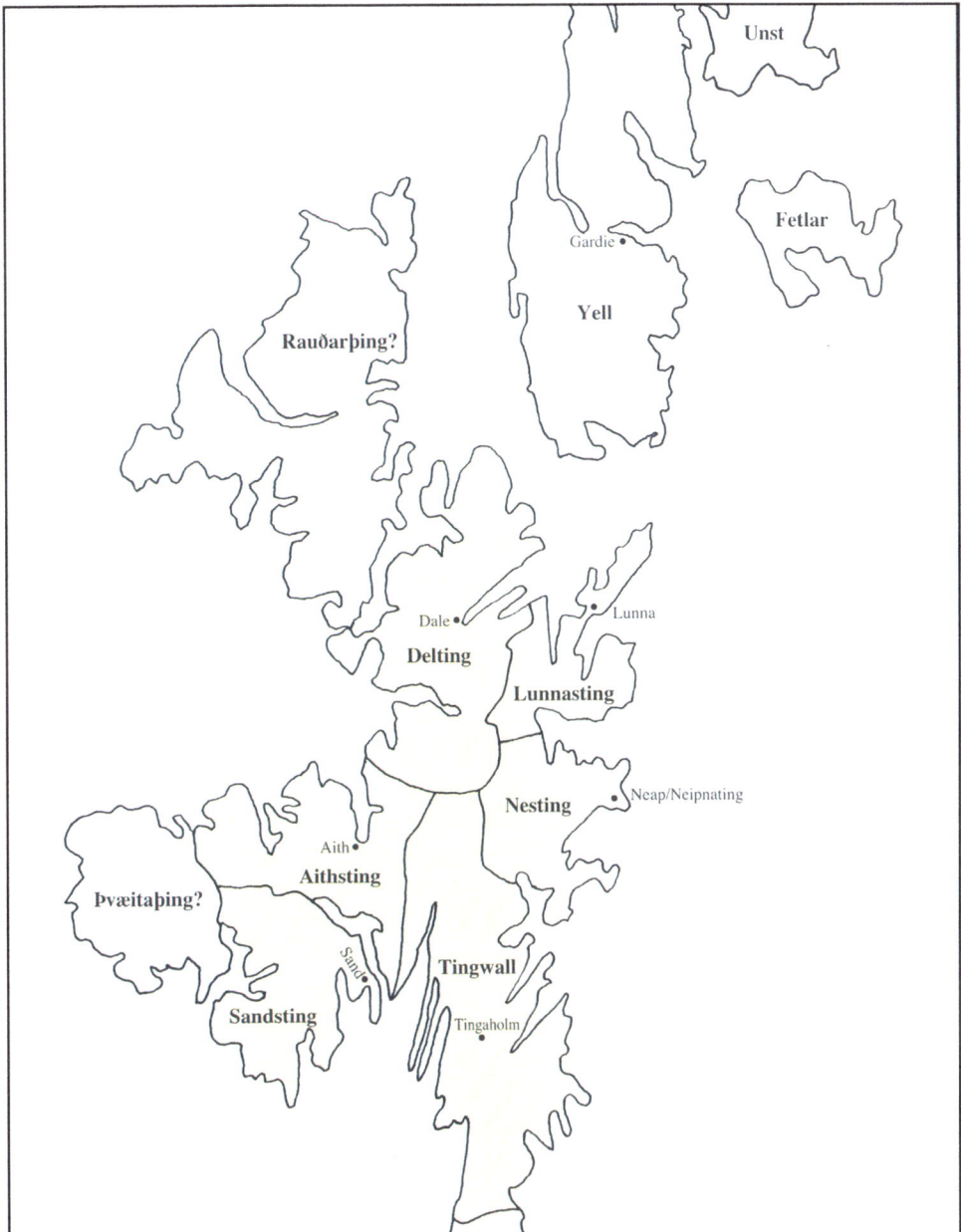

Map showing Ting parishes in Shetland. Originally published in *New Shetlander* 250 (Yule 2009), p.40. *Used with permission*

during King Magnus's reign (1263-80), and the participation of the lawman of Shetland indirectly tells that the new law code had been implemented in Shetland already. The next year we get to know that royal envoys had been travelling to and from Shetland and Norway frequently. Their job had probably been to reform the taxation-system. It is to Brian Smith's credit that we know that the old assessment units ounceland and pennyland now were replaced by the Norwegian *markebol*. This did not happen in any of the other tributary countries (Smith, 2000; cf. Smith, 2002).

Brian Smith is probably right when saying that place names with the suffix '-ting', like in Nesting, Lunnasting and so forth, which are unique to Shetland, bear witness to reforms in the administration of justice which were most likely instigated during the reign of King Magnus the Lawmender or one of his sons (Smith, 2009). The *-ting* names bear witness to a system of local courts corresponding to what we see in Norway after the introduction of the Landlaw in 1274-76. However, the reforms might have been introduced a bit earlier, for instance in 1271 when Magnus the Lawmender's revised law-code of the Gulating law-province was sanctioned in Iceland (called *Jarnsiða*) and in Faroe. There is reason to believe that Shetland, like Faroe and Iceland, was part of the west-Norwegian law-province. This corresponds to the Frostating law-province which, in 1223, in addition to the core-land Trøndelag, included Jemtland to the east and Hålogaland to the north, both provinces with their own lawmen and provincial tings. This may also explain why the lawman of Shetland consulted his colleague in Bergen on difficult matters, a tradition that continued until the middle of the sixteenth century.

Like in Norway, documents issued in Shetland in 1299 and 1307 tell us about a lawthing at Tingwall, a lawman, local delegates to the lawthing called lawrightmen, and royal hirdmen in the country (Ballantyne and Smith, 1999, nos.2 and 3). And, as already mentioned, the Shetlanders, like all other royal subjects, had to render *tegngjeld* and *fridkaup* to the king in order to obtain his protection in cases of homicide. In other words, the Norwegian system of criminal justice was introduced as well at the end of the thirteenth century (Imsen, 2009b).

This corresponds with what happened in the other tributary countries after 1280. In other words, a uniform system of law and administration was applied to all parts of the realm of the king of Norway as a useful instrument for royal rule as well as for provincial self-rule. We do not know for certain if the Shetland lawman had a seal like that of the Orkney community seal. The documents from 1299 and 1307 report that such a seal was not at hand, however Barbara E. Crawford (1978) holds that a seal for the community of Shetland was available later in the century. In a legal as well as in a political sense the tributary countries from now on should be characterised as provincial communes, and the realm of the king of Norway as a kind of commonwealth, a mainland with resident kings and a periphery of royal dominions, mostly ruled by natives.

A letter of witness issued in Kirkwall on 25 May 1369 illustrates how important the role of native participation might be, in practice as well as in principle. There had been an ongoing conflict between the bishop of Orkney and the king's governor in Orkney for some time. Since Orkney and Shetland still belonged to the same diocese, representatives from both countries had been summoned to reconcile the parties. In the letter, which is sealed by the native delegates together with the parties, we learn that 'the lord bishop and the most powerful men in Orkney and Shetland shall be first and foremost in all counsels henceforth affecting the king, the church, and the people, in accordance with the laws and customs of the land. And the lord bishop shall have good native men in Orkney and Shetland to serve him, as other bishops have had in the realm of the king of Norway' (Ballantyne and Smith, 1999, no.12 – two copies were drawn up, one for the bishop and one for the governor).

Local self-rule was strengthened during the late Middle Ages, not least because the Norwegian kings since the end of the fourteenth century were Danish and Swedish kings too, and they gave priority to the Baltic region and northern Germany. The Norse countries west-over-sea were stuck in a geopolitical backwater, so to say.

The pledge in 1469 did not have any immediate consequences for the Shetlanders. The province-communal system was intact until the second half of the sixteenth century, and the Norwegian Landlaw was abolished only in 1611. In spite of the transfer of sovereignty to Scotland, the Shetlanders still were oriented towards western Norway and Bergen, at least until the seventeenth century.

Since the twelfth century, Bergen had been some sort of capital for the tributary countries, commercially as well as administratively and politically. Even though the staple monopoly of the city was weakened in the fifteenth century as German merchants, mostly from Hamburg, sailed directly to Shetland and Faroe, Bergen's position was intact at the end of the Middle Ages. Jørn Øyrehagen Sunde says that until 'the second half of the sixteenth century Shetlanders like Orcadians, were counted as Norwegians and do therefore not appear in Norwegian custom records' (Sunde, 2009, p.12). In other words, Shetlanders and Orcadians enjoyed privileges, since they, in principle, were still royal Norwegian subjects. People from the Northern Isles were not considered foreigners, though they were not Norwegians either. However, local people in Bergen differentiated between Orcadians and Shetlanders – Orcadians were called Scots while the Shetlanders were 'hjelter' (Helle, 1990, pp.804-805, 828, 852). The name *Hjeltefjorden* at the seaward approach to Bergen bear witness to the enduring contact between west-Norway and Shetland.

Bibliography

Andersen, Per Sveaas (1991) 'When was regular, annual taxation introduced in the Norse Islands of Britain? A comparative study of assessment in North-Western Europe', *Scandinavian Journal of History* 16, pp.73.83

Ballantyne, John H. and Smith, B. (eds.) (1999) *Shetland Documents 1195-1379*. Lerwick: The Shetland Times Ltd.

Bull, Edvard (1931), *Det norske folks liv og historie* 3. Oslo: H. Aschehoug.

Cant, Ronald G. (1984) 'Settlement, society, and Church Organisation in the Northern Isles', in Alexander Fenton and Hermann Palsson (eds.) *The Northern and Western Isles in the Viking Age: Survival, Continuity and Change*. Edinburgh: John Donald Publishers, pp.169-80.

Crawford, Barbara E. (1978) 'The Shetland Lawthing Seal', *Orcadian*, 13 July.

Crawford, Barbara E. (1987) *Scandinavian Scotland*. Leicester: Leicester University Press.

Crawford, Barbara E. (2003) 'The Bishopric of Orkney', in S. Imsen (ed.) *Ecclesia Nidrosiensis 1153-1537*. Trondheim: Tapir Akademisk Forlag, pp.143-158.

Crawford, Barbara E. (2014) 'The Northern Half of the Northern Earldoms' Lordship. A Comparison of Orkney and Shetland', in Steinar Imsen (ed.) *Rex Insularum: The King of Norway and His 'Skattlands' as a Political System c.1260 – c.1450*. Bergen: Fagbokforlaget, pp.143-146.

Ekrem, Inger and Boje Mortensen, Lars (eds.) (2003) *Historia Norwegie*. Copenhagen: Museum Tusculanum Press.

Gundersen, Dag and Finn Hødnebø (eds.) (1979) *Norges Kongesagaer* 3, Oslo: Gyldendal Norsk Forlag.

Gunnes, Erik and Kjellberg, Halvor (eds.) (1979) *Regesta Norvegica* 4. Oslo: Norsk Historisk Kjeldeskrift-Institutt.

Hamre, Lars (1964) 'Kyrkans finanser', in *Kulturhistorisk leksikon for nordisk middelalder*, vol ix. Copenhagen: Rosenkilde og Bagger.

Haug, Eldbjørg (2009) 'Fra Stavangerkirkens eldste historie', *Historisk tidsskrift* 88.

Helle, Knut (1990) *Bergen bys historie*, vol. 1. Bergen: Universitetsforlaget.

Helle, Knut (2002) 'Thorvald Thoresson and the Political and Administrative Circumstances in Norway in 1299', in Barbara E. Crawford (ed.) *Papa Stour and 1299: Commemorating the 700th anniversary of Shetland's first document*. Lerwick: The Shetland Times Ltd, pp.45-58.

Helle, Knut (2001) *Gulatinget og Gulatingshslova*. Leikanger: Skald.

Imsen, Steinar (2009a) 'The Scottish-Norwegian Border in the Middle Ages', in Alex Woolf (ed.) *Scandinavian Scotland – Twenty Years After*. St Andrews: Committee for Dark Age Studies, University of St Andrews, pp.9-30.

Imsen, Steinar (2009b) 'Den gammelnorske drapsprosessen', *Historisk tidsskrift* 88, pp.185-229.

Imsen, Steinar (ed.) (2014) *Rex insularum: The King of Norway and His 'skattlands' as a Political System c.1260-c.1450*. Bergen: Fagforlaget.

Imsen, Steinar (2015) *Land og folk I den norrøne verda ca. 900 til 1450*. Oslo: Det Norske Samlaget.

Imsen, Steinar (2021) 'Nidarosnettverket', *Collegium Medievale* 34.

Jakobsen, Jakob (ed.) (1907) *Diplomatarium Færoense*, Tórshavn-København: H. N. Jacobsens Bokhandel.

Jesch, Judith (2015) *The Viking Diaspora*. London and New York: Routledge.

Karlsson, Gunnar et al. (eds.) (2001) *Grágás*. Reykjavík: Mál og menning.

Keyser, R. and Munch, P.A. (eds.) (1849) *Norges gamle Love 3*. Christiania.

Koht, Halvdan (1949) 'Historia Norwegiæ', *Historisk tidsskrift* 35, pp.49-56.

Kolsrud, Oluf (1913) *Den norske Kirkes Erkebiskoper og Biskoper indtil Reformationen*, Christiania: Det Mallingske Bogtrykkeri.

Krag, Claus (2003) 'Ragnvald Øysteinsson Mørejarl', *Norsk biografisk leksikon* 7, p.302.

Mundal, Else (2018) 'R gnvaldr Kali Kolsson. Orkneyinga Saga's portrait of a good ruler', *New Orkney Antiquarian Journal* 8, pp.24-31.

Oram, Richard (2011), 'Ouncelands, Quarterlands and Pennylands in the Western Isles, Man and Galloway: Tribute Payments and Military Levies in the Norse West', in Steinar Imsen (ed.), *Taxes, Tributes and Tributary Lands in the Making of the Scandinavian kingdoms in the Middle Ages*. Trondheim: Tapir Academic Press, pp.57-75.

Ritchie, Anna (1993) *Viking Scotland*. London: B.T. Batsford.

Semple, Sarah, et al. (2021) *Negotiating the north: Meeting-places in the Middle Ages in the North Sea Zone*. Abingdon and New York: Routledge.

Smith, Brian (1988) 'Shetland in Saga-Time: Rereading the Orkneyinga Saga', *Northern Studies* 25, pp.21-41.

Smith, Brian (1990) 'Shetland, Scandinavia, Scotland 1300-1700: the changing nature of contact', in Grant G. Simpson (ed.) *Scotland and Scandinavia 800-1800*. Edinburgh: John Donald Publishers, pp.25-37.

Smith, Brian (2000) *Toons and Tenants: Settlement and society in Shetland, 1299-1899*. Lerwick: The Shetland Times Ltd.

Smith, Brian (2002) 'The 1299 Letter about Papa Stour: a note' in Barbara E. Crawford (ed.) *Papa Stour and 1299: Commemorating the 700th anniversary of Shetland's first document*. Lerwick: The Shetland Times Ltd, pp.37-44.

Smith, Brian (2003) 'Archdeacons of Shetland 1195-1567', in Steinar Imsen (ed.) *Ecclesia Nidrosiensis 1153-1537*. Trondheim: tapir akademisk forlag, pp.161-170.

Smith, Brian (2009) 'On the nature of tings: Shetland's law courts from the middle ages until 1611', *New Shetlander* 250, pp.37-45.

Smith, Brian (2011), 'Some Shetland heiresses', 1360-1660', *New Shetlander* 258, pp.20-27.

Sunde, Jørn Øyrehagen (2009) *From Shetland Lairdship to a Norwegian Barony: the Mowat family and the Barony of Rosendal*. Lerwick: Shetland Museum and Archives.

Taranger, Absalon (1912) Norges gamle Love, 2nd series 1388-1604, vol. 1. Kristiania.

Thomson, William P.L. (1996) *Lord Henry Sinclair's 1492 Rental of Orkney*. Kirkwall: Orkney Press.

Thomson, William P.L.(2001) *The New History of Orkney*, Edinburgh: Mercat Press.

Woolf, Alex (2007) *The Edinburgh History of Scotland vol. 2: From Pictland to Alba 789-1070*. Edinburgh: Edinburgh University Press.

3

Kebister
– an ordinary and remarkable place

Olwyn Owen
(University of the Highlands and Islands)

Da draem o dem at no sae lang ago
Clang tae dis rock, loved, toiled, failed, wure awa –
An idder folk afore dem an benon –
Dir lives and deaths makkin da land we ken,
Dir caandleflames lightin wirs for wir onn.

From 'At da Croft Museum' by Stella Sutherland
(with thanks to Brian Smith for introducing me to Stella's poetry)

At first sight, back in 1985, the Kebister hillside seemed a very ordinary place by the standards of Shetland. It had a stark beauty by dint of bordering the majestic Dales Voe, but its northwest-facing aspect, cowering beneath and often overshadowed by the Hill of Gremista and Luggie's Knowe, lent it an unpropitious air and clearly inhibited its agricultural potential. Despite its proximity to Lerwick, only some 5km to the south, it felt remote and inaccessible. Before the road was built (in 1985 there was only a newly created, unsurfaced track), Kebister could only be reached with some difficulty, either on foot from the hinterland or by boat from the voe – a journey no doubt made by generations of inhabitants in earlier times.

Nevertheless, it was to Kebister that a team of young archaeologists was dispatched in March 1985 (Owen and Lowe, 1999). Our task was to investigate, at breakneck speed, the remains of a substantial and intriguing rectangular building lying in the path of the oil rig supply base that was then being built. The rest, as they say, is history. When I first stepped foot on the Kebister hillside is also when I first met Brian Smith, archivist and historian extraordinaire, who has made such a huge contribution to our understanding of historic Kebister, and much else besides. It was also the start of an enduring friendship.

The project aims were soon expanded in response to the unexpected discovery of a multi-period settlement site. Over three seasons between 1985-87, we toiled on that hillside as so many must have toiled before us, though for

Excavating the early Christian graves lying beneath Henry Phankouth's teind barn.   Photo: © Historic Environment Scotland, used with permission

different purposes. And from the first to the last day on site, the Kebister hillside never ceased to surprise us, with every lump and bump concealing a diverse array of traces of Shetland's rich past.

Among the more unexpected discoveries was evidence of early prehistoric settlement, from sometime in the 3rd to early 2nd millennium B.C.; and traces of a singular sub-rectangular wooden structure (Structure 1), dating probably from the early Bronze Age (first half of the second millennium B.C.). This timber building, still without parallel in Shetland, with its substantial hearth, water troughs and sophisticated water-management system, was interpreted as a cookhouse. The hillside also yielded a scatter of at least seven burnt mounds which are probably broadly contemporary with Structure 1; three Bronze Age cremation burials, one in a cist and two in pits, all adjacent to the remains of a funeral pyre; fragmentary remains of a probable late Bronze Age heel-shaped house (Structure 2); and rare remains of an early knapping floor for the production of sandstone agricultural tools.

There seems to have been a hiatus in activity on the Kebister hillside around the turn of the first millennium B.C., but sometime during the last two or three centuries B.C. (in the middle Iron Age), a small farming settlement was established. Shetland's Iron Age is normally synonymous with brochs – those great towers, like Mousa, that stud the coastlines of the Northern Isles – but very unusually, there was no broch at Kebister. Instead, we uncovered the remains of a cluster of small Iron Age buildings, making Kebister one of only a handful of unfortified domestic sites in Iron Age Shetland. From around 250 B.C. until about A.D. 400, a sequence of small houses formed the nucleus of a modest farming settlement.

The first to be built was a small oval dwelling of stone (Structure 4), only 4m wide internally, with its interior punctuated by orthostats forming small recesses in the walls, and two distinct levels of occupation discernible in its sunken interior. It seems the turf roof may have collapsed at some point, but was then replaced and strengthened with additional posts (hence the two main occupation levels). Some bloom-working debris was found in the lower level, together with pottery, while the finds from the secondary level were mainly spread around the edges of the room, suggesting periodic cleaning out. That said, it seems that the building was in a poor state of repair by then, even as the secondary deposits and a new hearth were laid. Radiocarbon evidence suggests this house was built probably in the last quarter of the first millennium B.C. and abandoned around the turn of the millennium or in the first century A.D.

Structure 3 was built around the same time as Structure 4, sometime between 300 and 100 B.C., but continued in use for much longer and was a somewhat different type of building, with no recesses or raised platforms within the walls. Although incomplete when excavated, it was probably roughly D-shaped or sub-circular originally, with a sunken interior in which the base of a single radial pier survived, terminating in an orthostat, and it had a sequence of four hearths at its centre. The structure was encircled by an enclosure wall forming a small yard around the building, and it was much later provided with an annexe, used probably for storage. Occupation seems to have been continuous, although the building was clearly reorganised and adapted several times. Interestingly, it is highly likely that it was still in use when Structure 5 was built, in the 1st century A.D.

Structure 5 was quite different to the earlier buildings at Kebister. Externally it was roughly oval in shape, but internally it was a cellular house – made up of a series of linked cells of different sizes, formed and separated by single-faced walls and orthostats. Ritchie (1977, p.182) has pointed out that one advantage of the cellular house (sometimes known as 'jelly baby' houses for obvious reasons) is that it reduces the roof span, with the intruding walls between the cells acting as roof supports. This building with its complex of cells seems to have been built in one phase, but there was plenty of evidence for internal additions and rearrangements, including the replacement of hearths and the insertion of a paved floor. The single-faced external walls were revetted with stone and turf.

All the excavated Iron Age structures seem to have been abandoned by about A.D. 400 on radiocarbon dating evidence. Overall, these small dwellings were lived in for several hundred years by a farming community who kept cattle, pigs and sheep or goats, and grew barley (bere) and black oats. The most emphatic evidence for Iron Age cultivation was an extensive spread of inter-cutting plough marks. In one case, the ploughshare's point had broken off at the end of an ardmark, confirming that flaked sandstone bars and ard points were still in use in the Iron Age at Kebister, and presumably, therefore, were also still being made on site. The Iron Age inhabitants clearly made use of all the locally-available resources, both as raw materials for building and for fuel: peat and heather, the sparse local woods and driftwood, and turf and seaweed. It must be admitted that the Iron Age artefact assemblage is notable more for quantity than quality, but sandstone, quartz, beach cobbles and pumice were clearly being exploited to produce a range of tools, and the copious amounts of coarse pottery (some 4,000 sherds were recovered from Kebister) were probably also being made locally, while evidence of small-scale iron-working survived in the yard of Structure 3 and elsewhere.

With the early historic, medieval and later periods at Kebister, we come to the meat of Brian Smith's important contributions to our understanding of the site. The substantial rectangular building we had first been dispatched to examine turned out not to be a Viking house as had been suggested, but a very different type of structure dating from the early 16th century. This was a huge building by pre-modern Shetland standards – some 17m long by 7.2m wide externally – and it was extremely well-built with its 1m-wide walls of dressed stone founded on a substantial plinth; and yet there was very little evidence of any domestic occupation or other function. Clearly this was no ordinary building – but who on earth had built it, and what for, and why at Kebister?

We thought we had the answer when we discovered an armorial stone lying face-down outside the sole entrance, almost certainly where it had fallen from its original position above the doorway. The stone, broken into five pieces when found, was beautifully restored by Stenhouse Conservation Centre and is now complete. It is a work of fine craftsmanship: 'The Kebister armorial panel stands out as particularly remarkable in the Northern Isles, where the later Middle Ages produced relatively little architectural sculpture' (Fawcett, in Owen and Smith, 1988, p.7). At first glance the design appears fairly typical for an armorial stone: a shield set within an elaborate Gothic tabernacle contains a raised chevron band with a gryphon's head and an inscribed motto: 'Sine paulusp', written in Gothic miniscule. At second glance, this 'veritable confection of heraldic elements' (Bertie, 2019, p.11) seems intentionally confusing. The ostentatious tabernacle design indicated an important ecclesiastical owner. The only trouble was – there was no immediately obvious candidate; and the enigmatic inscription, which translates as: 'permit (me?) for a little while', was puzzling to say the least.

It took Brian's dogged perseverance and typical ingenuity to come up with the answer (Smith, 1987; Owen and Smith, 1988; Smith, 1989; Smith, in Owen and Lowe, 1999, pp.219-220, pp.297-300). His forensic detective work unearthed the owner of the stone – and the building it had adorned – almost certainly as Henry Phankouth, archdeacon of Shetland from 1501-1529. Henry's antecedents had been a mystery, but Brian's research revealed the fascinating story of an educated man with a defect of birth, high aspirations, and a wry sense of humour.

Henry was the illegitimate son of Andrew Pictoris, Bishop of Orkney from 1477 to c.1505. German-born and educated (he may have matriculated in Cologne in 1488), Henry's distinctive surname is the common German occupational name Pfannkuch/en (pancake-maker). Henry followed in his father's footsteps when he came to Scotland to be ordained in St. Andrews in the 1490s. He received a papal dispensation on account of his illegitimacy in 1495, and his father procured letters of legitimation for him in 1497. After a political tussle (the archdeaconry of Shetland was a highly desirable office), Henry was appointed archdeacon in 1501. The Kebister township was an important part of the pre-Reformation archdeaconry estate (Erroll Charters), and the archdeaconry brought with it lucrative rights to a prebend [i.e. stipend or portion of revenue from a cathedral] in Orkney and extensive teinds and rents in Shetland. Henry was based in Kirkwall where he had several houses, but he also had a small estate in Shetland. It seems that he ordered the building of a substantial barn in which to store the rents and teinds on archdeaconry land at Kebister – and this was the impressive building we excavated in 1985. Recent reanalysis of the archaeological evidence for the teind barn has concluded that this building was almost certainly a full two storeys high originally, and probably resembled the surviving storehouse at St. Mary's in Orkney, built in 1649 (Holtermann and Grassel, 2023, pp. 18-20).

But what of the bizarre inscription on the armorial stone? Again, it was Brian (1987) who came up with an answer. The inscription most probably derives from the Roman comedian Terence's play *The Self Tormentor*. The words 'permit (me?) for a little while' form part of a dialogue in which Clitipho is pleading with his father's slave, Syrus, to be allowed to go and see his mistress, Bacchis. The tabernacle design on the stone echoes that of Henry Phankouth's contemporary, Bishop Edward Stewart (1498-1524/5), and it is likely that Henry set out to copy the stone of his superior on a more elaborate scale. If so, the Kebister armorial stone above the impressive teind barn's door was an exercise in epic one-upmanship, topped off with a lewd and highly irreligious joke. As Brian (in Owen and Lowe 1999, p.220) concluded: 'The stone and its legend is a not improbable piece of ostentation by an ecclesiastic with an important office, an important parent and a defect of birth'.

We had wondered whether fugitive traces of a Viking or later Norse farm might be found underneath Henry's teind barn, or might once have been present there but entirely swept away by the building of such a substantial structure in the 16th century. But once again, Kebister confounded all expectations when the very truncated remains of what was probably a small timber chapel were discovered beneath the teind barn, together with the poorly preserved remains of two Christian graves immediately beyond its east end. This episode in Kebister's long history has so far received rather less attention than it deserves, and merits further consideration, not least as it throws up some interesting conundrums for students of the early medieval period.

There were other indications of an early Christian presence on the site too, notably a handy palm-sized stone incised with a primary cross, likely of 8th- or 9th-century date (Owen and Lowe 1999, pp.220-222, plate 10); and a piece of exotic green porphyry, a material quarried in Greece in classical Greek, Hellenistic and Roman times (Owen and Lowe, 1999, pp.223-235, plate 11). A small corpus of these porphyry pieces is now known from early medieval sites in Scotland, Ireland

and elsewhere in the northern world, where they were primarily used for portable altars or to decorate shrines, tombs or fixed altars. They tend to occur on long-lived ecclesiastical sites (such as Whithorn in south-west Scotland), but they often also appear on sites with Norse connections, such as seven examples from 11th-century levels in Hiberno-Norse Dublin, and eight from Waterford. In Shetland, a very similar piece was found in the chapel on St. Ninian's Isle (Small et al., 1973, pp.31-32), but finding a piece at Kebister was more surprising. Unfortunately, the Kebister fragment was recovered from a redeposited midden just outside the teind barn, but it was brought to the site probably sometime between the 9th and 13th centuries.

Very little survived of the putative chapel at Kebister – only the rectangular outline of a small building formed by a slot (Structure 6) – but its east-west orientation and its position in relation to the two graves, which are aligned with the building, leaves little doubt but that this was the scant remains of a probably stone-clad, timber-built chapel with associated graves. It is well within the size range for the surviving examples of early medieval stone and timber chapels elsewhere in the British Isles, Faroe and Iceland, although it is unusually narrow. Nonetheless, the Kebister chapel entirely accords with Barrett's (2000) criteria for the identification of a Christian church, namely: the co-occurrence of supine east-west oriented burials; an east-west oriented structure (lacking domestic or industrial features such as a hearth); and the absence of grave goods from the burials. The two Kebister burials were unaccompanied save for their wooden coffins, which were unusually of Scots pine (most medieval coffins in Britain are of oak). No human remains survived, but the best-preserved coffin tapered from west to east, indicating (as would be expected) that the head lay at the west end. Two radiocarbon samples of coffin wood from Grave 1 produced very close results and gave a combined date of A.D. 930-1015 (one sigma range) and A.D. 890-1020 (two sigma) – suggesting a 10th- to 11th-century date for the chapel and graves, in which case the chapel must have been built within the Norse milieu.

This raises the thorny issue of whether vestiges of Christianity and Pictish religious institutions survived and endured after the arrival of Scandinavians, and when and how Christianity was adopted by Norse colonisers in the Orkney earldom. *Orkneyinga Saga* recounts the story of Earl Sigurd's enforced conversion to Christianity in A.D. 995, which has traditionally been cited as the date of conversion of the Norse; but the 9th-century hagiography, the *Life of Findan*, refers to a bishop in Orkney in around A.D. 850 (Thomson, 1986), which would seem to support the theory that some level of Christianity continued to be practiced into the Norse period. As an aside, this debate of course risks straying into the even more vexed question of what happened to the Picts when the Vikings arrived in Orkney and Shetland – a question on which Brian and I, and many others, have locked (metaphorical Viking) horns previously (e.g. Owen, 2004; Smith, 2017). In a nutshell – and at serious risk of caricature – the opposing arguments are that the native Pictish inhabitants were expelled or slaughtered en masse, or that the earliest Norse arrivals co-existed with the local population to a greater or lesser extent, which transmogrified over time into much less bloody integration. Both views have their scholarly advocates, and both views are regularly expounded with much more nuance and conviction than expressed here.

This argument may be difficult to settle once and for all, but recent research continues to cast light on different aspects of what remains a perennial debate. In an important paper attempting to date the earliest Christian burials in Viking Age Orkney, for example, Barrett *et al.* (2000) analysed the radiocarbon dates of 20 graves from the cemetery at Newark Bay and two graves associated with the two-phase chapel on the Brough of Deerness, both sites in the east Mainland of Orkney. They further calibrated the radiocarbon dates by applying a marine reservoir correction (to take account of the effects of the marine component in human diet in the Northern Isles, and other variables). The results strongly suggest that the Newark Bay cemetery originated as a Pictish burial place, and that there was continued or renewed use of the site by the mid 10th century at the latest – predating the traditional conversion of Orkney. The results from several of the Newark Bay graves and one of the Deerness graves (Barrett, 2000, p.541, Table 1) are very similar to that of the Grave 1 coffin at Kebister. A *terminus ante quem* for the earlier Deerness chapel was provided by a worn coin of Eadgar, who reigned from A.D. 959-75, which means that this timber chapel must date from the mid 10th century or earlier; and its excavators concluded that it was likely to belong to a Norse milieu based on its architectural characteristics (Morris and Emery 1986). In other words, there is a growing body of scientific and other dating evidence for either continuation of the Christian tradition in the earlier Viking period, or for its adoption by the incoming Scandinavians somewhat earlier than A.D. 995. As Barrett admits, the data so far cannot corroborate the continuity or adoption of Christianity in 9th-century Orkney implied by the *Life of Findan*, but 'it may have important implications regarding the relationship between "native" Picts and Norse "newcomers" in Viking Age Scotland' (Barrett, 2000, p.540).

The discovery of a chapel and associated graves at Kebister was entirely unexpected and poses other questions, notably its apparent lack of any contemporary context. Some comparable chapels, such as the early timber phase on the Brough of Deerness, appear to have been private chapels built to serve a chiefly stronghold (Morris and Emery, 1986; Barrett and Slater, 2009) – a habit that continued and multiplied in the late Norse and medieval period in the Northern Isles, including on another site I excavated, at Tuquoy, Westray, in Orkney (Owen, 1993). But no evidence was found at Kebister of any dwellings or other structures related to or broadly contemporary with the chapel. It is not impossible that any such remains were swept away in the early 16th century by the imposition of the substantial teind barn, and it is true that some elements of the artefactual assemblage betray Norse connections, such as fragments of steatite bowls and platters; but overall, had a Norse farmstead or chiefly stronghold once been present in the vicinity of the chapel, we would have expected to find more convincing evidence.

So was there a Norse element to this long-lived multi-period site at all? The place-name 'Kebister' is clearly Norse in origin and includes the common

Old Norse (ON) generic, *bústaðr*, meaning farm – a relatively common form in Shetland, seen today in names ending in '-bister'. The first element, 'Keb-', puzzled us for quite a while, until Brian's informant, Robert Leask, came up with the ingenious suggestion that it derived from 'kabe' (a boat rowlock in modern Shetland dialect, ON *keiþr*). By way of corroboration, Luggie's Knowe, towering behind the site, resembles a rowlock when observed from the sea and was also known locally as 'Da Kebb' (Smith, 1992). A topographical derivation for the first element would be entirely consistent with Norse place-naming habits, but the *bústaðr* element clearly implies that a Norse period farm was located somewhere on the Kebister hillside. As Brian (in Owen and Lowe, 1999, p.18) wrote: 'Kebister thus seems to bear a respectable, if quirky, ON name'. Moreover, palynological evidence (pollen analysis) suggests that Kebister was home to an active farming community around A.D. 1000. And yet, no trace of any Norse dwelling was found, either in the excavated area or identified in the hillside survey.

This brings us to the ruins of the crofting settlement of Handigert – where, yet again, Brian's contribution to the project was invaluable. Handigert, also called 'Da green toon' by its neighbours across Dales Voe, is the local name for an abandoned farmstead located less than 120m south of the teind barn, at the top of the lush grassy sward on the other side of the Burn of Kebister. In its final form it comprised seven conjoined rectangular buildings, all aligned NW-SE, with the walls still standing up to 1.6m high, and with attached enclosures. Trial excavations in four of the buildings revealed paved floors, areas of burning and drainage gulleys, and yielded pottery and other artefacts predominantly of 18th- and 19th-century date. So far, so ordinary – a typical ruined crofting settlement with a secondary (alternative) name to Kebister – or so we thought.

In Shetland, it is rare for a farmstead to have an alternative name, especially as the name Handigert never appears in documents: all those who lived there from 1577 to 1817 gave their address as Kebister. It was Brian (in Owen and Lowe, 1999, p.19) who unravelled the mystery, proposing that Handigert is the same place-name as Handegaard in Jondal, Norway, originally ON *hangðagarðr* (Rygh, 1898, p.xxiii, p.510). This Norse name means 'farm near or under a steep hill' – the steep hill probably being Luggie's Knowe – which would imply that Handigert, far from being a secondary settlement, might in fact be the site of the Norse and medieval settlement at Kebister.

The very limited trial excavations at Handigert did not produce evidence of occupation earlier than the post-medieval period, other than a single fragment of a fine, late Norse type of steatite bowl. Close examination of the cluster of buildings suggested there may have been an original longhouse at Handigert, some 19m long, which was later re-built and sub-divided into smaller units. However, the classic longhouse has 'at least a thousand years of tradition ... in the Northern Isles' (Fenton, 1978, p.114), which means that the tantalising probability of a longhouse at Handigert cannot in itself confirm that the farmstead originated in the Norse or medieval period. Nonetheless, 'Da green toon', set in its lush sward, is perhaps a more obvious place for a Norse or medieval farmstead than the site we excavated north of the Burn of Kebister; and it is significant that there was no evidence of domestic settlement later than the Iron Age on the excavated site. Nor is there any evidence that the medieval and later inhabitants at Kebister ever had more than one stance for their houses. As Brian concluded, all of these factors: 'strongly suggest that the medieval houses of the district had always been where the ruins of their successors remain today' (Smith, in Owen and Lowe, 1999, p.296). It is an archaeological truism that the absence of evidence is not evidence of absence, and it seems more likely than not that the fugitive traces of any Norse settlement may lie beneath the ruined crofting settlement at Handigert. For now, though, we may have to accept the Scottish verdict of not proven.

In the late medieval and post-medieval period, documentary research (by you-know-who, in Owen and Lowe, 1999, pp.17-22, pp.303-305) shows that Kebister, with its satellite farm Vatsland, was the focus of a township whose fortunes ebbed and flowed through the centuries in concert with the fortunes of Shetland as a whole. At Kebister, this general trend was punctuated by an extraordinary interlude in the early 16th century, by when Kebister was evidently part of the archdeaconry estates. It may have been a deserted township at this time: Kebister is absent from the scat-book of 1500 which suggests there was no tenant here then. The archdeacon's manse was inconveniently land-locked at Tingwall, and so Henry found a more accessible site for his teind barn – close to the sea and in a (probably) temporarily deserted township, where the rents and teinds could easily be delivered and safely stored – at Kebister.

The first named inhabitant appears in a document of 1577: 'Stephen of Kebustare' (Ballantyne and Smith, 1999, no.237). During the 17th and 18th centuries, Kebister appears to have been at most a two-household township, with regular changes of occupants, some of whom clearly struggled to make a living. In the later 18th century, the population of Kebister increased, as elsewhere in Shetland, and there were 15 inhabitants there in 1802. The last child born in Kebister was Agnes Morrison, in 1817, and shortly afterwards, probably around 1820, the remaining inhabitants were removed to make space for a sheep farm. Kebister has the dubious distinction of being the earliest Shetland township to be permanently cleared for sheep.

Since 1985, the Kebister hillside has been stamped indelibly by industries of the late 20th and early 21st centuries, and little survives of that fascinating archaeological landscape today. But the remains of the teind barn, now scheduled as a monument of national importance, are still there – to bear witness, albeit a little forlornly, to an extraordinary episode in the long story of an ordinary and remarkable place.

Postcript

It has been a huge pleasure to revisit the story of Kebister after all these years. It is sometimes said that archaeology is a footnote to history, or vice-versa. In the case of Kebister, history and archaeology (and historian and archaeologist) walked hand-in-hand to unlock the story of the recent and not-so-recent past.

Since that magic time of working together on Kebister, I've once or twice had the pleasure of editing Brian's writings, which led to some entertaining exchanges. On one occasion, Brian wrote: 'I think your ban on 'And' and 'But' at the beginning of sentences, and of words ending in 'n't' and 't's', is prehistoric' – he felt the same about my ban on use of the first person singular in academic papers. So I've written this paper not only to thank him for his friendship and his immense contribution to our understanding of the remarkable site at Kebister, but also to demonstrate that, as ever, he was right. And in a volume in his honour, so richly deserved, I couldn't have done anything else.

Bibliography

Ballantyne, John H. and Smith, Brian (1999) *Shetland Documents 1195-1579*. Lerwick: The Shetland Times Ltd.

Barrett, J.H., Beukens, R.P. and Brothwell, D.R. (2000) 'Radiocarbon dating and marine reservoir correction of Viking Age Christian burials from Orkney', *Antiquity* 74, pp.537-543.

Barrett, J H and Slater, A 2009 'New excavations at the Brough of Deerness: power and religion in Viking Age Scotland', *Journal of the North Atlantic* 2, 81-94.

Bertie, D.M. (2019) 'The Kebister armorial stone – a re-assessment', *Tak Tent* 84, pp.10-12.

Erroll Charters (in private hands): transcripts in NRA (Scotland) 925; archdeaconry document in section I, no 774; feu-charter of 10 June 1570 by Jerome Cheyne.

Fenton, A. (1978) *The Northern Isles: Orkney and Shetland*. Edinburgh: John Donald Publishers.

Holtermann, B. and Grassel P. (eds.) (2023) *Looking in from the Edge: Early Modern Trade in tthe Northern Isles*. Bremerhaven: Deutsches Schiffahrtsmuseum.

Morris, C.D. and Emery, N. (1986) 'The chapel and enclosure on the Brough of Deerness, Orkney: survey and excavations 1975-1977', *Proceedings of the Society of Antiquaries of Scotland* 116, pp.301-374.

Owen, O. (1993) 'Tuquoy, Westray, Orkney: a challenge for the future', in C.E. Batey, J. Jesch and C.D. Morris (eds.) *The Viking Age in Caithness, Orkney and the North Atlantic: Select papers from the proceedings of the eleventh Viking Congress, Thurso and Kirkwall, 22 August - 1 September 1989*. Edinburgh: Edinburgh University Press, pp.318-339.

Owen, O. (2004) 'The Scar boat burial – and the missing decades of the early Viking Age in Orkney and Shetland', in J. Adams and K. Holman (eds.) *Scandinavia and Europe 800-1350: Contact, conflict, and coexistence*. Turnhout: Brepols, pp.3-33.

Owen, O. and Smith, B. (1988) 'Kebister, Shetland: an armorial stone, and an archdeacon's teind barn?', *Post-Medieval Archaeology* 22, pp.1-20.

Owen, O. and Lowe, C. (1999) *Kebister: the four-thousand-year-old story of one Shetland township* (Society of Antiquaries of Scotland monograph series 14). Edinburgh. Society of Antiquaries of Scotland.

Ritchie A. (1977) 'Excavations of Pictish and Viking-Age farmsteads at Buckquoy, Orkney', *Proceedings of the Society of Antiquaries of Scotland* 108, pp.174–227.

Rygh, O. (1898) *Norske gaardnavne*. Kristiania: W. C. Fabritius and Sonners Bogtrykkeri.

Small, A., Thomas, A.C. and Wilson, D.M. (1973) *St Ninian's Isle and its treasure* (Aberdeen University Studies 152). London: Oxford University Press.

Smith, B. (1987) 'The Archdeacon of Kebister', *New Shetlander* 160, pp.6-9.

Smith, B. (1989) 'In the tracks of Bishop Andrew Pictoris of Orkney and Henry Phankouth, archdeacon of Shetland', *Innes Review* 40, pp.91-105.

Smith, B. (1992) 'Who was Luggie?', *New Shetlander* 179, pp.27-29.

Smith, B. (2017) 'The enigma and fate of the Picts in Shetland during the Viking Age', *Hugin and Munin* 1, pp.20-23.

Thomson, W.P.L. (1986) 'St Findan and the Pictish-Norse transition', in R.J. Berry and H.N. Firth (eds.) *The people of Orkney*. Kirkwall: Orkney Press, pp.279-283.

4

Revisiting -staðir place-names in Shetland

Peder Gammeltoft
(University of Bergen)

Shetland, the northernmost archipelago of Scotland, has a rich and diverse toponymy that reflects its complex cultural and linguistic history. A predominant element here are the place-names of Scandinavian origin, and of these Old Norse *staðir* m.pl. 'farm', now mainly written -sta, occupy a central position. This name type offers valuable insights into the social, economic, and environmental aspects of life in medieval Shetland. In this article, we will explore the origin, distribution, structure and meaning of *staðir* place-names in Shetland, as well as their relationship with other areas. We will also discuss some of the challenges and opportunities that *staðir* place-names pose for researchers in interpreting them.

Staðir place-names are found throughout a large area, their core distribution being in Scandinavia with outliers to Finland in the east as well as the North Atlantic Area in the West. In Norway, *staðir* place-names are very common throughout the entire country. It is one of the most frequently occurring settlement name types, with more than 2,250 examples. Sweden has slightly fewer names (approximately 2,000) in -sta (from Old Swedish *staþer*). The name type is also found in Denmark, albeit in much smaller numbers, with only 222 names in total. In Denmark, the usual form is today -sted (from Old Danish *stath*). In Denmark and Sweden, researchers agree that the name type originates in the Iron Age, possibly as early as the second century A.D. according to Swedish research, although Danish name researchers generally place the productivity period slightly later, c. 400-850. Since the name type does not occur in the Danelaw area, it is generally assumed that the name type had gone out of use by the beginning of the Viking Age. In Norway, however, research has suggested that the name type originates in the migration period, but with a period of productivity extending well into the Viking Age. As a result, we see an abundance of *staðir* place-names in the North Atlantic area, in the places where Norwegians settled: Iceland, the Isle of Man and Scotland.

Staðir place-names in the North Atlantic area

In Iceland, *staðir* place-names are very numerous and widespread, and they often indicate the location of farms or settlements that were established by the first settlers. They usually have personal names as their first element, such as Arnar*staðir* (from *Arnar*, m.) or Ingjalds*staðir* (from *Ingjaldur*, m). There are no place-names in -*staðir* in Greenland nor in the Faroe Islands. This is most likely an indication that the conditions for an agricultural settlement of the *staðir* -type were not present in these areas rather than the place-name type having gone out of use when these areas were settled.

One of the areas where we find a significant number of *staðir* place-names is in the Scottish Isles and in the Isle of Man. The exact number of place-names in ON *staðir* in the British Isles is somewhat uncertain. Two well-known, uncertain examples are found in the Wirral in northwest England: *Croxteth* (1257 Crocstad) and *Toxteth* (1212 Tokestath). These may either originate from either *staðir* 'farm' or gno. *stǫð* f. 'landing place for boats' (DSL, p.433). The remainder of the names, however, are either from the Isle of Man (cf. Broderick, 1994-), where we find about 12 names in *staðir*, or from the Scottish isles. There are some 60 *staðir* place-names known from the Northern Isles and just over 40 from the Hebrides (cf. Gammeltoft, 2006, pp.69-86; Marwick, 1952; Stewart, 1987, pp.251-257). The total known number of *staðir* names in the British Isles thus tallies at just under 120 names.

Old Norse *staðir* has played an important role in studies of the Norse settlement in Scotland and has been a cornerstone in the formation of theories about settlement processes and colonisation. Inspired by Hugh Marwick's ideas about naming and settlement chronology in Orkney (Marwick, 1952, pp.227-251), W.F.H. Nicolaisen (1969, pp.6-17) did a similar study of place-names in Old Norse -*staðir* , -*setr*, -*bólstaðr* and -*dalr*, but covering all Scotland. By plotting the known place-name examples of these types on maps, the following could be observed (see Figure 1): names of *staðir* were most frequent in Shetland and Orkney as well as in Lewis and northern Skye. The name type was virtually unknown in the southern Hebrides (Figure 1.1.). Names of *setr* were very frequent in Shetland, common in Orkney, Lewis and Harris. In addition, compared to *staðir*, there was a greater concentration in northern Caithness and in central Skye (Figure 1.2.). *Bólstaðr*, on the other hand, was found over the whole area from Shetland in the north to Islay in the south (Figure 1.3.). Finally, names in -*dalr* showed the greatest distribution, included Shetland, Orkney, Caithness, Sutherland and the whole of the Hebrides, as well as the adjacent mainland coastlines (Figure 1.4.). The differences in distribution led Nicolaisen to assume that *staðir* belonged to the oldest settlement name layer, a period he put at approx. 850-880, followed by a period in which *setr* was the most productive element (c. 880-900). The name type *bólstaðr* showed, by virtue of its slightly later period of productivity, the maximum spread of Norse settlement. At the same time, the settlement area commanded a considerable 'hinterland' or sphere of interest, an area represented by the natural name element *dalr's* large distribution far into the Scottish mainland.

Figure 1. Overview of the distribution of 1. *staðir*, 2. *setr/sætr*, 3. *bólstaðr*, and 4. *dalr*. All four illustrations from Nicolaisen 2001.

Nicolaisen's theory immediately resonated with Viking Age researchers and was widely accepted as the standard interpretation in the field, although a few critical voices have pointed out problems with the interpretation of the material (e.g. Crawford, 1987, pp.105-115). Nicolaisen has been criticised in particular for not having included the Isle of Man in the study. In addition, one can also object that the productivity period of the individual place-name types is very short (rarely more than 20-30 years) and that the theory assumes a colonisation movement from north to south, without taking into account that transport via the sea does not necessarily presuppose a gradual 'rings in the water' colonisation, but just as much can presuppose one or more support points anywhere in the Scottish islands from which colonisation and settlement could take place.

Staðir in the Northern Isles

As mentioned above, there are some 60 known place-names in *staðir* in the Northern Isles, in Orkney and in Shetland. In Shetland, Old Norse *staðir* in compounds have generally developed into *-sta*, e.g. Bailasta in Unst which is written *á Bollastöðum* in Magnus Barfod's saga, or occasionally into *-ster*, on analogy with the more frequent place-names originating from Old Norse *setr*, n. or *sætr*, n. In Orkney, on the other hand, *staðir* developed into *-ston*, which is due to mixing of the individual name in the original dative plural form with English and Scottish place names in *-ton* (Sandnes 2003, p.248).

Jakob Jakobsen pioneered place-name research in the Northern Isles with his *Shetlandsøernes Stednavne* in 1901 (translated into English in 1936). This was one of the earliest 'modern', linguistically based place-name works in the North Atlantic area. The book was the first result of Jakobsen's linguistic studies in Shetland – the other was his monumental *Dictionary of the Norn language in Shetland*, which was published a couple of decades later. Orkney followed with Hugh Marwick's *Orkney Farm Names* in 1952. Simultaneously, Shetland-born John Stewart started his own ambitious place-name project. He created a questionnaire for collecting place-names based on the *Skulebarnsoppskriftene* (now part of Norway's Documentary Heritage) from the University Museum of Bergen and asked school children to assist in the collection of local place-names. Although John Stewart unfortunately died before he could publish his work, the outcome, *Shetland Place-Names*, was published posthumously in 1987 – the first truly systematic place-name volume for Shetland. For the first time, more than 5,000 Shetland place-names were collected and interpreted in one publication – a similar number to that of *Norsk stadnamnleksikon* (1997), the Norwegian lexicon equivalent.

Shetland place-names and occurrences in *-staðir*

In *Shetland Place-Names*, Stewart listed 35 examples of the name type *staðir*. These examples are the focus of this article. Stewart's work was a significant contribution to the understanding of Shetland's past. Monumental as it may be, it is not without its flaws. Localisation is indicated through civil parish and a national grid numbering system. Unfortunately, the national grid numbers have not been supplied with initial letters (HP, HU, and HZ), making precise localisation ardous. Source forms usually indicate a year or a year range, but sources are not specified and interpretations are not always very in-depth.

In this article, these flaws will be addressed, albeit for one name type only. The examples will be listed in the same order as in *Shetland Place-Names* (see Figure 2). The numbering in the place-name interpretations below reflect both this order as well as that in Figure 2. There are a few minor changes to Stewart's spellings. They have been updated to reflect the modern written usage, as seen on maps and signs. The localisation is given according to the 1878 civil parishes (see Figure 3), which features almost the same divisions as Stewart. The only differences from Stewart's are the division of Yell into North Yell and Mid & South Yell and the incorporation of Foula in Walls, as well as Fair Isle into Dunrossness. A precise location is given as a six-letter National Grid Reference, here supplied with the correct initial letters.

The list of source forms has been heavily revised and supplied with forms from the most recent publications, including the two *Shetland Documents*

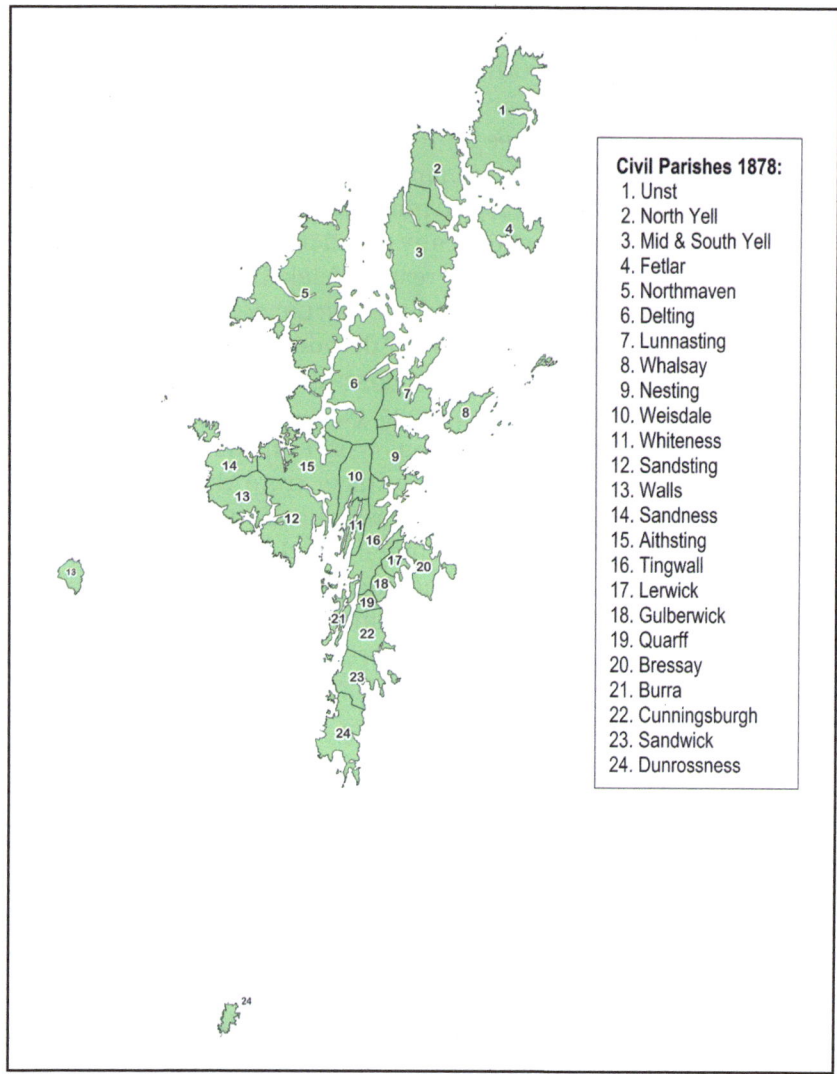

Figure 2. Map of the 24 civil parishes of Shetland in 1878 Borders are derived from the Ordnance Survey 1" map of the same year. *Illustration: Peder Gammeltoft*

volumes. When listed, a source form is followed by a date, as well as a source abbreviation. Source abbreviations are listed at the end of this article. The list of sources under each place-name is in no way exhaustive but represent the most readily available for the interested person.

Most importantly, however, is the inclusion of new interpretations. All interpretations take earlier studies into account but will feature current onomastic methods and make use of recent findings in the field. Interpretations have been made with source forms and pronunciation as an outset. The works consulted in this work are standard Old Norse and Icelandic-English dictionaries (Fritzner, 1886-96; Zoëga, 1910 and Cleasby & Vigfusson, 1874), as well as Jakobsen's dictionary (Jakobsen, 1928).

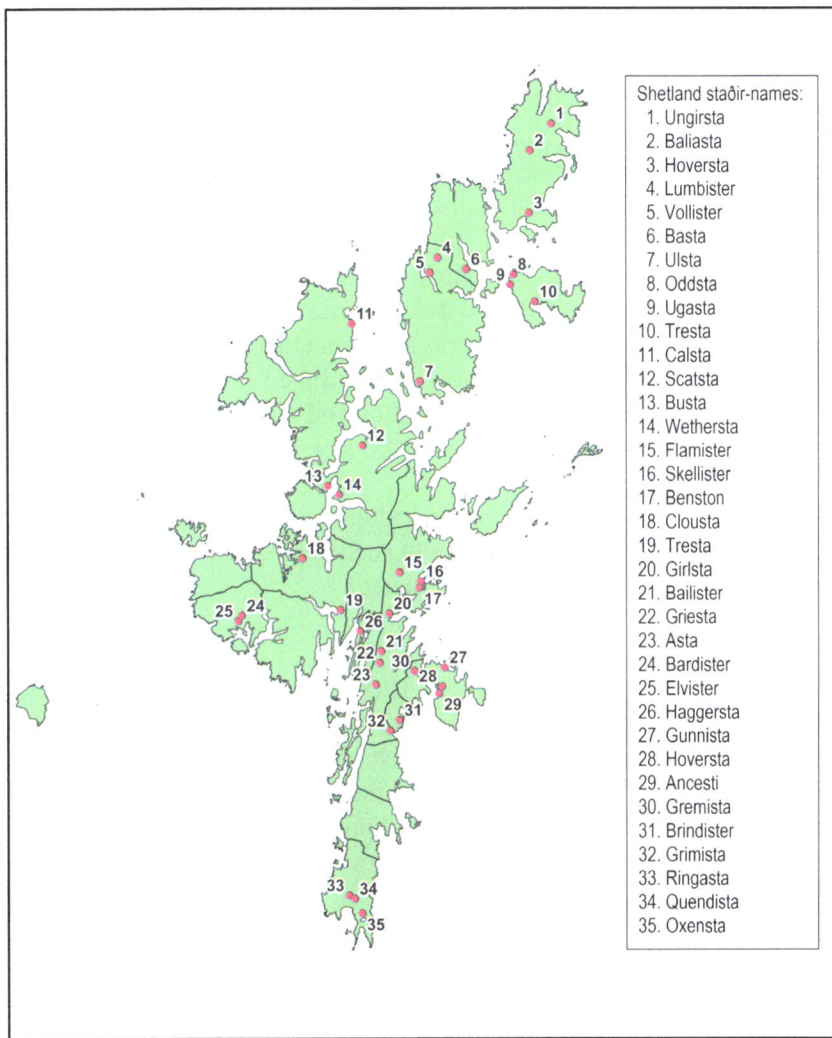

Figure 3. Map of the distribution of place-names in -*staðir* in Shetland. The numbers reflect the order in which the names are treated.   *Illustration: Peder Gammeltoft*

Place-names in -*staðir* in Shetland

1. **Ungirsta**, Unst, HP 629130.
Unustaðir (Longer Magnus Saga, ch. 34), Ungirsta 1621 (CBS), Ungasta 1716 (ROZ), Ungirsta 1878 (OS 1″), [uŋərsti] 1987 (Stewart, p. 252).

The Longer Magnus Saga shows an Old Norse form for this name, *Unustaðir*, that appears to be compounded with the female personal name *Una*, f. (cf. Stewart, 1987, p.252). And this is probably correct. The later source forms appear to suggest an original **Hungrstaðir*, compounded with Old Norse *hungr*, m. 'hunger, need for food', with regular loss of [h-] in the Shetland dialect. However, this derivation is probably not correct – but it is possible that the later forms are influenced by association with this word.

2. **Baliasta**, Unst, HP 602096.
á Bollastöðum (Longer Magnus' Saga, ch.34), Ballista 1543-44 (SD2, 72), Balyeistay 1578-79 (SD2, 260), Bailista 1580 (RJM), Balyistay 1589 (SD, 156), Balestay 1598 (SD, 274), Ballestay 1598 (SD, 275), Balyeastay 1599 (SD, 280), Ballazasta 1603 (SD, 354), Balyestay 1604 (SD, 377), Balzesta 1605 (SD, 410), Balzeasta 1613 (ROT), Balzesta 1613 (ROT), Bailaiesta 1615 (ROT), Balista 1716 (ROZ), Baliesta 1740 (RJM), Baliasta 1878 (OS 1"), [bæḷesta] (Stewart, 1987, p.252).

Baliasta is the second of two *staðir*-names from Shetland mentioned in the sagas. The saga form makes it fair to interpret the name *Bollastaðir*, as compounded with the personal name *Bolli*, m. (Jakobsen, 1936, p.149; Stewart, 1987, p.252). The pronunication shows a palatalised [-ll-], which is a common development from Old Norse [-ll-] in the Shetland dialect. The current root vowel [-æ-] is not a general development from Old Norse [-a-] but occurs occasionally before alveolar sounds.

There are a couple of possible parallel examples to this name in the Norwegian *staðir*-name material, namely *Balstad* in Selbu, Trøndelag (NG 15, 378) and *Bollestad* in Gjesdal, Rogaland (NG 10, 156).

3. **Hoversta**, Unst, HP 602017.
Hoverstay 1589 (SD, 156), Hovirsta 1628 (ROT), Hoverstay 1628 (ROT), Hoversta 1878 (OS 1"), [hovərsti] 1987 (Stewart, p.253).

This name has been interpreted as Old Norse **Hafrsstaðir* Stewart (1987, p.253), compounded with the Old Norse personal name *Hafr*, m. Just as likely, however, is the appellative, Old Norse *hafr*, m. 'a he-goat, buck'.

A parallel example from Norway is found in *Haverstad* from Sør-Fron, Innlandet (NG 4.1, p.125).

4. **Lumbister**, Mid & South Yell, HU 485959.
Limbista 1558-59 (SD2, 116), Lumbista 1569 (SD2, 178), Lumbista 1571 (SD2, 188), Lumbister 1605 (SD, 409), Lumbustaw 1610 (SD, 503), Lumbusta 1626 (DOH II, p. 81), Lumbesta 1672 (Retours O&S, 106), Lumbista 1698 (Retours O&S, 149), [lʌmbəstər] 1987 (Stewart, p.253).

Jakobsen (1936, p.27) interpreted *Lumbister* as an original place-name in Old Norse *bólstaðr*, m., although this has been refuted by both Stewart (1987, p.253) and Gammeltoft (2001, p.309), who both see this name deriving from *staðir*, m.

Stewart interprets the name as **Lambastaðir*, compounded with a personal name *Lambi*, m. Another possibility could be the animal designation, *lamb*, n. 'a lamb'.

However, none of these possibilities match source forms and pronunciation very well. This rather suggests an original root vowel in [-u-] in the specific. For this reason, Gammeltoft suggested an otherwise unattested **lumpr*, m., 'a lump, stump, block', with reference to the local topography.

5. **Vollister**, Mid & South Yell, HU 475940.
Volista 1577 (SD, 237), Volisdale 1646 (Janssonius), Volisdale c. 1650 (Johs. Mejer),

Volasta 1716 (ROZ), Volesta 1716 (ROZ), Vollister 1878 (OS 1"), [voləstər] 1987 (Stewart, p.253).

Stewart (1987, p.253) interpreted the specific as being an Old Norse personal name, *Vali*, m., the original form of the name would thus be *Valastaðir*. There is, however, also another, unexplored possibility. Vollister is situated by Whale Firth, a fjord with a very straight entrance (Whal-fyrth 1646 (Janssonius), Waal-Fyirt c. 1650 (Johs. Meyer)). Although this name seems to contain the word for whale, it is possible this is a transformation from an earlier fjord name Vala, f., derived from Old Norse *völr* m. 'a rounded stick, staff'. The original meaning of *völr* seems to have been used of anything being 'straight', a fitting description for the entrance to Whale Firth. If this is the case, then Volister would probably be an original *Valustaðir*. The position of the [-u-] would have made it prone for regular u-mutation, after which the name would have developed into *Volestað(ir)*.

6. **Basta**, North Yell, HU 522945.
Bosta 1577 (SD2, 237), Bastay 1578-79 (SD2, 260), Bastay 1599 (SD, 280), Bastay 1604 (SD, 377), Basta 1605 (SD, 409), Bastay 1613 (ROT), Basta 1615 (CBS), Basta 1648 (ROT), Basta 1716 (ROZ), Basta 1878 (OS 1"), [basta] 1987 (Stewart, p.253).

Jakobsen (1936, p.100) suggested that this name derives from *Bessastaðir*, presumably compounded with a byname *bersi*, m. 'little bear'. Stewart (1987, p.252), on the other hand interpreted Basta as *Bassastaðir*, with a byname *bassi*, m., also with the meaning 'little bear', or 'little fat guy'. An alternative possibility is that the specific of the name could be Old Norse *bast*, n., 'inner bark of the lime-tree', i.e., *Baststaðir*, although it is rather difficult to see why this could be a naming motive in a generally tree-less Shetland. The possibility forwarded by Jakobsen does not seem to fit neither the historical forms of the name, nor the present pronunciation of the name, so Stewart's suggestion is the most likely of the alternatives.

7. **Ulsta**, Mid & South Yell, HU 464802.
Vlstadh 1485 (SD2, 30), Ulstayth 1524 (SD2, App. 3), Ulstay 1576-77 (SD2, 235), Ulsta 1577 (SD2, 237), Ulstay 1613 (ROT), Olstay 1613 (ROT), Ulsta 1648 (ROT), Ulsta 1716 (ROZ), Ulsta (OS 1"), [ulsti] 1987 (Stewart, p.253).

Jakobsen (1936, p.101, 154) and Stewart (1987, p.253) both agree on an original *Úlfsstaðir*, compounded with the personal name *Úlfr*, m. The Norwegian examples in *Ulstad*, however, are generally taken to be derived from an original *Ölvisstaðir*, the specific from the personal name *Ölvir*, m., cf. *Ulstad* in Steinkjer, Trøndelag (NG 15, p.239). Both possibilities seem likely for this name.

8. **Oddsta**, Fetlar, HU 583939.
Odstay 1558 (SD, 112), Odsta 1577 (SD, 237), Odstay 1587-88 (SD, 106), Udsta (ROZ), Oddsta 1878 (OS 1"),[odsti] 1987 (Stewart, p.253).

Jakobsen (1936, p.100, 152) and Stewart (1987, p.253) interpreted this name as an original *Oddsstaðir*, compounded with the personal name, Old Norse *Oddr*,

m. Owing to *Oddsta's* situation close to the Ness of Hamar, it is perhaps more appropriate to see the name as a compound of Old Norse *oddi*, m. 'a tongue of land' and *staðir*, m.

A possible parallel example from Norway is found in Oddestad in Indre Østfold, Viken (NG 1, p.388). The specific of this name, however, is undoubtedly a personal name.

9. **Ugasta**, Fetlar, HU 579926.
Ugasta 1878 (OS 1"), Ugasta 1900 (OS 6"), [jugəsti] 1987 (Stewart, p.253).

Judging from the pronunciation, the specific could well be the male personal name *Jóðgeirr* or *Jólgeirr*, as Stewart (1987, p.253) assessed. It is also possible that the specific could be *Jógeirr*, m. Stewart sees this name as being a genuine place-name in -*staðir*, and this does indeed seem to be the case, judging from the pronunciation. However, the name is only very recently attested. In addition, it does not seem to be associated any settlement, being the name of a beach just off the settlement of Brough Lodge.

Macgregor (1987, p.151) suggested, more reasonably, that the name is a place-name in Old Norse -*stöð*, f., 'a landing-place, berth, harbour'. There is a landing-place at Ugasta, although the age of it is unknown.

10. **Tresta**, Fetlar, HU 611905.
Trestay 1587-88 (SD, 106), Trestay 1589 (SD, 136), Tresta 1589 (SD, 155), Trestay 1589 (SD, 156), Tresta 1602 (SD, 353), Tresta 1608 (SD, 442), Tresta 1610 (SD, 503), Traistay 1610 (SD, 516), Tresta 1716 (ROZ) / 1878 (oS1), [trɛsta] 1987 (Stewart, p.253).

Stewart (1987, p.253) suggested an original **Þrasastaðir*, compounded with the personal name *Þrasi*, m, cf. the parallel name, *Þrasastaðir* in Skagafjörður, Iceland. However, it is hard to see how [þra-] should develop into [tre-] in Shetland. Stewart is aware of this, and suggests instead an original *Tréstaðir*, from *tré*, n., 'a tree', occasionally with the meaning 'a wood'. His reasoning for suggesting this interpretaton was that the two Shetland *Tresta* examples, in Fetlar and in Aithsting, were both likely places for tree growth in Shetland. *Tresta* in Aithsting does today feature a small, wooded area, although this seems to be of recent date. A more likely interpretation of the names would be **Þrætustaðir*, from *þræta*, f. 'dispute, wrangle, litigation', as the development [þræ-] > [trɛ-] is regular. However, the pronunciation of the declined vowel of the specific must have been dropped early on to end up with today's pronunciation.

11. **Calsta**, Northmaven, HU 375874.
Calstay c. 1507-13 (SD2, App. 1, 2v), Calsta c. 1507-13 (SD2, App. 1, 7v), Coltsta 1576-77 (SD2, 235), Colsta 1576-77 (SD2, 235), Cauldstay 1613 (ROT), Caldstay 1628 (CBS), Calsta 1878 (OS 1"), [kalsti] 1987 (Stewart, p.254).

Jakobsen (1936, p.100) suggested the original form was **Kaldstaðir*, 'cold farm', finding support in the 17th century source forms. However, this is not supported in the earliest source forms. Stewart, on the other hand has interpreted the name as containing the personal name, Old Norse *Kali*, m., *Kalastaðir (Stewart 1987, p.254).

Comparing with Norwegian examples in *Kalstad*, the specific is usually interpreted as being a personal name *Karl*, m., or *Karli*, m. This seems to be an altogether more appropriate interpretation, although the appellative Old Norse *karl*, m. 'free man' – from which the personal name *Karl*, m., is derived – may well be more probable, *Karlstaðir. The development [-rl-] > [-l-] is commonly found in Norwegian and in the Shetland dialect.

Norwegian examples include *Kalstad*, Gausdal in Innlandet (NG 4.1, p.198), *Karlstad* in Kragerø, Telemark (NG 7, p.39), Karlstad in Fjaler, Vestland (NG12, p.280f.) *Karlstad* in Meldal, Trøndelag (NG 14, p.151), and *Karlstad* in Hamarøy, Nordland (NG 17, p.264).

12. **Scatsta**, Delting, HU 390720.
Schatsta c. 1507-13 (SD2, App. 1, 3r), Skatsta c. 1507-13 (SD2, App. 1, 6v), Skattistay 1524 (SD2, App. 3), Scatstadh 1537 (OSR), Skatstay 1560 (SD2, App. 4), Scatstay 1567-73 (SD2, App. 5), Scatistay 1574 (SD2, App. 5), Scattistay 1576 (SD2, App. 5), Scattistay 1578 (SD2, App. 5), Scatsta 1577 (SD2, 237), Scatstay 1577 (SD2, 237), Scatstay 1583 (SD, 54), Skattista 1584 (SD, 71), Scattistay 1586-87 (SD, 89), Scattistay 1586-87 (SD, 90), Scatstay 1586-87 (SD, 98), Scatsta 1586-87 (SD, 98), Skatstay 1589 (SD, 155), Skatsta 1589 (SD, 156), Scatza 1589 (SD, 161), Scattista 1602 (SD, 353), Scatsta 1606 (SD, 413), Skatstay 1608 (SD, 450), Scatstay 1620 (BOS), Scatsta 1716 (ROZ), Scatsta 1746 (BOS), Upper Scatsta 1878 (OS 1″), Lower Scatsta 1878 (OS 1″), [skatsti] 1987 (Stewart, p.254).

Stewart (1987, p.254) interpreted this name as an original *Skatastaðir. This is undoubtedly correct. However, his derivation of the specific as the Old Norse personal name *Skati*, m., is not the only possibility. Flanking the Voe of Scatsta is a prominent, pointing headland, Sella Ness. In Old Norse, such a feature could be termed a *skati, m. 'a point, something narrowing at the end, cf. Norsk Ordbok, *skata*¹, vb. 'something ending in a point' and *skate*¹, sb. 'a point'. The specific should thus rather be seen as either Old Norse *skati, m. 'a point', used topographically, or an original name of Sella Ness, *Skati, m.

13. **Busta**, Delting, HU 345668.
Byrstada 1490 (SD2, 32), Bousta c. 1507-13 (SD2, App. 1, 4r), Buistay 1578-79 (SD2, 260), Buistay 1579 (SD2, 261), Buistay 1589 (SD, 156), Buistay 1599 (SD, 280), Buista 1601 (SD, 325), Bustey 1604 (SD, 377), Buista 1695 (BOS), Busta 1716 (ROZ), Busta 1720 (BOS), Bustae 1730 (BOS), Busta 1878 (OS 1″), [bøsti] 1987 (Stewart, p.254).

There is consensus that the specific of this name is Old Norse *býr* 'farm, landed estate' (Jakobsen, 1936, p.27, 100; Stewart, 1987, p.254), and this is also supported by the earliest source form. Alternatively, the specific could also conceivably be Old Norse *byrgi*, n. '(fortified) enclosure, fence', although it is difficult to see what the reference should be, as there are – at least today – no remnants of neither fortifications nor enclosures in the area.

14. **Wethersta**, Delting, HU 360657.
Vodrist 1490 (SD2, 32), Vedderista c. 1507-13 (SD2, App. 1, 3r), Vedderista c. 1507-13 (SD2, App. 1, 4r), Vodderista c. 1507-13 (SD2, App. 1, 6v), Vaddesta 1560 (SD2, 119), Waddersta 1560 (SD2, 131), Wedderstay 1578-79 (SD2, 260), Weddirstay 1579 (SD2, 261), Wedderista 1581 (BOS), Wathersta 1583 (SD, 52), Wethersta 1583 (SD, 52), Waddirstay 1589 (SD, 156), Wedderstay 1591-92 (SD, 191), Wedderstay 1599 (SD, 280), Woddersta 1601 (SD, 325).Woddirsta 1602 (CBS), Weddersta 1602 (SD, 342), Wedderstay 1604 (SD, 377), Wedirsta 1605 (SD, 408), Weddersta 1607 (SD, 436), Weddersta 1608 (SD, 467), Wederstay 1608 (SD, 470), Wodderstay 1610 (SD, 518), Woddersta 1610 (SD, 518), Wedderstay 1614 (BOS), Wedderstay 1617 (CBS), Wedderstay 1620 (ROT), Wethersta 1716 (ROZ), Wethersta 1754 (BOS), Weathersta 1878 (OS 1″), [wadərsti] 1987 (Stewart, p.253).

The specific has been interpreted as containing the Old Norse personal name, *Viðarr*, m. (Stewart, 1987, p.254). However, this possibility finds little support in the early source forms. Thus, it seems more likely that the specific is the genitive or the plural form of Old Norse *veðr*, m., 'a ram, wether': *Veðrarstaðir or *Veðrastaðir. The current pronunication, as well as the modern spelling is most likely influenced by Shetland dialect word *wadder* 'a weather, wind' (from Old Norse *veðr*, m., 'a weather'), or from *wadder*, a Scots side form of *wedder* 'a ram' (cf. SND: *wedder*).

15. **Flamister**, Nesting, HU 440559.
Flamesta 1577 (SD2, 237) Flamista 1611 (SD, 529), Flamasta 1716 (ROZ), Flammester 1878 (OS 1″), [flaməstər] 1987 (Stewart, p.254).

Stewart (1987, p.254) suggested a derivation of Old Norse *flá*, f., 'ledge, small level part on a hillside' (cf. NG 12, p.115) for the specific of this name. This is probably a correct observation, as Flamister is situated in an isolated, flat area in the hills of South Nesting. The name is probably an original *Flámstaðir, from *flám*, the dative plural form. The current connecting vowel [-ə-] is probably a later added supporting vowel to avoid a [-mst-] consonant cluster.

16. **Skellister**, Nesting, HU 468548.
Schellesta c. 1507-13 (SD2, App. 1, 3r), Skalista 1560 (SD2, 119), Skellesta 1561 (SD2, 131), Skeldesta 1577 (SD2, 237), Skellista 1585-86 (SD, 80), Skellinstay 1601 (SD, 310), Skellesta 1606 (SD, 408), Skellinstay 1606 (SD, 408), Scelesta 1607 (SD, 436), Skelsta 1608 (SD, 467), Skellistay 1613 (ROT), Skelingsta 1629 (ROT), Skelingsta 1716 (ROZ), Skellister 1878 (OS 1″), [skıləstər] 1987 (Stewart, p.254).

There is general consensus that the original form of the name was *Skjaldarstaðir (Jakobsen, 1936, p.153; Stewart, 1987, p.254), compounded with the personal name *Skjöldr*, m. Superficially, this interpretation does not seem to fit the modern pronunciation, nor the source forms very well. A development from [skjaldar-] > [skılə-] is not regular. However, the Norwegian parallel, *Skjeldestad* in Sogndal, Vestland, does show a development from [skjaldar-] > [skjelde-] > [sjælde-], with a vowel change akin to the one seen here.

Interestingly, *Skjeldestad* occupies the same topographical position as Skellister, situated right on the peak of a hill. It thus seems probable that the specific is not a personal name, but rather the appellative *skjöldr*, 'a shield', in place-names used of shield-shaped elevations.

A third possibility is that the specific is Old Norse *skel*, f. 'a shell' (here also used topographically?). The original form would thus have been **Skeljarstaðir*. However, shells do not seem to have been a much used naming motive in Scandinavian place-names.

17. **Benston**, Nesting, HU 466540.
Bannasta c. 1507-13 (SD2, App. 1, 3r), Bennesta c. 1507-13 (SD2, App. 1, 7r), Bynstay 1557 (SD2, 109), Northe Beinstaye 1579 (SD2, 262), Beinsta 1577 (SD2, 237), Benestaye 1581 (BOS), Benista 1584 (BOS), Binstay 1589 (SD, 156), Beinstay 1592 (SD, 201), Beinsta 1597 (SD, 264), Benistay 1605 (BOS), Beinstay 1606 (SD, 415), Beinstay 1610 (SD, 509), North Binsta 1716 (ROZ), South Binsta 1716 (ROZ), Benston 1878 (OS 1"), [bınstən] Stewart (1987, p.254).

There are numerous possible interpretations for this name. Jakobsen and Stewart have both suggested that a personal name constitutes the specific of this name, either Old Norse *Beini* (Jakobsen, 1936, p.149; Stewart, 1987, p.254) or *Beinir* (Jakobsen, 1936, p.149). Another possibility is **Beinastaðir*, with Old Norse *beini*, m. 'hospitable treatment, hospitality' as the specific must also be taken into consideration. In that case, Benston would have been a place where officials would stay on visitations. However, there seems to be no historical evidence for this. There is a parallel example in the Norwegian *Beinestad* from Kristiansand in Agder (NG 9, p.22), which is interpreted as containing the Old Norse personal name, *Beini*, m. or *Beinir*, m.

Benston is the only Shetland *staðir*-name which ends in -ston, similar to *staðir*-names in Orkney. However, since none of the historical forms prior to the 19th century show any remnant of being in the dative form, *stöðum*, it is altogether more possible that the current form is due to analogy with Scots formations in -*ton*.

18. **Clousta**, Aithsting, HU 313576.
Cloustay c. 1507-13 (SD2, App. 1, 2r), Cloustay c. 1507-13 (SD2, App. 1, 5v), Cloustay c. 1507-13 (SD2, App. 1, 7r), Closta 1577 (SD2, 237), Cloistadtt 1582 (SD, 42), Cloustay 1589 (SD, 156), Clowstay 1606 (SD, 416), Cloustay 1607 (SD, 432), Cloustaw 1610 (SD, 503), Clousta 1628 (ROT), Clousta 1716 (ROZ), Clusta 1716 (ROZ), [klusta] 1987 (Stewart, p. 255), [klusta] 1987 (Stewart, p.255).

Jakobsen (1936, p.100) suggested an original **Klóstaðir*, from Old Norse *kló*, f., claw, used topographically about promontories and isthmuses (cf. NG, Indledning, p.29). This fits well with the topography, as Clousta is situated on an isthmus between the Voe of Clousta and the Loch of Clousta. Together with the North Voe of Clousta, these three water bodies create the appearance of the Clousta area as being a promontory – although this is only a reality at high water.

Stewart (1987, p.255) suggested the same word, *kló*, f., but rather used as a byname, but found it altogether more probable that it was more probably *Klaufastaðir* (cf. Klauvstad Østre Toten in Innlandet (NG, 4.2, p.55f.)), from the byname *klaufi*, m.

A fourth possibility is Old Norse *klofi*, m. 'a cleft or rift in a hill'. However, no such feature seems to exist in the vicinity of Clousta, so Jakobsen's original suggestion is probably the most likely.

19. **Tresta**, Aithsting, HU 363510.
Tresta c. 1507-13 (SD2, App. 1, 2r), Tresta c. 1507-13 (SD2, App. 1, 7v), Trasta 1577 (SD2, 237), Trestay 1589 (SD, 156), Trestrie 1609 (SD, 485), Trestay 1610 (SD, 508), Tresta 1619 (ROT), Tresta 1716 (ROZ), [trɛsta] 1987 (Stewart, p.255).

See above under *Tresta*, Fetlar.

20. **Girlsta**, Tingwall, HU 427506.
Girlistaye 1543 (SD2, 68), Girdilsta 1577 (SD2, 237), Griddilstay 1578-79 (SD2, 260), Gridilstay 1579 (SD2, 261), Girdilstay 1589 (SD, 160), Griddilstay 1599 (SD, 280), Gidilstay 1603 (CBS), Girdilstay 1604 (SD, 377), Gildersta 1604 (SD, 383), Girdilstay 1604 (SD, 388), Girlsta 1615 (CBS) / 1704 (BOS), Girlsta 1716 (ROZ) / 1878 (OS 1"), [gɪrlsti] 1987 (Stewart, p.254).

Traditionally interpreted as *Geirhildarstaðir* (Jakobsen, 1936, p.150; Stewart, 1987, p.255), from the woman's name *Geirhildr*, f. who, according to the Landnámabók, was the daughter of Hrafna-Flóki, who stayed briefly in Shetland before settling in Iceland. *Geirhildr* was drowned in the adjacent Geirhildarvatn, presumed to be the Girlsta Loch, and the nearby settlement subsequently named after her.

Although the association of Girlsta with Hrafna-Flókis daughter is anecdotal, there seems little doubt that the specific must be a personal name in *Geir-*. The Norwegian Gjervoldstad [jærelsta] in Kristiansand (cf. NG 9, 60f.) also lists the personal name possibilities, Old Norse *Geirulfr*, m. and *Geiraldi*, m., in addition to *Geirhildr*, f. The source forms of Girlsta, however, strongly suggests that the personal name in question should contain [-ld-], rendering *Geirhildr*, f. and *Geiraldi*, m. the most probable.

21. **Bailister**, Tingwall, HU 417458.
Belista 1570 (SD2, 185), Balyesta 1577 (SD2, 237), Belista 1587 (SD, 99), Balesta 1716 (ROZ), Balista 1716 (ROZ), Bailiester 1716 (ROZ), Bailister 1878 (OS 1"), [beːlistər] 1987 (Stewart, p.255).

Stewart (1987, p.255) interpreted this name as an original *Ballastaðir*, compounded with the Old Norse personal name *Balli*, m. However, it is not common to see an Old Norse [-a-] root vowel to develop into [-eː-] in the Shetland dialect, also visible in the earliest source form. On the other hand, Old Norse [-e-] commonly develops into [-eː-], so the specific is probably more likely to be the Old Norse appelative *belgr*, m. 'a bellows made from animal skin', used comparatively of 'bulging' natural features, such as evenly rounded hills. An original *Belgstaðir would thus carry the meaning of 'farm by the round hills'. Bailister is flanked by hills on its west side.

22. **Griesta**, Tingwall, HU 415443.
Grista 1570 (SD2, 185), Grista 1587 (SD, 99), Gristra 1587-88 (SD, 107), Gresta 1598 (SD, 267), Greissta 1621 (CBS), Grista 1878 (OS 1"), [grista] 1987 (Stewart, p. 255).

Jakobsen (1936, p.100) and Stewart (1987, p.255) both suggested the name originates from Old Norse *Griðstaðir, compounded with Old Norse grið, m., 'a sanctuary, refuge'. Stewart notes that tradition has it that criminals had sanctuary here after passing through the crowd assembled at Tingaholm 1.5 km away. Another possibility is that the specific is the Old Norse animal designation gríss, m. 'a young pig', thus *Grísstaðir.

23. **Asta**, Tingwall, HU 410415.
Astra (Asta) c. 1507-13 (SD2, App. 1, 1r), Hasta (Asta) c. 1507-13 (SD2, App. 1, 6v), Austa 1565 (SD2, 145), Asta 1574 (SD2, App. 5), Astay 1580 (SD, 5), Astay 1588-89 (SD, 135), Astray 1587-88 (SD, 110), Astay 1588-89 (SD, 135), Astay 1588 (SD, 113), Astay 1593-94 (SD, 218), Asta 1604 (CBS), Astay 1606 (SD, 418), Asta 1610 (SD, 506), Asta 1611 (SD, 539), Astay 1657 (BOS), Asta 1716 (ROZ), Asta 1878 (OS 1") [asta] 1987 (Stewart, p.255).

Asta has traditionally been interpreted as *Ásustaðir, compounded with the commonly occurring female personal name Ása, f. (Stewart, 1987, p.255). It is also possible that the specific may derive from Old Norse á, f. 'a stream', or áss, m. 'a ridge'. Since the settlement is not situated on a ridge, the last possiblity is ruled out. There is, however, a small stream running straight through the settlement, as is the area of Asta bordered to the north by the stream Garth Burn. Thus, it is not inconceivable that the origin is Old Norse *Ástaðir 'farm by the stream', rather than being compunded by a personal name.

There seems to be one parallel to this name from Gjemnes in Møre og Romsdal, Astad, although it is not interpreted in this way in NG (13, p.362). A possible parallel example to an origin in *Ásustaðir is found in Osestad, Larvik, Vestfold (NG 6, p.360).

24. **Bardister**, Walls, HU 234502.
Bardista 1649 (ROT), Bardesta 1716 (ROZ), Bardister 1878 (OS 1") [bærdistər] 1987 (Stewart, p. 255).

The origin of this name is probably *Barðastaðir, from the personal name, Old Norse Barði, m. (Stewart, 1987, p.255). Alternatively, it can be from Old Norse barð, n. 'verge, edge of a hill'. Bardister is situated on a distinct slope, which favours the second possibility, *Barðstaðir. The pronunciation and source forms thus show the development of a supporting vowel in the consonant cluster [-rðst-] > [-rðəst-].

A good parallel example is found in the Norwegian Barstad from Sokndal, Rogaland (NG 10, 18).

25. **Elvister**, Walls, HU 229495.
Illustay 1576-77 (SD2, 235), Elvestir 1582 (SD, 42), Elvesta 1629 (ROT), Ilvista 1648 (ROT), Elvister 1649 (ROT), Elvesta 1716 (ROZ), Elvister 1878 (OS 1"), [elvistər] 1987 (Stewart, p. 254).

This name is generally interpreted as containing a personal name. Jakobsen (1936, p.149) suggested that the specific was either *Eilifr*, m. *Ölvir*, m., or *Alvis*, m. Similarly, Stewart (1987, p.255) suggested the personal name *Ölvir*, m. Judging from the pronunciation and most of the source forms in [e-]/E-, only Old Norse *Eilifr*, m., appears to be a more probable origin of the specific. None of the other suggestions would regularly develop into the current form.

26. **Haggersta**, Whiteness, HU 389483.
Herrastad c. 1507-13 (SD2, App. 1, 3v), Herasater c. 1507-13 (SD2, App. 1, 7r), Hagrascath 1524 (SD2, App. 3), Hagasta 1525 (SD2, 47), Hagrista 1587 (SD, 99), Haggersta 1598 (SD, 267), Haggirstay 1599 (SD, 280), Haggristay 1602 (SD, 335), Haggerstay 1602 (BOS), Hagristay 1609 (SD, 485), Haggarsta 1610 (SD, 506), Hagrasetter 1610 (SD, 508), Hagarsta 1610 (SD, 510), Haggarsta 1610 (SD, 512), Hagarstay 1613 (ROT), Hagrastay 1621 (CBS), Haggerstay 1716 (ROZ), Hagraseter 1716 (ROZ), Haggersta 1878 (OS 1"), [hægərsti] 1987 (Stewart, p.256).

Stewart (1987, p.256) suggests an origin in either **Hallgeirsstaðir*, from the personal name *Hallgeirr*, m. or **Hallgerðarstaðir*, from *Hallgerðr*, f. This is certainly a possibility, although personal names in *Hall-* are not commonly occuring as specifics in Norwegian place-names, for some reason. Norske Gaardnavne only lists two names compounded **Hallgríms-* (NG 1, p. 213; NG 5, p. 459), otherwise there are no other instances. Judging from the earliest source forms and the pronunciation, the specific may rather be Old Norse *hegri*, m. 'a heron'.

Hegrestad in Eigersund, Rogaland (NG 10, p. 91), is taken to derive from either a stream name **Hegra*, f. or a byname **hegri*, m., both derived from the bird designation Old Norse *hegri*, m.

27. **Gunnista**, Bressay, HU 500438.
Gunnelista c. 1507-13 (SD2, App. 1, 2v), Gunnelista c. 1507-13 (SD2, App. 1, 4v), Gunnelista c. 1507-13 (SD2, App. 1, 6r), Gunneilestay 1581-82 (SD, 28), Guinneildstay 1589 (SD, 156), Gunneilestay 1592-93 (SD, 207), Gunneilsta 1639 (BOS), Gunielsta 1620 (BOS), Gunielsta 1716 (ROZ), Gunnelsta 1716 (ROZ), Gunilsta 1719 (BOS), Gunnista 1878 (OS 1"), [gɔiŋisti] 1987 (Stewart, p.256).

There is general consensus that the origin of this name is **Gunnhildarstaðir* (Jakobsen 1936, p.100, 151; Stewart, 1987, p.256), compounded with the female personal name *Gunnhildr*, f. A parallel name is found in *Gunhildstad* in Tønsberg, Vestfold (NG 6, p.129).

28. **Hoversta**, Bressay, HU 497414.
Houerista c. 1507-13 (SD2, App. 1, 2v), Hoverista c. 1507-13 (SD2, App. 1, 4v), Hoverista c. 1507-13 (SD2, App. 1, 6v), Howersta 1550 (SD2, 119), Howersta 1561 (SD2, 131), Hoverstay 1592-93 (SD, 209), Hoversta 1602 (CBS), Hoversta 1605 (SD,

408), Hoversta 1608 (SD, 467), Hoversta 1613 (ROT), Hoversta 1716 (ROZ), Hoversta 1878 (OS 1″), [huversti] 1987 (Stewart, p.256).

Jakobsen (1936, p.100, 151) interprets this name as Hoversta in Unst as *Hafrsstaðir, with the specific being the Old Norse personal name Hafr, m., see above. Stewart (1987, p.256), on the other hand prefers an original *Hávarðarstaðir, from the personal name Hávarðr, m., but acknowledges that Jakobsen's interpretation is also a possibility.

Equally likely, however, is an origin in *Hafrarstaðir, from the genitive plural form, hafrir, of Old Norse hafr, m. 'a he goat, buck'.

29. **Ancesti**, Bressay, HU 493405.
Ustensta 1577 (SD2, 237), Ancesti 1900 (OS 6″), [ɪntsjəsti] 1987 (Stewart, p.256).

This name is interpreted by Stewart (1987, p.256) as an original *Øysteinsstaðir, a compound of the personal name Øysteinn, m. and staðir, m. pl. This seems to be the case, judging from the earliest surce form. However, this place-name is not very well attested, so it is not certain that Ancesti is the same name as the Ustensta mentioned in 1577.

There are two parallels to this name in Norway, Namely Østenstad in Fjaler, Vestland (NG 12, p.273) and Østenstad in Asker, Viken (NG 2, p.159). Note the parallel development from Øysteins- to Østens-/Ustens-.

30. **Gremista**, Lerwick, HU 461433.
Gremistay 1610 (SD, 514), Grimesta 1716 (ROZ), Grimista 1878 (OS 1″), [grɪmɪster] 1987 (Stewart, p.254).

This name has been interpreted as containing the personal name Grímr, m. (Jakobsen, 1936, p.100, 150; Stewart, 1987, p.256). However, unless the vowel [-ɪ-] is a mere connecting vowel, this cannot be correct. The specific is rather either the Old Norse personal name Grímarr, m., *Grímarstaðir (cf. Grimastad in Voss, Vestland (NG 11, p.556)), or Gríma, f., *Grímustaðir (cf. Grimestad in Farsund, Agder (NG 9, p.209)). Another possibility is also the Old Norse appellatival equivalent gríma f. 'a hood or cowl covering the upper part of the face', used topographically. The specific could thus refer to the oblong-shaped Hill of Greenhead.

31. **Brindister**, Gulberwick, HU 442370.
Brynista c. 1507-13 (SD2, App. 1, 2v), Brynsta c. 1507-13 (SD2, App. 1, 6v), Brendistay 1525 (SD2, 47), Brindista 1570 (SD2, 185), Brindista 1587 (SD, 99), Brindistay 1589 (SD, 156), Bringesta 1602 (CBS), Bringyista 1603 (CBS), Brindista 1608 (SD, 444), Brindista 1620 (CBS), Brindistay 1620 (CBS), Brindista 1634 (CBS), Brindista 1716 (ROZ), [brɪndɪstər] Stewart (1987, p.256).

Stewart (1987, p.256) suggests that the specific of this name is the Old Norse personal name Brandr, m. However, this cannot be correct, as this goes against evidence from both the source forms as well as the pronunciation. Judging from the earliest source forms, the specific could be a form of Old Norse brýnn, m. 'brow, projecting ridge'. Brindister is situated towards the top of a slope near a marked ridge. This could be the naming motive. The later source forms as well as the pronunciation, however, rather suggests that the specific could be Old Norse *brenna*, vb. 'to burn', perhaps suggesting the area was originally cleared by burning. The current [-nd-] pronunciation is a regular development from original [-nn-] > [-ṇ-] > [-nd-].

32. **Grimista**, Quarff, HU 430356.
Gremsta c. 1507-13 (SD2, App. 1, 2v), Gremsta c. 1507-13 (SD2, App. 1, 6v), Grymbusta 1572 (SD2, 193), Grymbuster 1577 (SD2, 237), Grimesta 1716 (ROZ), Grimista 1878 (OS 1"), [grimıster] 1987 (Stewart, p.256).

Stewart (1987, p.256) correctly assumes the name is an original *Grímsstaðir*, with the Old Norse personal name *Grímr*, m. as specific. The name is possibly of the same origin as Gremista in Lerwick, see above, but the early source forms do not directly support this.

The name *Grim(e)stad* from *Grímsstaðir* commonly occurs in Norway. Norske Gaardnavne lists in the region of 20 names.

33. **Ringasta**, Dunrossness, HU 378143.
Regusta c. 1507-13 (SD2, App. 1, 1v), Reggasta c. 1507-13 (SD2, App. 1, 6r), Rygastay 1525 (SD, 47), Ringista 1570 (SD2, 185), Ringista 1577 (SD2, 237), Ringista 1578 (SD2, 255), Ringista 1587 (SD, 99), Ringistay 1589 (SD, 156), Rangista 1598 (SD, 267), Ringista 1598 (SD, 267), Ringista 1602 (CBS), Ringista 1606 (SD, 419), Ringista 1716 (ROZ), Ringasta 1878 (OS 1"), [riṇasti] 1987 (Stewart, p.257).

Both Jakobsen (1936, p.101) and Stewart (1987, p.257) interpret the name as an original *Hringsstaðir*, compounded with the personal name name *Hringr*, m. *Ringstad* is a commonly occurring place-name in Norway. Norske Gaardnavne lists fewer than 18 examples. However, the parallel example *Ringestad* in Vestre Slidre, Innlandet (NG 4.2, 283), suggests the female personal name *Ragnheiðr*, f., as the specific, i.e. *Ragnheiðarstaðir. With a transposition of [-gn-] to [-ng-], as is found in Norway and Shetland, this could also be a possible origin of Ringasta.

A third possibility could also be Old Norse *renna*, f. 'a watercourse' as the specific, as original [-nn-] is commonly palatalised to [-ṇ-]. The original form would thus be *Rennustaðir, presumably referring to the proximity to the small watercourse feeding the Loch of Hillwell.

34. **Quendista**, Dunrossness, HU 385139.
Cwndistay 1506 (SD2, 36), Quinnesta c. 1507-13 (SD2, App. 1, 5r), Quendista 1578 (SD2, 255), Quendestay 1578 (SD, 156), Quendista now Brew 1656 (Stewart, p. 257), Brow formerly Quendista 1733 (Stewart, p.257).

The farm does not exist any longer. It changed name in the 17th century to Brow and was later abandoned altogether. There is a signature on the first Ordnance Survey 1" and 6" maps of scattered stones called 'Old House of Brow', but nothing seems to remain of this today.

Stewart (1987, p.257) interprets the specific as the place-name *Quendale* (< *Kvern(á)dalr*, cf. Jakobsen, 1936, p.132 and Stewart, 1987, p.78), originally Old Norse *Kvern(á)dalstaðir. Quendale is situated some 1.5 km away, so this is a likely possibility. However, it is also possible that the specific could be Old Norse *kvenna*, f. 'a woman', judging from the early source forms. A third possibility is Old Norse *kvern*, f. 'a quern, millstone', but there does not seem to be any watercourse to a mill from anywhere near Quindista/Brow. Furthermore, it is also difficult to account for the occurrence of [-d-] from this suggestion. Thus, this possibility is very uncertain.

35. **Oxensta**, Dunrossness, HU 395120.
Oxinnasta c. 1507-13 (SD2, App. 1, 1r), Oxinasta c. 1507-13 (SD2, App. 1, 5r), Oxnasta c. 1507-13 (SD2, App. 1, 6r), Oxinsta 1578 (SD2, 255), Oknastay 1589 (SD, 156), Oxnesta 1716 (ROZ), Oxensta 1878 (OS 1").

The specific is Old Norse, *öxni*, a plural form of *uxi* or *oxi*, m., 'an ox', *Öxnastaðir*, cf. Stewart, 1987, p.257. Old Norse *uxi* has two plural forms in, a regular form, *yxni*, m. and a side form, *öxni*. However, since only Old Norse [ö] may develop into Shetl. [o], the side form derivation must be considered the most likely.

Revisiting the staðir-names of Shetland

As mentioned above, Stewart's work was the first comprehensive and systematic study of Shetland place-names since Jakobsen. His work differed from that of his predecessor in being encyclopedic in style. The section on Old Norse *staðir*, m. (Stewart, 1987, pp.251-257) followed the usual north to south movement and began with examples from Unst and ended in Dunrossness. The same sequence has been followed above. The study has shown that Shetland *staðir*-names have endings in *-sta* (25), *-sti* (1), *-ster* (8) and *-ston* (1). Nonetheless, the pronunciations given by Stewart show a greater range of spoken forms than what is visible in the written forms. Names ending in *-sta/-sti* usually developed into [-sti] (15) or less often [-sta] (7). Two examples in *-sta* even have a [-ster] pronunciation, and, finally, two examples do not have a given pronunciation. In the remainder of the cases, the written forms in *-ster* are pronounced [-stər] (8) and *-ston* as [-stɔn], as would be expected.

New insights gained?

True to the tradition of Jakobsen and contemporary Norwegian scholars, Stewart generally favoured a personal name as the specific of the Shetland *staðir* names. And indeed, this is generally true for a substantial number of examples – no fewer than 30 of 35 (86%). Since 26 of the 35 examples have been reinterpreted, this number is now somewhat lower. It is not possible to give an exact number. There two main reasons for this. Firstly, the source situation is not the greatest. The Shetland *staðir* place-names are usually not mentioned in sources prior to the early 16th century, that is, a minimum of five to seven centuries after their formation.

The exclusively Old Norse origin of the specifics in the *staðir* place-name material shows that the names were created in a completely Scandinavian-speaking environment. However, Old Norse underwent great changes during the High Middle Ages, especially after 1350. Therefore, there is quite a linguistic distance between formation to a first recording. In addition, Shetland underwent a gradual language change from Insular Norse to Scots. The change started in the late Middle Ages and had been completed by the time Jakobsen arrived in Shetland, although the local Scots dialect was still heavily mixed with words and phrases of Scandinavian origin. This means that most Shetland place-names were recorded in a language other than that of formation, creating yet another aspect of insecurity in tracing back to a plausible origin of the name.

These two factors, the poor source situation and language change, make interpretation of place-names of Scandinavian origin in Shetland challenging. Thus, the number of formal and possible origins of the specific increases considerably. Where Stewart usually had one possible specific origin, occasionally two, the norm is now generally three possibilities or more. This shows that Stewart's *Shetland Place-Names* gave an impression of certainty which is not present. This study of names has therefore not made it easier to say exactly what the origin is of a Shetland place-name in *staðir*; on the contrary.

This study has reinterpreted 28 of the examples. One of these, *Ugasta* is now interpreted as a place-name in Old Norse *stöð*, f., 'a landing-place, berth, harbour', as suggested by Macgregor (1987, p.151). The remainder are still considered to be genuine place-names in Old Norse *staðir*, m. As mentioned above, Stewart considered 30 of the *staðir* specifics to contain a personal name or a byname, whereas five contained an appellative or, rarely, another place-name. In addition, three names were seen to contain either a personal name or an appellative. The reinterpretation of this name material has reduced the number of possible personal name specifics to 22. Of these, 15 names may alternatively have an appellative as the specific. The four to seven possible appellative interpretations by Stewart, and the single place-name, in the specific material has been drastically increased to between 11 and 26 examples in this study. Additionally, there are now between one and three possible instances of a place-name in the specific.

The Shetland *staðir*-name material seems to have between 21-64% personal names as the specific, whereas between 31-77% of the names may have an appellative or occasionally a place-name, as in 3-9% of the cases. Compared with a previous study of -*staðir* place-names in the Hebrides, Gammeltoft (2006, p.82) concluded that personal names and bynames constituted around 49-58% of the material, whereas appellatives and adjectives made up 42-51% of the material. Although the percentage span is much greater in the Shetland material, it is still quite like the Hebridean material in as much as the personal name/appellative distributions is about fifty-fifty. In the Hebridean material, the potential number of personal name specifics seems slightly higher than appellatives and adjectives, whereas the Shetland material could have slightly more appellatives than personal names, judging from the range-spans.

Conclusion

All science, including name research, evolves over time. In the early years, the establishing years, research in this field was characterised by more 'system thinking', for lack of a better term. Certain name types were compounded by certain elements. As Oluf Rygh writes in his introduction (1898):

> The first part in staðir is in the vast majority of cases a personal name or a byname; In no other of the more widespread compositional parts does preposition of this kind have such a large predominance. It is not so very rare also to find as the specific the name of a river, a waterfall, or a stream in a river. Only in a few cases have names of mountains, hills, lakes, or fjords been identified so far in such a composition. (My translation)

Place-names in *staðir* were only seen to be compounded with proper nouns – names – usually in the form of personal names and bynames, more rarely in the form of place-names, particularly of water features. However, when one goes through the source material – both what was available at the time of Rygh and later published material – the specifics of *staðir*-names do not lend themselves only to the proper noun category. There is ample space for interpreting a significant number of *staðir* place-names in alternative ways, and this is what we see with the Shetland material. The Shetland *staðir* place-names generally conform to both the situation in Norway as well as in the Northern Isles. Interestingly, this is somewhat at odds with the contemporary place-name element Old Norse *bólstaðr*, which is slightly more frequent in Shetland. This name type is characterised by a much wider span of specifics than in Norway (cf. Gammeltoft, 2001).

The main difference between the Scottish material and the Norwegian material is a poorer source situation and a more complex linguistic situation of language change. Unfortunately, this situation often lends itself to a plurality of interpretations. However, the aim of science is not to offer a single, dogmatic truth. On the contrary, science must offer precise evidence-based interpretations and offer new insights on new findings. This article offers new insights into Shetland place-names. This would not have been possible without the tireless efforts of Brian Smith, whom we are celebrating with this festschrift, to make historical sources for Shetland more available for us all.

Abreviations

BOS – Bruce of Sumburgh papers
CBS – *Court Book of Shetland*
COS – *Court Book of Orkney and Shetland*
DSL – *Dictionaries of the Scots Language*
OS 1" – First edition Ordnance Survey Map, 1 inch to 1 mile
OS 6" – First edition Ordnance Survey Map, 6 inches to 1 mile

OSR – *Orkney and Shetland Records*
RJM – Diary of the Reverend John Mill
ROT – Register of Testaments in Shetland
ROZ – Rentals of Zetland
SD – *Shetland Documents 1580-1611*
SD2 – *Shetland Documents 1195-1579*
SND – *Scottish National Dictionary*

Bibliography

Ballantyne, John H. and Smith, Brian (1994) *Shetland Documents 1580-1611*. Lerwick: The Shetland Times Ltd.

Ballantyne, John H. and Smith, Brian (1991) *Shetland Documents 1195-1579*. Lerwick: The Shetland Times Ltd.

Barclay, Robert (ed.) (1962) *The Court Book of Orkney and Shetland 1612-13*. Kirkwall: W.R. MacKintosh, The Kirkwall Press.

Beito, Olav T., *et al.* (1966-2016) *Norsk ordbok – Ordbok over det norske folkemålet og det nynorske skriftmålet*, 12 vols. Oslo: Samlaget.

Bruce of Symbister Papers. Shetland Archives, D8.

Cleasby, R. and Vigfusson, G. (1874) *An Icelandic-English Dictionary*. Oxford: The Clarendon Press.

Crawford, Barbara E. (1987) *Scandinavian Scotland. Scotland in the Early Middle Ages*, 2. Leicester: Leicester University Press.

Donaldson, Gordon (ed.) (1954) *The Court Book of Shetland 1602-04*. Edinburgh: Scottish Record Society.

Donaldson, Gordon (ed.) (1991) *The Court Book of Shetland 1615-29*. Lerwick: Shetland Library.

Dictionaries of the Scots language. https://dsl.ac.uk/ (accessed 1 July 2023).

First edition Ordnance Survey Map, 1 Inch to 1 Mile, published 1878.

First edition Ordnance Survey Map, 6 Inches to 1 Mile, published 1900.

Fritzner, J. (1886-96) *Ordbog over det gamle norske Sprog*, 3 vols. Oslo: Den norske Forlagsforening.

Gammeltoft, Peder (2001) *The Place-Name element bólstaðr in the North Atlantic Area*. Copenhagen: C.A. Reitzel.

Gammeltoft, Peder (2006) 'Stednavne på gno. -staðir I Hebriderne og Man – et forstudie', in: Særheim, Inge, *et al.* (eds): *Busetnadsnamn på -staðir*. Rapport frå NORNAs 33. symposium på Utstein kloster 7.-9. mai 2004. NORNA-Rapproter 81, pp.69-82.

Goudie, Gilbert (ed.) (1889) *The Diary of the Reverend John Mill 1740-1803*. Edinburgh: Scottish History Society.

Jakobsen, Jakob (1901) *Shetlandsøernes stednavne*. København: Det kgl. Nordiske Oldskriftselskab.

Jakobsen, Jakob (1928) *An Etymological Dictionary of the Norn Language in Shetland*, 2 vols. Copenhagen: Vilhelm Prior.

Jakobsen, Jakob (1936) *The Place-Names of Shetland*. Copengahen: Vilhelm Prior.

Johannes, Mejer (c. 1650) *Charten über Norwegen mit Teutschen Beyschriften in 3 Th[eilen]*. Unpublished manuscript in Det Kongelige Bibliotek, Copenhagen.

Janssonius, Jan, 1644 (map). Map of Orkney and Shetland, copied from L.J. Waghenaer with only few alterations. British Museum.

Johnston, A.W. and Johnston, A. (eds.) (1913) *Orkney and Shetland Records 1072-1634*. London: The Viking Society for Northern Research.

Longer Magnus Saga = Vigfússon, Gudbrand (ed.) (1887): *Magnús saga hinn lengri, in Icelandic Sagas*, vol 1. London.

Macgregor, Lindsay (1986) 'Norse Naming Elements in Shetland and Faroe: a Comparative Study', *Northern Studies* 23, pp.84-105.

Macgregor, Lindsay (1987) *The Norse Settlement of Shetland and Faroe, c.800-c.1500: A Comparative Study*. PhD thesis, University of St. Andrews, St. Andrews. Available at: https://research-repository.st-andrews.ac.uk/bitstream/10023/2728/3/LindsayMacgregorPhDThesis.pdf (accessed: 1 July 2023).

Marwick, Hugh (1952) *Orkney farm-names.* Kirkwall: W.R. Mackinstosh.

Nicolaisen, W. F. H. (2001) *Scottish Place-Names,* New Edition. Edinburgh: John Donald.

Pálsson, H. and Edwards, P. (1972) *The book of Settlements – Landnámabók.* Manitoba: Manitoba University Press.

Register of Testaments in Shetland, 1611-1650. Shetland Archives, SA1/4.

Rentals of Zetland, 1716. Shetland Archives, SA4/292.

Retours O&S = Thomson, T. (ed.) (1811) *Inquisitionum ad Capellam Domini Regis Retornatarum, quae in publicis archivis Scotiae adhuc servantur, abbreviation,* vol. 2: 'Orkney et Shetland'. Edinburgh: The Great Britain Record Commission.

Rygh, Oluf (1897-1936) *Norske Gaardnavne. Oplysninger samlede til Brug ved Matrikkelens Revision, efter Offentlig Foranstaltning.* Kristiania/Oslo: W.C. Fabritius og Sønner.

Sandnes, Berit (2003) *Fra Starafjall til Starling Hill. Dannelse og utvikling av nørrøne stedsnavn på Orknøyene.* PhD thesis, University of NTNU, Trondheim. Available at: https://ntnuopen.ntnu.no/ntnu-xmlui/handle/11250/242760 (accessed: 1 July 2023).

Sandnes, Berit (2010) From *Starafjall to Starling Hill. An investigation of the formation and development of Old Norse place-names in Orkney.* Scottish Place-Name Society. Available at: https://spns.org.uk/resources/starafjall (accessed: 1 July 2023).

Sandnes, Jørgen and Stemshaug, Ola (1997) *Norsk stadnamnleksikon.* Oslo: Det norske samlaget.

Scottish National Dictionary, available online via *DSL.*

Stewart, John (1987) *Shetland Place-Names.* Lerwick: Shetland Library and Museum.

Zoëga, Geir T. (1910) *Concise Dictionary of Old Icelandic.* Oxford: The Clarendon Press.

5

The Shetland verses in Orkneyinga Saga ch. 85

Judith Jesch
(University of Nottingham)

On the lookout for Shetland and Shetlanders in the *Orkneyinga Saga*, Brian Smith drew attention to 'the result of a pure accident, that we find the most vivid description of Shetland and its society in the 12th century ... where we see the different classes of Shetland or Orkney society at their day to day work, cheek by jowl with each other' (Smith, 1988, pp.35-36). He was referring specifically to the anecdotes, accompanied by some skaldic verses by Earl Rǫgnvaldr Kali Kolsson, found in the first part of chapter 85 in most editions (e.g. Sigurður Nordal, 1913-1916, Guðmundsson, 1965) and translations (e.g. Taylor 1938, Hermann Pálsson and Edwards, 1981; all translations from the saga below are my own). Both the anecdotes and the verses are of great interest, providing a welcome Shetlandic interlude in this Orkney-heavy saga. They deserve closer attention and I will suggest that their presence in the saga is not just 'the result of a pure accident', but that a close reading provides some insight into not only the significance of Shetland for Rǫgnvaldr, but also how the saga was put together.

Chapter 85 comes at a major transition point in the narrative which culminates in the following chapter 86 when Earl Rǫgnvaldr and his followers set out on their long voyage to the Holy Land and back. Towards the end of chapter 84 we have been told that '[i]t was then quiet in the Isles and very peaceful'. Chapter 85 then prepares us for the next phase by having Rǫgnvaldr invited to Norway where the plans for the voyage are hatched. On the way back home, his two ships are wrecked on the coast of Shetland, and this provides an opportunity for a series of rather miscellaneous anecdotes set in Shetland, before Rǫgnvaldr and his party make it to Orkney and eventually embark on their voyage.

The first anecdote is of the shipwreck itself, so remarkable that it led in the 1970s to an expedition, ultimately unsuccessful, to try and locate the wreck somewhere off Gulberwick (Morrison, 1973; Collings *et al.*, 1974-77). Having noted that King Ingi of Norway had given two 'especially beautiful' ships (named *Hjálp* 'Help' and *Fífa* 'Arrow') to Rǫgnvaldr, and that Rǫgnvaldr had also received 'substantial gifts from his friends', the saga moves straight into a detailed account of what happened when he sailed west along with his junior co-earl Haraldr Maddaðarson:

> It was a Tuesday evening when the earls put out to sea, and they sailed through the night with an excellent wind. On Wednesday there was a great storm and during the night they became aware of land; it was very dark then; they saw breakers around them on all sides. They had previously sailed close together. Then there was no choice but to wreck both ships, and they did so. There was a rocky beach ahead, with little foreshore, and cliffs above. All were saved, but much cargo was lost; some of it came ashore during the night.

The saga text then includes a verse recited by Rǫgnvaldr which is ostensibly a part of the anecdote. However, despite an elaborate and unconvincing attempt by Roberta Frank (1972) to argue that it is about Rǫgnvaldr's ship, it is more likely simply to be misplaced (Finnbogi Guðmundsson, 1965, 196n.) and I will return to it below. Instead, I focus first on the description of the shipwreck and on those verses that are clearly related to that event, and then on the other Shetland verses in the chapter.

The detailed description of a shipwreck in chapter 85 is uncommon in saga literature. Reference to the days of the week, the account of the shifting weather and sea conditions, and the precise description of the spot where they came ashore, all give an usually specific feel to the narrative which suggests an eyewitness account (see Jesch, 2015 for more on treacherous sailing in skaldic poetry). This impression of personal experience is reinforced by one of Rǫgnvaldr's verses that stresses the impact of the shipwreck (all translations of the verses below are adapted from Jesch, 2009):

> And when they had carried the cargo up, they went ashore to look for settlements, because they were fairly sure they had arrived in Shetland. They quickly found a farm and men were then allotted to dwellings. The people there were pleased to see the earl when he came and people asked about his journeys. The earl recited a verse:

> *There was a loud noise when both Hjálp and Fífa were damaged;*
> *the wave caused men harm; the wet weather gave women sorrow.*
> *I see that that voyage of bold-hearted earls will be kept in memory;*
> *the crew got drenching work for sure.*

Although two fine ships and much cargo were lost, in the end nobody died and the well-known dandy Rǫgnvaldr could joke in his next verse about how the shipwreck ruined his clothes and forced him into inferior ones:

> The mistress of the house gave Earl Rǫgnvaldr a sheepskin instead of

his cloak; he stretched his hands out to take it and accepted it laughing and recited:

> *I shake out here a wrinkled leather garment; it provides me with very little finery; the prow-field [= sea] which surrounds our outerwear is big. Some day we'll go more finely dressed from a spray-swept horse of the eel-plain [= ship; eel-plain = sea]; surf drove the stallion of the mast-head [= ship] onto cliffs.*

Rǫgnvaldr seems to have had a soft spot for women and another Shetlandic woman comes briefly into the story:

> Then big fires were laid for them, and they warmed themselves at them. A serving-woman came in and was shivering a lot and spoke in her shivering and people did not understand what she said. The earl said he could understand her language:
>
> *You are [all] sitting around by the fire, while Ása—atatata!—is lying in the water—hutututu! Where shall I sit? I am rather cold.*

Rǫgnvaldr's own drenched state clearly gives him sympathy for this serving-woman, but why is she (or another one called Ása) lying in the water? The saga does not appear to say, though this does become clear when we consider the question of the manuscripts in which it is preserved.

It is important to remember that there is no single medieval manuscript which contains the whole of the text generally published as *Orkneyinga Saga*. All editions and translations present a text which is a patchwork drawn from a range of manuscripts which are all incomplete in some way, often very fragmentary, not always in Old Norse-Icelandic, and sometimes not even a text of the saga at all. (For more detail see the summary in Jesch, 2010, pp.156-159). The most extensive Old Norse text is in the late fourteenth-century manuscript known as *Flateyjarbók* (GKS 1005 fol.), which provides the main text for editors and translators. However, it is unsatisfactory in many ways, so whenever there is an alternative, editors replace its text with material from some of the other manuscripts and this can be seen in chapter 85 as elsewhere. Furthermore, in the case of the episode of the serving-woman, there is some relevant material which is not always included in the published translations.

This material is found in a manuscript kept in Uppsala and known as UppsUB R 702. This is not actually a manuscript of the saga, but rather an annotated collection of poetry and prose extracts from the saga compiled in the first half of the seventeenth century by the Icelandic priest Magnús Ólafsson. He owned an early copy of the saga (from the first half of the fourteenth century) which now survives only as a few leaves (AM 325 III α 4to), so it is a pity he did not copy out the whole saga when he had it. As well as being a collection of stanzas, Magnús Ólafsson's manuscript does include some prose passages which may derive from this early version of the saga and may thus represent a slightly different text than that which survives in other manuscripts. The only problem is that, although the verses are carefully reproduced, it seems that Magnús only included some prose passages in order to contextualise the verses and he seems often to have shortened or altered them to suit his purpose. But he does include a passage which gives an explanation for why the serving-woman is cold and another one is lying in the water (Sigurður Nordal, 1913-1916, 219n.):

> Ása was the name of a housemaid. She went out for water and another woman went with her. And when they came to the water, Ása stumbled into the source in the snowstorm, and the other one ran home very chilled.

It is likely that Magnús shortened this anecdote, as we would have expected it to be followed by some explanation of what happened when the other woman ran home, perhaps to get help for Ása. Or it may be that this passage is Magnús' attempt to explain the stanza, rather than an extract from the original saga (Guðmundsson 1965, 197-8n.), though in my view this is less likely. If it is original to the saga, then this short prose passage is indeed an insight into the working conditions of twelfth-century serving-women that would be of interest to Brian Smith and other readers, yet it is omitted from the Hermann Pálsson and Edwards translation (1981, p.158). Those who read Taylor's translation (1938, p.278) will find it included there, but unfortunately that translation is not entirely accurate, for in the original it is clear that it is not Ása (as Taylor has it) but the other woman who ran home.

More recently, Brian has alluded (Smith and Melton, 2019, p.119) to another anecdote from UppsUB R 702 in which 'Earl Rognvald and a peasant farmer go fishing'. This anecdote is included in the two main editions and the most recent translations into English, and most scholars seem to assume that, on this occasion at least, Magnús reproduces the original saga anecdote accurately. The passage is a long and well-written introduction to another verse by Rǫgnvaldr, and once again we get a glimpse of some Shetlandic women, among many other things:

> It happened one day south in Sumburgh Voe in Shetland that an impecunious farmer waited a long time for his crew, when all other boats were rowing out, each as it became ready. Then a man in a white cowl came to the old farmer and asked why he was not rowing out to the fishing as other men. The farmer said his crew had not arrived. 'Farmer', said the cowl-man, 'do you want me to row out with you?' 'I do want that,' said the farmer, 'and yet I want to have a share of my ship, because I have many children at home and I work for them as much as I am able.' Then they rowed out past Sumburgh Head and landward of Horse Island. There was a strong current where they stopped, and big eddies; they were going to sit in the eddy and fish from the roost. The cowl-man

Hundholm (or Horse Island) and its eddies from Scatness. Photo: Judith Jesch

sat in the bow and held the boat with the oars and the farmer was to fish. The farmer asked him to watch out that they were not carried into the roost, said that was likely to be dangerous. The cowl-man did not do as he said, and did not care if the farmer got into a testing situation. A little later they were carried into the roost, and the farmer became very frightened and said, 'I was ill-fated in my bad luck, when I took you on to row today, because I will die here, and my lot at home will be without provision and flung into poverty, if I pass away.' And the farmer became so frightened that he wept, since he feared his death. The cowl-man answers, 'Be cheerful, farmer, and do not weep, because he will drag us out of the roost who allowed us to come into it.' Then the cowl-man rowed out of the roost and the farmer then became very happy. They rowed to land and pulled up the boat, and the farmer asked the cowl-man to divide the fish. But the cowl-man asked the farmer to divide it as he liked, and said he did not want to have more than his third share. Many people had come to the beach there, both men and women, and many poor folk. The cowl-man gave the poor people all the fish he had been allotted during the day, and then prepared to leave. It was necessary to go up a bank, and many women were sitting on the bank. And when he went up the bank, his foot slipped, since it was thawing from the rain, and he fell down the bank. One woman saw this first and she laughed a lot at him and then other folk did. And when the cowl-man heard this, he recited:

The wise Sif of silk [= woman] makes fun of my outfit; the girl laughs a great deal more than would be right. Few are able to see the earl clearly in

> his fishing-gear, yet previously I pulled, gallant [as I am], the oak of the roller [= ship] from the waves in the early morning.

> Then the cowl-man went away and people later became certain that this cowl-man had been Earl Rǫgnvaldr. It later also became known to many that there were many of his deeds that were both helpful before God and amusing for people. People also knew the proverb which was in the verse, that 'few know an earl in fishing-gear'.

There is a detailed analysis of this anecdote by Paul Bibire in which he stresses its 'clerical, even hagiographic, tone' (Bibire, 1984, p.86) and sees parallels (1984, p.87, p.93) with the well-known pre-Christian myth of Thor fishing for the world serpent. These may both be over-interpretations. Rather than seeking some deeper meaning, it is more useful to consider this whole anecdote and its verse in conjunction with the other Shetland verses in chapter 85. Together, they form a coherent block of material about Earl Rǫgnvaldr that was originally in the version of the saga now represented only by that very fragmentary manuscript and Magnús Ólafsson's extracts from it. Some of this material, for whatever reason, never made it into other versions of the saga.

The coherence of this block of material is indicated by some parallels between the verse texts. Like the shipwreck stanza quoted above, the fishing anecdote involves the sartorial humiliation of Earl Rǫgnvaldr in connection with a maritime event. In the shipwreck anecdote, he laughs at himself in the verse when the housewife gives him an unsuitable alternative to his fine clothing. In the fishing anecdote, by contrast, he is laughed at by an assembly of female onlookers, but responds jovially enough in his stanza addressed to one of them. Again in contrast to the shipwreck anecdote, in this stanza his riposte emphasises his skill in bringing his craft safely ashore. And since the prose makes great play of the success of the fishing expedition, this also contrasts with the loss of valuable cargo in the shipwreck.

The fishing anecdote begins with 'It happened one day' and another anecdote found only in UppsUB R 702 also begins in the same way:

> It happened one day that a madman escaped his restraints and ran at Earl Rǫgnvaldr and grabbed him so firmly that the earl staggered so much that he nearly fell. Then the earl recited this verse:

> > The strong-gripped rascal grabbed the cloak of the leader; the man managed to jostle the generous war-leader severely. The Bjarki of weapons [= warrior/ man] was strong; they said the prince stumbled a bit; the speech-impeded destroyer of edges [= warrior/man] has strength instead of intelligence.

The placing of this anecdote in the narrative, and its location in Shetland, are both uncertain, as it is found only in UppsUB R 702, where it follows an episode that has a different cast of characters and is implicitly set in Orkney (explicitly so in the *Flateyjarbók* version). This uncertainty leads both editions of the saga to place the short madman anecdote and its verse in a footnote. Like the serving-woman anecdote, it is omitted from the Penguin (1981) translation, while Taylor (1938, p.281) does incorporate it into the text, but this time without indication or comment. Despite this uncertainty it seems most likely that the madman episode belongs with the other Shetland anecdotes. We cannot be sure that Magnús' collection of extracts exactly represents the order in which the anecdotes appeared in his source, and so it may have been misplaced in the order. More positively, there are clear parallels with the other Shetland anecdotes. Once again, we have the earl (nearly) sustaining a fall, and mentioning his own attire in the verse. Once again, we get a glimpse of a less-privileged member of society, in this case the 'madman', who has a speech impediment but is strong. His permanent speech impediment may even echo the more temporary speech impediment of the chilled serving-woman reporting on Ása's accident. In all of these anecdotes, the earl remains imperious and superior to the characters he encounters, yet he also shows some sympathy for them. The madman stanza implies that the earl has 'intelligence' in contrast to the madman's strength, and it is this intelligence which allows him to understand the speech of the serving-woman.

The episode, already mentioned, which is set in Orkney and which comes before the madman episode in 702, and is also found in *Flateyjarbók*, involves quite a different kind of competition, between Rǫgnvaldr and people who are more or less his equals, in this case two visiting Icelandic poets. In this episode, Rǫgnvaldr issues challenges; firstly to one of the poets to compose a poem about a spear; then to the other to compose a poem about a tapestry simultaneously with Rǫgnvaldr doing the same. Both the poets acquit themselves well in this competition, as does Rǫgnvaldr, and later they all go together to the Holy Land, with all three of them composing more poetry along the way. The elite, cultured and cosmopolitan relationships at Rǫgnvaldr's court in Orkney and on tour stand in stark contrast to his experiences among the frequently impoverished peasants of Shetland.

But not all Shetlanders were impoverished peasants evoking the earl's sympathy, and some presented more of a challenge, as pointed out by Brian (Smith, 1988, p.36). One more stanza, hardly an episode as such, comes in between the serving-woman episode and the fishing episode, and probably still relates to the arrangements after the shipwreck:

> The earl sent twelve of his men to Einarr in Gulberwick, and he said he would not take them in unless the earl came himself. And when Earl Rǫgnvaldr hears this, then he recited:

> *Einarr said that he wished to entertain none of the followers of Rǫgnvaldr except the earl himself; the roaring sea of Gautr [= poetry] comes to my palate.*

> *I know that* [the one] *not amiable to men overturned his promises; I went in where the fires of Yggr* [= swords] *burned late in the evening.*

Some of the meaning of this stanza may have been lost in the saga transmission and so it illustrates how the strict metres of skaldic poetry ensured its correct transmission, even when saga compilers or later scribes did not fully understand what was going on. While the stanza states that Einarr was only willing to offer hospitality to the earl, the saga says that Einarr would only accept the men if the earl came too. The prose context also implies that Rǫgnvaldr spoke this stanza before going in to Einarr's farm, while the final clause of the stanza suggests the opposite. The stanza itself has some notable features not found in the other Shetland verses discussed so far. The use of Óðinn's names in the poetry-kenning 'sea of Gautr' and the sword-kenning 'the fires of Yggr' hint at the elite cultural context of the earl's court, while also making a contrast with the earlier situation in Shetland. At Einarr's farm, Rǫgnvaldr is being received with hostility rather than the welcoming hearth at the farm where he first dries out, and where he meets the housewife with the sheepskin and the chilled serving-woman. In the light of this hostility, the earl has to assert his elite status as poet and earl to counter the challenge to his authority.

The stanza inserted into the prose narrative of the shipwreck, mentioned above, may also belong here:

> Earl Rǫgnvaldr managed the best of all, then as always. He was so cheerful that he played with his fingers and kept on composing poetry. He pulled a gold ring off his finger and recited a verse:
>
>> *I hang a snake of the bridge of the hawk* [= arm-ring; bridge of the hawk = arm]*, made round by the hammer, on the gallows of the tongs* [= arm]*; we reveal the drink of the Grímnir of hanged ones* [= poetry; Grímnir = a giant; a giant of hanged ones = Óðinn]*. The fir-tree of the gleaming-voice of the Gautar of the cave* [= woman; Gautar of the cave = giants; gleaming-voice of the giants = gold] *has gladdened me so much, that I play with my hollows of the backward-bending feller of the lagoon* [= hands; feller of the lagoon = oar]*.*

Once again, the prose contradicts the verse, not understanding that the ring in question is an arm-ring rather than a finger-ring. With its complex kennings (for further explication see Jesch, 2009, pp.583-584) and slightly inscrutable topic, this verse stands out from the Shetland group, though it does have some parallels with the stanza recited at Einarr's farm. The use of Óðinn's names (Gautr, Grímnir) in the kennings and the reference to the composition of poetry echo the themes that are more simply expressed in the Einarr stanza. Also, the reference to the gifting of an arm-ring suggests a generous lord in an elite context, and may represent some kind of resolution of the confrontational situation outlined in the Einarr stanza. Who the woman who gladdened him is, however, remains unclear. While the other stanzas in chapter 85 show Rǫgnvaldr interacting with the simpler residents of Shetland, these two remind his audience that he also belongs in a quite different context, that of his peripatetic court where poetry and a knowledge of Norse mythology are a part of the culture.

The sources of *Orkneyinga Saga* are varied and complex, yet it is clear that much of it derives from the life story and poetry of Earl Rǫgnvaldr Kali Kolsson. Paul Bibire (1988, p.211) has suggested that 'the author of the saga had access to an annotated collection of poetry associated with Earl Rǫgnvaldr Kali' and even that this collection was first recorded, or caused to be recorded, by Rǫgnvaldr himself. If this is the case, then this would have happened in the mid-twelfth century, and the material thus represents a very early example of prosimetrum, the embedding of verse into a prose narrative, that is so typical of the Old Norse-Icelandic sagas. Close attention to the manuscript preservation, and particularly the evidence of UppsUB R 702, shows both how this can have happened, and how such a prosimetrum could get mangled in the later manuscript transmission.

In addition to their significance for understanding the early history of the saga, the Shetland verses also have a special significance in the very varied body of Rǫgnvaldr's poetry, which covers many themes and takes in his adventures in a variety of places. Barbara Crawford (1984, p.71) has demonstrated how Shetland was the core of Rǫgnvaldr's power-base in the Northern Isles, as it was for his saintly uncle, Magnús Erlendsson, and the Erlendr branch of the earls generally. It is thus no surprise that Shetland figures quite largely in Rǫgnvaldr's poetry, while remarkably little of it has obviously Orcadian content. However, what Sigurður Nordal (1913-1916, p.ix) called the 'unhappy fate' of the saga manuscripts has tended to obscure the sigificance of this particular subset of his poetic output, even to the extent of some of the verses being excluded from the most recent, and most popular, translation of the saga, because they were also allowed to drop out in the medieval manuscript transmission. I hope Brian will be pleased to hear that this lack will be remedied, and the Shetland verses given full prominence, in my forthcoming annotated translation, to be renamed *The Saga of the Earls of Orkney*.

Bibliography

Bibire, Paul (1984) '"Few Know an Earl in Fishing-clothes",' in Barbara Crawford (ed.), *Essays in Shetland History: Heiðursrit to T. M. Y. Manson*. Lerwick: The Shetland Times Ltd, pp.82-98.

Bibire, Paul (1988) 'The Poetry of Earl Rǫgnvaldr's Court', in Barbara E. Crawford (ed.), *St Magnus Cathedral and Orkney's Twelfth-Century Renaissance*. Aberdeen: Aberdeen University Press, pp.208-240.

Collings, Lucy, Farrell, R. and Morrison, I. (1974–77) 'Earl Rögnvald's Shipwreck', *Saga-Book* 19, pp.293–310.

Crawford, Barbara E. (1984) 'The Cult of Saint Magnus in Shetland', in Barbara Crawford, (ed.), *Essays in Shetland History: Heiðursrit to T. M. Y. Manson*. Lerwick: The Shetland Times Ltd, pp.65-81.

Finnbogi Guðmundsson (ed.) (1965) *Orkneyinga saga*. Reykjavík: Hið íslenska fornritafélag.

Frank, Roberta (1972) 'Anatomy of a Skaldic Double-Entendre: Rǫgnvaldr Kali's Lausavísa 7', in Evelyn Firchow *et al.* (eds.), *Studies for Einar Haugen: Presented by Friends and Colleagues*. The Hague and Paris: Mouton, pp.227-235.

Hermann Pálsson and Edwards, Paul (trans.) (1981) *Orkneyinga Saga*. London: Penguin.

Jesch, Judith (2009) 'Rǫgnvaldr jarl Kali Kolsson, *Lausavísur*' in Kari Ellen Gade, (ed.), *Poetry from the Kings' Sagas 2: From c. 1035 to c. 1300*. Turnhout: Brepols, pp.575-609.

Jesch, Judith (2010). '*Orkneyinga saga*: a work in progress?' in Judy Quinn and Emily Lethbridge (eds.), *Creating the Medieval Saga: Versions, Variability and Editorial Interpretations of Old Norse Saga Literature*. Odense: University Press of Southern Denmark, pp.153-173.

Jesch, Judith (2015) 'The Threatening Wave: Norse Poetry and the Scottish Isles', in James H. Barrett and Sarah-Jane Gibbon (eds.), *Maritime Societies of the Viking and Medieval World*. Leeds: Maney, pp.320-332.

Morrison, Ian (1973) *The North Sea Earls: The Shetland/Viking Archaeological Expedition*. London: Gentry Books.

Sigurður Nordal (ed.) (1913-1916) *Orkneyinga saga*. Copenhagen: Samfund til udgivelse af gammel nordisk litteratur.

Smith, Brian (1988) 'Shetland in Saga-Time: Rereading the *Orkneyinga saga*', *Northern Studies* 25, pp.21-41.

Smith, Brian, and Melton, Nigel (2019). 'Historical evidence', in Nigel D. Melton *et al.* (eds.), *Excavations at Old Scatness, Shetland* vol.3. Lerwick: Shetland Amenity Trust, pp.119-131.

Taylor, Alexander B. (ed. and trans.) (1938) *The Orkneyinga Saga*. Edinburgh: Oliver & Boyd.

6

A parallel naming voyage through a familiar seascape

Andrew Jennings and Arne Kruse

(University of the Highlands and Islands / University of Edinburgh)

Introduction

This joint paper takes its inspiration from Brian's own keen interest in onomastics. In it we will explore the phenomenon of parallel naming, a feature of Norse naming practice in the Scottish maritime areas. When the Norse people were building a mental map of the coast, unsurprisingly they used the same place-name generics in the naming of Scottish islands, headlands and other coastal features, as they were wont to do in Norway. As a consequence, similar names and naming patterns turn up in Scotland and Norway, indicating that the Norse were effectively 'at home' when they were creating names in Scottish waters. Although there are examples of extended use in Scotland of certain generics, such as the frequent *geo,* from ON *gjá,* to denote a typically Scottish inlet of the sea with steep rocky sides, the Norse in general did not have to create new names or repurpose generics for a new and unfamiliar landscape.

Islands with personal names

Before examining the parallel use of generics, we would like to present a short excursus and look at a type of name which is not particularly common in Norway, although it does exist: islands with personal names as specifics. These seem to be a new phenomenon of the Viking era.

Among the many important onomastic papers that Brian has published, he has written about this type of name. In one paper (Smith, 1988) he explored the island name *Bressay,* which he convincingly argued takes its name from *Brúsi,* a jarl of Orkney with close connections to Shetland. Islands that take their name from a personal name are an interesting and under-researched phenomenon. However, Peder Gammeltoft (2005, p.123) has discussed a number of these from Shetland, including the islands of Vementry (< *Vémundr* m.), Hildisay (< *Hildir* m.), Trondra (< *Þrándr* m.), and Samphrey (< *Sandfríðr* f.) and he points out that 'The occurrence of a personal name as the specific in an island-name probably signals original ownership or it may possibly reflect a particular event involving the named person and the island in question' (Gammeltoft, 2005, p.123). Large islands containing personal names are relatively rare in Norway, but there are examples of smaller islands and skerries that commemorate certain persons, such as Persholmen, Paulgrunnen, Hansholmen, Ingebriktsholman (all from the coast of Trøndelag). In general, such names give the impression of not being particularly old coinages. For instance, these examples contain the personal names *Per*, *Paul*, *Hans*, all Christian names and *Ingebrikt*, which is of German origin.

Larger Norwegian islands, like Bokn, Solund, and Tustna, contain derivative suffixes that were no longer productive when the Viking *adventus* began (Nes, 1976; Kruse, 2020). Other naming practices had taken over. By far the majority of island names were now constructed with the generic -*ey* 'island' and following Viking era social changes, individuals now appear in place names coined all over the *landnám*.

Island names formed from personal names seem to be associated with the cultural context of exploratory and colonial conditions. We can think of them as mnemonics conserving the memories of events and people. The British Isles have a notable number of examples, and without being exhaustive in Orkney we have Rousay (< *Hrolfr* m.), South Ronaldsay (< *Rögnvaldr* m.) and Egilsay (< *Egill* m.), in the Outer Hebrides we have Eriskay (< *Eiríkr* m.), Grimsay (< *Grímr* m.), Hermetray (<*Hermundr*) and Berneray (< *Björn* m.) and in Wales, we have Ramsey (< *Hrafn* m., or the similarly named bird *hrafn*, m. 'raven') and Bardsey (< *Bárðr* m.) (Owen, 2015, pp.111-112). The latter may take its name from one of the kings called Bárðr who were active in the Irish Sea, perhaps Bárðr Óttarson defeated by Ragnald of York in 914. The Channel Islands probably have these examples, Guernsey (< *Grani* m.) and Jersey (< *Geirr* m.) (Everett-Heath, 2010).

There are a few such island names in Iceland, although perhaps not as many as one might expect. This is at least partly explained by the relative scarcity of islands. However, in this case, the traditions associated with the naming of places are sometimes preserved. For example, the Arctic skerry Kolbeinsay is called after Kolbeinn Sigurdsson, who, according to *Svarfdæla Saga*, was shipwrecked on the island, and according to *Landnámabók* Hergilsey in Breiðafjörður was named after Hergils *hnapprass* or 'button arse', who was driven from the island for helping Gísli Sursson. Iceland itself had a previous name with a personal name as a specific – *Garðarshólmi*, after Garðar Svavarsson, who was driven north by a storm in the Pentland Firth. To the west of Iceland there were the *Gunnbjarnasker*, Gunnbjörn's Skerries - in fact, the coast of Greenland. Greenland also had an *Eiriksey*, so called because that was where Eiríkr *hinn rauði* spent his first winter.

Islands with personal name specifics feature in research we are currently undertaking on the Norse maritime onomasticon of the sea-route between Norway and Dublin. For example, in Loch Linnhe, an area of particular interest, we have two examples which parallel those in the Outer Hebrides – Bernera (< *Björn* m.) and Eriska (< *Eiríkr* m.). Off the west coast of Mull we have Ulva (< *Úlfr* m.), and in a parallel with Iceland, we also have Colonsay (< *Kolbeinn* m.) (Watson, 1926, p.84). We will return to the islands of Loch Linnhe and the Firth of Lorne below. Presumably there were memorable events or traditions associated with these names, but unfortunately, we now no longer know what the stories were concerning Björn, Eiríkr, Úlfr or Kolbeinn; were they settlers, owners, or survivors of shipwreck? That information has been lost to time. However, their names were part of the mental map that Norse sailors carried with them as they sailed the coastal route.

These island names were mnemonic tools. Sailors had other ways of naming. Obviously, one of those was to name features according to their physical reality; a sandy beach would be named *Sandvík*, 'Sand bay' or a flat island might be called *Flatey* 'Flat island'. Nicolaisen (1978, p.46) argued that sailors had an onomasticon which they brought with them, a toolbox of appropriate names, which they delved into when they needed a name for a particular feature. Sailors from Norway would have a particularly appropriate toolbox for the Scottish islands and west coast. Brink calls this naming by analogy or association (2016, p.163). We can just call it parallel naming. If we think about island names, there are many examples. For example, in Norway a small island next to a larger can be called a 'calf', and this transferred metaphoric thinking is evident in Shetland names, like the Calf of Grunay in Skerries, the Calf of Daaey, the Calf of Linga, and the Calf of Score Holm. Along the Scottish coast we have Calbhsa Mòr, north of the Kylesku bridge. The Isle of Man also has its Calf, and Mull has Calve Island, which shelters Tobermory Bay.

As noted above, personal names attached to islands would once have had associated stories. Stories are the ideal mnemonic medium. One can imagine that over time sailors would have built up a bank of tales connected to landmarks which would have formed part of their mental map, just as much as sandy bays and rocky capes. In medieval Irish tradition this type of knowledge was called *dindshenchas* and produced a large corpus of material recounting the traditions and events associated with Old Irish place names (Gwynn, 1913). In Iceland a similar interest in the origin of names has given us *Landnámabók*.

The experienced seafarer heading from Norway to Dublin would have had his own collection of topographical stories, as well as a memorised list of place-names, to keep him orientated. We can speculate that these would have included the tale about the giantesses Fenja and Menja grinding out salt in the Pentland Firth, as related in *Litla Skalda* (Jesch, 2007). Wise sailors would avoid getting too close, and they might also have been aware that the *Hjaðningavíg*, or everlasting battle, was taking place on the hills of Hoy, as told by Snorri Sturluson in *Skáldskaparmál*.

Sailors had a practical reason for naming islands and coastal features. They needed to minimise their risk on potentially dangerous journeys. A crucial factor in this respect would be knowing one's exact position. In sheltered waters, and within sight of land, this involved being able to recognise known landscape features, and therefore knowing where your vessel was located in relation to the optimally safe course. A knowledge of landscape features along the route was of utmost importance, and place names are the mnemonic tool which allowed them to memorise features in the landscape. Names do not need to carry meaning to function as address tags, but semantically meaningful names are easier to remember, especially if they commemorate a notable event like a shipwreck or are descriptive, i.e. the name relates to what is actually seen. We can assume that it must have taken time for such stories to be attached to the coastal landscape and thus these stories are evidence for the existence of a well-established sea-route. It is, however, possible to identify earlier strata of names.

Ethnonyms

African and North American maps are peppered with names of areas or natural features stemming from an early contact period: Namibia, Wisconsin, Manitoba, etc. Preceding the exploitation and colonisation of the new land areas, these are names recorded by early explorers who have been told the names in communication with native people. Among this type of names are ethnonyms, i.e. names reflecting local groups of peoples or tribes, such as Swaziland (now Eswatini), Dakota, Miami. This way of naming, to recognise the local inhabitants, is also evident in the Norse names in the north of Scotland. Orkney, Caithness, the Pentland Firth and probably Shetland may reflect the names of the people inhabiting these locations when the Norse arrived. This type of naming is seen all over the Viking expansion area where Scandinavians met other peoples, such as *Bjarmaland* in the north and *Blámannaland* in the south, respectively referring to the land of Permeans in Northern Russia and to Africa (Kruse, 2017, pp.222-224).

It appears that the Norse had a relatively nuanced impression of the ethnic situation in Scotland. They appear to have been aware of Gaels and Britons viz. Great and Little Cumbrae ON *Kum[b]reyiar* 'Islands of the Britons' (Taylor, 2009, p.10), and in the north the Picts. While some have seen the Pentland Firth, *Pettlandsfjǫrðr*, as a name given from Orkney, registering that Picts were living to the south of the firth (Watson, 1924, p.30), it can be argued that the name actually denotes Picts living on both sides of the firth. That there were sub-groups on either side, seems to be evidenced by the names *Katanes* and *Orkneyjar*, originating from tribes bearing animal names, probably with the function as totems (Watson, 1924, p.29). The oldest documented name is *Orcades*, mentioned by Pytheas, c.300 B.C., corresponding with Old Irish *Innse Orc*. By adding an -n- the Norse adapted the native name to mean *erkn* or *ørkn* 'grey seal'. This type of seal is far more abundant in British waters than along the Norwegian coast and would therefore have been a noticeable feature to the Norse settlers. The Norse name is an adaptation of the tribal name *Orc* '(wild) boars'. As the modern Gaelic for whale is *mucmhara* 'sea pig', perhaps the earlier Celtic *orc* 'boar' originally meant a type of whale, although Watson dismissed the idea (1924, p.30). Interestingly OE had the same concept, having the word *mereswine* or 'seapig' for dolphin or porpoise, from proto-Germanic **mariswīnq*. Caithness developed from Old Norse *Katanes*, where the element *-nes*, 'headland', is added to the tribal name *Cat* 'Cats', reflected in the Old Irish for Sutherland *i Cattaib* 'among the Cats' and in the Modern Gaelic name for eastern Sutherland, *Cataibh* (Watson 1924, p.30). In a parallel with *Pettlandsfjǫrðr,* along the west coast, Norse sources call the indented coastline of sealochs *Skotlandsfirðir,* a calque on *Earra-Ghàidheal* 'Coastline of the Gael' (Jennings, 2017, p.120).

Similarly, *Papar*-names display a distinct concentration in the Northern Isles. Although the *papar* cannot be claimed as an ethnic group, there is close to a consensus that the term refers to Celtic monks, and as such they would have displayed sufficient common features to be classified as a recognisable group, clearly worthy of many place names. The *papar*-names show signs of being early (Gammeltoft, 2014), and justify a classification among the other names denoting the Norse mental mapping of a new land settled and distinguished by different peoples.

Unst, Yell and Fetlar

The three large northernmost islands in Shetland are oddly named. Unst, Yell, and Fetlar all lack the usual ending that derives from ON *-ey*. We should of course always allow for a degree of coincidence, but here is a cluster of three islands, located in relative geographical isolation but close to Norway, and on the straight lateral sailing course from Sogn and Solund, across the *Sólundarhaf*. Might their atypical character be explained by unusually early contact with Norway (Nicolaisen, 2003, p.141)? If the names Yell, Unst, and Fetlar had been located on the Norwegian coast, they would have fitted in nicely with most other names of large islands and be pre-Viking in date. For example, Unst, with its various ON forms *Ornyst, Örmst, Aumstr,* could be derived from the Indo-European root **aŭ-* 'wave, sea', like *Aumar,* the old name for Kvitsøy, near Stavanger (Særheim, 1989, p.16 ff. and 2007, p.23). A semantic content referring to heavy seas and strong currents would certainly fit Unst very well. The 'problem' with a classification among the old Norwegian island names is the *-st* derivation, which would place the creation of this island name hundreds of years before the Viking Age. Coates – although he offers a different derivation – agrees that the name is likely to be a suffixed derivative of a remote root (2021, p.7). Are we seeing here evidence of very early contact across the *Sólundarhaf*? Perhaps so, because the name *Shetland* itself has parallels with early pre-Viking names. Typologically the name fits into a group of old, pre-Viking names in *-land*, with people names as a specific, such as Rogaland and Hordaland (Kruse, 2017, pp.222-224), and in particular it seems to be a precise parallel with the island of Gotland (Jennings, 2010, p.137).

Semantic adaptation

An alternative explanation for the unusual character of the names of the three northernmost Shetland islands may be that they are Norse adaptations of original native names (Coates, 2007). This certainly seems to been the case with the large Hebridean islands Lewis, Uist, Skye and Mull. They also lack the element -*ey*. The respective Norse names for Lewis and Uist, *Ljoðhús* and *Ívist*, are both semantically transparent and, therefore, give the impression of being younger than Unst, Yell and Fetlar. Both are compound names, but although they appear to have meanings, semantically they are surprising as island names. *Ljoðhús* means 'peoples' house' or possibly 'house of sounds' and *Ívist* means 'in-dwelling'. They give the distinct impression of a semantic adaptation of an original name. Perhaps sailors' stories grew up around these strange names, which are now lost to us. We do not know for sure what the original pre-Norse form of Lewis was, unlike in the case of Skye and Mull which appear in Ptolemy, unless it is actually *Leoghus* recorded in the 12th century *Caithréim Chellacháin Chaisil*. This would make sense as the dental fricative [θ] was still pronounced in Gaelic at that time, so why change it to a velar fricative [ɣ]? In the case of Uist, ON *Ívist* reflects the pre-Norse Gaelic form *Ibdaig* (AU 672.2 *Deleti sunt Ibdig* 'The Ibdaig were destroyed'). Recorded in Ptolemy as *Eboudai*, which through scribal error gives us Hebrides (Jennings and Kruse, 2009, p.81; Clancy, 2018, p.32).

While the Norse names *Ljoðhús* and *Ívist* do not make topographical sense, Skye (ON *Skíð*) and Mull (ON *Múli*) are different. The two large islands again have known pre-Norse originals (*Scetis* and *Malaios/Maleus* on Ptolemy's map; and *Malea insula* in Vita C i.22), but the Norse adaptations carry semantically transparent and meaningful names that are paralleled in Norway. The ON *skíð*, f. 'straight piece of wood, split from the trunk', which gives us the word *ski*, is used in the name of the town Skien, either referring to the local river as straight or split (DSL). The Norse *Múli* has the original root vowel raised from *a* > *ú*. In Norway the metaphoric *múli*, m. 'muzzle, snout (of a cow or horse)', refer to prominent natural features, and the simplex Mulen is used several times along the coast for protruding mountains and headlands, for example Mulen and Lislemulen, headlands in Fedje, Mulen, a mountain in Tingvoll, and the farm Mule on Byneset, Trondheim. The adapted Norse names for the two Hebridean islands are semantically lucky strikes for the mountainous Mull and for Skye with the indented long and straight sea lochs. The loanword gave *mule* in Old Scots and is used for headlands, as in Mull of Galloway and Mull of Kintyre (DOST).

In the sailor's mind

Moving back north we find the interesting name Fair Isle. One could claim that this name has a clear origin because it is documented in *Orkneyinga Saga* as *Friðarey*, i.e. 'peaceful isle'. It is, however, important to remember that this source is written hundreds of years after the name is likely to have been coined. The pronunciation of the name actually points to a parallel with Faroe Islands,

Map 1 Extract from the area south of Bodø, northern Norway.
Copyright: A. Kruse

Neist Point.   *Copyright: Morten Hansen. Used with permission*

Stemshesten, seen from Tverrfjella, Romsdalen.
Copyright: Jan Erik Hansen. Used with permission

ON *Færeyjar* 'Sheep islands'. But there is a third possibility, namely a derivation from the verb *fara* 'travel'. A string of islands named Færøy are located along the coast of Norway, typically positioned as navigational points close to stretches of open sea. From a functional point of view, Fair Isle serves exactly this role. It is of principal importance for the navigation of *Solundarháf*, where it provides a visual contact between Shetland and Orkney, preventing a potentially dangerous sail-by on a westerly course from south-west Norway (Kruse, 2010).

Not surprisingly, the island Stroma, ON **Straumey*, in the Pentland Firth, with one of the strongest tidal currents in the world means 'stream island'. The name is also found in several locations along the coast of Norway, such as Straumøy next to the current Saltstraumen. (See Map 1.)

In Norway a pattern has been identified where dangerous islets and skerries are named after domestic animals, such as *ku* 'cow', *hest* 'horse', *gris* 'pig', and *okse* 'ox', obviously as a form of taboo naming. The name Swona in the Pentland Firth is a candidate for this type of naming. The name is probably from ON **Svíney* 'pig isle'. However, it might also have been inspired by the round shape of the back of a pig, which is also a likely motivation for the many Svinøy in Norway, such as the one on Map 2, outside Godøya, near Ålesund. The shape of a pig's posterior is the origin of the name Giltarump **Galtarump* 'Pig's bum' in Shetland. A horse appears to be referenced in the name Neist Point or *Rubha na h- Éist,* in Skye, from ON *hestr,* m. 'horse'. This name is paralleled in several Norwegian names for protruding headlands, for example Stemhesten, near Kristiansund (see pictures).

Continuing on our sailing route, after passing Hoy 'high island' (paralleled with many Håøy, from **Háey,* along the Norwegian coast) on the starboard, the course changes in a southerly direction at Cape Wrath, Gaelic *am Parbh,* from Old Norse *hvarf*, a very apt name seen from the navigator's point of view. Several names in Norway spring from the verb *hverfa*, 'turn' or the noun *hvarf*, n., used on locations where there are bends or protruding features in the landscape, such as Kvarv in Misværfjorden, near Bodø, which is evidently named for its location at a distinct bend in the fjord (see Map 1). The name is also paralleled in the Old Norse *Hvarf* in Greenland (Cape Farewell, in Greenlandic Nunap Isua).

Map 2 Extract from the area around Ålesund, west Norway.
Copyright: A. Kruse

The town of Ålesund with the island Godøya to the right and Stavneset and Kverve across the fjord.   *Photo: A. Jennings*

Assynt, from *ássendi*, 'hill end'. There are many Åsende in Norway.   *Photo: A. Kruse*

Parallel names along the western sea route

If we continue to follow the sea route south along the Scottish coast, we get more names paralleling coastal names in Norway, here illustrated with the names on three map extracts from respectively north, west and south in Norway. For example, there is the highly recognisable mountain Suilven, with its partly Gaelicised form, from Old Norse *súla* 'pillar', or a possible meaning 'cleft', referring to the jagged ridge. Both meanings are behind mountains and islands named Sula and similar in Norway (Map 2). Further south lies the aptly named Assynt, from ON **Ássendi* 'hill end', where there is the township of Stoer with its prominent sea-stack, which comes from Old Norse *staur* 'post, stake', and which is paralleled in several *Staur*-names on steep mountains in Norway. Sea-stacks, however, are not found in Norway, and consequently, Norwegian islands with *staur*, such as Staurøya, an island by Kinn, are more likely to refer to poles erected as navigational points, cf. names with *stafr*, discussed below.

Further south, off Skye there was a *Kerlingasteinn* 'hag's stone', now lost. It was recorded in *Hakon Hakonsson's saga* that King Hakon met King Magnus of Man there. The name may survive in the Gaelic form *Sgeir na Caillich* 'hag's skerry' near Kyleakin. Old Norse *kerling*, f., 'woman' mostly in the meaning 'married woman' and also 'old woman, hag', gives modern Norwegian *kjerring*, f., and is found in many place names, not least for mountains. The most well-known of these is Kjerringa, 497 m., which forms part of the headland of Stadt (Map 2). Kjerringa, Kjerringøy or Kjerringholmen are frequent island names. Some may be named after women who have lived there but most are small islands, too tiny to be inhabited. Typically in Norway, *Kjerringa* forms a pair with *Kallen* from Old Norse *karl*, m. 'man', mostly 'old man' (see Map 3). Kallen is a headland on an island in Kinn, and close by is Kjerringa, a small island off the larger. This name pair also occurs as two small islands in Bø, two submerged reefs in Averøy, two mountain tops next to each other in Lurøy, and on Godøy, by Ålesund. In the Faroe Islands at the north end of Eysturoy, Kellingin is paired with Risin the giant. There do not seem to be examples of the name pair along the western Scottish sea route. However, Old Norse *karl* is the likely origin of the island name Cara, interestingly off the coast of Gigha, which we will see has the same origin as Godøy. This is paralleled in Norway. Kalløya are islands in Sveio and in Alver on the west coast of Norway.

If we approach the area that we have been researching, Loch Linnhe and the Firth of Lorne with the islands of Argyll, we find a number of names paralleled in Norway which merit investigation – Glen Scaddle, Shuna, Shona, Ledaig, Dunstaffnage, Kerrera, Fladda, Lunga, Scarba, Torsa and Gigha.

Loch Linnhe is a particularly interesting area as it connects the coastal sea-route with the Great Glen. If the Great Glen was a portage, as seems likely, or at least a strategic through route for the Norse heading to Argyll from the Cromarty Firth (Crawford, 1987, p.67), Loch Linnhe was an area where communication routes converged. The most obvious onomastic indicator of a Norse presence in the area are the Gaelic place names noting the existence of *gall* 'strangers', the usual Gaelic term for the Norse. Although this term can

Sandwick, Shetland. Photo: A. Jennings

also mean both 'strangers' in general and 'Lowlanders' specifically, on the west coast it is generally assumed to mean 'Scandinavians'. On the westside of Loch Linnhe, at the start of Loch Eil, opposite the mouth of River Lochy, just across for the entrance to the modern canal, we have Camas na Gall 'The Bay of the Scandinavian (?)' and at the mouth of River Scaddle there is Eilean nan Gall 'Island of the Scandinavians (?)'. There are also names of Old Norse origin in Loch Linnhe, including the aforementioned River Scaddle, which flows from Glen Scaddle. This was originally *Skarðdalr, 'cleft valley', usually indicative of a mountain pass. It fits the nature of the glen. It occurs frequently as a name in Norway and gives us the Shetland word skord. On the other side of the loch was the particularly intriguing name Invershippinish, which appears in the 17th century History of the MacDonalds (Highland Papers I, 40). M.H.Brown (1992, p.336) in his PhD thesis suggested the name might refer to the inver 'mouth' of the River Kiachnish. This is possible. The modification appears to be a Norse one, changing Kiachnish to the Old Norse *Skipnes 'ship point'. Certainly, it seems to have been a known, important maritime destination, because in 1431, 600 men came in their galleys to that point in support of MacDonald. Was this a place for disembarking before heading up the Great Glen? In Norway we have many parallels, including Skibnes in Møre og Romsdal.

If we head south of the Corran ferry, Norse names become more abundant. There are a number on the strategically important Lismore, which retains its pre-Norse name. For example, there is Loch Fiart, which presumably derives from fjǫrðr 'fjord' (Johnston, 1991, p.225), presumably Loch Linnhe itself. It has been argued that Firth of Lorne, and therefore Loch Linnhe, was known at one time as Skotlandsfjǫrðr (Woolf, 2013, p.4). Just north of Lismore lies Shuna which shares the same name as Shona east of Luing. Both islands are relatively high, respectively 71 and 91 metres, and therefore can be seen from afar and used as markers for sailing. Also, from both islands respectively one can see far into Loch Linnhe and down south into the Sound of Jura. The island names mean 'sight island' and are derived from Old Norse *sjón*, f., 'sight'. A parallel to these Scottish island names is the fjord name Sjona in Lurøy, Nordland. The fjord's shape is straight and broad so that from the outer part one can see deep into its recesses (Rygh, 1896, s.63 and NG XVI s.117) It is likely that Channerwick in Shetland, recorded as *Schonarwyk* in 1525 (Stewart, 1987, p.294) also comes from this root, meaning 'Bay of Sight'.

To the east of Lismore lies the 13th century Dunstaffnage Castle, recorded as *Ard-Stofniche* in 1322 (Henderson, 1910, p.160). It shares the same root as the island of Staffa, from Old Norse *stafr* m. 'staff'. There are a number of Stavnes names in Norway. The name means 'headland with pole or staff' and is typically indicative of harbours or fjords which meet the common sailing route, such as Stavneset at Agdenes, which announces the course to Trondheim, and Stavneset by Ålesund, on the western side of Hessa, facing the island Godøy (Map 2). A raised pole here would have signalled the route to the medieval market town of Borgund. There is another Stavneset on Averøy, now a lighthouse, which indicates the harbour of Kristiansund, whose old name Fosna (from *folskn*, 'protection') informs the sailor that here is a safe haven along the dangerous open water of Hustadvika. At Dunstaffnage there was a castle here in the time of Somerled (MacPhee, 2004, p.63), and it has been suggested that the site was a stronghold of the Dál Riata, known as Dun Monaidh, as early as the 7th century (Grove, 2004, p.16). However, the name suggests that at the time of the Norse naming of this important location, the significant feature was not a fortification but a navigational aid in the form of a raised pole. One can only imagine what the pole looked like, but its placement effectively highlighted to someone sailing from Lismore the opening of Loch Etive and the dangerous Falls of Lora. Across from Dunstaffnage is Ledaig, which just might come from **Leiðvík*, 'bay by the sailing course'. However, one might have expected the /ð/ to have disappeared rather than have developed into the voiced consonant /d/. There are many compound names with *Lei-* along the coast of Norway, including Leivik in Solund and in Molde.

Heading further south and passing Oban, which is a Gaelic place-name *an -t Òban* 'the little bay', formed from a Norse borrowing into Gaelic of *hóp* n. 'small bay' (see Hopen on Map 1), lies the island of Kerrera 'Kjarbar's island' in *Hákonar saga*, This might be another example of an island name with a personal name as a specific. Although *Kjarbar* is not a personal name which is otherwise registered in Medieval Norse literature (Lind, 1915), it could be the Old Irish name *Cairbre*. As a number of Old Irish names were adopted by Norse speakers, for example *Niall* which gives *Njáll*, this is not impossible. However, it is also possible that the saga version of the island name is a misunderstanding. As with the example of Fair Isle, we must bear in mind that the saga recorded these names hundreds of years after the names are likely to have been coined. With Kerrara we may see a possible origin in *kjarr*, n., 'brushwood, mainly on wet ground', which is a usual element in Norwegian place names, like the river names Kjerråa, and Kjarará in Iceland. There is also the outside possibility that this might be a Norse adaptation of an older island name.

Continuing into the Firth of Lorne and beyond we come to a group of islands with topographical names paralleled in Norway and in other areas, Fladda, Lunga, and Scarba. These lie just to south of the slate island of Seil.

Descriptive island names

These three names clearly fit with Nicolaisen's idea of a Norse onomasticon, where Norse sailors delved into their onomastic toolbox, pulling out names appropriate to the topography, shape or some other feature of the island. These would have provided mnemonics for mariners, who would be able to associate the descriptive name with a fitting object. For example, if an island had a hole going through it such as Fiddra in the Forth, what better way of remembering its existence than naming it the fitting *Fuðey 'Fud island'. The same down-to-earth metaphorical thinking lies behind Ræva, 'Bum', a narrow gully over the fjord south of Bodø (Map 1). There would be no need for a sailor to think too deeply about such names. Sometimes a name motif can be both so obvious and so frequent that it even challenges the primary function of a place name, namely its distinctiveness as an address tag. This can perhaps be said about the island name Fladda Old Norse *Flatey 'flat island', and to a lesser degree Lunga, Old Norse *Lyngey 'heather island'. Flat islands are clearly common, because as well as Fladda, there is a Pladda south of Lismore, another Pladda, by Craighouse on Jura, Pladda, south of Arran, Flotta in Orkney and another Flotta in Weisdale Voe, Shetland. The name is found frequently in Norway and Iceland. Heathery islands are also common. Lunga is paralleled by another Lunga in the Treshnish Islands, Linga Holm in Orkney, Linga in the Scalloway archipelago, and Lyngøy in Norway which occurs very frequently (Map 3).

The third island name, unlike the other two examples, is not common. The rugged island of Scarba, which faces Jura on the other side of the Corryvreckan whirlpool, is named for its rocky, rugged aspect. We can safely dispense with the idea that it comes from Old Norse *Skarfrey 'Cormorant Island' (Gillies, 1906, p.132). Islands called after the bird tend to be small islands where the bird sits and dries its wings. Rather, the specific is the Old Norse adjective *skarpr,* cognate with English *sharp*, with the meaning 'barren, dried up'. For example, dry, coarse skin is *skǫrp húð*. There can be little doubt that Scarba comes from Old Norse *Skarpey 'Barren Island'. In Norwegian place names *skarp-* or *skorp-* refers to either poor, meagre vegetation or a complete lack of ground cover and names with *skarp-* or *skorp-* usually denote headlands, islands, and mountains at exposed locations. This is the case with the island Skarpøya by Kristiansand (just to the west of Map 3), where the exposed south and west of the island is bare rockface. An island with an older form of the name, without the element *-ey/-øy* is Skorpa, a tall, protruding island much used as an orientation point north of the dangerous crossing of the Stad headland (Map 2). Rugged, prominent Scarba would be an excellent marker for the equally dangerous Corrievreckan. In the poem *Runhenda* by Einarr Skúlason we find the name *Skǫrpusker* (in some manuscripts also *Skarpa-*), which have been identified as the Farne Islands, off the coast of

Map 3 Loch Melfort and the islands of Scarba, Lunga, Shuna and Torsa. Copyright: A. Jennings

Map 4 Extract from south of Kristiansand, southern Norway. Copyright: A. Kruse

Northumberland (Taylor, 1965, pp.132-133). The name is formed with the plural of the noun *sker*, n. 'skerries, rocks'. Two of the Farne Islands are still known as Little Scarcar and Big Scarcar, which seems to reflect the Old Norse name.

Theophoric island names

Flat and heathery islands were important markers for sailors, but they are perhaps not as interesting for place-name scholars. That cannot be said about the final two island names – Torsa and Gigha. Here we might be dealing with examples of that elusive class of placename generic, theophoric, or sacral names. The discussion about theophoric names in the British Isles is a complex one, and is tied in with the debate about the nature of Christianisation (Vikstrand, 2016). However, they exist in large numbers in Scandinavia (Brink,

2001) and they also appear in Iceland, particularly names containing Þórr 'Thor' (Sigmundsson, 1992). In the light of the relative frequency of theophoric names in Scandinavia and Iceland, there is a remarkable scarcity of such names in the Scandinavian settlement zones in Britain. It is as if the local gods at home in Scandinavia did not easily make the journey to lands that were already settled, and where the native people clearly had their own gods. However, there is a very small number of likely examples in the UK and Ireland e.g. the lost Caill Tomair probably the 'Wood of Þórr' (Holm, 2015) near Dublin, which was burned by the men of Munster in 1000 A.D. (Annals of Innisfallen), and Roseberry Topping in Yorkshire, written Othenesberg in 1199, which appears to be an Óðinsberg 'the hill of Odin' (Fellows-Jensen, 1992). We would suggest Torsa and Gigha could be added to the list.

Torsa is one of the Slate Islands. On its northern coast stands the ruin of the sixteenth century castle, *Caisteal nan Con*, 'The Castle of the Dogs', at one time a Campbell stronghold. It commands the approach to Seil Sound. It was of strategic importance to a seafaring community. The island itself is close to the mouth of Loch Melfort, presumably from Old Norse *Meðalfjǫrðr 'Middle Fjord' a name paralleled by Melfjorden, on Rødøy in Norway. We have to ask ourselves does the name Torsa contain the god's name Þórr? Was it originally Þórsey 'Þór's Island'? There is the possibility that this is another of the island names with a personal name as a specific. In this case it could be the name Þórir, which takes the genitive case Þóris. However, unlike in the case of the name Torosay on Mull, and which it is argued does come from Þórir (Whyte, 2017, p.97), there does not seem to be evidence of a vowel between /r/ and the /s/. There is also the possibility that Torosay itself might come from Þórsey, with the /o/ being an intrusive epenthetic vowel. Of course, these are by no means a definitive argument. However, similar names with –s- are in Norway taken to be from the name of the god, and the position of Torsøy at the entrance to Kristiansand (see Map 3) is similar to the position of Torsa *vis-a-vis* Loch Melfort, while Torsøya in Sunnhordland seems to be positioned near the beginning of Hardangerfjord. Perhaps these were islands on which some form of veneration was paid to Þórr before or after a sea voyage?

We are on firmer ground with the name Gigha. It is recorded several times in the 13th century *Hákonar saga Hákonarsonar* as *Guðey* 'God island'. We have to ask what kind of god? We are wrong to assume that it is the Christian god who is being referred to. There are Norwegian parallels – Gudøy, an island on the lake Vansjø in Våler, Østfold, Godøy, an island north on Tysnes, the old *Njarðarlǫg*, an island with an exceptional number of theophoric names (Heide, 2012), and the large island Godøya by Ålesund, written 'Gudœy' in 1351 (Map 2). In these cases, Sandnes and Stemshaug (1976, p.130) in their seminal work *Norsk Stadnamnleksikon* state that the first element is the genitive of *guð, goð* m.' heathen god', and that the names refer to worship of these heathen gods. Apparently, these were islands where the gods were venerated. Why? A sailor would be keen to increase his luck. When faced with the threat of a long sea voyage or dangerous waters, or returning from a perilous trip, an offering to the gods would make sense. The position of Gigha means that if you head north, you are faced with potentially hazardous sailing; you might have to go through the sound between Islay and Jura with its strong tidal race; and further north you have the Corryvreckan to contend with (Kruse, 2020, p.182). It appears to have been an important mooring place on the sea route. King Hákon moored his fleet twice on his campaign. The Norwegian cognates have similar positions (Kruse, 2020, p.182). Godøya by Ålesund is positioned before / after exposed sailing, and Godøya near Bodø is close to Saltstraumen, the world's strongest whirlpool. It flows between the islands Straumøya and Knaplundøya which were known collectively in Old Norse as the *Góðeyjar*, pl. 'The god islands' (NG XVI, p.209, p.211) (Maps 1 and 2).

Final Thought

Where better to end this short voyage of exploration through Norse maritime heritage than with reference to a strange story from Gigha, and a question. There is an anonymous tale associated with the island, which tells us that as late as the early 19th century Irish fishermen could be seen by the islanders visiting and paying homage to two sacred stones on the island. It is difficult to verify this story, but these peculiar stones called the *Bodach* 'Old man', the Gaelic equivalent of ON *karl*, and the *Cailleach* 'Old woman', the Gaelic equivalent of ON *kerling*, are still to be seen today near the farm of Achamore. Were these Irish fishermen part of a tradition that can be traced back to Norse maritime practices in the Viking Age? It is hard to prove, but it is enticing. Old traditions die hard as do place-names.

Bibliography

Anonymous, *Exploring Historic Kintyre and the Isle of Gigha.* Oban: Harlequin Press, n.d.

AU = *Annals of Ulster (to 1131)*, S. Mac Airt and G. Mac Niocaill (eds.). Dublin, 1983.

Binchy, D. A. (1966) 'Bretha Déin Cécht', *Ériu* 20, pp.1–66.

Bremner, R.L. (1904) 'Some Notes on the Norsemen in Argyllshire and on the Clyde', *Saga Book* 3, pp.338-380.

Brink, S. (2001) 'Mythologizing Landscape. Place and Space of Cult and Myth', in Michael Stausberg (ed.) Kontinuitäten und Brüche in der Religionsgeschichte. Festschrift für Anders Hultgård zu seinem 65 Geburtstag am 23.12.2001. Berlin: de Gruyter, 2001, pp.76–112.

Brink, S. (2016) 'Transferred Names and Analogy in Name-Formation', in *The Oxford Handbook of Names and Naming*. Oxford: Oxford University Press, pp.158-166.

Brown, M.H. (1992) 'Crown-Magnate Relations in Personal Rule of James I of Scotland (1424 – 1437)', PhD thesis, University of St Andrews, St Andrews.

Bugge, A. (ed.) (1905) *Caithreim Cellachain Caisil: The victorious career of Cellachan of Cashel; or, The Wars between the Irishmen and the Norsemen in the middle of the 10th century*. Christiania: Det Norsk Historiske Kildeskriftford.

Clancy, T. O. (2018) 'Hebridean connections: in Ibdone Insula, Ibdaig, Eboudai, Uist', *Journal of Scottish Name Studies* 12, pp.27-40.

Coates, R. (2007) 'Yell', *Journal of Scottish Name Studies* 1, pp.1-12.

Coates R. (2021) 'Unst', *Journal of Scottish Name Studies* 15, pp.1-9.

Crawford, B. (1987) *Scandinavian Scotland*. Leicester: Leicester University Press.

Everett-Heath, John (2010) *Concise Dictionary of World Place-Names* Oxford: Oxford University Press.

Fellows-Jensen, G. (1992) 'Cultic Place-Names: A View from the Danelaw', in G. Fellows-Jensen and B. Holmberg (eds.) *Sakrale navne: Rapport fra NORNAs sekstende symposium i Gilleleje 30.11–2.12. 1990.* Uppsala: NORNA-förlaget, pp.265-272.

Gammeltoft, P. (2009) 'Shetland and Orkney Island-Names – A Dynamic Group', in R. McColl-Millar (ed.) Vol 2: Northern Lights, *Northern Words. Selected Papers from the FRLSU Conference, Kirkwall 2009.* Aberdeen: Forum for Research on the Languages of Scotland and Ulster, pp.15-25.

Gammeltoft, P. (2007) 'Scandinavian Naming-Systems in the Hebrides – A Way of Understanding how the Scandinavians were in Contact with Gaels and Picts?', in B. Ballin Smith, S. Taylor and G. Williams (eds.) *West over Sea: Studies in Scandinavian Sea-Borne Expansion and Settlement Before 1300.* Leiden: Brill, pp.479-495.

Grove, D. (2004) *Dunstaffnage Castle & Chapel.* Edinburgh: Historic Scotland.

Heide, E. (2012) 'Sola og gudane på Tysnesøya', *Chaos* 58, pp.49-57.

Henderson. G. (1910) *The Norse Influence on Celtic Scotland.* Glasgow: James Maclehose.

Holm, P. (2015) 'The Naval Power of Norse Dublin', in E. Purcell, P. MacCotter, J. Nyhan and J. Sheehan (eds.) *Clerics, Kings and Vikings: Essays on Medieval Ireland in Honour of Donnchadh Ó Corráin.* Dublin: Four Courts Press, pp.67-78.

Jennings, A. (2011) 'Hjaltland Revisited: The Place-name Shetland and its Celtic Origin', in *NORNA Rapporter* 87, pp.132-141.

Jennings, A., and Kruse, A. (2009) 'One coast – three peoples: names and ethnicity in the Scottish west during the early Viking period', in A. Woolf (ed.) *Scandinavian Scotland – Twenty Years After: The Proceedings of a Day Conference held on 19 February 2007.* St Andrews: University of St Andrews, pp.75–102.

Jennings, A. (2017) 'Three Scottish Coastal Names of Note: Earra-Ghàidheal, Satíriseið, and Skotlandsfirðir', in D. Worthington (ed.) *The New Coastal History: Cultural and Environmental Perspectives from Scotland and Beyond.* London: Palgrave Macmillan, pp.119-129.

Johnston, A. R. (1991) 'Norse Settlement in the Inner Hebrides c. 800-1300; with special reference to the islands of Mull, Coll and Tiree', PhD Thesis, University of St Andrews, St Andrews.

Judith, J., 2008, 'The Swelchie and Why the Sea is Salt'. Available at: https://www.vikingeskibsmuseet.dk/en/professions/viking-ships-on-voyages/bigger-voyages/the-voyage-2008/armchair-comments/show/the-swelchie-and-why-the-sea-is-salt (accessed: 12 August 2023).

McTurk, Rory (ed.) (2017) 'Krákumál', in Margaret Clunies Ross (ed.) *Poetry in fornaldarsögur: Skaldic Poetry of the Scandinavian Middle Ages* 8. Turnhout: Brepols.

Kruse, A. (2007) 'Fashion, Limitation and Nostalgia: Scandinavian Place-Names Abroad', in A. Kruse and P. Graves (eds.) *Names Abroad, Images and Imaginations: Perspectives on Britain and Scandinavia.* Edinburgh, Lockharton Press, pp.3-33.

Kruse, A. (2017), 'The Norway to be: Laithlind and Avaldsnes', in C. Cooijmans (ed.) *Traversing the Inner Seas: Contacts and Continuity in and around Scotland, the Hebrides, and the North of Ireland.* Edinburgh: Scottish Society for Northern Studies, pp.198-231.

Kruse, A., 2020, 'On Harbours and Havens: Maritime Strategies in Norway during the Viking Age'. In *Viking Encounters. Proceedings of the Eighteenth Viking Congress*, Denmark, August 6-12, 2017. Aarhus University Press

Kruse, A., 2020, *Namnet Smøla og andre øynamn.* In Smølaminne, pp.71-79

MacPhee, K., 2004, Somerled: *Hammer of the Norse*, Vital Spark. *Metrical Dindshenchas*. Pt. 3, Text, translation and commentary. Gwynn, Edward John. Published Dublin: Dublin Institute for Advanced Studies,School of Celtic Studies, 1991

Owen, H.W., 2015, The Place-Names of Wales, University of Wales Press.

Nes, O. 1997, Øynamn. I: Norsk stadnamnleksikon

Nicolaisen, W.F.H., 1978, 'Are There Connotative Names', *Names* 26, pp.40-47.

Nicolaisen, W.FH., 2003, 'Perspectives on the Pre-Norse Language(s) of Orkney'. In J. Downes and A. Ritchie (eds.) Sea-Change: Orkney and Northern Europe in the later Iron Age AD 300-800, Balgavies, The Pinkfoot Press, pp. 139-144.

Pálsson, H. and Edwards, P. 2006, *The book of settlements. Landnámabók*. Translated with introduction and notes by Herman Pálsson and Paul Edwards, Winnipeg, University of Manitoba Press.

Sandnes, J. and Stemshaug, O., 1976, Norsk stadnamnleksikon, Det Norske Samlaget, Oslo.

Smith, B., 2022, 'Þursasker: A Note'. In *Islands of place and Space: A Festschrift in Honour of Arne Kruse*, Edinburgh, Scottish Society for Northern Studies.

Smith, B., 1988, 'Shetland in Saga-Time: Re-reading the Orkneyinga Saga', *Northern Studies*, Edinburgh, Scottish Society for Northern Studies, 25, pp. 21–41

Somerfelt, A., 1958, 'On the Norse form of the name of the Picts and the date of the first Norse raids on Scotland', *Lochlann* I.

Svavar Sigmundsson, 1992, 'Átrúnaður og örnefni'. In Úlfar Bragason (ed.) Snorrastefna. 25.–27. júlí 1990, Reykjavik, Stofnun Sigurðar Nordals.

Snorrastefna25.–27. júlí 1990. Reykjavik: Stofnun Sigurðar Nordals. 241-254.

Særheim, I., 1989, *Kvitsøy : namn og stader*, Stavanger : Rogaland fylkeskulturstyre.

Taylor, A. B. 1965. 'Eysteinn Haraldsson in the West, *c*. 1151: Oral Traditions and Written Record'. In Small 1965, pp. 119-34.

Taylor, S., 2009, 'Ayrshire Place-Names: a rich seam still to mine'. *Ayrshire Notes* (38), pp. 4-18.

Vikstrand, P., 2016, 'Place Names and Viking Age Religion'. In *Names and Their Environment. Proceedings of the 25th International Congress of Onomastic Sciences*, Glasgow, 25 - 29 August 2014. Vol. 2. *Toponomastics II* . Carole Hough and Daria Izdebska (eds .) First published 2016 by University of Glasgow under Creative Commons licence (CC BY -NC -ND 4.0)

The Saga of the People of Svarfadardal. Translated by Fredrik J. Heinemann. In The Complete Sagas of Icelanders IV. Ed. Viðar Hreinsson Reykjavík, Leifur Eiríkson Publishing, 1997.

Townend, M., 1998, *English Place-Names in Skaldic Verse*. English Place-Name Society extra ser. 1. Nottingham, English Place-Name Society.

Whyte, A.C., 2017, *Settlement-names and society: analysis of the medieval districts of Forsa and Moloros in the parish of Torosay, Mull*. PhD thesis University of Glasgow.

Wold, H. A., 1991, *I paradisets første krets*. Oslo, Cappelen.

Woolf, A,, 2013, 'The song of the death of Somerled and the destruction of Glasgow in 1153'. Journal of the Sydney Society for Scottish History, vol. 14, pp. 1-11.

7

Baliasta and Stembelshoull – two thing sites in the island of Unst

Alexandra Sanmark
(University of the Highlands and Islands)

This chapter examines two potential *thing* sites (ON *þing*, i.e. court and parliament) located at Baliasta and Stembelshoull in Unst (Shetland), dating from the Viking Age (A.D. 750-1050) and/or Late Norse period (A.D. 1050-1468/9). The locations and characteristics of Shetland *thing* sites is an interest that Brian Smith and I share and have discussed on many occasions. Over the years Brian has been immensely helpful in finding and passing on local information, above all details about place-names and oral traditions, which meant that I could study Shetland *things* sites in greater depth than would otherwise have been possible.

In this vein, a few years ago an e-mail arrived from Brian, which contained the suggestion of a *thing* site at Baliasta. At the time, a quick exploration made it clear to me that this suggestion certainly merited further study. When the opportunity to write a chapter for this *festschrift* arose it provided me with the perfect opportunity to finally investigate the possibility of a *thing* site at Baliasta. This investigation in turn led me to the discovery of another possible *thing* site in Unst, at Stembelshoull in the southern part of the island. It turned out, of course, that Brian Smith knew of this site too and this chapter therefore draws on both published sources and information gathered by Brian and other people active in Unst. One such person is Les Smith, originally from Unst, whose advice to me has been invaluable for the writing of this chapter.

Thing sites have been a focus of my research for many years (see e.g. Sanmark, 2017 and Semple et al., 2020). These sites were widely distributed across Scandinavia as well as in the areas of Norse settlement in the west, which shows the significance of the *thing* institution and the practice of law to Viking Age and Norse society. If the *thing* had not served its purpose the Norse settlers could have left it behind. Instead, both in Scandinavia and in their new homes, the people of the Viking Age and the Late Norse period created an ever-shifting pattern of elaborate *thing* sites. Put simply, a range of different features were available for creators of *thing* sites to choose between. These features are found at *thing* sites in different combinations, depending on what message the creators – the elite – wanted to transmit to the wider population (Sanmark, 2017, pp.56-57). The list is rather long, but the most important characteristics can be summarised as follows:

- A location on the convergence of communication routes, often both land and water routes. A location by fords, isthmuses (portages) or on islands, often with good landing places.

- A location by large mounds and prehistoric cemeteries.

- *Thing* sites frequently have long biographies with evidence of use stretching far back into prehistory.

The overriding characteristic in the selection of *thing* sites, both in Scandinavia and the areas of Norse settlement, was a location on important communication routes. Land routes, water routes, portages and fording places, were used for travelling to the assembly. Streams and rivers supplied fresh water, formed symbolic boundaries, and could also function as communication routes (Sanmark, 2017a, pp.122-131; Brink, 2004). It would have been in the interest of the rulers, and of the wider elite, to make sure that as many people as possible attended the meetings. The larger the number of people who attended and thus approved a decision or verdict, the stronger the position of the ruler. Therefore, in order to facilitate wide participation, assembly sites needed to be in places that could easily be reached (Sanmark, 2017, p.43, p.117).

Another commonly occurring *thing* sites feature is mounds. Large mounds and cemeteries provided the assemblies with links to the past, and there are examples of *thing* sites with burials starting in the 1st and 2nd centuries A.D. Mounds and other elevations moreover made the assembly-sites easy to spot from afar and they could also be used as platforms to address the people gathered (Sanmark, 2017, pp.57-58). Many sites thus have very long biographies of use, although long-term trajectories do not necessarily mean that assemblies were held at the very same spot for very long periods of time, but on many occasions they seem to have been part of wider areas in which judicial and political power was increasingly focused. A striking example of this comes from the county of Södermanland in Sweden, where detailed study showed that the distance between the oldest assembly site identified within the administrative unit of the *härad* (from Old Norse *herað*) and the late medieval/early modern *thing* site (often located by the parish church) was in no case more than 10 km (Sanmark, 2009, p.230).

Thing sites in Scotland, and indeed Shetland, share many of the same features as Scandinavian *thing* sites. In terms of communication routes, they are mostly situated by water routes as *thing* sites in Scotland tend to be close to the sea, frequently on isthmuses or within firths. Such isthmuses often have place-names containing Old Norse *eið*, which can be translated as 'portage', i.e. a narrow strip of land across which boats were pulled (Stewart, 1987, p.80; Waugh,

2010, pp.545-546). In Shetland, several *thing* sites of this type have been identified (Sanmark, 2013, pp.102-104), for example Lunnasting, derived from *hlunnr-eið*, where Old Norse *hlunnr* refers to the wood rollers used for pulling boats across land. At Lunna, there is a narrow isthmus recorded as a portage in modern times (Stewart, 1987, p.80; Waugh, 2010, pp.545-546; McCullough, 2000, pp.183-185; Sanmark, 2013, pp.102-103). Sand in Sandsting was also located on a rather narrow strip of land, possibly a portage, or alternatively, a channel for boats. Similar circumstances are seen at Gardiestaing[1] in Yell, and Aithsting, named after Æiði farm (from Old Norse *eið*), may be another example (Ballantyne and Smith, 1999, p.1; Jakobsen, 1936, p.125; Stewart, 1987, p.80, 300; Sanmark, 2013, pp.103-104). In Shetland a number of *thing* sites are moreover found in close proximity to churches or chapels, including for example Delting, Lunnasting, and Tingwall (Sanmark, 2013).

Unst *thing* sites

It is now time to evaluate the evidence at Baliasta in the light of the research presented above. Baliasta is located approximately in the middle of Unst, c. 2 km west of the current coastline. The name Baliasta is derived from *Bollastaðir*, which translates as 'Bolli's farm' (Stewart, 1987, p.252). As stated above, the possibility of this *thing* site was brought to my attention by Brian Smith, who in turn had been contacted by Les Smith. Brian and Les discussed potential *thing* site remains in the light of the publications of George Low (Low's 1774 account was published in 1879) Samuel Hibbert (1822 and 1832) and Jessie Saxby (1905-06), all of whom refer to local assembly traditions.

George Low, in his description of a tour around Orkney and Shetland, stated that he was 'shown on the top of a precipice called the Heog (or Height), a heap of stones called by tradition a place of execution, and at the foot of the rock another heap, called the House of Justice, from which one ascends by steps to the former. Tradition says that whatever criminal ascended the steps of Hanger Heog never came down alive.' (Low, 1879, p.154). Low added that two bodies, supposed to be executed criminals', were 'found some years ago in the bottom of the lower heap' (Low, 1879, p.154). Hibbert raised many of the same points, referring to the three focal points 'Hanger Heog', 'Place of Justice' and 'Place of Execution' (Hibbert, 1822, p.405; 1832, p.195). This information was also picked up by Saxby, who referred to Hibbert and a *lawting* site at Baliasta (Saxby, 1905-06, pp.28-29).

The site description provided by Hibbert is rather long and fanciful, referring to 'three concentric circles...into which boulder stones or earth were thrown' as well as 'a small central tumulus of stones in the middle of the inclosure, 12 feet in diameter, the presence of which is no unfrequent indication of a Scandinavian temple' (Hibbert, 1822, p.405). This is followed by details of supposed Norse legal and judicial rituals, involving for example human sacrifices to the god Thor,

---

1 This name is most likely derived from Gardiesting (Sanmark, 2009, p.102).

Baliasta, Unst

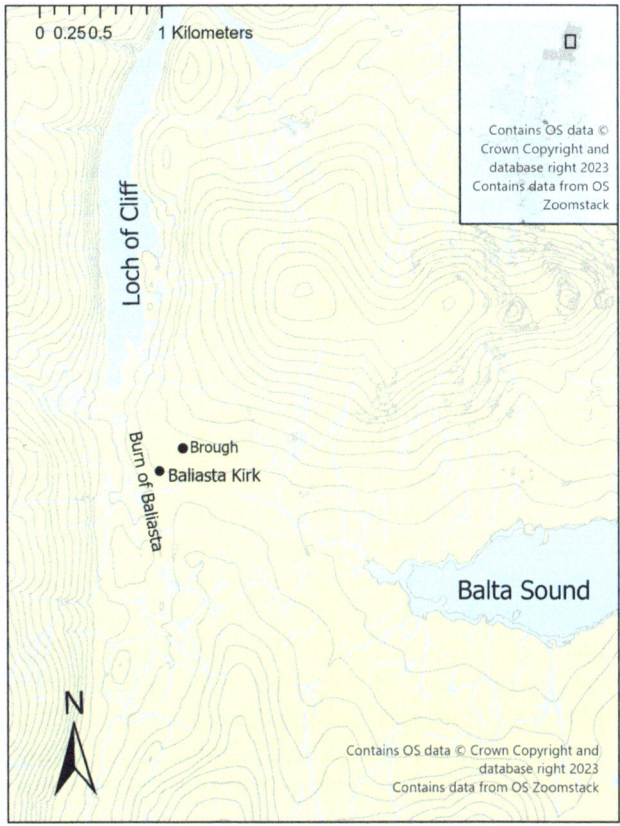

none of which can be verified in the primary sources, written or archaeological (Hibbert, 1822, p.405). It is moreover important to note that there is some confusion in Low's and Hibbert's texts, as Hanger Heog is not located at Baliasta, but instead a hill called Muckle Heog situated around three km to the northeast (NGR HP 6315 1081; Coolen, 2016, p.95). In addition, Brian Smith has argued that the name Hanger Heog does not refer to an execution site, but rather 'a steep, overhanging hill' (Smith, 2006) and this site has therefore been excluded from this study.

As indicated above, the area around Baliasta has a number of other *thing* site traits and features. The location is highly indicative of an assembly, as it is found at the narrowest point of Unst, between two major bodies of water, Baltasound and the Loch of Cliff, which in turn connects to Burra Firth in the northwest of Unst (Fig. 1). This is highly reminiscent of Gardiestaing, which is situated in the narrowest part of Yell, between two major firths (Sanmark, 2013). Today, in Unst the distance from Baltasound on the east coast to the southern end of the Loch of Cliff is 2.8 km as the crow flies. There are strong indications, however, that in the past much of this low-lying area – which is largely below 10 m above sea level – would have been open water and/or wetland. According to Ordnance Survey maps this area has been heavily drained as part of agricultural improvements, especially to the south of the Baliasta kirk, where the Burn of Baliasta now runs. Drainage ditches are also observed southeast of the kirk in the area leading towards the sea. The presence of past wetlands and therefore potential shallow waterways is further supported by the remains of an Iron Age broch c. 200 m to the north of the kirk, suggested by 19th century reports (Canmore ID 104) as well as the place-name Brough (Stewart, 1987, p.46). Brochs are consistently placed by water, often in coastal locations, but also frequently by inland water routes and freshwater lochs (Canmore; Rennell, 2010).

The exact location of the *thing* meetings at Baliasta is difficult to determine. Les Smith drew attention to two archaeological features: one west of the kirk, as alluded to in the antiquarian accounts, and a mound (now badly damaged), situated c. 100 m southeast of the kirk. He suggested that the former was the Viking Age assembly and the latter was a Late Norse one. In view of previous knowledge, it is definitely possible that the *thing* site has been moved over time. To my mind, the most likely location is the mound, as mounds are so frequently occurring at *thing* sites in both Scotland and Scandinavia. *Thing* meetings may have been held here already in the Viking Age, although such an early date is far from certain.

The documentary record contains further evidence of judicial proceedings at Baliasta. In 1543-4, a purchase of land was witnessed at 'Balliasta' by several men including both the Shetland *fold* (*foud*, i.e. governor / chamberlain) and the Shetland lawman (Ballantyne and Smith, 1999, no.72). Some years later, in 1571-2, a meeting of the sheriff court was held at the Kirk of Baliasta (Ballantyne and Smith 1999, no.190). In addition, there are two documents dated 21 August 1598, which evidence an agreement between two parties, stating that the sum of £300 should be handed over at Baliasta Kirk on Whitsunday (Ballantyne and Smith, 1994, nos.274 and 275). These documents, together with the Scandinavian *thing* site features discussed above and the later recorded traditions, support the idea that Baliasta was the location of an earlier outdoor *thing* site.

The shift from outdoor *thing* meetings to judicial gatherings held in the kirk cannot be pinpointed. It is not known when a kirk was erected, although it may date from the Viking Age/Late Norse period (McCreadie, 2021, pp.39-41). By the time of the earliest recorded meetings, the courts had most likely been moved indoors, and the 1543-4 meeting was presumably held in the kirk, even though that is not specifically stated. By comparison, in Scandinavia *thing* meetings were frequently held outdoors at well-established *thing* sites until the 15th or 16th centuries when they started being held by/in parish churches and '*thing* cottages' (Sanmark, 2017, pp.247-248).

Returning to Unst and Baliasta, Gardiestaing again serves as a useful parallel. The documentary record shows that in 1538 and 1586 courts were held in 'Giærd'/'Gerde' (Ballantyne and Smith, 1999, no.59; 1994, no.88), which must be seen as 'Gardiesting' meetings. Moreover, in 1588 the commissary court

Stembelshoull, Unst

was held in the kirk of St John in 'Rafirtht in Yell' (Ballantyne and Smith, 1999, no.135).[2] This is a ruined church, located some 800 m south of Gardiestaing. Its location, and the presence of some cruciform stones presumably dating to the 9-11th centuries, has led to the suggestion that a kirk was founded here in the Viking Age/Late Norse period (McCreadie, 2021, pp.39-41; Canmore ID 1395). In this way, a similar pattern of shifting sites can be observed as at Baliasta. It is unlikely, however, that St John's Kirk was used for *thing* meetings as early as the Viking Age.[3] Another useful comparison for Baliasta is a meeting of the Shetland *lawthing* that according to a document from 1307 was held in Tingwall

---

2   'Rafirtht' is important in this context as it refers to Reafirth, which is derived from *Ræyðar fyrðe*, the old name for Mid Yell Voe, which presumably lent its name to the thing parish of *Rauðarþing*, recorded in the 14th century (Sanmark 2009, p.102).
3   Another possible location for indoor court meetings in Mid Yell is the 'Tollbooth of Zetland in 1400' which is marked on a map from 1868, a few km west of Gardiestaing (Mathewson (c. June 1868), Shetland Archives, D23/33; Brian Smith, pers. comm.). This building is not known from other sources and no courts have, to my knowledge, been recorded here.

Kirk, rather than at Law Ting Holm in the Loch (Ballantyne, and Smith 1999, no.2; Sanmark, 2017, p.233).

The 1307 document is noteworthy also from another angle, as it lists a number 'lawrightmen', one of whom is 'Sigurðr a Kallbak' (Ballantyne and Smith, 1999, no.2). Brian Smith has identified Kallback as Caldback, which is situated c. 2.5 km south of Baliasta (Brian Smith, pers. comm.). Caldback farm seems to have been used for judicial purposes too, as a doom [i.e. judicial decision or sentence] was issued here on 28 June 1431 (Ballantyne and Smith, 1999, no.21). This is very interesting as it further adds to the judicial traditions in the area around Baliasta.[4]

As mentioned in the introduction to this chapter there is another possible *thing* site in the southern part of Unst. This is suggested by the two intriguing place-names of Stembelshoull[5] and Umbot/Winbat[6] in southwest Uyeasound. At both sites suggested Norse farm remains have been recorded (Smith, 2005, p.129). Stembelshoull is derived from Stefnuboðshóll, which contains the elements *stefnuboð* 'summons to a public meeting' and *hóll* 'hill' (Stewart, 1987, p.140; Smith, 2005, p.129). *Stefna* is an Old Norse term for 'assembly' and at times found in *thing* site names. Examples include Stevnuválur ('assembly oval/hollow') on Eysturoy in the Faroe Islands and Stevnebø ('assembly farm') by the Gulathing in western Norway (Sanmark, 2017, p.77, p.181). Umbot is a very unusual and intriguing name, which according to John Stewart was recorded as Umboth in 1613-1869 and Umbuth in 1622-32 and therefore derives from *umboð*, which he translated as 'authority, office, commission' (Stewart, 1987, p.281; cf. Zoëga, 2004, p.448). It is not clear what type of office this might denote, but the reference to administration is very interesting, especially in such close vicinity to Stembelshoull. In this context, the 1586 document from 'Gerde' becomes interesting again, as it refers to Willom Monssøn who is 'lawrightman' of Unst and 'umbothsman' for two brothers representing one side of the case (Ballantyne and Smith, 1994, no.88), thus demonstrating that terminology derived from *umboð* was used for legal officials at this time.

Additional judicial setting is provided by the presence of a Gallow Hill, situated directly above Stembelshoull and Umbot. At the Gallow Hill summit a large undated cairn was excavated in 1865 which revealed 'a human skeleton with some limpet shells', and 'several skulls', i.e. most likely a prehistoric burial

---

4   There is also a recorded *thing* tradition relating to a carved boulder found c. 200 m southeast of the township of Gunnister in the Hamarberg district (c. 3 km south of Caldback), which is said to rest 'on top of a low circular heap of small stones'. It has been reported that this is where 'the earliest Law Ting Court in Shetland' was held, which later was moved to Tingwall (Canmore ID 41). This tradition is not, to my knowledge, supported by any written sources. It should, however, be noted that this site seems to share some features with Steelaheelenagro in North Yell, a possible execution site, where there is a big boulder on top of a cairn (Jamieson and Smith, 2022, p.22).

5   Stembelshoull is now known as Skuda as the original name disappeared as a result of clearance. The name Stembelshoull is not found on OS maps but has been located by Les Smith with the help of Robert Hughson, the crofter at Rockfield, who added that he associates the place-name with the slope behind that croft house. (Les Smith, 2005, p.129 and pers. comm., NGR HP 5862 0070).

6   Winbat is the name found on OS maps, but as pointed out by Stewart, this spelling is not reflective of the local name and its etymology (Stewart, 1987, p.281).

monument (Canmore ID 43). The combination of gallow hills and prehistoric cairns is commonly occurring. It is however rare for the Shetland gallow hills to be found in connection to *thing* sites or indeed later judicial arrangements, although the *lawthing* at Tingwall is overlooked by a Gallow Hill, which also has a prehistoric cairn (Coolen, 2016).

Returning to Unst, the place-names are highly suggestive of a *thing* site by Stembelshoull and Umbot, and as they are of Norse origin, the site is likely to have been in use at least by the Late Norse period. In terms of location, they are found by the very sheltered bay of Uyeasound, close to Bluemull Sound between Unst and Yell, which must have been a frequently used water route. Uyeasound is derived from Old Norse *Øyjarsund* and contains the name of the island Uyea, signifying that this island protects the eponymous harbour and settlement (Stewart, 1987, p.263). Just as Baliasta, Stembelshoull may well have been located next to open water or wetlands prior to the agricultural improvements, since the area just to the north has a number of watercourses and drainage ditches, signifying agricultural improvement. It is not known exactly where the *thing* meetings would have been held, although a possibly anthropogenic platform about 10 m in diameter, shown on the OS map as the 20m contour (NGR HP 5862 0073) has been suggested (Les Smith pers. comm.).

In conclusion, this short chapter has highlighted two potential *thing* sites in Unst, which have previously not been examined in detail. I hope to have illustrated the possibility that further *thing* sites and other places of administration in Shetland are still to be identified through the wealth of place-names, oral traditions, and archaeological remains. I am grateful to Brian Smith for his never-ending enthusiasm and assistance in my search for deeper knowledge of the Norse legal landscape in Shetland.

Bibliography

Ballantyne, J. H. and Smith, B. (eds.) (1994) *Shetland Documents 1580–1611*. Lerwick: Shetland Islands Council and The Shetland Times Ltd.

Ballantyne. J. H. and Smith, B. (eds.) (1999) *Shetland Documents 1195–1579*. Lerwick: Shetland Islands Council and The Shetland Times Ltd.

Canmore - Catalogue of archaeological sites, buildings, industry and maritime heritage across Scotland. Compiled and managed by Historic Environment Scotland. Available at: https://canmore.org.uk/ (accessed: 21 May 2023).

Coolen, J. (2016) 'Gallows, Cairns, and Things: A Study of Tentative Gallows Sites in Shetland', *Journal of the North Atlantic*, Special Volume 8, pp.93–114.

Hibbert, S. (1822) *A Description of the Shetland Islands: Comprising an Account of their Geology, Scenery, Antiquities, and Superstitions*. Edinburgh: Archibald Constable and Co.

Hibbert, S. (1832) 'Memoir on the Tings of Orkney and Shetland', *Archaeologia Scotica* 3, pp.103-210. Available at: http://journals.socantscot.org/index.php/arch-scot/article/view/221 (accessed 21 May 2023).

Jakobsen, J. (1936) *The Place-Names of Shetland*. London: David Nutt.

Jamieson, D. and Smith, B. (2022) 'Steelaheelenagro and Skuldigert: rough justice in medieval Shetland, *New Shetlander* 298, pp.6-11.

Low, G. (1879) *A tour through the islands of Orkney and Schetland: containing hints relative to their ancient, modern, and natural history, collected in 1774 / by George Low, with illustrations from drawings by the author, and with an introduction by Joseph Anderson*. Kirkwall: W. Peace.

McCreadie, S. (2021) 'Evangelists of Stone: Chapels within Landscapes of Conversion in Viking Age and Late Norse Shetland', *Northern Studies* 51, pp.38-51.

Mathewson, A. D. (c. June 1868), Copy sketch plan of Setter, Mid Yell. Shetland Archives, D23/33).

Rennell, R. (2010) 'Islands, islets, experience, and identity in the Outer Hebridean Iron Age', *Shima: The International Journal of Research into Island Cultures* 4(1), pp.47-64.

Sanmark, A. (2009) 'Assembly Organisation and State Formation. A Case Study of Assembly Sites in Viking and Medieval Södermanland, Sweden', *Medieval Archaeology* 53, pp.205-241.

Sanmark, A. (2013) 'Patterns of Assembly: Norse Thing Sites in Shetland', *Journal of the North Atlantic, Special Volume* 5, pp.96-110.

Sanmark, A. (2017), *Viking Law and Order. Places and Rituals of Assembly in the Medieval North*. Edinburgh: Edinburgh University Press.

Saxby, J. (1905-06) 'Sacred Sites in a Shetland Isle', *Saga-Book* IV, pp.24-35.

Semple, S., Sanmark, A., Iversen, F., and Mehler, N. (2020) *Negotiating the North: Meeting Places in The Middle Ages in The North Sea Zone*. Final project monograph by The Assembly Project. The Society for Medieval Archaeology Monograph Series: Routledge.

Smith, B. (2006) 'Gibbets and gallows: Local rough justice in Shetland, 800–1700'. Available at http://normblog.typepad.com/normblog/2006/09/gibbets_and_gal.html. (accessed: 21 May 2023).

Smith, B. (2009) 'On the Nature of Tings: Shetland's Law Courts from The Middle Ages until 1611', *New Shetlander* 250, pp.37–45.

Smith, L. H. (2005) 'Norse Farmsteads (Unst parish)', *Discovery and Excavation in Scotland*, 6, pp.128-129.

Stewart, J. (1987) *Shetland place-names*. Lerwick: Shetland Library and Museum.

Waugh, D. (2010) 'On *eið*-names in Orkney and other North Atlantic islands', in J. Sheehan and Ó. Corráin (eds.) *The Viking Age: Ireland and the West. Papers from the Proceedings of the Fifteenth Viking Congress, Cork, 18–27 August 2005*. Dublin: Four Courts Press, pp.545–554.

Zoëga, Geir T. A. (1910) *Concise Dictionary of Old Icelandic*. Oxford: Clarendon Press.

8

Shetland's foreign trade before 1500

Mark Gardiner and Natascha Mehler
(University of Lincoln / University of Tübingen)

The broad outlines of Shetland's trading contacts in the late Middle Ages and Early Modern period are well understood. During the fifteenth, and particularly the sixteenth centuries, trade with Norway was supplemented by growing contact with German merchants. That reorientation was part of a wider trend in the North Atlantic world by which Bergen's role as the staple port for the region ceased to be effectively enforced and then lapsed entirely, and its trade was, at least in part, superseded by the direct contact between merchants from northern Europe and the tributary territories of Norway. German merchants no longer had to wait for dried fish to be brought to Bergen from Iceland, the Faroes and Shetland, but instead could trade directly, first tacitly, and later increasingly openly, with the North Atlantic islands (Gardiner and Mehler, 2019, pp.13–17). For Orkney and Shetland, the legal requirement to channel trade goods through Bergen may, in any case, have been barely enforceable after the transfer of those islands to the kingdom of Scotland in 1468 and 1469 respectively (Crawford, 1969; Grohse, 2020). Brian Smith (2010, p.6) has pointed out that this did not prevent the Danish king, Hans, from behaving as if Shetland was still part of his realm. For example, he granted Dutch merchants the right to trade in Shetland in 1490, and as well as Bergen and Iceland, on the same terms as the merchants of the German Hanse (*Diplomatarium Norvegicum* 6, pp.643-664, no. 609). The net result was that by the sixteenth century, 'the vast majority of Shetland's trading ties ... were with Germany' (Smith, 2010, p.8).

The present paper seeks to examine the changing character of Shetland's trade in the period before and immediately after the transfer of control of the islands to Scotland. It is a subject which Brian Smith himself has addressed with regards to the Norwegian aspects of trade. He has summarised the problem with the pithy statement, 'Finally, trade. Here we are almost completely in the dark about the relationship between the two countries' (Smith, 1990, p.28). Such a remark by Shetland's leading historian makes clear that any consideration of the subject is always going to be difficult. Faced with a paucity of documents from the period before the mid-sixteenth century, we have necessarily to be inventive in how we approach the problem. First, we have to review the very sparse documentary evidence that does survive and determine how far it is possible to construct an understanding of trade. Second, we need to use non-written sources to investigate the extent and the manner to which Shetland was engaged in foreign commerce in this period.

We must begin with what we know. Trade in the period after 1550 is fairly well understood due to studies by Hance Smith (1984), Brian Smith (2019) and most recently by Bart Holterman (2020). Every spring, ships sailed from the German ports, mainly from Bremen and Hamburg, and anchored in the ports in Shetland allotted to them for trade. They established booths onshore where they exchanged dried and salted fish caught and prepared by local fishermen who were in turn offered imported goods, namely clothing, fishing gear, and also tobacco and spirits. The rates of exchange for this trade were fixed each year by the *foud* (sheriff). In addition to this trade in fish, the German merchants also bought butter, fish oil and *wadmal* (coarse cloth), quantities of which had been collected as rental payments. The ships that were anchored in the voes served as floating warehouses, and were gradually filled with goods over the summer, until they left in late August or September, before the onset of autumn storms. There were, therefore, two suppliers of goods to the Hanse merchants: the fishermen on the one hand and the tacksmen and lairds on the other. The fishermen provided fish in exchange for goods brought by the merchants. The tacksmen and lairds supplied butter and wadmal in exchange for goods or cash, although lairds also were active participants in the fishing industry.

Historians have been dismissive of the commercial value of butter and wadmal. They have argued that the butter was of little worth to the Germans, being of such low quality that it was suitable only for greasing cartwheels and smearing sheep (Donaldson, 1958, p.28; Fenton, 1978, p.440). But this is too sweeping a judgement and the result of reading history backwards. Certainly, by the seventeenth century both commodities were of diminishing commercial value and the most important export was fish, but that was a consequence of changes in the market. Previously, there had been a significant trade in these goods. For example, the Bergen *Kontor* [trading post] complained in 1514 that merchants from Hamburg, Bremen and Amsterdam were shipping butter, tallow, wool and feathers from Shetland and the Faroes without the trade passing through Norway (*Hanserecesse*, III, 9 (1477–1530), p.920 no.737). The loss of trade in those items was evidently felt in the Norwegian port. Shetland wadmal is also listed amongst the goods lost by merchants in a riot in Bergen in 1523 (Helle, 2019, p.49). The demand for wadmal fell away in the early seventeenth century and rent payments of cloth were commuted to money (Smith, 1984, p.37), but it strains credulity to imagine that before that time Shetland tenants regularly paid rents in the form of commodities which were of little commercial value, and it is clearly contrary to the evidence.

Before we pursue the implications of this further, it is necessary to consider systems of currency in Shetland before the advent of Germans. Land was assessed in silver marks, but this was an entirely theoretical measure as relatively little silver seems to have been in circulation in the island. For example, tithes to the value of 186 marks were owed by the bishop of Orkney to the archbishop of Trondheim in 1327, but it was agreed that this debt would be paid from the 'goods and rents' from Shetland (*SD* 1, no.7). So, though accounted in marks, the payments were to be made in other forms. Not all debts were measured in terms of silver. Tax and rents might be valued in 'commodity money', that is, values based upon goods produced on the typical Shetland farm – butter and wadmal (see Gullbekk, 2011, pp.103-104). Just as payments defined in terms of silver did not need to be paid in silver, so too debts in terms of commodity money were not always paid in that form, though often they were. When Margaretta Eilifsdottir granted land to the monastery of Munkeliv in Norway in 1418, the rent was described as five *laupar* of butter from lands in Norway and three pieces of cloth from those in Shetland (*SD* 1, no.19). A rental of the same monastery made some fifty years later included rents from Hascosay near Yell of one barrel of butter in one year and 30 ells of wadmal in the alternate years (*SD* 1, no.23). That second record leaves little room for doubt that what was given was actual butter and actual cloth, for why otherwise define the forms of rent paid in different years?

The commodity money system provided both a standard against which value could be measured and also arose out of the material in which payments could be made. It was both 'flexible and adaptive to changes in society' (Gullbekk, 2011, p.108), so it could be extended to, or indeed superseded by, other materials as the need arose. In Iceland, for example, as demand from German and English merchants increased *skreið* (dried fish) had by the fifteenth century superseded *vaðmál* (wadmal) as the main commodity money (Gelsinger, 1981, p.187; Mehler and Gardiner, 2021, p.41). However, in Shetland butter and cloth were so important as traded items it was not until the sixteenth century that fish began to appear as a form of commodity money. Fish appeared in the list of *scat* (tax) owed for Shetland which has been attributed to *c.* 1507×1513, but only under three entries for the Brecks, Churchton and Olligarth, all in Whiteness, and for *Meklagar*, apparently near Laxfirth (*SD* 1, p.262, 267). The exchange rate for Shetland fish is also provided in a mid-sixteenth-century list of drawn up in Bergen (*SD* 1, no.91). It explains that a mark of silver is equivalent to one Shetland *gulden*, and a gulden was equal to one *pund* of butter, 6 ells of cloth or 2 *punds* of fish. Once again, it is evident that these were not just units of account, but items which could be used in payment.

Fish was adopted as a form of commodity money in Shetland by the mid-sixteenth century as it became established that it had a clear exchange value and was being produced in greater quantities. Its previous absence suggests that neither had been the case. The upturn in the supply of fish and the activity of the fishing industry in Shetland appear to occur around 1500. In 1498 the Hanse noted that supposedly inferior fish from Shetland was being passed off with better fish from elsewhere, suggesting that it was entering the market in some quantity and creating a problem (*Hansercesse*, III, 4 (1497–1504), p.82 no.12, pp.114–115 nos.194, 198). Shetland fish was brought to Bergen by both German merchants and Scottish ones. German traders had been operating in Shetland from at least the mid-fifteenth century when Henrik Soost, a merchant in

Bergen, sold a small piece of land in Papa Stour (*SD1*, no.22). He was apparently a pioneer in the trade in Shetland, but by the end of the century he had been followed by others. Two Bremen ships sailed there in 1494 and another Bremen merchant, Hinrik Kummertho, was said to have gone there every year to purchase dried fish (*Hanserecesse*, III, 4 (1497–1504), p.69 no.68). Although the Hanse officially forbade direct trade with Shetland in 1498, it clearly had little effect, and nine years later the trade had grown to such a degree that merchants were complaining that fish bought there were undercutting prices in Bergen (Helle, 2019, p.33). A further Bremen captain, Johan Baller, is mentioned in Burravoe in 1539 with a merchant, Kenert Springar (*SD* 1, no.61). He became so well established that he was still trading there in 1550 (Focke, 1916, p.99).

It was not just German merchants that were shipping fish from Shetland. Merchants from the Scottish mainland and the Northern Isles, some of whom were based in Bergen, were also making the voyage to Shetland. The riot of 1523 in Bergen, already mentioned, was the outcome of commercial rivalry which had developed between Scottish and German merchants settled in the port. The Scots were well placed in this trade and able to use their knowledge of the Northern Isles to buy fish and other products, in a field of trade formerly dominated by Hanse merchants (Pedersen, 2005, pp.137–139)

The fragments of evidence we have are consistent in suggesting that the nature of trade with Shetland changed rapidly in the decades around 1500. It raises the question, what was it like before the advent of German merchants in Shetland? There is an important earlier record alluding to the transport of goods from Shetland to Bergen. In 1429 Hermen Wiitstok, a Lübeck merchant in Bergen, left money in his will to write-off the debts of sailors coming from Iceland, Shetland and the Faroes who had traded with him (Bruns, 1900, p.61, no.88). They are referred to in the will as *nordervaren*. The term *nordvar* was applied more commonly to those from northern Norway who brought dried fish to trade at Bergen, but the will indicates that there were similar merchants coming with cargoes from Shetland to Bergen. Such cargoes would certainly have included butter and wadmal, and perhaps some fish.

The details of the trade largely elude us, but by turning to the archaeological evidence we can suggest how it may have operated. The bulking of goods in Shetland for the sea journey to Bergen, whether dried fish or payments of butter and wadmal, must have taken place in suitable buildings which offered secure, dry storage. Only a single example is known from that period in the Northern Isles of Scotland, but the 'lords of Norway', as major Scandinavian landowners were known, are likely to have had similar warehouses at which they assembled payments from their Shetland estates before shipping them to Bergen. Excavations at Kebister uncovered the one known building, a barn-like structure probably built for Archdeacon Henry Phankouth (1501–29) (Owen and Lowe, 1999, p.90 ff.). He had extensive estates in Shetland and the goods collected in the warehouse would have included the rent paid by his tenants, as well as tithes paid from Tingwall parish (Donaldson, 1995, pp.84–88). Coastal locations, such as that of Kebister, were most suitable to bulk goods, because they could

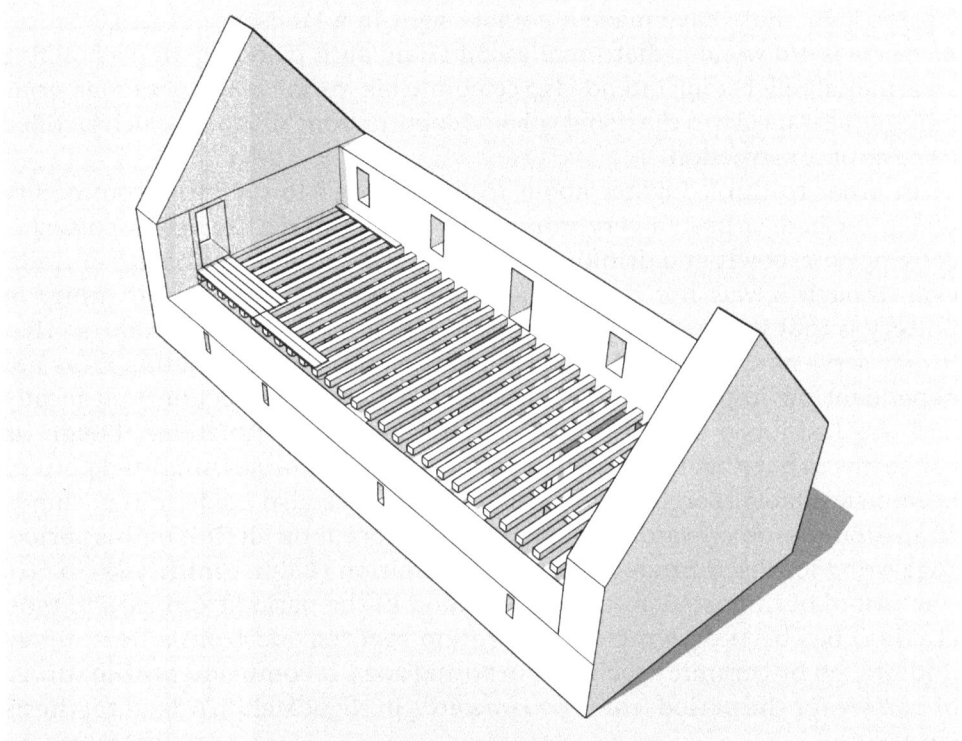

Reconstruction of the building at Kebister, Shetland viewed from the south-east. The position of the doors and windows is speculative. Two girding beams run the length of the building under the upper floor supporting a series of joists. The floorboards, of which only a small number are shown, were laid on the joists.

be brought there by boat and subsequently loaded on to ships for sale overseas. The excavated building at Kebister was constructed of stone bonded with clay. It had glass windows and a timber floor at ground level. The interpretation of the form of the building given in the excavation report poses a number of problems (Owen and Lowe, 1999, pp.298–300). Here it is necessary only to consider those aspects which relate to the form of the building. There were two internal stone walls and also a pair of posts. These were all interpreted in the excavation report as supports for tiebeams. This is highly unlikely: tiebeams do not need to be supported on walls or posts, because their ends sit on the head of the wall. They are more likely to have been for weight-bearing girding beams, which in turn supported joists. While this may seem like a detail of interpretation, it is in fact fundamental. First, it suggests that the upper floor was carrying a very considerable load: joists alone would have been sufficient for lesser weights. Second, it removes the connection between the internal walls and the roof structure. Both these factors lead to the conclusion that the building was a full two-storeys high. To call this, as the report does, a *teind* (or tithe) barn may give a too-limited idea of its role. It was intended as a substantial warehouse for the goods to be shipped. It had an internal floor area of 157 sq m. and, being two-storeys high, must have made a notable sight in a landscape of single-storey farmsteads. No wonder that Archdeacon Phankouth placed upon his building an armorial relief stone intended to celebrate his work. This ostentatious stone building also speaks to the rising value of exports from Shetland which justified its costs of construction.

In order to think further about trade, we need to turn to a commodity which formed, at best, a very minor part of commerce. Imported pottery – cooking pots, bowls and drinking vessels – can serve as an indicator of trade, even though it was not a significant component. The particular utility of pottery is that it can be dated and located to an area of production, so that it may serve as a marker of the movement of other goods. Shetland was not dependent on imported pottery. Soapstone (steatite) was quarried locally and was fashioned into vessels of various forms and functions though its use seems to have been declined in the fifteenth century as imported pottery became available (Forster, 2009, p.68). Pottery was also made in the islands from around 1100 onwards, though it does not occur on all sites of this period, suggesting localised production and distribution (Ballin Smith, 1999, p.134). The record of imported pottery in Shetland in the period from 1200 to 1500 (Table 1) has been drawn from excavation reports, and from a new survey undertaken by ceramic specialists in spring 2023. It complements the survey of pottery for the period from 1500 onwards in Nigel Melton's doctoral thesis (2001).

English and German pottery is assumed to have been imported not directly from the countries of manufacture, but from Bergen where it occurs in large quantities (Blackmore and Vince, 1994; Lüdtke, 1989) The route by which Scottish pottery reached Shetland is less certain, since, while it might have come directly from the Scottish mainland, it too could have gone via Bergen where Scottish east coast white gritty ware dating to the 12th and 13th centuries has been found (Haggarty, 1984, p.396). The quantities found on all sites is small, but it is not the volume which is significant, but the fact that it occurs at all. It is not merely on high-status sites, but also on more modest farmsteads, such as at Belmont and Soterberg which lie in areas of rather poor soils. It implies that all farms were involved in the trading nexus well before 1500. They were producing commodities for export and received in return goods from Bergen. This pattern can be compared to the farms in northern Norway. Sites here were also involved in trade with Bergen with the goods being taken to that port town by *nordvar* and goods brought back in return. In northern Norway imported pottery of the thirteenth to fifteenth century is found on farm sites, but mainly those in the vicinity of the port of Vågan or the administrative centre of Trondenes (Demuth, 2019, p.128). The contrast may reflect the easier transport of goods by sea from most farms in Shetland compared to the inland positions of some of those in Norway.

To put these discoveries in perspective, Table 2 records sites of the same period from which no imported pottery is reported. The site at Lower Underhoull and Hamar house 1 may have been abandoned before imports

Table 1

Imported pottery in Shetland 1200-1500

Belmont, Unst	Site occupied at least as late as 11th to 13th century and probably beyond. A small group of green-glazed fragments from late 13th- or early 14th-century date (Turner *et al.* 2013, p.205).
The Biggings, Papa Stour	One sherd of Paffrath ware (German); eleven sherds of Lower Saxon stoneware; one vessel of a highly decorated redware jug from Lübeck, c. 1250-1350 (missing in the publication, not identified there); fourteen sherds of 14th- to 15th-century English and Scots wares (Ballin Smith *et al.* 1999; identifications revised by Derek Hall in February 2023).
Jarlshof, Dunrossness	Sherds of '13th century type' found on the floors of the medieval farmstead. Four rim sherds with splashes of yellow glaze and cooking pots of the same fabric; also pottery of 14th and 15th centuries (Hamilton 1956, 193). These have not been re-examined.
Kebister, Mainland	Eight sherds of Scottish gritty white ware, 13th to 15th centuries (Crowley and Mills 1999, p.200).
Muness Castle, Unst	One fragment of 14th-century English whiteware; two fragments of 15th-century Dutch or German floor tiles (Ames 1975; identifications by Derek Hall and Michiel Bartels, February 2023).
Sands of Breckon, Yell	One fragment of 12th- or 13th-century Scottish gritty white ware; six pieces of 14th- or 15th-century East Anglian unglazed redware (stray finds in Shetland Museum identified by Derek Hall, February 2023).
Sandwick, Unst	Site occupied from 12th to late 14th, or early 15th century. A few fragments of English Scarborough and Grimston pottery, along with some proto-German stoneware (Bigelow 1985, p.121).
Scalloway Castle, Mainland	One sherd of Low Countries greyware pitcher; two Scottish bowl sherds; numerous 'northern European' earthenware from 16th century onwards (Hall and Lindsay 1983, p.566–67).
Scalloway broch, Mainland	Pottery of late 15th- to 17th-century date of Dutch and German origin (Sharples 1998, p.201).
Old Scatness, Dunrossness	A sherd of green-glazed Scarborough Ware dating to 13th or 14th century; one sherd of Langerwehe stoneware from Germany of 15th-century (Melton 2019, p.64).
Soterberg, Harold's Wick, Unst	'A number of sherds from glazed pottery' from excavated late Norse house (Stummann Hansen *in lit.*; see also Stummann Hansen 2000, p.93).

Other sites excavated by Stummann Hansen (2000) are not considered here as they are not fully published.

from Bergen started to arrive in Shetland. There was very limited excavation at Hamar house 2, but that is not true at Upper Underhoull which was extensively dug. Of course, the absence of finds does not prove that pottery was not reaching those sites, but merely it did not remain on the site to be excavated. The predominant pattern remains that the greater number of

Table 2

Sites occupied 1200-1500 without imported pottery

Hamar house 1, Unst	Final abandonment dated to a period within of the 12th to the first quarter of the 14th century (Turner et al. 2013, p.134).
Hamar house 2, Unst	Limited excavation of earlier phase of building suggested it was abandoned sometime in the period of mid-15th to mid-17th century (Turner et al. 2013, p.138).
Lower Underhoull, Unst	Occupation may have lasted until at least 12th century, but no pottery was noted (Small 1967).
Upper Underhoull, Unst	Radiocarbon analysis suggests activity ceased in the period mid-13th to the end of the 15th century (Swindles et al. 2019).

farms were receiving at least some pottery and therefore engaged in overseas trade in the period before 1500.

We can now reach some preliminary conclusions about the character of trade in the period before 1500. Shetland's trade was largely with Bergen, though some ships may have travelled southwards to the Scottish mainland. Cargoes of surplus butter and wadmal were assembled by *nordervar* from various farms, both big and small, for shipping abroad. We have not identified the sites from which these merchants operated, but it is likely to be at those protected inlets which were later used by German ships. In return the *nordervar* brought back various commodities from Bergen for which pottery has to serve as an indicator. In addition to that trade, goods collected in rent, tax and tithe were also shipped abroad. The building at Kebister gives some indication of the scale and mechanism of that commerce, although it belongs to the beginning of the sixteenth century. From the 1490s onwards, the trade began to alter very considerably. German merchants started to increase in numbers and it is unlikely to be coincidence that this was also the time when fish becomes more important as an exported commodity. The evidence is scant, but piecing the fragments together it is possible to outline the nature of Shetland's overseas trade in the period before the influx of German merchants. The arrival of these merchants from 1500 onwards, and particularly after 1550, was not the beginning of Shetland's foreign trade, but rather marks a stage in the reorientation from Scandinavia to the European continent.

Acknowledgements

We are grateful to Bart Holterman for commenting on an earlier version of the text. Thanks also to the group of pottery specialists who in February 2023 examined the medieval and early modern pottery imported to Shetland: Michiel Bartels, Torbjörn Brorsson, Volker Demuth, Derek Hall, Harald Stadler and Frauke Witte. This paper forms part of the AHRC-DFG project, Looking in from the Edge.

Abbreviations

SD 1 – Ballantyne and Smith (eds.) (1999) *Shetland Documents 1195-1579*
SD 2 – Ballantyne and Smith (eds.) (1994) *Shetland Documents 1580-1611*

Bibliography

Ames, H. E. (1975) 'Interim report of the excavation at Muness Castle, Unst, Shetland'. Unpublished report for Historic Buildings and Monuments, SDD, pp.133–34.

Ballantyne, John H. and Smith, Brian (eds.) (1994) *Shetland Documents 1580-1611*. Lerwick: Shetland Islands Council and The Shetland Times Ltd.

Ballantyne, John H. and Smith, Brian (eds.) (1999) *Shetland Documents 1195-1579*. Lerwick: Shetland Islands Council and The Shetland Times Ltd.

Ballin Smith, B., Blackmore, L., Stephan, H.G. and Will, R. (1999) 'Ceramics', in B.E. Crawford and B. Ballin Smith, *The Biggings, Papa Stour, Shetland: The History and Excavation of a Royal Norwegian Farm*. Edinburgh: Society of Antiquaries of Scotland, pp.144–68.

Bigelow, G. (1985) 'Sandwick, Unst and the late Norse Shetland economy', in B. Smith (ed.), *Shetland Archaeology: New Work in Shetland in the 1970s*. Lerwick: The Shetland Times Ltd, pp.95–127.

Blackmore, L. and Vince, A. (1994) 'Medieval pottery from south-east England found in the Bryggen excavation 1955-68', in A. Herteig (ed.) *The Bryggen Papers, Supplementary Series* 5. Bergen: University of Bergen, pp.9–160.

Bruns, F. (1900) *Die Lübecker Bergenfahrer und ihre Chronistik*. Berlin: Pass & Garleb.

Crawford, B. (1969) 'The pawning of Orkney and Shetland: a reconsideration of the events of 1460-1469', *Scottish Historical Review* 48, pp.35–53.

Crowley, N. and Mills, S. (1999) 'The medieval and post-medieval pottery', in O. Owen and C. Lowe, *Kebister: The Four-Thousand-Year-Old Story of One Shetland Township*. Edinburgh: Society of Antiquities of Scotland, pp.200–206.

Demuth, V. (2019) 'Medieval and early modern ceramics in urban and rural Norway as evidence of trade within the Hanseatic world', in N. Mehler, M. Gardiner and E. Elvestad (eds.), *German Trade in the North Atlantic c. 1400–1700: Interdisciplinary Perspectives*. Stavanger: Arkeologisk museum i Stavanger, pp.121–132.

Diplomatarium Norvegicum (1847–). Christiana, Oslo.

Donaldson, G. (1958) *Shetland Life under Earl Patrick*. Edinburgh: Oliver and Boyd.

Donaldson, G. (1995) 'The archdeaconry of Shetland', in B.E. Crawford (ed.), *Northern Isles Connections: Essays from Orkney and Shetland presented to Per Sveaas Andersen*. Kirkwall: Orkney Press, pp.77–89.

Fenton, A. (1978) *The Northern Isles: Orkney and Shetland*. Edinburgh: John Donald Publishers.

Focke, J (1916) 'Das Seefahrtenbuch des Brüning Rulves', *Bremisches Jahrbuch* 26, pp.91–144.

Forster, A. (2009) 'Viking and Norse steatite use in Shetland', in A. Forster and V. Turner (eds.), *Kleber: Shetland's Oldest Industry*. Lerwick: Shetland Amenity Trust, pp.58–69.

Gardiner, M. F. and Mehler, N. (2019) 'Introduction: German trade in the North Atlantic', in N. Mehler, M. Gardiner and E. Elvestad (eds.) *German Trade in the North Atlantic c. 1400–1700: Interdisciplinary Perspectives*. Stavanger: Arkeologisk museum i Stavanger, pp.9–24.

Gelsinger, B. E. (1981) *Icelandic Enterprise: Commerce and Economy in the Middle Ages*. Columbia: University of South Carolina Press.

Grohse, I. P. (2020) 'The lost cause: kings, the council, and the question of Orkney and Shetland, 1468–1536', *Scandinavian Journal of History* 45, pp.286–308.

Gullbekk, S. H. (2011) 'Norway: commodity money, silver and coins', in J. Graham-Campbell, S. M. Sindbæk and G. Williams (eds.), *Silver Economies, Monetisation and Society in Scandinavia, AD 800-1100* (Aarhus: Aarhus University Press, pp.93–111.

Haggarty, G. (1984) 'Observations on the ceramic material from Phase 1 Pits BY and AQ', in C. J. Tabraham, 'Excavations at Kelso Abbey', *Proceedings of the Society of Antiquaries of Scotland* 114, pp.395–397.

Hall, D and Lindsay, W. J. (1983) 'Excavations at Scalloway Castle, 1979 and 1980', *Proceedings of the Society of Antiquaries of Scotland* 113, pp.554–593.

Hamilton, J. R. C. (1956) *Excavations at Jarlshof, Shetland*. Edinburgh: HMSO.

Hanserecesse (1878–). Leipzig, Weimar.

Helle, K. (2019) 'Bergen's role in the medieval North Atlantic trade', in N. Mehler, M. Gardiner and E. Elvestad (eds.), *German Trade in the North Atlantic c. 1400-1700: Interdisciplinary Perspectives*. Stavanger: Arkeologisk museum i Stavanger, pp.43–51.

Holterman, B. (2020) *The Fish Lands: German trade with Iceland, Shetland and the Faroe Islands in the late 15th and 16th Century*. Berlin: Walter de Gruyter.

Lüdtke, H, (1989) *The Bryggen Pottery I: Introduction and Pingsdorf Ware* (*The Bryggen Papers, Supplementary Series* 4). Bergen: University of Bergen.

Mehler, N and Gardiner, M. (2021) 'Coinless exchange and foreign merchants in medieval Iceland (A.D. 900-1600)', in L. Rahmstorf, G. Bajamovic and N. Ialongo (eds.), *Merchants, Measures and Money: Understanding Technologies of Early Trade in a Comparative Perspective*. Göttingen: Wachholtz Verlag, pp.35–54.

Melton, N. D. (2001) 'Archaeological Visibility of Cultural Continuity, Contact and Change in Southern Shetland from the Sixteenth to Eighteenth centuries A.D.'. PhD thesis, University of Bradford, Bradford.

Melton, N. D. (2019) Ceramics, in Nigel D. Melton *et al.*, *Excavations at Old Scatness, Shetland Volume 3: The Post-Medieval Township*. Lerwick: Shetland Heritage Publications, pp.63–88.

Owen, O. and Lowe, C. (1999) *Kebister: The Four-Thousand-Year-Old Story of One Shetland Township*. Edinburgh: Society of Antiquaries of Scotland.

Pedersen, N. Ø. (2005) 'Scottish immigration to Bergen in the sixteenth and seventeenth centuries', in A. Grosjean, and S, Murdoch (eds.), *Scottish Communities Abroad in the Early Modern Period*. Leiden: Brill, pp.135–165.

Sharples, N. (1998) *Scalloway: a broch, late Iron Age settlement and medieval cemetery in Shetland*. Oxford: Oxbow Books.

Small, A. (1967) 'Excavations at Underhoull, Unst, Shetland', *Proceedings of the Society of Antiquaries of Scotland* 98, pp.225–248.

Smith, B. (1990) 'Shetland, Scandinavia, Scotland, 1300–1700: the changing nature of contact', in G. G. Simpson (ed.), *Scotland and Scandinavia 800–1800*. Edinburgh: John Donald Publishers, pp.25–37.

Smith B. (2010) 'When did Orkney and Shetland become part of Scotland? A contribution to the debate', *New Orkney Antiquarian Journal* 5, pp.1–18.

Smith, B. (2019) 'Shetland and her German merchants, c. 1450–1710', in N. Mehler, M. Gardiner and E. Elvestad (eds.) *German Trade in the North Atlantic c. 1400–1700: Interdisciplinary Perspectives*. Stavanger: Arkeologisk museum i Stavanger, pp.147–152.

Smith, H. (1984) *Shetland Life and Trade 1550–1914*. Edinburgh: John Donald Publishers.

Stummann Hansen, S. (2000) 'Viking settlement in Shetland: chronological and regional contexts', *Acta Archaeologica* 71, pp.87–103.

Swindles, G. *et al.* (2019) 'Viking peat formation and settlement abandonment: a multi-method chronological approach from Shetland', *Quaternary Science Reviews* 210 (15), pp.211–225.

Turner, V. E., Bond, J. M. and Larsen, A.-C. (2013) *Viking Unst: Excavations and Survey in Northern Shetland 2006-2010*. Lerwick: Shetland Heritage Publications.

9

Earl Patrick's domra of Shetland in the name of the old law

Jørn Øyrehagen Sunde
(University of Oslo)

Evil genius

In 1954, lecturer Gordon Donaldson, later Sir William Fraser Professor in Scottish History and Palaeography in Edinburgh, published *The Court Book of Shetland 1602-1604* (Donaldson, 1954). The year before, the court book for the Jæren and Dalane district in south-western Norway from 1613 was published (Aurenes and Thorson, 1953).[1] Both court books are a product of the application of the Magnus Code of 1274. The Code was applied in Shetland until 1611, when Norwegian law in general was replaced with Scots law, and in Norway until 1687, when the medieval lawbook was replaced by Christian V's Norwegian Law.[2] Secondly, both court books are sources which tell us about everyday life, as well as law and state formation in what remained of the Norwegian medieval realm in the first part of the Early Modern period. They have hence been investigated when writing Shetland and Norwegian history. However, the books have not been compared. There are several reasons why such a comparison would be of interest. One is to better understand Earl Patrick's use of the legal system for his own benefit.

In his Introduction to *The Court Book of Shetland 1602-1604*, Donaldson notes that '[v]ery likely it was the earl's policy to exploit the situation by maintaining such features of Shetland usage as upheld or extended his own authority', and '[t]he Court Book is certainly a momentum to Earl Patrick's concern for his "gain and commodity"' (Donaldson, 1954, p.v). In short, Donaldson finds it likely that the old Norwegian law in Earl Patrick's court in the early 17th century was applied for the earl's gain. The general character of the reign of Earl Patrick,

---

1 The earliest Norwegian court book for urban areas in Norway is the court book for the city Bergen from 1592-1594. Available at https://xml.arkivverket.no/tingboker/Bergen-raadstueprotokoll-1592.pdf (accessed: 13 August 2023).
2 The Magnus Code was printed and to some extent altered already in 1604 with the Norwegian Code of Christian IV. See Hallager and Brandt, 1855, pp.III-XXVI; Leslie-Jacobsen, 2020-21.

nicknamed Black Patie, supports Donaldson's assumption. By contrast, Peter Anderson claims that much of Earl Patrick's bad reputation is based on 'folk tales of mysterious origin', 'family legends' and 'literary offerings of greater or lesser merit' (Anderson, 1992, p.45). However, in *Robert Stewart – Earl of Orkney, Lord of Shetland 1533-1593* (Anderson, 1982), he finds that Earl Robert misused his powers as Lord, and that 'the legal problem regarding the government of Orkney and Shetland (...) would not be solved (...) until the fall of Robert's son [Earl Patrick]' (Anderson, 1982, p.94). By this, Anderson implies that Earl Patrick pursued 'his selfish interests' like his father, and is therefore the kind of villain that Donaldson described him as three decades earlier.

Anderson and Donaldson also agree on the reason for the brutal character of the reign of Earl Robert and Earl Patrick: the opportunity to misuse power that was embedded in the old Norwegian law – both men used the obscurity of the law to their own advantage. Anderson bases his judgement on the reading of the Shetland complaint against Earl Robert and his half-brother sheriff Laurence Bruce of Cultmalindie, from 1575 and 1577 (see Ballantyne and Smith, 1999, nos.216, 237). Donaldson based his judgement on the reading of the Shetland court book of 1602-1604, which he devoted a whole chapter to in *Shetland Life under Earl Patrick* (Donaldson, 1958, pp.106-129). In this book, he concludes on one hand that 'Earl Patrick's administration, while undoubtedly burdensome, was not oppressive in an arbitrary way', and on the other hand that 'half-forgotten branches of the law were brought to light in order to provide the opportunity for imposing a fine' (Donaldson, 1958, pp.10-11). However, Donaldson does not point at how the law was misused, and with good reason.

The problem when studying the Shetland court book of 1602-1604, is that any deviation from the Magnus Code cannot be taken as evidence for Earl Patrick's villainous rule of Shetland. The time span from 1274 to 1602 justifies in itself such deviations, since law has to change to meet the needs of society. The practice of passing country acts, which for Shetland's account is well documented from 1615 (Donaldson, 1958, p.12), was a response to a mismatch between law and society (Donaldson, 1991, pp.x-xi; see also the collection of acts in Gifford, 1879, pp.74-79). However, by comparing the Shetland court book of 1602-1604 with the court book for Jæren and Dalane from 1613-1625, in light of the Magnus Code, we might be able to move from justified assumption to more certain knowledge. The hypothes is that a legal practice not intended in the Magnus Code as being for the advantage of the earl and the disadvantage of Shetlanders, and which is only found in the Shetland court book of 1602-1604, is evidence of the evil intent of Earl Patrick.

In this article I will firstly compare the practices of law in the earl's court as recorded in the court book with the Magnus Code of 1274, to see if the law was applied in Shetland as it was recorded in the 39 preserved manuscripts of the code. We do not have the lawbook referred to in the Shetland court book of 1602-1604, which says that the 'essyse taking lang and mature deliberatioun, by the inspectioun of the chepturies of the law buik' (Donaldson, 1954, p.43). However, the 39 surviving manuscripts from mainland Norway ought to indicate what was for long the common understanding of the medieval code.[3] Secondly, I will compare the court books of Shetland with those of Jæren and Dalane in Norway, to investigate if the practice of the old law was understood and applied in the same way in these two jurisdictions, in a close time period, and in areas with similar landscapes and economies.

My conclusion is that Earl Patrick and his stewards very cunningly interpreted and applied the Magnus Code in order to increase fines and control the public. It was not primarily substantial law that was bent in the favour of the earl, but procedural law. The reason is that the procedural law was far more obscure, since it was found in different and non-interrelated parts of the Code, and in the first amendment to the lawbook from 1280. This is why Donaldson assumes Earl Patrick used the Magnus Code to his advantage, but cannot pinpoint how and when. However, the application of the lawbook in the earl's courts did not only increase the revenues of the earl, but also his hold on the population. Procedural law was applied to set different parts of the population against each other. It could be assumed that it was the Norwegians against the Scots. However, the earl seems to deliberately dismantle the solidarity between Shetlanders. In 1982, Anderson was hesitant to call Earl Robert an 'evil genius', but I do not hesitate to label his son in this manner, and would like to stress that Shetland suffered from Earl Patrick's cynical policy for centuries.

Domra

The foud has in Shetland history acquired a bad name, partly due to the conduct of Laurence Bruce of Cultmalindie, half-brother of Earl Robert Stewart. The foud – in Norwegian *fogd* and best translated into modern English as sheriff – was also unpopular in Norway in the 16th and 17th centuries. This is partly due to the recruitment of unscrupulous characters like Laurence Bruce in Shetland. However, the recruitment policy must also be understood as a necessary political move to gain control after more than a century of weak central control. With the Calmar Union of 1397, Norway was governed by monarchs situated outside the realm, and mainly advised by non-Norwegian aristocrats. Outlying Norwegian districts, like Shetland, Jæren and Dalane, were regionally governed and fouds were recruited locally. However, in early 14th century Norway the foud, then called *sýslumaðr*, would have been a part of the *national* elite, and was therefore very much the king's vassal (see Moseng et al., 2007, pp.199-211). This was for instance the case with Thorvald Toresson, who we know as the king's *sýslumaðr* from the Papa Stour document of 1299 (*Diplomatarium Norwegicum* vol.1, no. 89; Ballantyne and Smith, 1999, no.2).

---

3   While the 39 surviving medieval manuscripts of the Magnus Code have been thoroughly investigated and all variations recorded (Rindal and Spørck, 2018) approximately 120 manuscripts made between 1550 and 1604 have not. It is not likely, but it is possible, that the Shetland manuscript was not a medieval one, but one of the many Early Modern variations. However, this more recent manuscript tradition was harmonised in Christian IV's Norwegian Law of 1604. Shetland legal practices in 1602-1604 will hence also be compared to this edition of this Early Modern standardisation of the Magnus Code.

The foud in the 15th century, and onwards into the 16th century, would have fewer ties to the king and was more dependant on cooperation with the rest of the regional elite. With increased royal interest, and presence, in Shetland and Norway in the second half of the 16th century, the foud's loyalty was again pulled away from the region towards the ruler. In Shetland that was the Stewart earls, and in Norway the king's governors. This does not justify unscrupulous behaviour, but it explains why rulers wanted to recruit fouds from outside the regional elites in the 16th century, and could explain why they might have viewed the misbehaviour of the fouds as a favourable quality, since the enmity of the population made them more dependant on their Lords.

The foud of the 16th century was never as powerful as the *sýslumaðr* of the 14th century, partly due to recruitment from lower strata of society and greater distance from central power. However, they both had the right to call the parties in a conflict to them, and to suggest a solution. This was a power vested in the *sýslumaðr* already in the first amedment to the Magnus Code in 1280 (Keyser and Munch, 1849, pp.8-9 (art.24); Sunde, 2014, pp.151-152). In the Shetland court book of 1602-1604 and in the court book for Jæren and Dalane, we find that this was a frequently used way of resolving conflicts, partly because the conflict could be resolved faster than waiting for the *ting* to meet and decide the case. For Jæren and Dalane, as for the rest of Norway, it was also partly because the foud was not bound by law, and could propose a more equitable settlement. However, in Shetland it was different.

The foud's proposed settlement was not a judgement. According to the amendment of 1280, the case would simply go on to the lawman – the *logmaðr* in Old Norse – if one of the parties would not accept the foud's suggestion (Sunde, 2014). Probably, because the Norwegian lawmen had already retreated to the cities before 1350 instead of going on a yearly circuit, it became customary that such cases went to the local *ting* – the local assembly – to be decided, instead of going to the lawman. This seems to also have been the case in Shetland. However, not yielding to the foud's suggested settlement would, in Shetland, be regarded as a *domra*, a practice we do not find any evidence of in Jæren and Dalane. A domra is defined by Donaldson in his glossary to the court book as 'a fine for contempt of court' (Donaldson, 1954, p.viii). Ebbe Hertzberg, in his glossary to the medieval Norwegian laws, defines it as not yielding to a judgement (Hertzberg, 1895, p.136). Domra, or *dómrof* in Old Norse, literally means the robbery (*rof*) of a judgement (*dóm*). According to the Magnus Code, book 1 chapter 5 (I-5) and IV-20, 'domra' carried a fine. But in both cases, 'domra' is linked to a judgement by the assembly or assize, and not dealt with outside the court by what became the foud.

Domra is only found once in the court book of Jæren and Dalane between 1613 and 1625, whereas it is frequently used in the Shetland court book between 1602 and 1604. This is because the decision of the foud was regarded a judgement passed in a court in Shetland and not in mainland Norway (see, for example, Donaldson, 1954, p.27). This practice could have developed already in the Middle Ages. In the 1200s there were complaints of greedy *sýslumaðr*, and King Håkon

V established in 1308 a system of controlling their practice (Moseng *et al.*, 2007, p.138, p.180; see also Keyser and Munch, 1849, pp.74-81). This was also the essence of the accusations against Thorvald Toresson in 1299 in Papa Stour, and later in 1307 (*Diplomarium Norvegicum* vol.I, no. 109; see Smith, 1990, p.26). The possibility of taking advantage of the system increased as bonds between mainland Norway and Shetland weakened after the Black Death and the Calmar Union in the 14th century, with a subsequent weakening of control. However, domra is a practice, contrary to the law, that only benefitted the Shetland ruler and not the foud. Misuse of the power to call the parties in a conflict, and to suggest a solution, was, in the Middle Ages, linked to the *sýslumaðr* taking a share of the monetary settlement. This was quite different from the earl's court fining a person who would not obey the foud, which only the earl would benefit from. This misuse of domra can be explained by Shetland lacking a strong central power up to the time that Robert Stewart became Earl of Orkney and Shetland (see Anderson, 1982, pp.89-91). There are hence good reasons to assume that the practice of fining for domra emerged with Laurence Bruce as foud and Robert Stewart as earl some time before 1575.

The practice we can identify in the Shetland court book of 1602-1604 concerning domra is therefore not in line with the Magnus Code, and is contrary to the practice we find in the court book for Jæren and Dalane. It is not the only example of a misuse of the procedural law in the Magnus Code in Shetland in the early 1600s.

Oaths and 'Failying thereof'

All the cases of people failing to follow the foud's suggestion of settlement and being fined for domra give an impression of a lawless Shetland in the early 17th century. This impression is strengthened by the accused failing to swear an oath to free themselves of the charge of many different crimes, like theft, illegal fishing and – more rarely – witchcraft. Oaths were an important instrument of proof in the Magnus Code, and dealt with in the ninth book in the Code named the *þiofa bolk*, the book on theft. The main instrument of proof was two witnesses, as stressed already in I-4 in the Magnus Code, and repeated in V-17. However, theft was a crime committed in the secrecy of darkness, hills, etc., and oath swearing replaced two witnesses as the dominant instrument of proof in such situations. That was also the case in other crimes that were otherwise hard to prove.

The Magnus Code operates quite often with a one-man oath to free yourself from less serious accusations. Taking something of low value was in the Magnus Code IX-10 called *huinzska*, and seems to be covered in Shetland by the term 'gripstair' (see, for example, Donaldson, 1954, p.26). In such cases you could free yourself with an one-man oath. If it was the second or third time a small theft was committed, the accused had to free his- or herself with a 'laryct aith', or *lyritar eið* in Old Norse, swearing an oath of innocence with four other men or women. In the case of a graver theft, the accused could swear an oath of innocence with six other men or women, the so called *settar eid* in Old Norse, called 'sixter aith' in the Shetland court book. Swearing an oath of innocence with 12 other men, the *tylptar eid,* was only an option when someone was accused of a theft punishable by death, according to IX-1 in the Magnus Code.

In the earl's court, the accused could bring on an acquittal by swearing an oath of innocence for many different crimes. For instance, in 1603 we read in the court book:

> The haile tennentis and commonis of Quhytnes, Weisdale, Sandsting ar dempt to quite thame themeselffies of the fisching with their haddock lynis within their vois fra Beltane to Hallowemes according to the auld actis and that with the laryth aith, and failying thairof ilk person to pay x il. under the pain of poynding. (Donaldson, 1954, p.92)

Fishing by the tenants of the four communities was not a crime that took place in secret – the fishermen were in their boats on open water, not hiding in bushes on the shore. It should be more than possible to prove the offence with two witnesses, if it actually took place. Instead, the court asked every person in the four communities to find two persons to swear an oath of innocence with, and the court – or rather the foud – appointed the two other oath swearers to complete a 'larycht aith'. This is a misuse of oath as an instrument of evidence, which in the Magnus Code was only to be used when two witnesses could not be found due to the character of the crime. However, it increased the possibility of income for the earl, since any person who failed the oath of innocence – and only one person unwilling to swear would cause the oath to fail – would have to pay a fine. By rounding up all inhabitants in four communities and making them swear an oath in this manner, with oath keepers also appointed by the foud, there ought to be some financial gain for the earl.

The fishery case of 1603 is not the only one where a large number of people had to swear an oath of innocence for a crime that should have been possible to prove with two witnesses (see Donaldson, 1954, pp.59-60). However, this tactic was much more commonly used by the earl's stewards when a single person was accused of a crime: when someone was accussed of an illegal action, they were asked to swear an oath of innocence, and if they failed, they could be fined. For instance, we read the following from a court held in South Yell in 1603:

> Olaw Mansoun is dempt to quite himself, his wyf and houshald, that thai nawayis knew the half codling inbrocht be Erasmus Manisoun to roist wes stollin, and that with the larycht aithe within xxiiii houris, and fayling thairof to pay ii merkis and to underly the law for the resset of stowth. (Donaldson, 1954, p.73)

The court book does not inform us of the evidence that calls for Olaw Mansoun to swear an oath of innocence, but it does say that, if he fails, he will have to pay a fine for the failure and for the theft. The Shetland court book of 1602-1604 shows how this method of increasing the earl's income was well-established and frequently used during the reign of Earl Patrick (see, for instance, Clouston, 1914, pp.171-172n). It might be that it originated under Earl Robert and his sheriff Laurence Bruce, since a special version of this way of increasing income was mentioned in the Shetlanders' complaint of 1577: when an oath failed, the oath swearer had to prove his innocence by swearing another oath with even more oath helpers, and – when failing again – payed a higher fine (Ballantyne and Smith, 1999, no.237, p.204).

In the court book of Jæren and Dalane we find no evidence of this, while in Shetland the number of people that had to pay fines for failing an oath of innocence was large. The practice we can identify in the Shetland court book of 1602-1604 concerning oath-swearing is not in line with the Magnus Code, is contrary to the practice we find in the court book for Jæren and Dalane, and is hence another example of the misuse of procedural law in the Magnus Code in Shetland in the early 1600s.

Social unrest

In Dunrossness 36 people paid fines for breaking the foud's domra in 1602, while 12 paid fines for failing their oath, making up around half of all persons that paid a fine in the parish that year. This means that the earl increased his revenues by interpreting the Magnus Code to his advantage. It might also mean that the Earl not only looted Shetland, but also attacked the vertical and horizontal structures of local society, leaving it boneless and destroyed.

36 of 88 cases in which fines were paid in Dunrossness concerned domra. This means that the foud aggressively pushed his decisions on the Shetlanders as judgements. It also indicates that many Shetlanders did not accept the judicial power the foud claimed to have, and protested by not obeying the earl's officer.[4] The collective protest that forced the unpopular Laurence Bruce out of office in the 1570s seems, to some extent, to have continued on an individual level. This must have been damaging to the vertical trust between inhabitants and officers in Shetland for a long while.

To make sure that the result of an oath was not decided by personal relationship, the accused could only pick half of his oath helpers; the other half was appointed by the foud. Domra-cases indicate that there was tension in Shetland between the earl's officers and the population. We cannot be sure that the foud would not appoint oath helpers reluctant to swear in favour of the accused. We must keep in mind that an oath helper put his own salvation at stake when swearing someone's innocence. Hence, not knowing the accused well enough to decide if that person had the potential for mischief could make the person reluctant to take the risk. To increase the chance of an oath failing, the foud did not have to look for enemies of the accused when appointing

---

4   We have to keep in mind that some did not obey simply because they did not have the financial means to fulfil the foud's suggested settlement.

oath helpers, but only people who were unfamiliar with the accused. With all the oaths that had to be sworn every year in every part of Shetland, the tactic of accusation and then demanding an oath of innocence, with oath helpers appointed by the accused and by the foud, must have increased social tension. The horizontal distrust among the inhabitants must hence have increased over the years. It might be that we already see the result in the court book of 1602-1604.

In the early 17th century there was a surprisingly large amount of crime in Shetland: accusations of theft, witchcraft, violence, slander, etc were common. Also in Norway there were a fairly high number of such crimes in the first half of the 1600s. This can be explained by a central government taking back control after more than a century of regional, as opposed to central, government, and a new understanding of violent interactions as crimes, rather than conflictts to be settled (See the discussion in Sandmo, 1999, pp.244-248; see also Donaldson, 1958, pp.109-117). At the same time, the Reformation strengthened a feeling of low morals and flourishing sin in society (See Sunde, 2005, p.196), partly because morality became a question for ordinary courts and not those of the Church (Sunde, 2015, p.187; Donaldson, 1958, pp.121-129). In both Norway and Scotland, this gave rise to a tough-on-crime approach by central government. However, the level of crime in Shetland, as seen from the court book, was still unexpectedly high. Was this a result of a collapse of vertical and horizontal structures of trust? If that is the case, it is a long-lasting consequence of the misuse of legal power by Earl Robert and Earl Patrick.

Bibliography

Anderson, Peter (1982) Robert Stewart: *Earl of Orkney, Lord of Shetland 1533-1593*. Edinburgh: John Donald Publishers.

Anderson, Peter (1992) 'The Stewart Earls of Orkney and the History of Orkney and Shetland', *Northern Studies* 29, pp.43-52.

Aurenes, Ola and Thorson, Per (eds.) (1953) *Ting og stevne i Rogaland, Rogalands tingbøker, serie A: Jæren og Dalane 1613-1625*. Stavanger: Dreyer Aktieselskap.

Ballantyne and Smith (1999) *Shetland Documents 1195-1579*. Lerwick: The Shetland Times Ltd.

Clouston, J. Storer (1914) *Records of the Earldom of Orkney 1299-1614*. Edinburgh: Scottish History Society. *Diplomatarium Norwegicum* vol.I (1848). Christiania: Grøndahl.

Donaldson, Gordon (ed.) (1954) *The Court Book of Shetland 1602-1604*. Edinburgh: Scottish Record Society.

Donaldson, Gordon (1958) *Shetland Life under Earl Patrick*. Edinburgh and London: Oliver and Boyd.

Donaldson, Gordon (ed.) (1991) *The Court Book of Shetland 1615-1629*. Lerwick: Shetland Library.

Gifford, Thomas (1879) *Historical Description of the Zetland Islands in the Year 1733*. Edinburgh: Thomas George Stevenson.

Hallager and Brandt, (1855) *Kong Christian den Fjerdes Norske Lovbog af 1604*. Christiania: Feilberg & Landmark.

Hertzberg, Ebbe (1895) 'Glossarium', in Gustav Storm and Ebbe Hertzberg (eds.) *Norges gamle love* vol.5. Christiania: Grøndahl.

Keyser, Rudolf and Munch, P.A. (eds.) (1849) *Norges gamle Love* indtil 1387, 3. Bind. Christiania: Grøndahl & Søn.

Leslie-Jacobsen, Helen F. (2020-21), 'The Fracturing of the Law: The Motivation Behind the Norwegian Law of 1604', *The Retrospective Methods Network Newsletter*, pp.15-16.

Moseng, Ole Georg, *et al.* (2007) *Norges historie I, 750-1537*. Oslo: Universitetsforlaget.

Rindal, Magnus and Spørck, Bjørg Dale (eds.) (2018) *Kong Magnus Håkonssons Lagabøtes landslov – Norrøn tekst med fullstendig variantapparat*, 1. Part. Oslo: Arkivverket, Oslo.

Sandmo, Erling (1999) *Voldsamfunnets undergang – Om disiplinering av Norge på 1600-tallet*. Oslo: Universitetsforlaget.

Smith, Brian (1990) 'Shetland, Scandinavia, Scotland, 1300-1700: the changing nature of contact', in Grant G. Simpson (ed.) *Scotland and Scandinavia 800-1800*. Edinburgh: John Donald Publishers, pp.25-37.

Sunde, Jørn Øyrehagen (2014) 'Daughters of God and counsellors of the judges of men – a study in changes in the legal culture in the Norwegian realm in the High Middle Ages', in Stefan Brink and Lisa Collionson (eds.) *New Approaches to Early Law in Scandinavia*. Turnhout: Brepols, pp.151-152.

Sunde, Jørn Øyrehagen Sunde (2005) *Speculum legale – Rettsspegelen. Ein introduksjon til den norske rettskulturen si historie i eit europeisk perspektiv*. Bergen: Fagbokforlaget.

10

Research into the destruction of the 17th century Broo township, Shetland Islands, through burial in aeolian sand: an update

Gerald F. Bigelow

Institute of Archaeology, University of the Highlands and Islands / Burroughs & Chapin Center for Coastal and Wetland Research, Coastal Carolina University

Introduction

The township of Broo was a property of four farms located at the southwest end of Mainland, Shetland. Its earliest history is unknown, but there is considerable evidence of prehistoric settlement on the east flank of its most prominent geographical feature, Quendale Bay (CANMORE, 2023). During the historic period it appears that Broo consisted of four farms – Quindista, Visligarth, Husabroo and Heughe – and these names are either identifiably Norse or contain Norse elements suggesting the settlements existed there during the Viking or medieval periods (A.E. Jennings, pers. comm., 2022). However, Broo today is remembered largely for its almost complete destruction, a human catastrophe wrought by an extreme environmental transformation that we now know occurred in the 17th century (Bigelow et al., 2013; Bampton et al., 2017; Kinnaird et al., 2014; Kelley et al., 2018). This paper will: a) outline the catastrophe's relevance to local and wider historical questions, b) discuss research questions and completed field and laboratory activities focused on determining causes and consequences of the event, c) provide an update on current findings of this work and d) outline important, remaining questions about this dramatic event and its larger significance.

Before we move on to the main points of the paper, it should be noted that the township's name appears in several forms in original records and in later scholarly works. 'Brow', 'Brew and 'Broo' all refer to the same township, but this project uses the spelling "Broo" on the advice of Brian Smith, the Shetland Archivist, for its possible reference to a local geographical feature; its close relationship to the phonetic value of the Norse ancestor word *brú*, meaning "bridge" (Gordon, 1974, p.377); and its most common pronunciation in the Shetland dialect (B. Smith, pers. comm., 2004).

Historical relevance of Broo

The first, known historical document that refers to Broo dates to 1525 (Ballantyne and Smith, 1999, no.46). The next reference is in a document from 1559, and it provides our first, if indirect, link between Broo and the Sinclair family (Ballantyne and Smith 1999, no.118). The Sinclairs were among the wealthiest of the Scottish families that began to move into Shetland in the later Middle Ages, with much acquisition of lands in the 16th and 17th centuries. The story of Broo includes certain details of the life of possibly the most famous of the Shetland Sinclairs, Ola Sinclair, who is thought to have purchased Broo in the mid-1500s when he was the *Great Foud* – the magistrate or later, sheriff of Shetland (DSL, 2023) - a measure of the family's status at the time (Grant, 1893, pp.241-242). Ola is best-known popularly for an important role he is believed to have played in a successful battle with marauders from the island of Lewis who were bent on revenge for deaths at the Battle of Summerdale in 1529, a conflict involving several branches of the Sinclair family (Irvine, 1987, p.20). This brief report on scientific research is not the place for a detailed account of the Sinclair family at Broo, but their tenure involved many examples of the kinds of local, political and economic inter-family power-plays that were common among Scottish elites of the 16th, 17th and 18th centuries. The Broo Sinclairs were integral to many important aspects of Shetlandic early modern history, with economic ties extending far from Dunrossness, including important marriage connections with the Bruces of Muness, Unst, a branch of another very powerful family from Scotland that settled in Shetland (Irvine, 1987, p.19).

Although we have relatively little evidence of direct involvement in specifically fish trading commerce by the Broo Sinclairs in the 16th and 17th centuries, their township was one of the most valuable properties in southernmost Shetland (Low, 1879, p.184), and the southern tip of Mainland was an important area for trading activities by Hanseatic German, and Scottish, fish merchants. In general, the shores of Quendale Bay, Scatness, the West Voe of Sumburgh, Grutness and the Pool of Virkie together were a kind of gateway to Shetland for voyagers coming directly from Orkney or stopping while rounding the northern tip of Britain via the Sumburgh Roost. The Pool of Virkie, or the 'German Pool', and Grutness have been proposed as particularly important trading sites for fish and other commodities (Smith, 1984; Melton, 2004). Farther up the west coast, Bigton was another possibly significant international trading site. And, as discussed further below, what was then the Voe of Spiggie near Bigton, the Pool of Virkie and the Broo township were all subject to a kind of severe environmental change that caused much general economic stress in southernmost Shetland in the later 17th century: the loss of agricultural lands and changes in economically important coastal morphology from sand blowing inland from the beaches at West Voe, Quendale Bay and Scousburgh (Smith, 1984, p.41; Smith and Melton 2019).

While these adverse changes in the environmental infrastructure for both agriculture and trade depressed the local economy in the later 17th century in the general area of Broo, much larger contemporary political and macroeconomic trends also discouraged trade in that area and elsewhere in Shetland. By the beginning of the 18th century, the institution of tariffs, and the banning of importation of salt in non-British ships by the British government in the later 17th century, had contributed to the cessation of Hanseatic trade, a step that was most damaging to Shetlanders because it hampered the profitable, international commerce in dried fish (Smith, 1984, p.46; Riddell, 2019, p.9). This period was the beginning of a critical transition in Shetland, as in the early 18th century local landowners gradually stepped in to manage the trade in dried fish, and the *haaf* fishery was born (Smith, 1984, p.40; Smith, 2019, pp.1-4; Riddell, 2019, p.9). The development of this intensified form of fishing under local control proved to have an extensive impact on the islands' demography, socioeconomic structures, agriculture and other aspects of Shetland life. The historical, archaeological and environmental evidence of Broo is thus a time capsule of important economic changes in a formerly prosperous Shetland township during a time of crisis that preceded the beginning of the haaf period.

Broo as a case study in catastrophe and the role(s) of climate

The destruction of Broo is a prominent example of how human communities can be impacted by burial in sand transported inland from beaches by the wind. Once on land, these aeolian sands may form dune fields, and / or sand sheets, and when their deposits continue moving inland, they are known as 'transgressive dune fields' or 'transgressive sand sheets' (Hesp, 2013). The complete burial in sand of settled landscapes is the ultimate hazard to humans presented by these geological processes. The primary sources of coastal sand transgressions, sand beaches, are found around the world, and their related dune fields and sand sheets are also common. As our research has shown that the Broo catastrophe resulted in the formation of both a transgressive dune field and transgressive sand sheet (Kelley et al., 2018), the terms 'sand drift' or 'sand movement' will be used here in a general way to describe the process of aeolian sand burial: from the perspective of communities destroyed by sand, the ultimate surface forms taken by that sand are irrelevant, although they might disclose information about formation processes.

Scotland is a place that offers many iconic, historically recorded examples of the human impacts of coastal sand drift, particularly in the Northern and Western Isles, and along the east coast. In addition to the Broo catastrophe, prominent sand movements that destroyed settlements on Scottish coasts include historically recorded events at Culbin in Moray (Ross, 1993, pp.51-55; Lamb, 1991, pp.51-55); Forvie in Aberdeenshire (Willis, 1986); and along extensive stretches of the shell-sand *machair* on South Uist in the Outer Hebrides (Gilbertson et al., 1999). Many smaller events occurred elsewhere, and archaeological and geological evidence demonstrate that some sand beaches and shorelines have mobilised repeatedly in certain locations over millennia during the Holocene (e.g. see Gal, 2019, for Orkney).

Depositions of sand on settlements may occur over different timescales, from weeks to centuries, and the severity of their impacts range from ephemeral challenges to vegetation from seasonal and light deposits, to the complete transformation of arable landscapes and related settlements into vast dune fields or sand sheets, their surfaces punctuated by mounds hiding buried ruins of abandoned houses, farm buildings and churches. The Broo catastrophe is an example of the latter dimension of complete devastation.

Though historical accounts of settlement destruction from mobilised sand transgressions may stress the speed with which burial processes can occur, these events are not Pompeii scenarios. In contrast with volcanic ashfalls, the great majority of aeolian impacts from mobilised beach sands occur over weeks to decades. From the standpoint of seeking information about social resilience to environmental hazards, this aspect of sand catastrophes is critical, as it means that affected communities may have time to find ways to mitigate or make adaptations to the associated environmental changes. One important goal of the Broo research has been to explore the ways that the proprietors and tenants of the township responded to the gradual loss of their lands: this information could be a useful contribution to the growing interdisciplinary research on social resilience to extreme events (van Bavel et al., 2020), and in particular, 'disaster archaeology' (Cooper and Sheets, 2012). Disaster archaeology paradigms have been applied to multiple prehistoric cases, particularly involving volcanism (Riede and Jackson, 2020), but the Broo research has high potential for yielding nuanced evidence, because of its prospects for a much more finely calibrated dating of environmental events and human responses. This has been made possible by utilising high resolution imaging, early modern historical sources, and a range of archaeological and environmental evidence.

An additional and fundamental goal of the Broo research project has been to determine the cause, or causes, of the large-scale 17th century sand drift that occurred there (Bigelow et al., 2005). Starting in the 1970s, the influential historical climatologist H. H. Lamb promoted a model that linked episodes of northern hemisphere cooling to increased frequencies and severities of northeast Atlantic storms, which in turn theoretically destabilized sand shorelines and coastal dune fields in northwest Europe, leading to mass sand movements that in many areas affected human settlements (Lamb, 1977, p.129). Lamb proposed that these events clustered in periods of cooling from 1700-500 B.C., A.D. 400-700, and A.D. 1300-1700 which, in terms of European archaeological cultural chronologies, correspond to the Neolithic to early Iron Age, the late Iron Age and the later medieval and early modern periods. The last phase of widespread coastal sand mobilisation was proposed as the most severe, and in climate history terminology it occurred during the period most often referred to as the 'Little Ice Age' (Grove, 2004). The Broo catastrophe has been one of the most commonly cited examples of straightforward climatic forcing of transgressive dune field and sand sheet formation (e.g. see Dawson, 2009, p.125) but, as discussed below, the results of our work so far are inconclusive regarding the potential complexity of interactions through which the climate may have contributed to the catastrophe.

Research activities

When the Broo research began in the 2000s, it was clear that, in order to learn about an event that involved the movement and distribution of many tonnes of sand inland to a distance of over two kilometres, and the resulting destruction of a community of four farms, we would need to examine documentary, geological, archaeological and other environmental history evidence. To evaluate the role that Little Ice Age climatic changes may have played in the event, our historians, geologists, archaeologists and other environmental history specialists needed previous experience working with northern climate history information.

Historical research by Michael E. Jones has required many hours of work with original documents and secondary sources in the Shetland Archives, the National Library of Scotland, the Advocates Library of the National Library of Scotland and the British Museum Library, (Bigelow et al., 2007; Bampton et al., 2017; Oehler, 2017). Documents on landholding and taxation, and early descriptions of Shetland have proved to be particularly useful to the project's goals.

It was obvious from the nature of the Broo catastrophe that geological investigation would also play a prominent role in exploring the causes and processes of the event. Multiple methods of geological research have been employed thus far in studies of the Quendale links and greater Broo landscapes, including coastal geomorphology analyses accomplished through Ground Penetrating Radar (GPR) surveys (Kelley et al., 2018; Sorrell, 2013), traditional sediment analyses (Gilbert, 2012; Halsted, 2014), and lake sediment analysis of cores taken from the Lochs of Brow and Spiggie (Lindelof et al., 2012; Lindelof, 2012). In addition, Optically Stimulated Luminescence (OSL) dating has been an important means of both geological and archaeological dating for the project, because the 17th and early 18th centuries, when the last and most massive sand movements took place, is a period for which radiocarbon dating is unusually imprecise (Kinnaird et al., 2014). OSL dating also offers useful information on the process of burial, because it specifically measures time elapsed since a sediment was buried and excluded from light, a feature lacking from chronologies based on radiocarbon analyses.

It was also clear from the outset that the influences of human activities and weather on soils and vegetation may have played important roles in enhancing the vulnerability of any existing near-shore dunes and adjacent sandy farm fields to transport by winds of unusual or normal magnitudes. Therefore, analysis of soils through micromorphology, which provides direct evidence of soil formation processes, has been performed (Saunders and Simpson, 2012).

The centrepiece of our efforts to reconstruct the causes and consequences of the Broo sand transgression has been the archaeological excavation of a previously unknown 17th century farm site that was found through survey in 2002 and dated through test excavations in 2003 (Bigelow et al., 2005). Although the site is near the Loch of Huesbreck, and may be the ruin of the 17th century farm of 'Heughe' (Ballantyne, 2016, no.1526, p.578), in the absence of a firm association

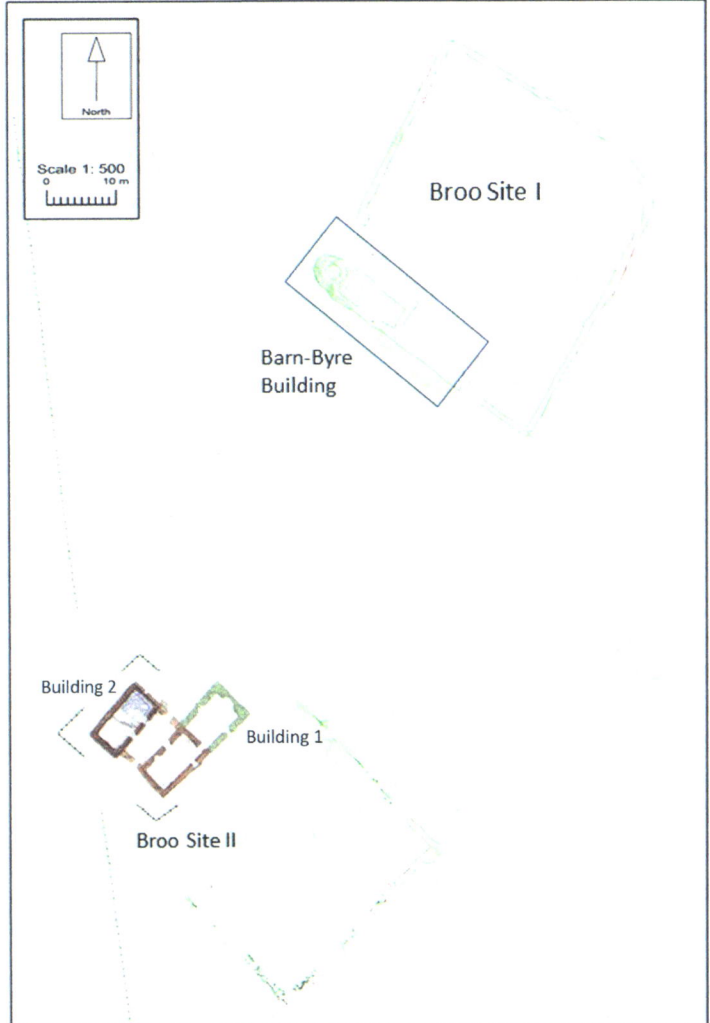

Figure 1. The Broo Site Complex, Dunrossness, Shetland Islands.
Map produced by Robert M. Friel and Zoe Outram

between the two we have labelled the site 'Broo Site Complex', as it consists of two large, stone-walled enclosures with building ruins at one corner of each enclosure (Figures 1&2). Test excavations of Broo Sites I and II in 2005 indicated that the building ruin in Site I was an agricultural structure with a corn-drying kiln, a bere processing barn, and possibly a cow-byre. Broo Site II clearly had a greater range of functions because it contained two buildings, one a dedicated dwelling house with an adjacent structure that appears to have had both human and animal housing within it (Bigelow et al., 2013). The stone buildings in both areas are very well-preserved because their walls were protected through burial in sand. The architecture and artefacts found in and around the buildings have provided key information about the settlement's inhabitants and the impact on their lives as their home was progressively buried in sand.

Interim findings

We have conducted a substantial amount of field, archival, and laboratory research on the Broo catastrophe to date and only selected highlights of the new information from these activities will be presented here. Several unrelated factors have centred these interim findings in the later history of the township and the later stages of its destruction. Firstly, more documentary records and historical information about Broo survive from the later 17th century than from earlier periods. Secondly, archaeological excavation normally proceeds from the uppermost and latest surface deposits down through progressively earlier strata, and since the Broo Site Complex was covered with up to two metres of sand during its catastrophic burial, we have not yet been able to investigate most of its earlier archaeological contexts. Finally, the Broo Site Complex farm was located 1.5 kilometres downwind from the Quendale beach sand source, and so it naturally would have been affected in the later stages of any sand drift event than farms closer to the beach.

The Quendale and Broo environment

The extensive dune field that was formed by the last sand mobilisation spans what was two townships, Broo and Quendale. In addition, sand was blown farther inland to the east and most likely mixed there with sand similarly transported northwards from the beach at West Voe. Unfortunately, a tragic medical emergency during the year of our most intensive geological survey activities prevented a full analysis of this very large sand landscape, and at this point detailed knowledge of the sand deposition and erosion history is restricted to areas near the Quendale beach and the vicinity of the Broo Site Complex. From dating of relict, marginal dunes on the side of Quendale Bay, it is clear that sand was being deposited by the wind there as early as the Neolithic period, c.2380 B.C. (Kinnaird *et al.*, 2013, SUTL2526), in former shoreline areas that have since been eroded by the sea 450 metres back to today's 10 metre high foredune (Kelley *et al.*, 2018, p.1299). Sand movements at this early period did not extend inland to the area of the Broo Site Complex. Similar evidence of Neolithic period sand blow episodes has been found at Shetland's earliest known human settlement site at West Voe (Gillmore and Melton, 2011), and at many sites in Orkney (Gal, 2019; Sommerville, *et al.*, 2003). OSL dates record that additional drift episodes occurred near today's shore after the Neolithic sand movements; however, the sand mobilisation of the 17th century appears to have been by far the largest and most extensive of these events, resulting in the loss of a significant area of arable land in the Quendale township, as well as the almost total destruction of the Broo township (Kinnaird *et al.*, 2014).

An important methodological finding from this geological research was the extent to which OSL dating of transgressive sand deposits may be strongly shaped by complex cycles of aeolian deposition, subsequent remobilisation, and redeposition in changing patterns over sand landscapes. The resulting selective preservation or destruction of early deposits is graphically reflected by OSL samples taken from sand directly overlying the original soil land surfaces from both areas outside the Broo Site II enclosure and inside the enclosure from a context that was protected from prevailing winds by the walls of structures: the lowest 'first sand' sample from the exposed, unenclosed deposit was dated to A.D. 1810±25 years (Kinnaird et al., 2013, SUTL2519), while there were records of sand being deposited in the mid-1300s and mid-1500s A.D, as well as the late 17th and early 18th centuries 'terminal' and catastrophic event from contexts that were sheltered from the prevailing winds (Kinnaird et al., 2013, A.D. 1370±40 SUTL2608, A.D. 1550±60 SUTL2606, 1710±60 SUTL2606; Kelley, et al., 2018, p.1290). The resulting complexity of OSL and other chronometric dating frameworks for aeolian landscape formation has also been observed elsewhere in archaeological studies (Carter and Fraser, 1996; Gal, 2019), and it undoubtedly reflects the fragility of open, unvegetated dune fields and sand sheets in places with inherently windy environments. These dynamic cycles of deposition and erosion underline the need for careful design of OSL sampling strategies and caution in interpreting dating series, particularly when attempts are made to correlate sand deposition sequences with historical records of storms.

The Broo Site Complex: early phase occupation

Although the development of Broo Site II in its later phases seems relatively clear at this point, our knowledge of its nature before the late 17th century is still incomplete. At this point it appears that, by the mid-17th century, the site consisted of two stone-walled buildings roughly 7 x 3.8 metres in interior dimensions, located side by side and separated by a formal passageway or linear corridor (Figure 2). Building 1, to the southwest, was the primary dwelling and it had a hearth built against the southwest gable wall. A simple hearth built against a gable wall was also found in Structure 26, a small 17th century dwelling at the Old Scatness Broch site (Melton et al., 2019, pp.18-20), and the form also appears in another Broo Site II context, so it could have been a common feature in Shetland houses of the post-medieval period, as well as in the 19th century (Tait, 2012, p.250).

The earlier phases of the Broo Site II house interior have not been completely excavated (Figure 2, Building 1, southwest room), and other contemporary internal features are not fully known at this point. However, the excellent preservation of the walls reveals that there were doorways in both long walls, one opening into the passageway between the two buildings, and one opening into the enclosed yard. The early house also had two windows, one in each long wall. If the building's interior was subdivided, it must have been achieved through building a timber partition which has left no trace visible at this stage of the excavation.

Building 2, located next to and parallel with the dwelling in Phase 1, appears to have been divided into two activity areas during its somewhat complex life. The northeast end was most likely an animal stable, as its floor was neatly paved with flagstones, one of which had a hole bored through it containing the remains of an iron bolt *in situ*: it may have been a tethering point for a large animal such as a cow or pony. This room also had a small

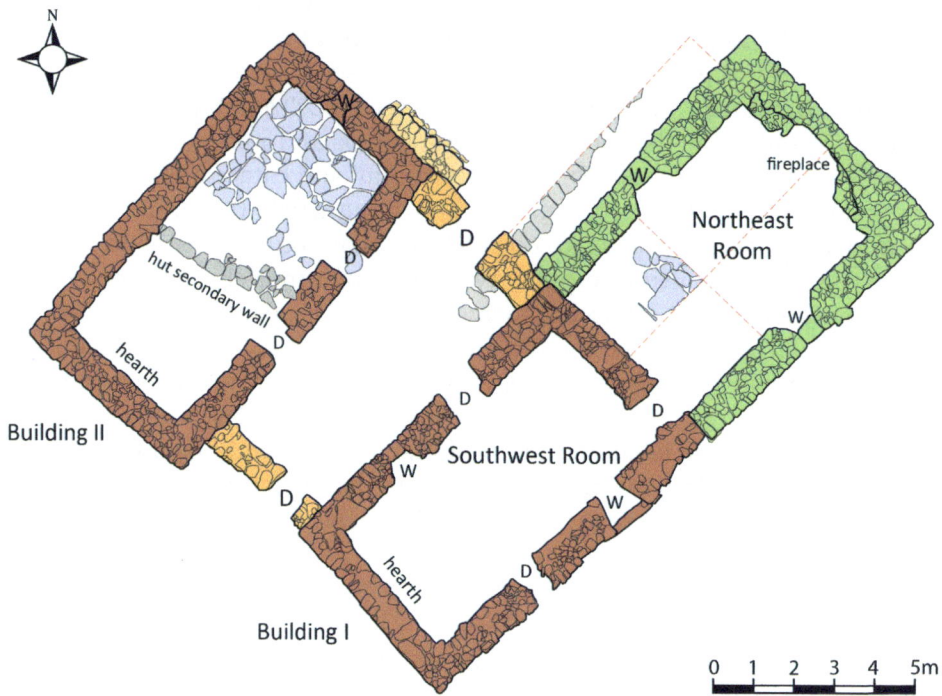

Figure 2. Broo Site II Building Plans. Building Phases: Early – Brown; Intermediate – Yellow; Late – Green. W = windows, D = doorways.   Plan by Robert M. Friel and Zoe Outram

window opening in the northeast gable wall that still had a preserved iron hinge hanger embedded in the wall stonework to support a casement window or wooden shutter.

The southwestern half of Building 2 appears to have been a human habitation or heavily used work area during the life of the structure. As in the dwelling, a hearth was built against the centre of the southwest gable wall. It was equipped with a small hearthstone on the floor and ash from the hearth had been spread throughout the room to a depth of 30+ cm and packed to form a smooth floor. Both the extensive accumulation of ash and the highly heat-damaged condition of the hearthstone suggest that this small room was used frequently. Soil samples from a formally built, small stone enclosure in a corner of the room next to the hearth revealed that it was used a nook for the storage of peats, another sign of intensive use. There were no other features in the room to suggest a specialized use as a defined activity area.

Although it is possible that some later Shetland crofthouse ruins incorporate parts of 17th century farm structures, these two buildings, which have walls standing over two metres high in most places, are likely to be the only well-preserved simple farm structures of that period in the islands, and our research has shown that no part of them post-dates the 1720s at the latest. Although there are better preserved 17th century buildings in Shetland, they were all laird's houses or special-purpose structures for use by the government or merchants (Finnie, 1990; Finnie, 1996; Strachan, 2008). At least for southern Shetland, the Broo Site Complex thus plays an important role in bridging our knowledge of the now relatively well-known vernacular farm architecture of the medieval Late Norse period and the 18th-19th centuries (Tait, 2012).

Broo Site I, located just 60 metres to the north of Broo Site II, has been extensively test excavated but not fully uncovered. Like Broo Site II it consists of a stone-walled yard enclosure, with the wall standing around 140 centimetres high in some locations. A structure approximately 18 x 5 metres in external dimensions stands at its southwest corner, and from the start of our research it was clear that the building was an agricultural structure, as a well-preserved circular corn-drying kiln forms its southwest gable wall. This kiln is most likely the earliest known example of its well-known type, which is restricted to the southernmost part of Mainland and Fair Isle, and may have spread to Shetland from Orkney (Fenton, 1978, pp.380-384; Tait, 2012, pp.387-394).

Surface indications in the larger structure's interior indicate that it was divided into two rooms by a stone-built partition. The room ending in the corn-drying kiln had a very smooth, packed clay floor and two opposed doorways in the building's long walls: it almost certainly was a grain processing area where bere was threshed and winnowed when poor weather prevented these activities, which required dry working conditions, from being performed outdoors.

The other end of the building was the only part of the overall archaeological site complex that was extensively disturbed by later human activities, as much of its long walls and gable were salvaged to build a *krogabøl* or sheep storm shelter on the south wall of the site's enclosure in the early 20th century (Tait, 2012, p.335). However, given the room's spatial relationship to the corn barn, the absence of a drain in the Broo Site II Building 1 stable room, and the lack of an alternative location on the site for housing a group of large farm animals, it is very likely that the easternmost room was a cow-byre.

An extensive soil coring survey in the interior of the Broo Site I enclosure did not reveal evidence of whether it was used as an area for storing bere before processing, as a seasonal livestock penning area, or for both purposes. Much of the enclosure's interior was on a slope that faced the prevailing southwest winds, and it is possible that its pre-sand deposition soils were deflated before the 17th century sand movements took place.

The Broo Site Complex: later phases occupation

The later phases of occupation of the Broo Site Complex settlement were marked by changes that seem in many cases likely related to the onset and progress of the sand invasion over the township and around the settlement site. Although architectural and possible land use changes discussed below may testify to a series of gross, strategic decisions that were made to counter physical losses in the landscape, evidence of changing consumption of material culture hints at less obvious and expected responses to the growing crisis. Artefacts recovered through archaeological excavations may reflect many aspects of the lives of their owners: e.g. their daily and seasonal activities; their ability to make, barter for and purchase goods; their social interactions, transactions and attempts to identify themselves as members of religious and ethnic groups and economic classes; their contacts with other communities, regions and countries; and, when people leave their settlements, their decisions about what is important to take and what can be abandoned (Schiffer, 1996). The locations in which artefacts are found may also reveal much about how different areas of a settlement were used over time, and changes in the organization of those activities. The finds recovered from the Broo Site Complex thus far reflect some common economic and consumption patterns known from existing historical and archaeological information on Shetland's 17th century lifeways. However, certain categories of finds, their conditions and final resting spots in the settlement, give us detailed, and in some cases surprising, information on how a family or families responded to an existential threat to their livelihoods in the final phases of the farm's life.

When we combine information from selected types of artefacts recovered from the house in Broo Site II with architectural features of its late phase form, it strongly suggests that a wealthy family moved to the farm, took over the existing tenant farmhouse and modified it to better represent their higher status. Although there are considerable methodological risks in making firm associations between historically known individuals and archaeological sites of settlements where even their place-names have been lost over time, in reviewing the available chronological and historical evidence it is quite likely that the northeast room of the Broo Site II house was added by the family of Charles Sinclair, the laird of Broo, sometime between the 1670s, when the sand catastrophe may have started (Smith 1984, p.41), and the 1690s to 1700, when it reached its climax (Grant, 1893, p.246). Supporting evidence for this interpretation consists of what had to have been expensive goods abandoned in the house's northeast room, especially three artefacts made from elephant ivory, including a complete, double-side, hair comb that was left lying on the room's flagstone floor when the house was abandoned. Although there is as yet no conclusive proof that the Sinclairs were involved in this transition in the new occupation of the farm (and the settlement's location may indicate that it was always the Sinclair home farm (Smith, pers. comm. 2011), it is quite possible that the Broo proprietors moved to the inland tenant settlement after their own home farm, located closer to the shore or lower in the Quendale valley (-dale, from Shetland Norn *dal,* valley (Jakobsen, 1985, p.95), had been affected by the sand.

In addition to the artefactual evidence of a change in occupants, there was an expansion in the scale of the Broo Site Complex Site II early phase house from containing an interior floorspace of approximately 26m^2, to its Phase III size of roughly 54m^2, through the addition of the northeast room (Bigelow *et al.*, 2013). Along with more than doubling the size of the house, the northeast room

Figure 3. Aerial view of the Broo Site II Complex facing southwest, with Quendale Beach in the background. *Drone photo: Robert M. Friel, Take the High Point*

also introduced architectural features that strongly diverge from those of the earlier buildings. For example, the new room's dominant feature was a large, chimneyed or canopied (Tait, 2012, p.252) fireplace in the northeast gable wall that was approximately 2 metres wide. Constructing this large hearth must have been challenging, as both the early and later phase walls of all the Broo Site Complex buildings were of double-faced construction with rubble cores bonded together lightly with clay, not with lime mortar as found in surviving, larger and more elaborate buildings of the time. Construction of the fireplace wall was additionally complicated and weakened by the placement of two storage *gliggs*, aumbries, or storage alcoves (Tait, 2012, pp.374-375) flanking the fireplace opening. Tait's 2012 study discusses the multiple applications of wall gliggs in vernacular dwellings, barns and byres of post-medieval Shetland, but the close proximity of one or two in a wall close to a fireplace opening may have been related to some specialized use in specifically elite structures of the 16th-17th centuries, as there were two gliggs built into the opposing inner cheeks of the largest 'ceremonial' fireplace in the Scalloway Castle hall, probably the most important, formally defined political space of its time in early 17th century Shetland, and one gligg directly adjacent to and one in an inner cheek wall of the hall fireplace in the contemporary Muness Castle. These storage niches are also present in walls flanking various fireplaces in the 17th century Earl's Palace and 16th century Bishop's Palace in Kirkwall, Orkney.

The chimney breast wall of the fireplace, if it had one, is not preserved, and it is likely it or a smoke-directing canopy was supported by a stout crossbeam, as no large lintel stone or fragments of a possible lintel were found in the considerable wall rubble that fell into the room in front of the fireplace.

The northeast room had two windows, one in each long wall, that were wider than window openings in the other Broo Site II contexts. A subtle but striking similarity in the construction of the room's fireplace and the window openings was the careful, almost artisanal, laying up of wall stones to produce smooth, shallow and curved interior wall faces for the hearth's firebox and the wall surfaces below the window openings where the walls were indented, perhaps to allow people to stand in the windows (see Tait, 2012, Fig. 3/74 'No-cill' window openings). That the large windows were glazed was demonstrated by the find of a complete but fragmented rectangular pane of glass below the southeast window opening (Figure 4). In general, a significant number of window glass fragments were recovered from around the Broo Site II dwelling.

The initial impression given by the Phase III northeast room, with its large fireplace, unusual stone-laying methods, relatively large glassed windows, and expensive, imported artefacts is that it may have served the socioeconomic functions of a hall in a newly high-status house. However, the room's relatively small size and its clay-bonded walls suggest its builders were a formerly wealthy family who could no longer afford to construct a more suitable, larger, *haa*-type residence with mortared stone walls (Finnie, 1996; see also Strachan, 2008). It is important to remember, though, that the room has not been fully excavated and that this interpretation should be considered preliminary.

It is very likely that, at some point in the late 1690s or early 1700s, sand began to cover the landscape around the farm and the buildings were abandoned. The barn and byre structure in Broo Site I contained stratigraphic evidence which suggests that it remained roofed for an unknown period of time while sand accumulated around its exterior, before the roof was removed or collapsed and the building was inundated with sand (Bigelow et al., 2013). The Broo Site II house sand fill stratigraphy suggests that its roof may have been removed early in the catastrophe and the house stood as a slowly decaying ruin until it was completely overwhelmed by a large sand deposition event that capped the entire settlement site in the first half of the 18th century. The find of a corner fragment of a roof slate indicates that the house may have had a slate roof, another indicator of elite status in its last occupation phase (Bigelow, 2011, p.171).

The Broo Site Complex: last phase occupation

The multi-purpose Building 2 across from the Broo Site 2 house was most likely the last occupied space on the farm. Like the house, it was abandoned and its ruin was allowed to fill with sand, but after an unknown period of time the accumulated sand in the southwest end of the ruin was excavated down to the former packed peat ash floor. A transverse, single-faced revetment wall incorporating large orthostat stones was then built against the remaining sand fill, most likely with stones robbed from the north wall of the adjacent

Figure 4. Fragmented 17th century window pane found in the destruction layer of the Northeast Room, Building 1, Broo Site II. The colors in the glass are from decay.   *Photo: G.F. Bigelow*

Figure 5. Oblique view of the Late Phase Hut, Building 2, Broo Site II during the 2011 excavation. The secondary transverse wall with orthostat construction is visible on the upper left (the backing sandfill was removed earlier).   *Photo: G.F. Bigelow*

dwelling ruin, and a resulting 4 x 4 metre hut was roofed, protecting its interior from further sand deposition.

Whoever lived and/or worked in this small, marginal space burned peat in the room's original wall hearth and added more ash to its packed floor (Figure 5). There was no obvious changing distribution of finds or environmental evidence to differentiate this final use of the room from its earlier functions, when it was part of a full-fledged farming settlement. The adaptive decision to reuse a structural space equipped with a hearth and well-made floor may suggest that these secondary occupants were acquainted with the building and the salvaged room from before its first abandonment.

During the time when the hut was occupied, sand deposition continued over the ruined settlement and the landscape rose upward around the ruins, the hut and inside the large enclosures. Sand stratigraphy located between the hut and the former dwelling reveals that the last occupants of the hut made attempts to clear the passageway, which continued as a foot traffic route for a while. However, the area nevertheless slowly filled with sand and, in some locations, light midden debris, until the hut's occupants had to insert a few makeshift stone steps in the rising sand to assist them in climbing out of the hut and onto what must have looked like a landscape of disaster. The general stratigraphy of sand over the site indicates that, during this time, multiple cycles of active deposition were interrupted by periods of stability when vegetation temporarily grew on the site, allowing humus to form in the sand. Even during active sand deposition events, the continued presence of human activities was represented by light distributions of peat ash and occasional midden bones and artefacts within the otherwise sterile accumulating sand (Saunders and Simpson, 2012). After the sand reached the eaves of the hut structure it was abandoned and then, along with the rest of the site, its ruin was capped by pure sand, with no anthropogenic content indicating continued settlement.

A petition to declare the great majority of Broo township lands worthless for taxation purposes was submitted in 1706 (Shetland Archives, D24/108/23) and it is likely that the Broo Site Complex settlement was abandoned by its Sinclair proprietors sometime between the later 1690s and that date. However, coins dating to 1702, 1711 and 1716 were recovered from sand overburden near the house, from a stratum very likely contemporary with the occupation of the hut (Murray, 2020). In addition, terminal phase artefacts include clay pipe bowl fragments and pipe stem bore diameter evidence that reinforce the idea that the hut's occupation could have extended into the second decade of the 18th century. Finally, OSL dates for the beginning and end of the period of cyclical sand depositions and vegetation growth episodes (which may have been seasonal) are A.D. 1720±15 SUTL2576 and 1780±35 SUTL2577 (Kinnaird et al., 2014, p.25): given what we have learned about deflation and redeposition cycling on open sand landscapes, taken together with OSL information from other areas of the site, the earlier date most likely reflects a bias towards recording later phases of sand deposition, rather than the actual onset, especially since the sample location was in a site context that would have had a moderate to strong exposure to prevailing winds. Similarly, the date for the end of vegetation cycles represents sand that accumulated on a dense paleosol that would have been resistant to deflation, and it is extremely likely that possibly multiple deflation events removed earlier deposits on that surface until, around 1780, sand deposition was so rapid, extensive and deep that no further episodes of deflation exposed the much earlier soil horizon. This information all suggests that the Broo Site Complex settlement had a relatively prolonged period of destruction and developed a secondary use or uses after the majority of its township was legally declared a wasteland. At this interim stage of the project, it seems likely that, except for a narrow strip of land on its northern border unaffected by the last mobilisation, the definitive abandonment of the core of Broo occurred within a few years of 1720.

Remaining questions

The investigation of the Broo catastrophe will continue, as there are many important aspects of the story that are still unknown. Some of the resulting questions may remain unanswered because key forms of information may simply have not been preserved. However, there is a clear need to complete further fieldwork and laboratory analyses, in particular to recover relevant environmental and archaeological data that relate to the following unresolved issues.

The Broo Site Complex early history

At present, the end of the Broo Site Complex settlement occupation has been well-dated from documentary, archaeological and geological evidence. However, the beginnings of the settlement and the construction of its buildings are still very poorly understood. At the time of writing, the earliest well-dated pottery that has been recovered is a fragment of a stoneware Bartmann jug very similar to one from the Dutch East India ship *Kennemerland* that foundered off Out Skerries in 1664 (Martin and Martin, 2018), but such objects may have stayed in use for extended periods. However, test pits excavated on the lee side of prevailing winds behind Site II, Buildings 1 and 2, yielded OSL dates for periods of blowing sand dating to the 14th and mid-16th centuries (Kinnaird *et al.*, 2014). It is likely that these sand layers would not have been preserved in the absence of the protective architecture at those earlier periods, but we currently lack artefactual evidence of such an early occupation of the site. This contradictory evidence for the first occupation of the site should be resolved through further excavation of the Site II building contexts and the Site 1 corn barn and byre structure.

Causes of the catastrophe

A primary goal of the project was to determine whether the sand drift that destroyed the 17th century Broo township was triggered by Little Ice Age storm activity, as specified by H.H. Lamb's model that linked sand movements to storm effects on coastlines during periods of climatic cooling (Lamb, 1977, p.129). Although two previous publications of Broo project data have either implicitly (Bampton *et al.*, 2017) or explicitly (Bampton *et al.*, 2018) attributed the onset of catastrophic sand movements at Broo to a synergistic interaction of Little Ice Age storm activity with anthropogenic factors, at this stage of the project *there has been no clear geological or documentary evidence recovered to suggest impacts made by storms on the Quendale beach shoreline or its sandy hinterlands were a primary cause of the catastrophe.*

There is an array of other potential factors that may have acted singly or in combination to increase the vulnerability of Broo sandy coastal areas to deflation and transport inland. These factors include intensifications of cultivation and/or grazing activities on sandy areas of the township's landscape; human harvesting of plants for craft purposes, fodder or fuel; or the burrowing and grazing of rabbits that were introduced to Shetland as early as the 16th century (Smith, 1984, p.20; Bigelow *et al.*, 2005; Bigelow *et al.*, 2007; Kelley *et al.*, 2018). In addition, discussions with local residents of modern occurrences of sand movements in the vicinity of the Quendale links suggest that weather-related levels of soil moisture seem critical to the mobilisation of sand by the wind (SMCHG, 2008-2019).

Results from recent advances in coastal geological research methodologies have also underlined the importance of importance of vegetation in stabilising sandy shoreline coastal strips against aeolian transport, and in allowing transgressive mobilisations to occur when disturbed (Jackson *et al.*, 2019a; Jackson *et al.*, 2019b). Thus, to better define what caused one of the most valuable properties in 16th and 17th century Shetland to be overrun and ruined by blowing sand, further geological analysis of the bathymetry and wave environment of Quendale Bay, and the history of the Quendale beach foredune, should be conducted. In addition, further archaeological and soil micromorphological surveys should be expanded to seek evidence for changes in land use and vegetation in the period prior to the later 17th century. Evidence collected through these activities may yet indicate that storms triggered geological processes that led to the 17th century sand transgression. However, it is also possible that archaeological and soils development evidence will suggest that Little Ice Age cooling instead contributed to the catastrophe indirectly by encouraging farmers to expand their use of the sandy coastal strip in response to diminished basic agricultural productivity, and in the process increased the land's vulnerability to aeolian erosion and transport (Kelley *et al.*, 2018, p.1299).

Responses to the catastrophe

Abandoning the farms and fields that were disappearing under the sand was the ultimate adaptation to a possibly unpreventable or irreversible catastrophe for the Broo inhabitants. To obtain a fuller understanding of earlier efforts to stem the growing crisis, we need to complete the excavation of the well-preserved Broo Site Complex and obtain artefact, zooarchaeological and archaeobotanical samples that represent a full time series of the farm's economic activities from before the 17th century sand movements began, to the final abandonment of the core of the township; *contra* Bampton *et al.* 2018, there are still many as yet undefined variables to be discovered, explored and assessed before the Broo catastrophe is understood in a meaningful way as a scenario of adaption or maladaption. For example, did the farmers change the balance of their livestock holdings between cattle and sheep, animals with different grazing needs and landscape impacts? Similarly, can we detect any changes in the production or purchase of cereals, a resource that was at one time so prominent in the area that two local place-names, *Quendale* and *Quindista*, contain the Old Norse 'kvern' and Shetland Norn 'kwern' words for 'mill' (Jakobsen, 1985, p.482), implying much local cereal production occurred there in earlier centuries (Smith, pers. comm., 2004).

The likely arrival of the township proprietors and their seizure of the Broo Site Complex tenant farm settlement may be seen as a kind of gross adaptation to the loss of their own home farm to the advancing sand. If their original farm could be located in a place that was affected by sand earlier than the Broo Site Complex farm, it would support this quite specific interpretation. Unfortunately, surveys have not located other conspicuous ruin sites within the sand transgression area, but one of the very few surviving, pre-catastrophe place-names marks a spot in the Quendale valley about 300 metres from the Broo Site Complex, at a significantly lower elevation. 'The Old House of Brow', which likely refers to the original 'Husabrow' farm (Ballantyne, 2016, no.1526, p.578), is distinguished today only by some scattered stones and low mounds. If test excavations there revealed the presence of costly 16th-17th century goods such as tin-glazed ceramic wares, or dressed building stones, that would support the identification of the site as the original Sinclair farm. It is unfortunate that there is virtually no chance of determining the steps taken by the Broo Site Complex farm's likely tenant occupants in response to the sand event, unless previously unknown historical records emerge that reverse the anonymity that so often accompanies past peoples of their status.

Conclusion

At the beginning of this research project, the best-known record of the destruction of the Broo township was an account by the Reverend George Low who visited Shetland in 1774:

> Here lay the estate of Brow, once worth 3000 Merks (near £22 Ster.) a year, now a mere wilderness; occasioned by the blowing of a small dusty kind of sand, which never can possibly rest, as the least puff of wind sets it all in motion, in the same manner as the drifting snows in winter. We still see the foundations of the farm houses, but the ridges, &c., have entirely disappeared. (Low, 1879, pp.184-185).

After much research we now know that the destruction Low witnessed very likely started over 60-70 years earlier and was complete by 1710-1720. The dunes and sand sheet had advanced from shore areas to over 1.5 kilometres inland by the late 1690s, smothering four farms in the process, the last one most likely what we now call the Broo Site Complex. The cause or causes of the mobilisation of the sand, after what may have been over a century of landscape stability, are still unclear. This aeolian event or process peaked during the 1690s, believed by many climate researchers to be have been one of the coldest decades in the last two millennia (Ljungqvist, 2010, p.345), and which contained notable storms and sand movements in other parts of Scotland (Dawson et al., 2011; Dawson et al., 2004). Thus, there was a close chronological association between the sand movements and a colder climate, as Lamb had proposed. However, at any period, Shetland and other places in northern Scotland would have experienced major oceanic storms because of the islands' general location within a a particularly dynamic zone of atmospheric and oceanic circulation. Yet major periods of aeolian deposition at Broo and in many other places were demonstrably sporadic and episodic events, a pattern which repeatedly allowed humans to utilise their coastal environments. In addition, a significant weakness in Lamb's theory, pioneering as it was, is that it proposed no critical thresholds of storm intensity or frequency that would have pushed beaches over structural tipping points at which existing topography and vegetation could no longer absorb the combined effects of surf and wind, and the sand would start to move inland in transformative quantities. It is possible that the colder temperatures of the deep Little Ice Age contributed to the Broo catastrophe and other related sand movements of the time, but the connections among those phenomena may have been through influences on economic production practices that enhanced the vulnerability of coastal landscapes to aeolian processes from so-called normal, as well as unusual, wind conditions. Although we have learned a great deal about the ecological and human dramas that unfolded around Quendale Bay over 300 years ago, more field and laboratory research on the area's rich environmental and archaeological records is needed to fully grasp the lessons the Broo story may hold for our own time of challenging environmental changes.

Acknowledgements

The work reported here was supported by the US National Science Foundation, Office of Polar Programs, Arctic Social Sciences Program, under grants no. 0444078 and no. 1026911. Additional support of various types was provided by Bates College, the University of Southern Maine, the University of Bradford, the Shetland Amenity Trust, the Shetland Museum & Archives, the South Mainland Community History Group, and the Dunrossness Primary School. The author would also like to thank the owner of the Broo Site Complex, John Leslie, and Les Smith, Andy Duffus and Allison Duncan for continued assistance with the project. Finally, the Broo project owes a large debt of gratitude to Brian Smith for invaluable information and inspiration.

Bibliography

Ballantyne, John H. and Smith, Brian (eds.) (1999) *Shetland Documents 1195-1579*. Lerwick: The Shetland Times Ltd.

Ballantyne, John H. (ed.) (2016) *Shetland Documents 1612-1637*. Lerwick: The Shetland Times Ltd.

Bampton, M., Kelley, A., Kelley, J., Jones, M. and Bigelow, G.F. (2017) 'Little Ice Age catastrophic storms and the destruction of a Shetland Island community', *Journal of Archaeological Science* 87, pp.17-29.

Bampton, M., Kelley, J. T. and Kelley, A. (2018) 'The hyperlocal geography of climate change impacts: long-term perspectiveson storm survivability from the Shetland Islands', *Historical Geography* 46, pp.129-150.

Bigelow, G.F. (2011) 'Broo; survey, paleoenvironmental research and excavation', *Discovery and Excavation in Scotland* New Series 12, pp.170-171.

Bigelow, G.F., Ferrante, S.M., Hall, S.T., Kimball, L.M., Proctor, R.E. and Remington, S.L. (2005) 'Researching catastrophic environmental changes on northern coastlines: a geoarchaeological case study from the Shetland Islands', *Arctic Anthropology* 42, pp.88-102.

Bigelow, G.F., Friel, R.M. and Outram, Z.M. (2013) 'Shetland Islands, Dunrossness. Broo, survey, paleoenvironmental research and excavation' *Discovery and Excavation in Scotland* New Series 14, pp.172-174.

Bigelow, G.F., Jones, M. and Retelle, M. (2007) 'The Little Ice Age, blowing sand and a lost township', *New Shetlander* 240, pp.6-12.

CANMORE (2023) *Links of Quendale*. Edinburgh: Historic Environment Scotland. Available at: https://canmore.org.uk/site/575/links-of-quendale (Accessed: 4 August 2023).

Carter, S. and Fraser, D. (1996) 'The Sands of Breckon, Yell, Shetland: archaeological survey and excavation in an area of eroding windblown sand', *Proceedings of the Society of Antiquaries of Scotland* 126, pp.271-301.

Cooper, J. and Sheets, P. (eds.) (2012) *Surviving Sudden Environmental Change: answers from archaeology*. Boulder, Colorado: University Press of Colorado.

Dawson, A. (2009) *So Foul and Fair a Day: a history of Scotland's weather and climate*. Edinburgh: Birlinn.

Dawson, S., Dawson, A.G. and Jordan, J.T. (2011) 'North Atlantic climate change and Late Holocene windstorm activitiy in the Outer Hebrides, Scotland', in D. Griffiths and P. Ashmore (eds.) *Aeolian Archaeology: the archaeology of sand landscapes in Scotland*. Edinburgh: Scottish Archaeological Internet Report.

Dawson, S., Smith, D.E., Jordan, J. and Dawson, A.G. (2004) 'Late Holocene coastal sand movements in the Outer Hebrides', *Marine Geology* 210, pp.281-306.

DSL (2023) *Dictionaries of the Scots Language*. Available at https://www.dsl.ac.uk/ (Accessed: 4 September 2023).

Fenton, A. (1978) *The Northern Isles: Orkney and Shetland*. Edinburgh: John Donald Publishers.

Finnie, M. (1990) *Shetland: an illustrated architectural guide*. Edinburgh: Mainstream Publications (Scotland).

Finnie, M. (1996) 'An introduction to the hall houses of Shetland', *Vernacular Building* 20, pp.39-52.

Gal, E.L. (2019) 'The archaeological potential of windblown sand and its impacts on prehistoric settlements and landscapes in the Orkney Islands, Scotland', PhD thesis, University of St. Andrews, St Andrews.

Gilbert, N.J. (2012) 'Crossing the sand barrier: a geomorphological study into the changing form of Quendale Links', BSc (Hons) Geography, University of Edinburgh, Edinburgh.

Gilbertson, D.D., Schwenninger, J.L., Kemp, R.A. and Rhodes, E.J. (1999) 'Sand-drift and soil formation along an exposed North Atlantic coastline: 14,000 years of diverse geomorphological climatic and human impacts', *Journal of Archaeological Science* 26, pp.439-469.

Gillmore, G.K. and Melton, N.D. (2011) 'Early Neolithic sands at West Voe, Shetland Islands: implications for human settlement', in L. Wilson (ed.) *Human Interactions with the Geosphere: the geoarchaeological perspective*. London: Geological Society.

Gordon, E.V. (1974) *An Introduction to Old Norse*. Oxford: Clarendon Press.

Grant, F.J. (1893) *The County Families of the Zetland Islands, Being Genealogies of Local Families Compiled from Public Records and Other Sources*. Lerwick: T. & J. Manson.

Grove, J.M. (2004) *Little Ice Ages: Ancient and Modern*, second edition, vol.2. London: Routledge.

Halsted, C.T. (2014) 'A physical and mineralogical analysis of Late Holocene sand deposits: a case study of Little Ice Age coastal change in the Shetland Islands UK', BSc (Hons), Bates College, Lewiston ME.

Hesp, P.A. (2013) 'Conceptual models of the evolution of transgressive dune field systems', *Geomorphology (Amsterdam, Netherlands)* 199, pp.138-149.

Irvine, J.W. (1987) *The Dunrossness Story*. Lerwick: A. Irvine Printing.

Jackson, D.W.T., Costas, S., González-Villanueva, R. and Cooper, A. (2019a). 'A global "greening" of coastal dunes: An integrated consequence of climate change?', *Global and planetary change* 182, no.103026.

Jackson, D.W.T., Costas, S. and Guisado-Pintado, E. (2019b) 'Large-scale transgressive coastal dune behaviour in Europe during the Little Ice Age', *Global and planetary change* 175, pp.82-91.

Jakobsen, J. (1985) *An Etymological Dictionary of the Norn Language in Shetland*. Lerwick: Shetland Fok Society.

Kelley, J.T., Kelley, A.R., Sorrell, L., Bigelow, G.F. and Bampton, M. (2018) 'Evidence for a former transgressive dune field: Shetland Islands, United Kingdom', *Journal of Coastal Research* 34, pp.1289-1302.

Kinnaird, T.C., Sanderson, D.C.W. and Bigelow, G.F. (2014) *Luminescence dating of wind-blown sands from archaeological sites in Shetland: early modern farmstead, Broo Peninsula, Norse settlement, Sandwick South, Unst*. East Kilbride: Scottish Universities Environmental Research Centre.

Kinnaird, T.C., Sanderson, D.C.W. and Simpson, I.A. (2013) *Luminescence investigations at Quendale (Broo Peninsula, Shetland)*. East Kilbride: Scottish Universities Environmental Research Centre.

Lamb, H.H. (1977) *Climate: past, present and future*, vol.2. London: Methuen.

Lamb, H.H. (1991) *Historic Storms of the North Sea, British Isles and Northwest Europe*. New York: Cambridge University Press.

Lindelof, J.A. (2012) 'Using sedimentary and geochemical proxies for Little Ice Age climate change reconstructions, South Mainland, Shetland', BSc (Hons), Bates College, Lewiston ME.

Lindelof, J.A., Johnson, B.J., Retelle, M.J. and Bigelow, G.F. (2012) 'Sedimentary and geochemical proxies for Little Ice Age paleoenvironmental reconstructions, South Mainland, Shetland', *47th Annual Meeting (18-20 March 2012) Geological Society of America, Northeastern Section*. Hartford, CT: Geological Society of America.

Ljungqvist, F.C. (2010) 'A new reconstruction of temperature variability in the extra-tropical northern hemisphere during the last two millenia', *Geografiska Annaler* 92, Series A, Physical Geography, pp.339-351.

Low, G. (1879) *A Tour Through the Islands of Orkney and Schetland: containing hints relative to their ancient modern and natural history collected in 1774*. Kirkwall: William Peace & son.

Martin, P. and Martin, C.J.M. (2018) *Record of work carried out on the finds from the wreck of the Kennermerland (1664), Out Skerries, Shetland: Data structure report for Historic Environment Scotland*. Edinburgh: Historic Environment Scotland.

Melton, N.D. (2004) 'Cod and ships: Scottish merchant activity in southern Shetland in the seventeenth century' in R.A. Housely and G. Coles (eds.) *Atlantic Connections and Adaptations: economies, environments and subsistence in lands bordering the North Atlantic*. Oxford: Oxbow Books.

Melton, N.D., Dockrill, S.J., Bond, J.M., Turner, V.E., Brown, L.D., Smith, B., Bashford, D.J., Cussans, J.E.M. and Nicholson, R.A. (2019) *Excavations at Old Scatness, Shetland, Volume 3: The Post-Medieval Township*. Lerwick: Shetland Heritage Publications.

Murray, W. (2020) 'Conservation report for finds from Broo, Shetland'. Edinburgh: The Scottish Conservation Studio.

Oehler, C. (2017) 'Broo Township' A Case Study in South Mainland Shetland History, 1550-1710'. BA Honours, Bates College, Lewiston ME.

Riddell, L. (2019) 'Shetland's German Trade – On the Verge of Colonialism?', *Northern Scotland* 10, pp.1-9.

Riede, F. and Jackson, R. (2020) 'Do Deep-Time Disasters Hold Lessons for Contemporary Understandings of Resilience and Vulnerability? The Case of the Laacher See Volcanic Eruption' in F. Riede and P. Sheets (eds.) *Going Forward by Looking Back: Archaeological Perspectives on Socio-Ecological Crisis, Response, and Collapse*, first edition. New York: Berghahn Books.

Ross, S. (1993) 'The Culbin Sands - A Mystery Unravelled' in W.D.H. Sellar (ed.) *Moray: Province and People*. Edinburgh: Scottish Society for Northern Studies.

Saunders, K. and Simpson, I.A. (2012) 'Environmental hazards and cultural adaptations: characterising sand blow events and human responses in the early modern township of Broo, Shetland', unpublished techical report, University of Stirling, Stirling.

SMCHG (2008-2019) South Mainland Community History Group oral history interviews.

Shetland Archives (1706) D24/108/23, Declaration by heritors and udallers of Dunrossness

Schiffer, M.B. (1996) *Formation Processes of the Archaeological Record*. Reno: University of Utah Press.

Smith, Brian (2019) 'Shetland and her German Merchants, c.1450-1710' in Natascha Mehler et al. (eds.) *German Trade in the North Atlantic c.1400-1700: Interdisciplinary perspectives*. Stavanger: Arkeologisk Museum.

Smith, Brian and Melton, N.D. (2019) 'The Historical Evidence' in N.D. Melton *et al., Excavations at Old Scatness, Shetland, Volume 3: The Post-Medieval Township*. Lerwick: Shetland Heritage Publications.

Smith, H.D. (1984) *Shetland Life and Trade 1550-1914*. Edinburgh: John Donald Publishers.

Sommerville, A.A., Hanson, J.D., Sanderson, D.C.W., Housley, R.A. (2003) 'Optically stimulated luminescence of large storm events in Northern Scotland', *Quaternary Science Review* 22, pp.10-13, 1085-1092.

Sorrell, L. (2013) 'Periodic episodes of aeolian sand deposition, Shetland, UK', MSc, University of Maine, Maine ME.

Strachan, S.R. (2008) 'The Laird's Houses of Scotland: from the Reformation to the Industrial Revolution, 1560-1770', PhD thesis, University of Edinburgh, Edinburgh.

Tait, I. (2012) *Shetland Vernacular Buildings 1600-1900*. Lerwick: The Shetland Times Ltd.

Van Bavel, B., Curtis, D.R., Dijkman, J., Hannaford, M., De Keyzer, M., Van Onacker, E. and Soens, T. (2020) *Disasters and History: The Vulnerability and Resilience of Past Societies*. Cambridge: Cambridge University Press.

Willis, D.P. (1986) *Sand and Silence: lost villages of the north*. Aberdeen: Centre for Scottish Studies.

11

The phonology of Shetland Norn – preaspiration and vowel length in Jakobsen's Etymological Dictionary

Remco Knooihuizen
(University of Groningen)

Introduction

Scandinavian Shetland is a theme that runs through the work of Brian Smith and many of the contributions to this *Festschrift*. While Shetland politically became Scottish in the events of 1468–1472 (Crawford, 1969, 1983), this of course did not mean that culture and identity followed course immediately. Trade connections between Shetland and Norway continued to thrive for some time until the mid-17th century (Smith, 1990) and the population only became more Scottish through substantial migration from the Scottish mainland in the 16th century.

Few aspects of Shetland's Scandinavian past tickle the imagination as much as its now-extinct language, Norn. Much of the language is shrouded in mystery. The few sources of any meaningful size were recorded after the language had already gone out of use as a medium of regular communication, so that we know little for sure about its phonology and syntax. Michael Barnes's (1998) book-length treatment of the language is a mere 50 pages long, over half of which is historical context. The rest consists of annotated source material, where the annotations often underline the uncertainty of our interpretations. The only area in which we know more about Shetland Norn is its lexicon, due to the many loanwords that have survived in especially older Shetland Scots. Melchers (1981, p.261) claimed that her informants knew exactly which dialect words were of Scandinavian origin, suggesting the importance of this cultural heritage for Shetland speakers.

At this point, it is important to note that Shetland's Scandinavian connection is an easy vehicle through which islanders can highlight an identity different from the mainland, and there is a danger of romanticising these elements in Shetland's language and culture (Millar, 2007, p.132). This is especially salient now that the use of Shetland dialect is rapidly declining among younger generations (Smith & Durham, 2011, 2012). As an example of such romanticisation, we can mention the etymology added to the placename sign for Lerwick: it comes from Old Norse *Leirvík* 'muddy bay'.[1] Similarly, the motto of the Shetland coat of arms, granted in 1975, is Old Norse *Með lögum skal land byggja* 'By law shall the land be built up'. There even is a fringe revivalist movement attempting to promote *Nynorn* 'New Norn', but given how little we know about Shetland Norn, this is nothing more than an Old Norse- and Faroese-inspired conlang. If it were ever to be successful, it would be invented tradition on a par with Up Helly Aa.

This paper focuses on what we do know about Shetland Norn. It aims to provide an overview of some details of Shetland Norn that have come to light over the past decade or so in a re-investigation of one of the chief sources of the language, Jakobsen's *Dictionary*. An analysis of two aspects of phonetic detail in the transcriptions in the *Dictionary*, preaspiration and vowel length, shows that these include a great deal of systematicity. These systematic patterns are consistent with what we find in other West Scandinavian languages, especially when we take into account the long-term and intensive language contact with Scots. Together, they add to our understanding of the phonology of Shetland Norn.

Shetland Norn and language reconstruction

The life and death of Shetland Norn

Shetland and Orkney were settled from Scandinavia around the year 800. The Scandinavian settlers brought with them their language, Old Norse, or as they called it, *norrœna* — hence the name for the Shetland and Orkney vernaculars, Norn. When exactly Norn developed into a language different from other West Scandinavian languages (Norwegian, Icelandic, and Faroese) is unclear. The few surviving documents contain some features that may indicate specific Shetland and/or Orkney developments, but it is uncertain what this should mean. It is not certain that these documents were written by Shetlanders or Orcadians, and even if they were, they most certainly remained within a Norway-centred writing tradition (Barnes, 1998, pp.11–16).

A key event the islands' history was their pledging by the Danish king in 1468 (Orkney) and 1469 (Shetland) to King James III of Scotland, as pawn for the agreed-upon dowry for his daughter Margaret of Denmark (Crawford, 1969, 1983). The islands had been incorporated into the Scottish administrative system by 1472 (Thomson, 1987, p.125). Such an administrative change need not have direct effects on the ground, but it appears that it did in Shetland: the first

---

[1] Note that the etymology provided is one in Old Norse, not in Shetland Norn. Perhaps the intention is to highlight a Scandinavian connection further back in time, or perhaps the reason is more pragmatic: we simply do not know for sure what the Shetland Norn form for 'Lerwick' was. Not many places in Shetland have an etymology added to the placename sign.

Scots-language document from Shetland is from 1525 (Barnes, 1991, p.447) and almost all Scandinavian-language documents since then appear to have been written in mainland Scandinavia (Smith, 1990, p.29).

Although some scholars have suggested that Scottish authorities prohibited the use of Norn as they did Scottish Gaelic (Wiggen, 2002, p.62; Jakobsen, 1957, p.20), there is no actual evidence to that effect (Donaldson, 1958, p.76; Smith, 1990, p.32). Rather, the demise of Norn appears to have been a direct effect of substantial migration to Shetland from the Scottish mainland in the 16th century. Donaldson (1983) has argued, based on personal name evidence, that approximately a third of the islands' population just after 1600 had Scots origins. That proportion alone may be enough to promote a language shift from Norn to Scots, but the same evidence also shows substantial intermarriage between people with Scottish and Scandinavian names, which further increased the demographic pressure on the language (Knooihuizen, 2008b).

When exactly Norn eventually died is a matter of dispute. Contemporary comments (see Stewart, 1964) are contradictory and imprecise, and may not be entirely reliable. Although some scholars see the language survive much longer (Rendboe, 1984), most believe the language to have died in the early 18th century (Barnes, 1984, p.355; Smith, 1996, p.33). The fact that a list of common Scandinavian words collected in 1774 was likely part of Shetland fishermen's taboo language suggests that by that time, the language must no longer have been used for regular communication (Knooihuizen, 2008a). This is usually what is seen as language death (Sasse, 1992).

But Shetland Norn did not simply disappear. Rather, at least by the late 19th century, many lexical traces of it remained in the Shetland Scots dialect that replaced it: Jakobsen collected more than 10,000 of them for his *Dictionary*. It is likely that Shetland Scots originated through intense dialect contact between the varieties of Scots spoken by immigrants to Shetland from the Scottish mainland (Millar, 2008). But another variety played a role in this new-dialect formation: the second-language variety of Scots spoken by those who had Shetland Norn as their first language. Historical and linguistic evidence support such a reading of how elements of Shetland Norn appeared in Shetland Scots (Knooihuizen, 2009): while some elements such as the vowel system are fairly clearly Scots, the influence of Shetland Norn can be seen in features such as *th*-stopping (pronouncing the fricatives /θ/ and /ð/ as stops /t/ and /d/, respectively) and *hw*-confusion (the merger of /hw/ and /kw/, so that, e.g., *what* can be pronounced as either /ʍɒt/ or /kwɒt/). Understanding how varieties in contact mix to form a new dialect (Trudgill, 2004) can perhaps help us reconstruct what these original varieties were like.

Linguistic sources for Shetland Norn

There are extremely few reliable linguistic sources for Shetland Norn from when it was still a living language. A few medieval documents survive, but even though these can be localised to Shetland, they fall under a Norwegian writing tradition (Barnes, 1998, pp.11–16). The first sizeable source dates from 1774, most likely after the language died, and consists of some fragments collected by Orkney minister, George Low (1879). These fragments include a version of the Lord's Prayer (Rendboe, 1989, 1990), the *Hildina Ballad* (Hægstad, 1900), and a list of thirty words with English translations (Rendboe, 1987; Knooihuizen, 2008a). These texts have given us a reasonable view of the structure of Shetland Norn in its latest stages, but as Low had no knowledge of Scandinavian languages or linguistics and his informant does not appear to have had a full grasp of the language, the material is difficult to assess and there is a clear risk of over-interpretation (as in, e.g., Rendboe, 1984, 1987).

Notwithstanding the work of Lindqvist (2015) on the basis of the medieval material, most of what we can tell about the lexicon and phonology of Shetland Norn comes from Jakob Jakobsen's *An Etymological Dictionary of the Norn language in Shetland* (Jakobsen, 1908–1921, 1928–1932). Jakobsen, a native speaker of Faroese and a trained phonologist with a background in Scandinavian linguistics, did the fieldwork on which the dictionary is based in 1893. This was at least well over a century after Shetland Norn language death, which raises a host of questions about the reliability of the material, but the sheer size of the corpus and the level of detail provided — Jakobsen provides precise phonetic transcriptions, localisations and etymologies — makes it the most important source for the historical study of the language.

Can Shetland Norn be reconstructed?

With so few sources of Shetland Norn surviving, and what survives being filtered through at least one century of Shetland Scots speech, attempting to analyse smaller details in the phonological system seems like an impossible endeavour. Of course the data may sometimes show clear positive evidence of a Scandinavian feature, but it is more likely that we need to assess what influence the Scots filter may have had on what we see. If the filter language is less complex than the filtered language – i.e. if Scots had fewer phonemic oppositions or a system with less complicated rules than Shetland Norn – we may not be able to identify the original Shetland Norn (cf. Lehiste, 1965).

Alternatively, what we may find could be a distortion in the filter: a pattern that is not quite what we would expect from Scots. In such cases, we can use our knowledge of the languages in contact and our theoretical knowledge of language contact to reconstruct what input may have resulted in the observed patterns. Older Scots is a fairly well-known quantity (Johnston, 1997a), and for all the mystery that surrounds the linguistic structure of Shetland Norn, we have extensive contemporary and historical descriptions of closely related languages, in particular Faroese (Thráinsson *et al.*, 2004; Lindqvist, 2003), to assist us in this comparative work on language reconstruction.

Norn phonology in Jakobsen's *Dictionary*

Although the data was collected up to two centuries after the death of the language, Jakobsen's *Dictionary* is by quite some distance the best source for an investigation of the phonology of Shetland Norn. His phonetic transcriptions of Norn words surviving in 1890s Shetland Scots dialect have been characterised as "phonetics run riot" (Stewart, 1964, p.172), or in other words, as being *too* precise, but as the case studies in this section will show, an investigation of patterns in the *Dictionary* transcriptions reveals a clear underlying sound system. With the caveat that our view is filtered through Shetland Scots, we may identify this sound system as the phonology of Shetland Norn.

Preaspiration

The first case study concerns *preaspiration*.[2] Preaspiration can be described as a period of voicelessness, an *h*-like sound, before a voiceless stop, as in Faroese *nátt* 'night' [nɔʰtː]. Another way of viewing this phenomenon is as the spreading of voicelessness from the stop to a preceding vowel. If the preceding sound is a nasal or a liquid, voicelessness may also spread there, resulting in, e.g., Faroese *gult* 'yellow (neut.)' [kʊl̥t]. Although both these phenomena fall under the umbrella term "preaspiration", they are more properly distinguished as "stop preaspiration" and "sonorant devoicing", respectively (Hansson, 2001, p.157).

Preaspiration is an areal feature in the North Atlantic. It occurs in Icelandic and Faroese (Helgason, 2002; Thráinsson *et al.*, 2004), in Scottish Gaelic (Clement, 1984; Oftedal, 1956), and to some extent also in Scottish Gaelic-influenced Hebridean English (Shuken, 1984, 1985). It appears never to have been a feature of Scots dialects, be it in the Older Scots period of the first large-scale Scottish migration to Shetland (Johnston, 1997a), or in the 20th century (Mather & Speitel, 1986; Johnston, 1997b). Recent phonetic investigations of Shetland speech do not show it even in older, conservative speakers (Scobbie, 2005, 2006; Sundkvist, 2007). From a contact-linguistic perspective, this suggests that any preaspiration that is found in Jakobsen's *Dictionary* transcriptions must have come from Shetland Norn, and any patterns in the occurrence of the feature are indicative of Shetland Norn phonology.

For the analysis, all transcriptions were collected of words from the H, I, and J sections of the *Dictionary* where preaspiration could be expected to occur based on the constraints on the feature in Scandinavian and Scottish Gaelic. This applied to just over 500 lemmas in this part of the *Dictionary*. Taking into account that there may be multiple phonetic transcriptions of a word, and that Jakobsen often added transcriptions for different regions within Shetland, the analysis is based on many more individual tokens than that. Each token was coded for the presence or absence of preaspiration, and for the relevant subtype of preaspiration.

An overview of the results is given in Table 1. What is immediately clear is that stop preaspiration is a very rare occurrence in the data. Only 11% of the tokens where stop preaspiration could occur were actually pronounced that way. On the other hand, sonorant devoicing is extremely common, as it was

---

2   A more in-depth discussion of this study appears in Knooihuizen (2013).

Table 1
Occurrence of stop preaspiration and sonorant devoicing in Shetland Norn, by region

	stop preasp.		son. devoicing	
Region	%	N	%	N
Central Mainland	0%	0	100%	2
Foula	9%	11	91%	44
Northern Mainland	0%	13	94%	36
Northern Isles	11%	159	90%	250
Northmavine	5%	42	94%	62
Southern Mainland	17%	41	98%	41
Westside	7%	14	95%	65
Total *(incl. no location)*	11%	349	92%	613

found in 92% of possible cases. Geographical variation was not statistically significant for either type of preaspiration.

If we generalise over these results, it is fair to say that the Shetland Norn as it was recorded in Jakobsen's *Dictionary* did not have stop preaspiration as a normative feature in its phonology, but that it did have sonorant devoicing. Of course there was variation, but also here we see clear patterns. The majority of occurrences of stop preaspiration involve the vowel [oɪ] followed by a [t] — stemming from Old Norse -*átt*- or -*ótt*- — and of the tokens that lacked sonorant devoicing, most contain an [n]. Sonorant devoicing is also uncommon when the sonorant and the triggering stop occur across a morpheme boundary in a compound word. As these are exceptions to a very strong pattern, and token counts are low, we may afford to see this variation as noise.

The occurrence of sonorant devoicing but not stop preaspiration in Shetland Norn is somewhat surprising, as Faroese, the language thought to be most similar to Norn, has both. On the other hand, the Shetland pattern is found in some dialects of Norwegian (Kristoffersen, 2000), so it is not unheard of even in a Scandinavian context. It is possible, however, to explain the Shetland pattern as a result of language contact between Scandinavian and Scots. In Scandinavian languages with preaspiration (e.g., Faroese), stop preaspiration is one of the cues involved in distinguishing meaning, while sonorant devoicing is simply a by-effect of having a sonorant followed by a voiceless stop. This means that speakers have a different awareness of the two types of preaspiration. When speakers learned Scots, a language without preaspiration, they were able to 'switch off' the stop preaspiration that they were aware of, but not the sonorant devoicing they were not aware of. Sonorant devoicing therefore continued to exist even after the language shift to Scots (Knooihuizen, 2013, p.66). Sonorant devoicing eventually also disappeared as a result of migration patterns and increased dialect contact in the late 19th century.

Vowel length

The second case study revolves around patterns of vowel length in Shetland Norn.[3] A well-known feature of Shetland Scots is that consonant and vowel duration are inversely correlated: a long vowel is typically followed by a consonant of shorter duration, and a short vowel by a consonant of longer duration. As this pattern also occurs in many Scandinavian varieties, it is often thought that it is a substrate remainder of Shetland Norn (van Leyden, 2004; Sundkvist & Gao, 2015). However, this claim has never been properly scrutinised.

In spite of the potentially Scandinavian-influenced production of vowel and consonant duration in modern Shetland Scots, the phonological system appears fairly unambiguously Scots. That is to say, whether a vowel is pronounced as long or short (and the following consonant, subsequently, as short or long) is determined by the Scottish Vowel Length Rule (SVLR; Aitken, 1981). This is a somewhat complicated system stemming from the 16th century (Aitken, 2002) in which lax vowels are always short, while tense vowels are short *unless* they are followed by a morpheme boundary, a voiced fricative /v ð z ʒ/, or /r/. The system as it appears in the Shetland data for the Linguistic Atlas of Scotland (Mather & Speitel, 1986) follows Aitken's generalisation with only few exceptions (Knooihuizen, 2009). Of course, this Scotland-wide survey did not include Shetland words of Norn origin, so it may not tell us anything about the vowel length system of Shetland Norn.

In Shetland Norn's ancestor language, Old Norse, vowel length was not constrained by any rules. Syllables could have a short vowel and a short consonant (as in *kyn* 'kin'), a long vowel and a short consonant (*kýr* 'cows'), a short vowel and a long consonant (*kyrr* 'quiet'), or a long vowel and a long consonant (*kýll* 'bag') (Árnason, 1980). This system underwent a radical language change, the "Great Quantity Shift", in most varieties of Scandinavian. After the shift, only two syllable types were allowed: with a long vowel and a short consonant or with a short vowel and a long consonant — the Shetland pattern that is seen as so typically Scandinavian. The other two syllable types changed mostly by altering their vowel length as appropriate; the weight of phonemic distinctions was now carried by vowel quality instead (Küspert, 1988). Importantly, however, Lindqvist (2003) dates the completion of the Great Quantity Shift in Faroese to around 1600. If the timing in Shetland Norn was anything similar, this would be after the transfer of the islands to Scotland, and concurrent with a large-scale immigration of Scots speakers from the mainland.

The vowel length system of Shetland Norn itself has never been surveyed in detail. Hægstad (1900, pp.72–73) sees "many exceptions", and Barnes (1991,

---

3 This section is based on ongoing work in collaboration with Dr Pavel Iosad of the University of Edinburgh. The discussion here presents only the larger patterns; an in-depth analysis is in preparation for publication in another venue.

p.437) laments that the inverse correlation of vowel and consonant duration in Shetland "never seems to have been observed by Jakobsen". The latter claim is true to the extent that Jakobsen's transcriptions in the *Dictionary* are only marked for vowel length, whereas the transcriptions of Faroese he made a few years earlier for Hammershaimb's *Færøsk Anthologi* (1891, pp.439–460) also mark length on consonants. Nevertheless, by investigating the Shetland Norn transcriptions at hand in combination with Old Norse etymologies and the constraints of the SVLR, it is in fact possible to uncover some of the systematicity of vowel length in Shetland Norn.

The data for our analysis consists of all transcriptions from the *Dictionary* lemmas starting with G and H, provided that Jakobsen offers a (putative) Old Norse etymology. This amounts to a total of over 1,500 tokens, which we coded for vowel quality and vowel length in Shetland Norn and Old Norse, following consonant in Shetland Norn and Old Norse (to investigate the effect of the SVLR), and syllable type in Old Norse. In order to ease interpretation, some of Jakobsen's idiosyncratic vowel transcriptions were collapsed into a single vowel, while maintaining long/short and tense/lax distinctions.

As a first check on the reliability of the transcriptions, we can see evidence in Jakobsen's transcriptions of some common West Scandinavian developments. Old Norse *á*, whether long or short, appears in the data as [o] or some other rounded vowel. This is parallel to what we find in continental Scandinavian languages (*å*, pronounced short [ɔ] or long [ɔː]) and Faroese (*á*, pronounced short [ɔ] or long [ɔaː]). Old Norse *ó* predominantly appears as short [ø] or long [uː]. The short development is nearly identical to what we find in Faroese; the long development in continental Scandinavian (e.g., *sol* 'sun' [suːl]). Finally, also in line with other Scandinavian languages, Old Norse *i* is often laxed and lowered when it turns up as a short vowel. These findings were recorded already by Hægstad (1900) and by Jakobsen (1928–1932) himself. That we find them so clearly in our data suggests that our sample and method are reliable, and moreover, that Jakobsen's transcriptions are systematic enough to attempt to analyse the historical development of vowel length in Shetland Norn.

A cross-tabulation of vowel length in Shetland Norn by syllable type in Old Norse is given in Table 2. If Shetland Norn were a well-behaved Scandinavian language undergoing the Great Quantity Shift, we would expect long vowels in syllable types A (through lengthening) and B (original), and short vowels in syllable types C (original) and D (through shortening). Even allowing for some exceptions, the distribution of vowel length in Shetland Norn is very different from this expectation. We find a much higher proportion of short vowels in syllable types A and B, and a much higher proportion of long vowels in syllable type D. The system of vowel length in Shetland Norn, therefore, was not a straightforward development from Old Norse.

An alternative scenario could be that Shetland Norn vocabulary was fully incorporated into Shetland Scots at the time of Jakobsen's fieldwork, so that his *Dictionary* transcriptions simply reflect a Scots vowel length system. In such a scenario, we would expect a vowel to be long only when it is tense *and* when it

Table 2

Occurrence of short and long vowels in Shetland Norn, by Old Norse syllable type

ON syllable type			short vowel		long vowel	
			%	N	%	N
A	short V, short C	e.g., *kyn*	68%	238	32%	112
B	long V, short C	e.g., *kýr*	47%	173	53%	199
C	short V, long C	e.g., *kyrr*	91%	647	9%	65
D	long V, long C	e.g., *kýll*	69%	125	31%	55
			73%	1183	27%	431

occurs before one of a specific set of consonants. As can be seen from Table 3, lax vowels are indeed (almost) always short. For tense vowels, phonological context matters, but only to some extent: the prediction based on the SVLR is borne out in just under two-thirds of cases. This means that the Shetland Norn vowel length system did not straightforwardly carry over from Scots, either.

Table 3

Occurrence of short and long vowels in Shetland Norn, by tenseness and SVLR context

Tenseness	SVLR context	short vowel		long vowel	
		%	N	%	N
lax	SVLR-long	99%	122	1%	1
	SVLR-short	98%	628	2%	12
tense	SVLR-long	35%	60	65%	110
	SVLR-short	62%	371	38%	229

The Shetland Norn vowel length system as it appears in Jakobsen's *Dictionary*, then, contains clear traces of both Scandinavian influence — Old Norse syllable type and the Great Quantity Shift – and Scottish influence – the effect of tenseness and SVLR context — but cannot be fully explained by either in isolation. It is likely, therefore, that both influences interact with each other. As an illustration, Table 4 gives the distribution of short and long vowels in Shetland Norn by Old Norse syllable type and SVLR context. (The table only shows the data for tense vowels, as lax vowels show negligible variation.) It is clear that the highest percentages of long vowels are found when both syllable type (A and B) and SLVR context (long) favour long vowels; the highest percentages of short vowels are found when both (C and D; short) favour short vowels.

Table 4

Occurrence of short and long vowels in Shetland Norn, by Old Norse syllable type and SVLR context; tense vowels only

ON syllable type		SVLR context	short vowel %	N	long vowel %	N
A	short V, short C	SVLR-long	31%	9	69%	20
		SVLR-short	50%	67	50%	68
B	long V, short C	SVLR-long	20%	18	80%	71
		SVLR-short	44%	92	56%	118
C	short V, long C	SVLR-long	63%	33	37%	19
		SVLR-short	87%	171	13%	26
D	long V, long C	SVLR-long	–	–	–	–
		SVLR-short	71%	41	29%	17

In ongoing work, we aim to chart the Shetland Norn vowel length system in more detail using more advanced statistical techniques that allow us to differentiate the influence of these factors in various combinations. For example, it is possible that SVLR context had a greater influence on vowel length in words of syllable type A, which lengthened in the Great Quantity Shift, than in words of syllable type B, which were already long before the Great Quantity Shift. It also allows us to investigate whether certain vowels developed in different ways from others, and to examine the effect of following consonant in more detail than the generic SVLR context has done in this paper.

Our working hypothesis is that the Shetland Norn vowel length system originated in a scenario of intensive language contact, potentially as early as the first large-scale migration wave from the Scottish mainland to Shetland in the late 16th century. This is a significant time, as both languages in contact were undergoing change themselves: remember that both the Scottish Vowel Length Rule and the Great Quantity Shift are dated to exactly this period. In such a situation with a lot of variation, the hypothesised outcome of contact is unclear (cf. Trudgill, 2004). It is remarkable, therefore, that such strong traces of both the Scottish and especially the Scandinavian system can be found in Jakobsen's transcriptions.

Conclusion

Taking together the results from these studies on preaspiration and vowel length in Shetland Norn, it is clear that the criticism of Jakobsen's *Dictionary* transcriptions as overly precise is unwarranted. In fact, they form a very clear signal of an underlying sound system: the distributions of preaspiration and vowel length pattern consistently by phonological context. These patterns are entirely in line with what we would expect from a cross-linguistic Scandinavian and/or Scots perspective. They also support a story of contact-induced language change, where from prototypical Scots and Scandinavian input we would expect an output not unlike what we find in the *Dictionary*.

Naturally it is exactly this language contact scenario that stands in the way of the most important question: are the patterns we find really representative of Shetland Norn phonology? It is unclear how much of what we find can be traced back to the Scots filter through which we are investigating Shetland Norn: ultimately, the speakers Jakobsen transcribed were first-language speakers of Shetland Scots, not Norn. Should we expect to find stop preaspiration in this data, given that Scots does not normally have preaspirated stops? And how significant is it that the strongest constraint on vowel length is whether the vowel is tense or lax — exactly the main constraint in our description of the Scottish Vowel Length Rule?

On the other hand, we have also identified patterns that cannot be straightforwardly traced back to Scots. Sonorant devoicing is a clear sign of transfer from a Scandinavian language, and it is safe to interpret this to mean that Shetland Norn had the feature as well. Similarly, the influence on vowel length of Old Norse syllable type suggests that the Great Quantity Shift also applied to Shetland Norn, perhaps even with the inverse correlation of vowel and consonant duration in present-day Shetland Scots as a direct remnant. This is evidence of Shetland Norn phonological features that could be unearthed despite the Scots filter.

Jakobsen's *Dictionary* thus constitutes an important language archive for the study of Shetland Norn. The enormous amount of phonetic detail contained within it may have kept earlier scholars from embarking on a structural analysis, although what Jakobsen himself managed to conclude on the basis of his data is exceptional. Over a century later, we have the computational power and statistical techniques available to dig deeper and to begin to chart the more complex parts of the structure of the language, but we can only do this because the material was preserved in the *Dictionary*. It will be exciting to see what the future holds for the history of Shetland Norn.

Bibliography

Aitken, A. J. (1981) 'The Scottish vowel-length rule', in Benskin, M. & Samuels, M. L. (eds.), *So meny people longages and tonges*. Edinburgh: Middle English Dialect Project, pp.131–157.

Aitken, A. J. (2002) *The Older Scots vowels: A history of the stressed vowels of Older Scots from the beginnings to the eighteenth century*. Glasgow: Scottish Text Society.

Árnason, K. (1980) *Quantity in historical phonology: Icelandic and related cases*. Cambridge: Cambridge University Press.

Barnes, M. P. (1984) 'Orkney and Shetland Norn', in P. Trudgill (ed.), *Language in the British Isles*. Cambridge: Cambridge University Press, pp.352–366.

Barnes, M. P. (1991) 'Reflections on the structure and demise of Orkney and Shetland Norn', in P.S. Ureland & G. Broderick (eds.), *Language contact in the British Isles: proceedings of the Eighth International Symposium on Language Contact in Europe, Douglas, Isle of Man, 1988*. Tübingen: Niemeyer, pp.429–460.

Barnes, M. P. (1998) *The Norn language of Orkney and Shetland.* Lerwick: The Shetland Times Ltd.

Clement, R. D. (1984) 'Gaelic', in P. Trudgill (ed.), *Language in the British Isles.* Cambridge: Cambridge University Press, pp.318–342.

Crawford, B. E. (1969) 'The pawning of Orkney and Shetland: a reconsideration of the events of 1460–9', *Scottish Historical Review* 48, pp.35–53.

Crawford, B. E. (1983) 'The pledging of the islands in 1469: the historical background', in D.J. Withrington (ed.), *Shetland and the outside world 1469–1969.* Oxford: Oxford University Press, pp.32–48.

Donaldson, G. (1958) *Shetland life under Earl Patrick.* Edinburgh: Oliver & Boyd.

Donaldson, G. (1983) 'The Scots settlement in Shetland', in D.J. Withrington (ed.), *Shetland and the outside world 1469–1969.* Oxford: Oxford University Press, pp.8–19.

Hægstad, M. (1900) *Hildinakvadet, med utgreiding um det norske maal paa Shetland i eldre tid.* Christiania: Dybwad.

Hammershaimb, V. U. (1891) *Færøsk Anthologi I: Tekst samt historisk og grammatisk indledning.* København: Møller.

Hansson, G. Ó. (2001) 'Remains of a submerged continent: preaspiration in the languages of Northwest Europe', in L.J. Brinton, L. J. (ed.), *Historical Linguistics 1999.* Amsterdam: Benjamins, pp.157–173.

Helgason, P. (2002) *Preaspiration in the Nordic languages: synchronic and diachronic aspects.* Ph.D. dissertation, Stockholms Universitet, Stockholm.

Jakobsen, J. (1908–1921) *Etymologisk ordbog over det norrøne sprog paa Shetland.* København: Prior.

Jakobsen, J. (1928–1932) *An Etymological Dictionary of the Norn language in Shetland.* London: Nutt.

Jakobsen, J. (1957) 'Nøkur orð um Hetlands søgu', *Varðin* 32, pp.18–27.

Johnston, P. (1997a) 'Older Scots phonology and its regional variation', in C. Jones (ed.), *The Edinburgh history of the Scots language.* Edinburgh: Edinburgh University Press, pp.47–111.

Johnston, P. (1997b) 'Regional variation', in C. Jones (ed.), *The Edinburgh history of the Scots language.* Edinburgh: Edinburgh University Press, pp.433–513.

Knooihuizen, R. (2008a) 'Fishing for words: the taboo language of Shetland fishermen and the dating of Norn language death', *Transactions of the Philological Society* 106, pp.100–113.

Knooihuizen, R. (2008b) 'Inter-ethnic marriage patterns in late sixteenth-century Shetland', *Local Population Studies* 80, pp.22–38.

Knooihuizen, R. (2009) 'Shetland Scots as a new dialect: Phonetic and phonological considerations', *English Language and Linguistics* 13, pp.483–501.

Knooihuizen, R. (2013) 'Preaspiration in Shetland Norn', *Journal of Language Contact* 6, pp.48–72.

Kristoffersen, G. (2000) *The phonology of Norwegian.* Oxford: Oxford University Press.

Küspert, K.-C. (1988) *Vokalsysteme im Westnordis- chen: Isländisch, Färöisch, westnorwegisch.* Tübingen: Niemeyer.

Lehiste, I. (1965) 'A poem in *Halbdeutsch* and some questions concerning substratum', *Word* 21, pp.55–69.

Lindqvist, C. (2003) 'Thesen zur Kausalität und Chronologie einiger färöischer Lautgesetze', *Arkiv för nordisk filologi* 118, pp.89–178.

Lindqvist, C. (2015) *Norn im keltischen Kontext.* Amsterdam: Benjamins.

Low, G. (1879) *A tour through the islands of Orkney and Schetland containing hints relative to their ancient, modern and natural history, collected in 1774.* Kirkwall: Peace.

Mather, J. Y. & Speitel, H. H. (eds.) (1986) *The Linguistic Atlas of Scotland. Volume III: Phonology.* London: Croom Helm.

Melchers, G. (1981) 'The Norn element in Shetland today: a case of "never-accepted" language death', in E. Ejerhed & I. Henrysson (eds.), *Tvåspråkighet.* Umeå: n.p., pp254–261.

Millar, R. M. (2007) *Northern and Insular Scots.* Edinburgh: Edinburgh University Press.

Millar, R. M. (2008) 'The origins and development of Shetland dialect in light of dialect contact theories', *English World-Wide* 29, pp.237–267.

Oftedal, M. (1956) *The Gaelic of Leurbost, Isle of Lewis.* Oslo: Aschehoug.

Rendboe, L. (1984) 'How "worn-out" or "corrupted" was Shetland Norn in its final stages?', *NOWELE* 3, pp.53–88.

Rendboe, L. (1987) *Det gamle shetlandske sprog*. Odense: Odense Universitetsforlag.

Rendboe, L. (1989) 'The Lord's Prayer in Orkney and Shetland Norn (1)', *NOWELE* 14, pp.77–112.

Rendboe, L. (1990) 'The Lord's Prayer in Orkney and Shetland Norn (2)', *NOWELE* 15, pp.49–111.

Sasse, H.-J. (1992) 'Theory of language death', in M. Brenzinger (ed.), *Language death: Factual and theoretical explorations with special reference to East Africa*. Berlin, New York: Mouton de Gruyter, pp.7–30.

Scobbie, J. M. (2005) 'Interspeaker variation among Shetland Islanders as the long term outcome of dialectally varied input: speech production evidence for fine-grained linguistic plasticity', *QMU Speech Science Research Centre Working Paper* 2.

Scobbie, J. M. (2006) 'Flexibility in the face of incompatible English VOT systems', in L. Goldstein, D.H. Whalen & C.T. Best (eds.), *Laboratory Phonology 8*. Berlin: Mouton de Gruyter, pp.367–392.

Shuken, C. R. (1984) 'Highland and Island English', in P. Trudgill (ed.), *Language in the British Isles*. Cambridge: Cambridge University Press, pp.152–166.

Shuken, C. R. (1985) 'Variation in Hebridean English', in M. Görlach (ed.), *Focus on Scotland*. Amsterdam: Benjamins, pp.145–158.

Smith, B. (1990) 'Shetland, Scandinavia, Scotland, 1300–1700: the changing nature of contact', in G.G. Simpson (ed.), *Scotland and Scandinavia 800–1800*. Edinburgh: Donald, pp.25–37.

Smith, B. (1996) 'The development of the spoken and written Shetland dialect: a historian's view', in D.J. Waugh (ed.), *Shetland's Northern links: language & history*. Edinburgh: Scottish Society for Northern Studies, pp.30–43.

Smith, J. & Durham, M. (2011) 'A tipping point in dialect obsolescence? Change across the generations in Lerwick, Shetland', *Journal of Sociolinguistics* 15, pp.197–225.

Smith, J. & Durham, M. (2012) 'Bidialectism or dialect death? Explaining generational change in the Shetland Islands, Scotland', *American Speech* 87, pp.57–88.

Stewart, J. (1964) 'Norn in Shetland', *Fróðskaparrit* 13, pp.158–175.

Sundkvist, P. (2007) 'The pronunciation of Scottish Standard English in Lerwick, Shetland', *English World-wide* 28, pp.1–21.

Sundkvist, P. & Gao, M. (2015) 'A regional survey of the relationship between vowel and consonant duration in Shetland Scots', *Folia Linguistica* 49, pp.57–83.

Thomson, W. P. L. (1987). *History of Orkney*. Edinburgh: Mercat.

Thráinsson, H., Petersen, H. P., Jacobsen, J. í. & Hansen, Z. S. (2004) *Faroese: an overview and reference grammar*. Tórshavn: Føroya Fróðskaparfelag.

Trudgill, P. (2004) *New-dialect formation: The inevitability of colonial Englishes*. Edinburgh: Edinburgh University Press.

van Leyden, K. (2004) *Prosodic characteristics of Orkney and Shetland dialects: an experimental approach*. Utrecht: Landelijke Onderzoekschool Taalwetenschap.

Wiggen, G. (2002) *Norns død, især skolens rolle: kommentarer til en disputt om nedgangen for det nordiske språket på Orknøyene og Shetland*. Oslo: Novus.

12

Peer Gynt meets the Trow of Windhouse

Terry Gunnell
(University of Iceland)

In 2022, the new Shetland section of the Icelandic *Sagnagrunnur* database of folk legends in the North Atlantic islands was opened for the first time. It contains summaries of, and information about around 1000 printed and recorded folk legends from Shetland which are connected to an interactive map, and, where available, links to those original recordings of legends made for Edinburgh University's School of Scottish Studies accessible on the Scottish *Tobar an Dualchais/ Kist o Riches* web site. This exciting new database can be said to owe a great deal to the support of the inimitable Brian Smith, along with that of the late Davy Cooper (to whom this part of the web site is dedicated, alongside Laurence Tulloch and Bo Almqvist). Indeed, it was Brian who put me in contact with Eileen Brooke-Freeman of the Shetland Amenity Trust (who kindly followed up the University of Iceland in providing us with financial support for two summers), and Eileen who connected me with Mona Walterson and Shetland ForWirds (who have kindly provided additional financial support). *Sagnagrunnur: Shetland* can be said to take the cultural treasure trove of Shetlandic legends to a new level. In addition to putting them in a wider international (and especially Nordic) context, the mapping aspect of the programme can be said to bring them directly back to the landscape and the communities from which they originally sprang.

Both aspects of the database have key roles to play in this present article which focuses on a famous legend from Mid Yell, an area I came to know well from my earlier work with Shetlandic guising traditions (something else for which I need to thank Brian for his invaluable assistance) (see further Gunnell, 2001, 2007, and 2012).

As of now, the database contains seven versions of the legend of the "Trow of Windhouse" (https://ismus.is/leit/Windhouse), four of which are told by Brucie Henderson (see, for example, Henderson 2022a and 2022b [recorded in 1955 and 1970], and *The Green Man of Knowledge*, 1982, pp.80-84); while a further two are told by Tom Tulloch (2022 [recorded in 1975]) and his son Laurence Tulloch (2014) (see further the discussion of these legends in Vilborg

Davíðsdottir, 2011, pp.137-139, 164, 208 and 261). Here, it should suffice to quote the version recorded by Laurence Williamson (1855-1936) (who, like both Brucie Henderson and the two Tullochs came from Yell), who credits "A. D. M." (the teacher Andrew Dishington Mathewson [1799-1887] also from Yell: see Stuart, 1991) as the source for his recording:

> Windhouse was haunted by a trow every Yule een, and the family always flit to Reafirth all night. One Yule een when they were about to go a stranger came in and said that a ship had been wrecked at the Daal o Lumbister, and he alone had been saved, and asked for lodgings. They said that they could not lodge themselves that night and told him why. He said that if they would let him remain he was not afraid of that. At last they consented. Next morning he was not to be found, till peering into the "gjudman's" bed they found him asleep. When he awoke he related that he sat at the fire till he heard a noise as if a force were straining the roof and waxing ever louder. He went outside and before him was a black lump and he followed it down the Byarky park and towards Mid Yell Voe. When it was near the sea, he concluded that it was a sea-trow and would soon escape him, so he threw his battle axe at it and down it came a shapeless grey mass. After telling this he went alone and recovered his axe and buried the trow. Stones were taken out of the place when building a boathouse. (Johnson, 1971, p.137; see further Johnson, 1971, p.155, where Williamson repeats the information about where the stranger's ship was wrecked).

In general, the same features are found in all of the other versions noted above:

> Those living in the house (the Spence family according to Brucie Henderson [see Henderson, 2022b]) are troubled by loud disturbances on Christmas night, which have been associated with a person being found dead next morning.

> They eventually decide to leave the house for Christmas night.

> One year, just as they are about to leave, an unnamed shipwrecked sailor arrives. Brucie Henderson suggests that he was Norwegian (Henderson, 2022a; also noted by Brucie in the version told to Tom Anderson).

> The visitor offers to stay for the night.

> At midnight, the house grows totally dark, no light coming in through the windows. Brucie Henderson also talks of noise. Tom Tulloch says that "the whole house seemed to be enveloped by a creature of some description" (Tom Tulloch, 2022).

The man inside grabs an axe (a battle axe in Laurence Williamson's account quoted above).

Using the axe (which in Henderson, 2022a is regularly thrown), the being is chased down to the voe, and killed.

Where it has been buried, the ground turns green.

A key feature of all the stories is the way in which the huge being is described. Laurence Williamson describes it as a "shapeless grey mass", a "black lump", a "hush of blubber" (Henderson, 2022a and 2022b; and in *The Green Man of Knowledge*, 1972, p.83), while Tom Tulloch says it "had no shape, no appearance", and was "an enormous lump of blubber". Laurence Tulloch echoes his father in stating that it was "a black, shapeless and flexible lump" (Laurence Tulloch, 2014, p.201). It seems evident that even though the word "trow" is used for this being, the creature in question seems to have been quite different to the way that trows were and are usually understood in Shetland (see, for example, Bruford, 1997; Marwick, 2000, pp.30-46; and the various stories in Laurence Tulloch, 2014).

What is clear from the accounts noted above (and the similar wording in them) is that we are dealing with a community of master storytellers who evidently knew each other. Also evident, however, is that in its present form, the story belongs to a well-known Nordic type of migratory legend classed by the Norwegian folklorist Reidar Th. Kristiansson as ML (Migratory Legend) 6015: The Christmas Visitors, which is known all over Scandinavia (see Christiansen, 1958, pp.144-156; see also af Klintberg, 2010, p.186 [Swedish Legend type K97] and Gunnell, 2004). These are legends telling of how people need to move out of their homes at Christmas because supernatural visitors [trolls, *álfar*, or the dead] take over the premises on Christmas night, and how those living in the house are saved by a brave unnamed guest who dares to stay the night, and frightens off the supernatural beings. As we all know, one can see echoes of such narratives in the modern *Die Hard* movies, which have ancient roots in the Viking era in narratives like that of the "Fróða wonder" in the Icelandic *Eyrbyggja saga* (1935, pp.139-152) and that of the combat between the saga-hero Grettir and the ghost Glámr in *Grettis saga* (1936, pp.119-122), both of which are also associated with the Christmas period. One can also see a close relationship to the account of Beowulf and Grendel in the Old English *Beowulf* (see further Gunnell, 2004). The key difference in the Windhouse stories is the nature of the huge and shapeless antagonist, which is not only unlike the beings traditionally encountered in the Nordic legends noted above, but also all of the other types of supernatural being that tend to be encountered in other Shetlandic or Orcadian legends.

This leads us back to mainland Scandinavia and Henrik Ibsen's *Peer Gynt*, first published in 1867, in which, in a central scene from the second act of the play, the hero, Peer Gynt encounters a being called "den store Bøygen" (the great Bøyg, *bøyg* meaning literally "obstacle", but with a reference to the verb *bøyje* meaning "bend"). Peer is alone in the middle of the night in the mountains, and suddenly finds himself in pitch darkness. He flails around himself with a branch, trying to fight whatever it is that has suddenly surrounded him:

Peer Gynt: What are you?

The Voice: The Great Bøyg.

Peer Gynt: Oh? Is that so? The riddle was black, now it seems to be grey. Out of my way Bøyg!

The Voice: Go round about, Peer!

Peer Gynt: No, I'll go straight through you! (Hacking and slashing) He's down! (He tries to go forward but always finds himself obstructed.) Are there others?

The Voice: The Bøyg, Peer Gynt, the one and only. The Bøyg who was wounded – the Bøyg who is whole – the Bøyg who was slain – the Bøyg who is alive!

Peer Gynt: (Throwing away the branch): My weapon's bewitched, but still I have my fists. (Hitting out.)

The Voice: Yes, trust to your fists and trust to your sinews – ho ho, Peer Gynt – then you'll come out on top.

Peer Gynt: Backwards or forwards, it's just as far, out or in, it's just as narrow. He's here, he's there, he's all about me! When I'm sure that I'm out, then I'm back in the middle! What's your name? Let me see you! What sort of thing are you?

The Voice: The Bøyg.

Peer Gynt (groping about): Neither dead nor alive... mist... and slime. Shapeless, too. (Norwegian: "Ikke dødt. Ikke levende. Slimet. Ingen skikkelse heller": Ibsen, 1994, p.53)

(Translation from Ibsen, 1970, pp.78-79; for the whole scene, see pp.77-81; for the original, see Ibsen, 1994, pp.51-54).

While for Ibsen, the Bøyg becomes a philosophical concept that rules Peer Gynt's life ("Go round about"), it is clear that here, as with much of the material in this part of the play, Ibsen is drawing on recognised motifs from western Norwegian folklore. He himself had collected folklore in Gudbrandsdal, Sogn,

Sunnfjord, Nordfjord, and Romsdal in 1862 (see Meyer, 1974, pp.205-208), and it is thus probable that he had encountered the narrative that Peter Christian Asbjørnsen published about the hunter Peer Gynt as part of the story collection "Rensdyrsjagt ved Ronderne" (Reindeer hunting in Ronderne) in *Norske Huldreeventyr og Folkesagn* (see Asbjørnsen, 1848, pp.77-85; also Bø, Grambo *et al.* [1981], pp.186-190; translation in Asbjørnsen, 1881, pp.145-150; on Ibsen's knowledge of the story, see Liestøl, 1927, p.146).

In Asbjørnsen's collection, the story of Peer Gynt and the Bøygen runs as follows (in my own translation):

> There was a hunter from Kvam in the old days, and he was called Peer Gynt. [...] When he got up to Høvringen, where he was going to stay in a mountain dairy for the night, it was so dark that he could not see his fists in front of him, and the dogs started barking, it was so ghostly. At that moment, he came into contact with something, and when he took told of it, it was both cold and slippery and big (original: "var det baade koldt og sleipt og stort"), and he sensed that he hadn't left the road either, so he had no idea what it was; but it was pretty nasty (original: "ohoglé var det").
>
> "Who is that?" said Peer, because he noticed it was moving.
>
> "Oh, it's the Bøyg," it answered. And that didn't help Peer Gynt much. But he stepped aside a little. That's one way of getting away, he thought. And at that moment, he came into contact with something again, and when he took hold of it, it was both big and cold and slippery.
>
> "Who is that?" said Peer Gynt. "Oh, it's the Bøyg," it answered again.
>
> "Well, either you are right or wrong. You'd better let me pass," said Peer, for he sensed when he had walked in a circle that the Bøyg had encircled the dairy (original: "Bøygen hadde ringt seg omkring selet"). And then it moved a little so that Peer could get into the dairy. And when he got in, it was no lighter inside than it had been on the outside, and he started feeling around the walls and was going to put away his rifle and hang up his bag, but as he was groping about, he again felt something cold and big and slippery.
>
> "What is that, now?" shouted Peer.
>
> "Oh, it's the great Bøyg", it answered, and wherever he felt and wherever he tried to move forward, he again felt the circle of the Bøyg. It's not good being here, thought Peer Gynt, since this Bøyg is both inside and outside, but I'll try and get this thing out of the way. So he took his rifle and went out again and felt his away forward until he found the head.

"What are you?" said Peer.

"Oh, I'm the great Bøyg from Etnedal," said the great troll. And then Peer quickly shot it in the head three times.

"Shoot one more time!" said the Bøyg. But Peer knew better, because if he had shot one more time, the shot would have come back at him. And then both Peer and the dogs got hold of the great troll and dragged it out so that they could get comfortably into the mountain dairy. (Translated from Asbjørnsen, 1848, pp.77-79.)

The account is followed by two others, ending with yet another version of the earlier-mentioned "Christmas Visitors" migratory legend (Asbjørnsen, 1848, pp.82-84) in which the hunter is said to have frightened away the Christmas visitors with the help of a polar bear (a common feature of the Norwegian versions of this legend: see Liestøl, 1933; and Gunnell, 2004).

As Knut Liestøl notes in his detailed examinations of the legends of Peer Gynt and the Bøyg (Liestøl, 1927 and 1948), Asbjørnsen had been told these stories by the 15-year old Engebret Hougen when he had visited Gudbandsdal, and Hougen later admitted that he had added two other local hunter stories to the single narrative he knew about Peer Gynt (that relating to the Bøyg: see Liestøl, 1948, pp.148-149; and Bø, Grambo et al., 1981 pp.292-293). Liestøl nonetheless mentions yet another account from Skåne in Sweden ("Bøj-om I Ramsadal") in which, as in both Shetland and in Asbjørnsen's account, both the Bøyg story and a version of the "Christmas Visitors" legend were once again found together, suggesting that they both belonged to a package of stories told about hunters ("Ramsadal" here perhaps referring to Romsdal in Norway) (Liestøl, 1927, pp.24-25). Indeed, as part of the same discussion, Liestøl also points to two other potential parallels to the Bøyg legend from Jylland in Denmark in which a huge creature blocks the way. (See further Granberg, 1935, pp.224-228, and Kart [map] 34 for further examples of the use of the appearance of the name Bøyg (in forms such as Böjom, Böjiom, Bajom, Böjåmm, and Bøje) in two other types of legend relating to forest workers in in southern Sweden and Denmark; see also af Klintberg, 2010, p.109 [legend type E62].

With regard to the Bøyg legend itself, Liestøl underlines that the account (always using the name "Bøyg" in one form or other) seems to have been most well-known on the eastern side of Langfjelli in the centre of Norway, running south from Gudbrandsdal to Vest-Telemark, and lists seven versions (including that of Asbjørnsen), two from Gudbrandsdal, one from Valdres (involving the sharpening of an axe), and four from Telemark (Liestøl, 1927, pp.21-22).

If we return to Shetland, it is evident (to my mind at least) that we are dealing with yet another version of the same legend, not least because of the similar nature of the being. As noted above, while the words "trow" and "troll" are used for the being in both the Shetlandic legend and some of those from Norway, as noted above, it would seem questionable that we are dealing with such a being as understood by most Shetlanders and Norwegians. Liestøl's idea (see Liestøl, 1927, p.23) that this is a shape-changing troll (like the potentially shape-changing *jǫtnar* of Old Norse mythology) receives no support from either the narratives themselves or the local traditions. The nature of the creature (the curvature implied by its Norwegian name and its ability to surround a building), and its blubber and apparent return to the water in the Shetland accounts would instead seem to imply that we are dealing with something more like a serpent, similar perhaps to the Nordic *lindorm* and the Orcadian "muckle mester Stoor Worm" (Marwick 2000, p.20, 139-144; see also Dennison, 1995, pp.22-25; Muir, 1998, pp.3-9; and 2014, pp.13-22; Künzler, 2021).

Also evident is that it is unlikely that any of the Shetland storytellers noted above picked up the story from books (either the original Norwegian collections of Asbjørnsen's legends, which were regularly republished after 1848, or from Bæksted's translation of 1881), or from Ibsen's play (apparently first performed in Shetland in 2004). While the heart of the story is the same, here the creature has become nameless, there is no conversation, and the hunter has become a nameless shipwrecked sailor (essentially an outsider to the community like the heroes of the "Christmas Visitors" legends). (Interestingly, one notes that the hero of the version from Skåne in Sweden noted above is from Asia!) While the time-setting of the narrative (Christmas) firmly reflects that of the other "Christmas Visitors" legends, it is also evident that, as in Iceland, for that migratory legend to be able to be adapted to suit the local Shetlandic worldview, its form clearly needed to be altered. Unlike in Norway, where the supernatural visitors in such legends were commonly members of the wild ride (*Oskoreia* or *Juleskrei*) which was composed of trolls or the dead, Shetland evidently had no such beliefs of travelling groups of supernatural beings, and no other "Christmas Visitors" legends. (For similar reasons, in Iceland the group of visitors needed to become *álfar*: see Gunnell, 2004.)

While we are therefore dealing with an oral account with a background in the Norwegian oral tradition (something perhaps lent support by Brucie Henderson's suggestion that the shipwrecked sailor was Norwegian [see above]), it nonetheless seems apparent from the extant recordings that the story has not become a traditional Shetlandic narrative that could be adapted to be connected to different parts of the islands (like those legends dealing with trows or brownies). It is quite firmly a Yell narrative, linked to a particular deserted building that everyone in the area knew, in other words, a large ruined building that stood on a hill outside the local community which had a number of other ghost stories associated with it (see https://ismus.is/leit/Windhouse; and Adventure Shetland, 2022). This building, like the green area of heather mentioned in several of the stories, would have effectively served as what Pierre Nora called a "lieu de memoire" (Nora, 1989). As the recordings show, and as has been noted above, the narrative itself seems to have largely been confined to storytellers from Mid Yell, Brucie Henderson (in the recording made with Tom Anderson) saying that he had first heard it from Laurence Williamson, while Tom Tulloch credits Brucie with being the best man to recount the story.

So how old is the story? As has been noted above, Laurence Williamson's source died in 1887, and while Williamson himself mentions no names, Brucie Henderson connects the story to the Spence family who lived at Windhouse in the nineteenth century (Henderson, 2022b; see also Grant, 1893, pp.286-289). At the same time, however, one notes the way in which the rifle used as a weapon in the Norwegian stories is here regularly substituted with an axe (a battle axe in Laurence Williamson's account), and, in the earliest of Brucie Henderson's accounts, an axe that is thrown several times. Even though Knut Liestøl was highly wary of the idea earlier suggested by Asbjørnsen that we might be dealing here with a development of a much older narrative that might have been associated with the Old Norse god Þórr and his struggles with the Middle Earth sea-serpent, Jǫrmungandr (see Liestøl, 1927, p.23; and 1948, pp.150-151), to my mind, this possibility has to remain (see Gunnell, 2021, p.666; for the original Old Norse narratives of Þórr and Jǫrmungandr which are also depicted on the Gosforth stone, see *Eddukvæði* (2014), I, pp.399-407 [*Hymiskviða*] and Snorri Sturluson, 2005, pp.44-45). Of course, while we have no evidence to suggest that the Windhouse legend was known in Shetland before the time of Laurence Williamson, as Ernest Marwick notes (Marwick, 2000, p.20), narratives were sometimes told in Shetland of how "away, far out to sea, near the edge of the world lived a monstrous sea-serpent that took about six hours to breathe in its breath, and six hours to let it out". As noted above, we also have the Orkney account of "Ashipattle and Mester Stoorworm" (see also Künzler, 2021, pp.164-165 on potential connections with Þórr mythology).

Naturally such speculations about faint memories of ancient preserved narratives remain nothing more than speculation (something with which I am certain that the honoured recipient of this present volume would agree). The fact remains nonetheless that, where possible, it is important to consider local folk legends and folk beliefs (like folk traditions) in an international context. If nothing else, the existence of the stories of the Trow of Windhouse not only demonstrate the narrative art of the Shetland storytellers of the past (see, in particular, Vilborg Davíðsdóttir, 2011), but also the close connections that Shetland evidently maintained over the course of time with western Norway and Norwegian folk tradition, even after it had become part of Scotland.

(I would like to express my thanks to Nicolai Lanz, Amanda Green, Mark Smith, Jennifer L. Porath, and Bengt af Klintberg for their assistance with this article.)

Bibliography

NOTE: Icelanders are named by given name in line with Icelandic custom. Most Icelanders use patronyms rather than surnames.

Adventure Shetland (2022) *Spooky Shetland Part 5: Windhouse: Shetland's Most Haunted*. Available at: https://www.youtube.com/watch?v=_ioFDSzF_RM (accessed: 10 May 2023).

af Klintberg, B. (2010) *The Types of the Swedish Legend*. Helsinki: Suomalainen Tiedeakatemia/ Acta Scientiarum Fennica. Folklore Fellows Communications 300.

Asbjørnsen, P. C. (1848) *Norske Huldreeventyr og Folkesagn, fortalte af P. Chr. Asbjørnsen*. 2nd collection. Christiania: Jakob Dybwad and W. C. Fabritius, 1848.

Asbjørnsen, P. C. (1881) *Round the Yule Log*. H. L. Brækstad (trans.) (with an introduction by E. W. Gosse). London: Sampson Low, Marston, Searle and Rivington.

Bruford, A. (1997) 'Trolls, Hillfolk, Finns, and Picts: The Identity of the Good Neighbours in Orkney and Shetland', in P. Narváez (ed.), *The Good People: New Fairylore Essays*. Lexington: University Press of Kentucky, pp.116-141.

Bø, O.; Grambo, R.; Hodne, B.; and Hodne, Ø. (ed.) (1981) *Norske Segner*, Oslo: Det Norske Samlaget.

Christiansen, R. (1958) *The Migratory Legends: A Proposed List of Types With a Systematic Catalogue of the Norwegian Variants*. Helsinki: Suomalainen Tiedeakatemia/ Acta Scientiarum Fennica. Folklore Fellows Communications 175.

Dennison, W. Traill (1995) *Orkney Folklore and Seas Legends*. T. Muir (ed.). Kirkwall: The Orkney Press.

Eddukvæði (2014) Jónas Kristjánsson and Vésteinn Ólason (eds.) 2 vols. Reykjavík: Hið íslenska fornritafélag. Íslensk fornrit.

Eyrbyggja saga (1935) Einar Ólafur Sveinsson and Matthías Þórðarson (eds.). Reykjavík: Hið íslenzka fornritafélag, pp. 1-184. Íslenzk fornrit, IV.

Granberg, G. (1935) *Skogsrået i yngre nordisk folktradition*. Uppsala: A.-B. Lundeqvistska Bokhandeln. Skrifter utgivna af Gustav Adolfs Akadamien för folklivsforskning 3.

Grant, Francis (1893) *The County Families of the Shetland Islands*. Lerwick: T.&J. Manson.

Grettis saga Ásmundssonar (1936) Guðni Jónsson (ed.). Reykjavík: Hið Íslenzka fornritafélag. Íslensk fornrit VII.

Gunnell, T. (2001) 'Grýla, *grýlur*, "*grøleks*" and *skeklers*: Medieval Disguise Traditions in the North Atlantic?', *Arv: Nordic Yearbook of Folklore*, pp.33-54.

Gunnell, T. (2004) 'The Coming of the Christmas Visitors: Folk Legends Concerning the Attacks on Icelandic Farmhouses Made by Spirits at Christmas', *Northern Studies* 38, pp.51-75.

Gunnell, T. (2007) 'Masks and Mumming Traditions in the North Atlantic: A Survey', in T. Gunnell (ed.), *Masks and Mumming in the Nordic Area*. Uppsala: Kungl. Gustav Adolfs Akademien för svensk folkkultur, pp.275-326. Acta Academiae Regiae Gustavi Adolphi XCVIII.

Gunnell, T. (2012) 'Skotrarar, Skudlers, Colloughs and Strawboys: Wedding Guising Traditions in Norway, Shetland and Ireland, Past and Present'. In Bo Almqvist, Cróstóir Mac Cárthaigh, Liam Mac Mathúna, Séamas Mac Mathúna and Seosamh Watson (eds.), *Atlantic Currents: Essays on Lore, Literature and Language: Essays in Honour of Séamas Ó Catháin on Occasion of His 70th Birthday, 31.12.2012*. Dublin: University College Dublin Press, pp.241-268.

Gunnell, T. (2021) 'George Marwick's Account of "The Muckle Tree or Igasill"', in Frog and J. Ahola (eds.) *Folklore and Old Norse Mythology*. Folklore Fellows Communications Communications 323. Helsinki: The Kalevala Society, pp.665-688.

Henderson, B. (2022a) 'The Annual Visit of the Windhouse Troll Each Christmas Is Followed by a Death in the House'': School of Scottish Studies Archive SA1955.095: Tobar an Dualchais/ Kist o Riches. Available at: https://www.tobarandualchais.co.uk/track/31660 (accessed: 17 May 2023).

Henderson, B. (2022b) 'How a Shipwrecked Sailor Killed the Trow That Haunted Windhouse', School of Scottish Studies Archive SA1970.240: Tobar an Dualchais/Kist o Riches. Available at: https://www.tobarandualchais.co.uk/track/65348 (accessed: 17 May 2023).

Henderson, B. (1972) 'The Trow of Windhouse', *Tocher* 8, pp.252–256;

Ibsen, H. (1970) *Peer Gynt*. Peter Watts (trans.). Harmondsworth: Penguin.

Ibsen, H. (1994) *Peer Gynt*. Oslo: Gyldendal Norske Forlag.

Johnson, L. G. (1971) *Laurence Williamson of Mid Yell*. Lerwick: The Shetland Times Ltd.

Künzler, S. (2021) 'A Male Cinderella and a Sea Serpent's Teeth: Scandinavian Echoes in an Orkney Folk-Tale', in J. Glauser and P. Hermann (eds.) in collaboration with S. Brink and J. Harris and the editorial assistance of S. Künzler, *Myth, Magic, and Memory in Early Scandinavian Culture: Studies in Honour of Stephen A. Mitchell*. Turnhout: Brepols, pp.159-174.

Liestøl, K. (1927) 'Den store Bøyen', in *Festskrift til Hjalmar Falk*. Oslo: H. Aschehoug and Co., pp.135-142.

Liestøl, K. (1933) 'Kjetta pa Dovre: Til spursmålet um pilagrimsvegar og segnvandring', *Maal og minne* 24, pp.24-48

Liestøl, K. (1948) 'Segnfiguren Per Gynt', *Arv: Nordic Yearbook of Folklore*, 4, pp.146-156.

Marwick, E. (2000) *The Folklore of Orkney and Shetland*, 2nd ed., Edinburgh: Birlinn Ltd.

Meyer, M. (1974) *Ibsen*. Penguin: Harmondsworth.

Muir, T. (1998) *The Mermaid Bride and Other Orkney Folk Tales*. Kirkwall: The Orcadian Ltd./ Kirkwall Press.

Nora, P. (1989) 'Between Memory and History', *Representations* 26, pp.7-24.

The Green Man of Knowledge and Other Scots Traditional Tales from Tape Recordings of the School of Scottish Studies University of Edinburgh (1982). Alan Bruford (ed.). Aberdeen: Aberdeen University Press.

Sagnagrunnur Shetland (2022) The Arnamagnean Institute for Icelandic Studies. Available at: http://sagnagrunnur.arnastofnun.is/en/shetland/. (accessed 12 May 2023).

Snorri Sturluson (2005) Prologue and *Gylfaginning*. Anthony Faulkes (ed.). London: Viking Society for Northern Research/ University College London.

Stuart, M. (1991) *Sons and Daughters of Shetland 1800-1900*. Lerwick: Shetland Publishing Company.

Tobar an Dualchais/ Kist o Riches (2022) The School of Scottish Studies, The Canna Collection and BBC Radio nan Gàidheal. Available at: https://www.tobarandualchais.co.uk/ (accessed 28 April 2023).

Trail Dennison, W. (1977) 'Assipattle and the Mester Stoorworm', G. Douglas (ed.), *Scottish Fairy and Folk Tales*. New York: Arno Press, pp.58-72 and 299-303.

Tulloch, L. (2014) *Shetland Folk Tales*. Stroud: The History Press.

Tulloch, T. (2022) 'The Windhouse Trow; A Violent Family Quarrel', School of Scottish Studies Archive SA1975.169, Tobar an Dualchais/Kist o Riches. Available at: https://www.tobarandualchais.co.uk/track/102120 (accessed 1 May 2023).

Vilborg Davíðsdóttir (2011) ,'"An Dat's de Peerie Story": Rannsókn og túlkun á sögnum tveggja Hjaltlendinga'. MA thesis, University of Iceland, Reykjavik. Available at: http://hdl.handle.net/1946/10174 (accessed 28 April 2023).

13

Genetic genealogy of Fair Isle
– an extreme Northern Isles microcosm

James Flett Wilson
(Usher Institute, University of Edinburgh)

Fair Isle, despite lying midway between Orkney and Shetland, is geologically, linguistically, culturally, politically and, as we'll see here, genetically, part of Shetland. Since the evacuation of St Kilda in the Outer Hebrides in 1930, it holds the title of the most isolated inhabited island in the British Isles. "Da Isle" is famous the world over for its knitting patterns, migrant birds, musicians and the many shipwrecks, including the Spanish Armada hulk flagship *El Gran Grifón*. However, my interest stems from the fact that my father is one of the last few full-blooded Fair Islanders alive, with 64 out of 64 of his great great great great grandparents coming from the Isle; that is why I've studied its genealogy and genetics for nearly 40 years.

Isolated islands are akin to natural laboratories, magnifying the effects that are actually present in all populations due to kinship, but which can't always be easily observed. The finite size of populations does unusual things to pedigrees, such that it is common to be related in several ways to other people, or to descend from multiple siblings from one family.

All this is true of the rest of Shetland, a few more generations further back in time, as it is for the wider population in Scotland even further back. But it is fun to probe the extremes, as they teach us what we'd find if only we had deeper pedigrees in other, larger populations.

The six traditional families of Fair Isle

Like all small places and genetic isolates, there are a limited number of surnames in Fair Isle, and indeed six account for the great majority of the population over the last 250 years: Wilson, Stout, Eunson, Irvine, Williamson and Leslie (Wilson, 1994). A small number of much rarer names were either introduced (e.g. Anderson in 1871) or were represented by only one family and died out over 150 years ago (e.g. Mather, Smith, Brown). I will take each of the traditional families of Fair Isle in turn and discuss their origins and genetic genealogy. These analyses use the Y chromosome, a piece of DNA passed down the generations from father to son and which contains many markers and is thus invaluable for tracing lineages. Of the six families, only Wilson and Stout survive as surnames in Fair Isle in 2023, even if a number of other islanders are descended in the female line from the six families.

Wilson

Oral tradition passed down from acclaimed family historian Aest Aggie (Agnes Wilson of Springfield 1877-1961) relates that the first Wilson in Fair Isle was a David Wilson and that he was a covenanter. David Wilson has in fact been found in the records, e.g. in the Dunrossness court in 1604, where he was convicted of selling ale at dearer than regulation prices. His father was Robert Wilson (c.1540-1603), who owned a house at Westshore in Scalloway. They are too early to be covenanters, but perhaps they came to Shetland to escape persecution of some other kind. Jerome Wilson, probably a son of David, was in 1626 servitor to James Sinclair, the laird of Quendale, who bought Fair Isle.

Wilson is not an indigenous name in Shetland and there are very few others on record outside Fair Isle, apart from an early branch in Unst/Fetlar. Indeed, genetics has revealed matches to Wilsons from Fife, which ties in well with David Wilson actually being a burgess of St Andrews (i.e. owning land and with the right to trade, a merchant). The Fair Isle Wilson Y chromosome actually belongs to a Pictish group, R1b-S190, which arose about 1,700 years ago. R1b-S190 is most common around Fife and Stirlingshire, reaching a frequency of 2.4% in Central Scotland, but has spread across the nation, as well as to Ulster.

Detailed analysis of the whole Y chromosome sequence has revealed that within the R1b-S190 group, the S425 marker defines a subgroup made up of Wilsons and Sloans, among others, linking about the year 1000 A.D. Then, within that, the S422 and S302 markers define a Fife Wilson lineage, and under that, S303 defines the Wilsons of Fair Isle, the marker having occurred in an ancestor of Andrew Wilson of Busta, Fair Isle (born 1708). The Wilsons of Sanday, Orphir and Hoy in Orkney are all genetically distinct from those in Fair Isle (and from one another).

Stout

Tradition relates that the first Stout in Fair Isle was a teacher, supposedly from Yorkshire. We do find Thomas Stout as a teacher in early records, probably the same man as Thomas Stout of Shirva (born 1717). Genetic testing has revealed that all the Stouts of Shetland (with traceable male-line descendants), from Dunrossness, Lerwick and Fair Isle, belong to one deep genetic family (including Sir Robert Stout, prime minister of New Zealand 1884-87). The Shetland Stouts are not related to the Stouts of the south isles of Orkney, who belong to a distinct genetic group. The Stouts of Westray and Stronsay, in the north isles of Orkney, migrated from Fair Isle in 1832.

Where exactly the Shetland Stout lineage, R1b-S5952, comes from, is not as clear. Only very few individuals match the father group, R1b-S6898, and these appear in England, but in the West Country, not the North of England. As genetic genealogy expands, we can hope to find further matches to help clarify the origins of the Stouts of Shetland. Recruitment and testing of ancestral Yorkshire Stouts will be required to assess if they are of the same genetic stock.

Eunson

Oral history suggests that the Eunsons (sometimes Ewensons or Younsons) originally came from the Netherlands. The earliest on record in Fair Isle are Thomas Eunson of Busta, whose mother was a Jean Steansgarth (born 1707 – the name is now rendered Stanger, from Birsay in Orkney), Walter and Charles Eunson of Shirva, all on record in the 1750s. A similar situation exists as for the Stouts, as there are Eunsons in other parts of Shetland and also in the east Mainland and south isles of Orkney. Genetic testing has also revealed the same pattern: all of the Shetland Eunsons – Quendale, Whalsay, Aithsting and Fair Isle – are related in one deep genetic group, whereas the Orkney Eunsons are from a different genetic lineage.

The deeper origins are very clear in the case of the Eunsons, for their group, R1b-S3201 (and the father group R1b-S4034), is Swedish in origin. Within this group, the Eunsons of Shetland share the S6979 marker with the Corse/Corsie families of Orkney (Rousay and Sanday) and both likely descend from a Swedish Viking settler. There is no evidence of a connection to the Netherlands. The last Eunsons left Fair Isle in 1993.

Irvine

Outside of *Orkneyinga Saga*, the earliest named inhabitants of Fair Isle are Irvines: William Irvine had a contract with Earl Patrick Stewart to divide the spoils from *El Gran Grifón* in 1588, and John and Henry are there in 1604. The surname dominates in the earlier records, however many left the Isle in the first half of the 19th century. There are two large Irvine genetic clusters in Scotland, but the Irvines of Fair Isle do not relate to either, nor to the Irvines of Orkney (Shapinsay or Sandwick), nor other Irvines in Shetland (Whalsay, Delting, Tingwall); thus far we have not discovered any other Irvines they match.

Their lineage belongs to R1b-S389, another group with Pictish subgroups, concentrated in central Scotland, where it reaches 1.8% in frequency (and 1.2% in north-east Scotland). Whether this is an Insular Pictish lineage and thus represents continuity through the Pictish-Norse transition or a Pictish lineage brought to Shetland by a Lowland Scot is unclear, but the name itself would suggest the latter, as a man from Irvine may have taken or been given the name. In Fair Isle, the surname died out in 1952.

Williamson

Williamsons were also more common longer ago, and a John Williamson also appears in 1604. It is likely that Williamson is, like Eunson, a local patronymic. It remains to be seen whether they match other Shetland Williamsons, of which there are various genetic groupings. One Fair Isle Williamson lineage has been tested at low resolution and belongs to the widespread group, R1b-S9257. Testing of representatives of further 18th century patriarchs is required, and at higher resolution. The last Fair Isle Williamson died in 1911.

Leslie

Charles Leslie of Shirva (born 1692) is the first on record in Fair Isle, and the namesake of many later Leslies. As with Eunson, Stout and Irvine, there are Leslie families in both Orkney and Shetland and yet again they do not match one another; the surname arose or arrived independently in each archipelago. The Leslies of Fair Isle match the Leslies of Dunrossness and Sandwick (Shetland) and not the Leslies of Westray, Orkney (although there are Leslies of Fair Isle origin in Westray and elsewhere in Orkney, as is the case for Stouts), belonging to the widely spread R1b-S206 group.

Like most north-west European groups and indeed all the other Fair Isle R1b lineages, this group arose in the Bronze Age, among the Beaker folk. It is at present unclear exactly how it came to Shetland and at what time (higher resolution testing is required), although both the surname itself and the relative rarity of the group in Scandinavia suggest a Lowland Scots proximate origin. Barkland Janet (Janet Leslie 1881-1969) was the last Leslie in Fair Isle. The judge Harald Leslie, Lord Birsay, 1905-82, claimed relationship to Janet, but this will need to be tested genetically as paper genealogy shows no link to Fair Isle.

Maternal lineages

The assortment of Fair Islanders into six families is based on patrilineal descent, but it's equally possible to analyse matrilineal descent, using a piece of DNA called mitochondrial DNA (mtDNA). This is inherited from mother to daughter to granddaughter down the generations. Matrilineal descendants of eight independent ancestresses c.1750 have been identified and tested, revealing only four distinct haplotypes or genetic lineages. Indeed, the first and second maternal lineages each account for three ancestresses, so that two women are together the matrilineal ancestresses of roughly three quarters of the people.

The first lineage belongs to the H4a1a1 group. This group shows a founder effect in Shetland: it has been in Shetland long enough to rise in frequency so that many individuals today are descendants of the original founder. It reaches 1.7% frequency across all of Shetland and is seen on the west Mainland, Delting and Yell, with derivatives in Whalsay and Unst. The Fair Isle subtype has the 16355t variant, which has not been seen elsewhere in Shetland.

The second lineage belongs to H1b1g, with the hypervariable region motif 16182c 16183c 16189c 16356c. A founder effect is also seen here, with 0.6% of a large Shetland sample carrying this type, all of them from Cunningsburgh! The minority mtDNA groups are H5a, a Dunrossness mtDNA lineage, also seen in the north Mainland and Whalsay, and finally a V lineage. Over the generations, women have moved around more than men, and so mtDNA lineages tend to be more mixed up than Y chromosomes. It is therefore difficult to infer the deeper origins beyond Shetland, but it's clear that the mtDNA diversity is very low, with only four female founders of the Fair Isle population.

Autosomal genetics

While the Y chromosome and mtDNA provide insights into two ancestral lineages (patrilineal and matrilineal) for each individual, they ignore all the other hundreds of ancestors we all have. The analysis of the rest of the genome, called the autosomes, brings their contributions into focus. In analyses looking across the British Isles (Gilbert, 2019), it was possible to identify 43 clusters of genetically related individuals. Fair Isle formed its own genetic cluster, which was part of the larger Shetland grouping, and closest genetically to the Dunrossness cluster. This might be expected, with the sharing of five Fair Isle surnames with Dunrossness (Leslie, Irvine, Eunson, Williamson and Stout).

It is also possible to estimate the contribution of deeper ancestral populations to the present population, in the case of Shetland the Scandinavian and British contributions. Fair Isle is something of an outlier in Shetland with an estimated Scandinavian component of 14%, the second lowest of any parish or isle in Shetland, more akin to the Orkney estimates (average 16%, vs. 23% for Shetland). This is possibly due to the large component of Wilson heritage, coming from Fife, together with Irvines and Leslies probably also having Lowland Scots ancestry, with Stouts possibly of ancient English heritage. There was no sign of Spanish ancestry, giving no support to the fanciful idea that there was genetic interchange between the Armada sailors and the local population.

Beyond individual genetic genealogy, it can be interesting to pursue 'statistical genealogy', counting and categorising ancestors, ancestral places, surnames and dates, looking for patterns, similarities and differences across the population.

Genetic drift of surnames

When Prince Philip and Queen Elizabeth II visited Fair Isle in 1960, Philip quipped "If in doubt, just say Stout", as a way to remember the names. Indeed, in the 20th century Stout was the most common surname in Fair Isle. For instance, in 1911 34% of the islanders (excluding the light-keepers) were Stouts (24% were Eunsons and 21% Wilsons). By the 1950s, 11 of the 18 inhabited crofts (61%) were in Stout hands. However, all these Stouts descended from only three brothers and a distant cousin, and as we go back into the 19th century, Wilson was the most common name.

For example, in 1841, 28% of the population were Wilsons, followed by Irvine (20%), Williamson (17%), Stout (10%), Leslie (8%) and Eunson (7%). By 1861, there were 103 Wilsons (29%) and they became even more dominant from 1862 onwards as none of them emigrated in the large movement to New Brunswick in Canada that year, thus Wilsons accounted for 46% of the population in June 1862. They participated heavily in the emigrations to Kirkwall and Edinburgh in the second half of the 19th century, however, and thus declined, while the Stouts became more common.

Going further back in time though, the Irvines dominate, as in 1798, when 52 of the 221 inhabitants (24%) were Irvines, with Williamsons in second place (18%). The changes in frequency are a form of what is called genetic drift, because some families have many sons, while others run to daughters or indeed have very few offspring at all. Thus some surnames drift upwards in frequency, while others drift downwards. These chance effects are exacerbated in small Scottish islands through the powerful effects of emigration, and the fact that kin may emigrate together or decide to emigrate because their relatives have already left (kin-structured migration). In 2023, the Wilsons and Stouts hang on by a thread with only one and three households, respectively, remaining, while all the other traditional surnames of Fair Isle are already gone.

Inbreeding

Over one billion people on earth today practice the cultural tradition of cousin marriage, commonly with first or second cousins, or even in some communities, double first cousin or avuncular (e.g. uncle-niece) unions. While close cousin marriage is not common in the Northern Isles, the marriage of more distant relatives, however, was routine before the Second World War, as in the rural parishes and isles most people were related. While such distant kinship meant that almost every couple in Fair Isle were related to each other, the Wilson family practiced closer inbreeding, very commonly marrying other Wilsons.

Between 1789 and 1945, 50 Wilson men married, 27 of them (54%) to Wilson women. Comparing all other surnames together, only 22 out of 154 marriages (14%) were between spouses with the same surname (isonymous), meaning the levels of isonymous marriage among Wilsons was significantly higher than among other surnames (P<0.00001; χ^2). The most *distantly* related of these Wilson-Wilson spouses were second cousins once removed, but 89% were as closely related as first cousins once removed (or closer), with one pair being *double* first cousins *and* simultaneously double second cousins once removed *and* double third cousins.

Population structure

Why did this close cousin marriage occur? One important factor was that there was a subdivision within Fair Isle, or what is known as population genetic structure, between people living south of the Meadow burn and belonging to the Wesleyan Methodist faith (worshipping in the Chapel), and those north of the burn who were Church of Scotland and worshipped in the Kirk. There was considerable mating isolation between the two groups (potentially even before the arrival of Methodism in 1828), meaning that the population of an area of less than a square mile, where the crofts are, was divided in two, in terms of who was an eligible marriage partner! The Wilsons were almost entirely Methodist (and four generations were lay preachers in the Chapel), which will have limited their choice of mates, but we can speculate that there may also have been an element of arranged marriage, as is the case in many consanguineous communities today.

Sibset exchange

The marriage of multiple siblings from one family to multiple siblings from another (sibset exchange) was also practiced on the Isle, with 49 of 205 marriages (24%) between 1789-1945 being of this type. The most extreme example crossed the Kirk-Chapel divide, where between 1924 and 1933 four sisters and one brother – Stouts from South Busta – married four brothers and one sister – Stouts from Taft! Despite the shared surname, the families' closest relationship was only third cousins, at the more distant end of the kinship scale in Fair Isle. The next generation were therefore double first cousins, but none of them married islanders.

The consequences make for rather interesting genealogy! Firstly, as is the case in other small communities with limited numbers of both surnames and given names, extreme care is required in reconstructing family trees, for instance at one point in the 1870s, three different Stewart Wilsons are married to three different Agnes Wilsons, with two of the couples producing children with the same first names, and all of them related to each other.

Given names

Like many parishes, certain given names were used much more often than others, in particular Jerome/Jeremiah (called Jarm or Jerry): there is even a picture of eight Jeromes taken in Fair Isle in 1928. Andrew, William and John were the most common male first names, with Stewart mostly among Wilsons and George mostly among Stouts. For women, Barbara (Baaby), Mary (sometimes known as Polly), Jane (Jean) and Agnes (Aggie or Nanny) were most common, and more unusually Jacobina (Koby or Jackie). The given name or middle name Strong (pronounced Strang) was passed down the generations in the Eunson and Wilson families (originally named after James Strong, the tacksman).

We are very lucky, though, in Fair Isle genealogy, to have a document (part of the Old Statistical Account) which lists the entire population in 1798, arranged in families, as well as some rentals from the 1740s-60s, which list the heads of households by township, without which things would be much less clear.

Entangled pedigrees

The pedigrees themselves are extraordinary, being full of inbreeding loops, where an individual descends from an ancestor in more than one way, so the family tree loops round in a circle. This leads to unusual situations. For example, I descend from Polly Wilson (born 15 May 1791) and also from her twin Koby, as well as two of their brothers! This isn't even the only time I descend from four siblings in one Wilson nuclear family.

Despite their nearest relationship being third cousins, my grandfather and grandmother were related to each other in at least 33 different ways, and my father descends from Andrew Wilson of Busta (born 1708), through 20 different genealogical paths! It is not such a surprise when we consider that of his eight great-grandparents, six were Wilsons. This also leads to what is known as pedigree collapse, such that where an outbred individual has 32 pairs of GGGG grandparents, my father has only nine, of whom at least four of the individuals were siblings. A large part of his DNA comes down from a very small set of ancestors – four couples having children between 1769-1791 accounting for 81% of my father's DNA.

Super-ancestors

This is not out of the ordinary among full-bred Fair Islanders, when the same analyses are repeated for two further representative (and not too closely related) full-bred islanders, they each had 15 descents from Andrew Wilson. The first had only 12 pairs of GGGG grandparents, only one from outwith Fair Isle, and the same four couples account for 53% of his DNA. The second had 22 pairs of GGGG grandparents, 9 from outwith Fair Isle (because a great-grandparent and a great-great-grandparent were among the seven people to marry into the Fair Isle families between 1789-1900), but still 47% of his DNA will have been inherited from the same four couples as the other examples.

The other Fair Isle ancestors also overlap, such that 13 pairs of ancestors account for all the local ancestry of the three individuals and we can project that about one quarter of the entire island's ancestry comes from Thomas Wilson (born c.1745) and Jean Irvine of Gaila, the couple contributing the most to each of the three subjects. A further seventh of the island's ancestry comes from each of the three other super-ancestor couples (Jerome Wilson (born c.1750) and Ellen Thompson of Busta; Alexander Eunson (born c.1750) and Agnes Irvine of Busta; and John Irvine (born c.1740) and Mary Stout of Leogh). For people with part-Fair Isle ancestry, clearly the percentages of their genome deriving from these same ancestors would decrease in proportion to the amount of Fair Isle ancestry. In fact, only 16 ancestral couples born c.1740-1765 and seven incomers account for the entire ancestry in all ascendant lineages of all 20th century Fair Islanders.

Studies in Iceland have shown the same phenomenon: tracing the matrilineal and patrilineal genealogies of over 100,000 Icelanders born since 1972 back to a cohort of ancestors b. 1698-1742 revealed that 62% of women descend from only 7% of the potential matrilineal ancestresses, and 71% of the contemporary men descend patrilineally from only 10% of the potential ancestors (Helgason, 2003). These are examples of genetic drift in action, how gene pools become different from one another over the generations.

The extensive sharing of deep ancestors leads to an upward bias in estimates of kinship based on the algorithms of direct-to-consumer genetic testing companies, as is also seen in other isolated populations, such as Ashkenazi Jews. People whose closest relationship to me is second cousin twice removed share as much DNA as would be expected for a grand-uncle or first cousin, because all of the distant cousinships add to the sharing.

Effects

It's no surprise that my grandfather, Aest Jimmy (James Wilson of Springfield and then Schoolton 1915-1994) remarked "Hit's a winder we wir da wye we wir!" (It's a wonder we were the way we were). No obvious ill effects of inbreeding were apparent on Fair Isle, with islanders following comparable life paths to other Shetlanders, being subject to the similar social and economic forces of the times. After leaving the tenant crofting life, islanders and their descendants flourished in many professions, including notable sets of Wilson and Stout master mariners, doctors, vets, lawyers, professors and a bishop.

It is important to be aware that one generation of outbreeding removes any effects of earlier cousin marriage. The negative consequences of inbreeding come from the bringing together in one person of disease-causing genetic variants that only have their effects if present in two copies. One copy is inherited from their mother's side and one down the father's side of their family tree (Ceballos, 2018). If no such variants are present, or are by chance not in the pieces of DNA that are brought together in this way, then inbreeding causes no harm. Large genetic studies show that close parental relatedness decreases height, fertility and cognitive function (Joshi, 2015; Clark, 2019) and it is notable that none of the offspring of the double first cousin marriage produced children, and six out of eight died of infectious diseases (mostly measles). It is exactly like the luck of a draw, but inbreeding raises the odds of a poorer outcome.

Shared ancestors

It often used to be said that "wir aa Jock Tamson's bairns" and it has, in fact, been shown that deep enough in the past, everyone on earth shares ancestors and thus we are all very distantly related (and so are our parents, so we are all inbred to some degree). Think about how many ancestors you have at different generations in the past: 2 parents, 4 grandparents, 8, 16, 32 … it soon becomes very large, 1,024 at 10 generations, over 15,000 at 15 generations and over 1 million by 20 generations. For someone middle-aged, that is about the year 1360, during the Scottish Wars of Independence and just after the Black Death. But the population of Scotland c.1360 was only around 500,000.

This is called the ancestor paradox and is solved by the fact that many of the ancestors at this generation must be the same people – and so everyone in Scotland is related to everyone else, at about 21st cousins at the most distant. By 29 generations back (one generation after William the Conqueror), everyone in the world is related. This point is called the most recent common ancestor (MRCA) point – where everyone in a population is related by descent from at least one common ancestor. The number of common ancestors increases as you go further back and work shows that there is deeper time-point, called the identical ancestors point, where if someone is the ancestor of anyone today, then they are the ancestor of everyone (Chang, 1999; Rohde, 2004). This is why people like Charlemagne, Alfred the Great and Kenneth MacAlpin are ancestors of all of us. The fact that people tend to marry someone from nearby complicates these calculations only slightly; simulations have shown that even if 98% of ancestors are local, short and long distance migrants eventually mean you descend from everyone in distant places as well (Coop, 2017).

Most recent common ancestor

How deep in the past you have to go for these effects to be seen depends on the population size of your ancestors' community. If they were all from Shetland, given the historical size of the population, everyone will share ancestors around 1550, but in Fair Isle, due to the extreme isolation and small number of ancestors, the MRCA point happens already by the late 18th century. Jerome Wilson of Springfield (1775-1832) and his wife Barbara Eunson (1779-1864) are in fact the ancestors of all native Fair Islanders today, and indeed all those born in the last century. Rather similarly, pedigree analysis has shown that Donald MacCrimmon born c.1750 was the ancestor of all St Kildans alive at the time of the evacuation in 1930.

For comparison, in Westray, Orkney (maximum population over 2,000 in the mid-19th century, somewhat analogous to Yell, Shetland), a prominent forebear, e.g. Thomas Stevenson (born 28 May 1749), is the ancestor of about one third of the islanders today, meaning that the MRCA point will only be reached deeper in the past. Because the number of ancestors doubles every generation, it is not a linear process and so it's very likely this point is reached by about three generations further back, probably by 1650. Unfortunately records don't survive to allow us to explore most relationships at this remove of time, but for individual parishes or isles in Shetland or Orkney, the MRCA point is likely around 1650-1700, depending on how populous the parish was.

Isolate breakdown

Marriage in Fair Isle was remarkably strictly local (endogamous) until the 1940s, with both spouses in almost every marriage coming from the isle (only seven non-islanders contributed to the gene pool from the 1780s till the 1940s). The last marriage between islanders occurred in 1943, and the last full-bred Fair Islander was born in 1954. Around this time, an unusually long line of baby boys was born in the island (1930-1950) until a girl was finally born in 1951. It was said that nature was taking action to counteract the inbreeding, although of course this was just chance. Newspaper articles started to appear and even a documentary about the "Island of Men". Together with the decline in population and increased movement, the genetic isolate began to break down, and even islanders who stayed took spouses from elsewhere in Scotland or England. Immigration from the 1960s onwards further altered the make-up of the isle and eventually the distinctive "Frisle" dialect of Shaetlan – like Whalsay and Skerries dialects rendering *brae* and *hae* as *broi* and *hoi* – was no longer spoken in the school and will in time become extinct.

Diasporas

Given that the population today is only around 50, having declined from a peak of 380 in 1861, it is clear that Fair Islanders have emigrated and, indeed, their descendants are found from Dorset to British Columbia and New York to Queensland. A number of large scale emigrations, however, brought islanders to Orkney during the time that Fair Isle was owned by Stewart of Brough in Westray. To combat overpopulation, a number of islanders were resettled in Westray in 1832, and a larger group (of about 50) went to Stronsay around the same time to expand the herring fishing. Further individuals followed, bringing the number of Fair Islanders in Westray to above 30 by 1851.

About 14 families also moved to Kirkwall in the 1870s, because of increasingly hard conditions and sometimes destitution. Many hundreds of people in Orkney today descend from the Stouts who moved to Westray in 1832, and large numbers also come down from the Leslies and Williamsons, who were in Whitehall village in Stronsay. The later movement to Kirkwall, mostly of Wilsons, but also some Eunsons and Leslies, has left fewer descendants, as many families used Orkney as a stepping stone for one or two generations, before moving further afield to the cities of Scotland or the colonies.

Another important emigration was to Edinburgh and Leith (around the 1880s-90s), where many Fair Isle men worked in the biscuit factory for McVities, with smaller numbers also moving to Aberdeen, County Durham and New Zealand, following a broader pattern of Shetland emigration. Throughout the 19th and 20th centuries, there has been a steady flow of Fair Isle people to the Shetland Mainland – in earlier days to Dunrossness specifically, but also to Lerwick, as would be the case with other isles.

The most unusual exodus from Fair Isle, however, was that of 137 adults and children in 1862 to New Brunswick in Canada, again to alleviate overcrowding (but this movement has also been interpreted as a form of clearance – see Hutchison, 2023). Census records show the diaspora of Stouts, Irvines, Williamsons, Browns, Mathers and Johnsons (Eunsons in disguise!) in the province in the latter half of the Victorian era, and there are still descendants there today.

While celibacy was quite common in the rural farming parishes of the Northern Isles in the 19th century (e.g. in Sanday – see Brennan, 1981), it is notable that many Fair Isle emigrants to the cities of Scotland did not marry. For example, there were two families of Wilsons, each with ten siblings, only two of whom married, and another three families of eight (Wilsons and Eunson), where only one or none married. This perhaps reflected difficulties fitting in to urban Victorian life, a society where Highlanders and Islanders faced prejudice and discrimination. Many succumbed to infectious diseases such as measles as well. Parallels are perhaps to be seen in the families of St Kilda, with high rates of tuberculosis, but the Hiorteachs appeared to have no trouble marrying on mainland Scotland (or elsewhere in the Hebrides).

Disease genetics

The population demography described here can also lead to disease-causing genetic variants rising to much higher frequencies than elsewhere, due to genetic drift. In the Viking Genes study (ed.ac.uk/viking), we have seen this in Aithsting, Shetland for a KCNH2, heart arrhythmia risk variant (Kerr, 2019), in Westray, Orkney for a BRCA1, breast and ovarian cancer risk variant (Kerr, 2023) and for other, as yet unpublished, variants in further subpopulations in Orkney and Shetland. While none of these are observed in Fair Isle, it does have one of the highest, if not the highest, rate in the world of the CFTR gene variant called DF508, which causes cystic fibrosis in children with two copies. Evidence suggests that, unfortunately, one of the most recent common ancestors, Jerome and Barbara Wilson, carried this variant and it has been passed down the generations to many of their descendants. It is a small miracle that more cystic fibrosis babies were not born, given the perfect storm of most people descending from carriers and a preference for cousin marriage. Fair Isle has also given rise to its own form of the genetic condition ichthyosis, where the skin in certain areas grows more quickly than normal, causing it to become hardened and scaly. This appears to have arisen by a novel mutation in the 1890s and has been inherited through the family in the generations since.

A tour of the genetic genealogies of Fair Isle has highlighted many features arising from its being an extreme microcosm of the Northern Isles. Similar phenomena are observed in very deep pedigrees, such as royal genealogies and, in fact, will be ubiquitous at greater time depths. The study of such a small and isolated natural laboratory provides a rare opportunity to see how ancestry and inheritance play out within the time-depth of the genealogies of ordinary women and men. I hope that the deep study of the genealogy and genetics can act as an exemplar for the other parishes in the Northern Isles and Hebrides.

Acknowledgements

I thank Gerry Wilson, Karen Nielsen, Andrew Stout, Carol Tweedie, Lucija Klaric, Craig Sinclair and Alan Beattie for helpful suggestions. Too many people to mention assisted with the genealogy of Fair Isle over the decades but I'd like to particularly thank Aest Jimmy (Wilson), Skeul Andy (Eunson), Myres Jimmy (Stout), Busta Tommy (Stout), Anne Sinclair, Annie Thomson, Houll Willie (Stout), Muriel Eunson and Hazel Wilson.

Bibliography

Brennan E.R. (1981) 'Kinship, Demographic, Social, and Geographic Characteristics of Mate Choice in Sanday, Orkney Islands, Scotland', *American Journal of Physical Anthropology* 55, pp.129-138.

Ceballos F.C., *et al.* (2018) 'Runs of homozygosity: windows into population history and trait architecture', *Nature Reviews Genetics* 19, pp.220-234.

Chang J.T. (1999) 'Recent Common Ancestors of All Present-Day Individuals', *Advances in Applied Probability* 31, pp.1002-1026.

Clark D.W., *et al.* (2019) 'Associations of autozygosity with a broad range of human phenotypes', *Nature Communications* 10, p.4957.

Coop G. (2017) 'Your ancestors lived all over the world', gcbias blog. Available at: https://gcbias.org/2017/11/28/your-ancestors-lived-all-over-the-world/ (accessed: 24 August 2023).

Gilbert E., *et al.* (2019) 'The genetic landscape of Scotland and the Isles', *Proceedings of the National Academy of Sciences* 116, pp.19064-19070.

Helgason A., *et al.* (2003) 'A Populationwide Coalescent Analysis of Icelandic Matrilineal and Patrilineal Genealogies: Evidence for a Faster Evolutionary Rate of mtDNA Lineages than Y Chromosomes', *American Journal of Human Genetics* 72, pp.1370-1388.

Hutchison I. (2023) 'The 1862 Fair Isle Clearance to New Brunswick', *Scottish Historical Review* 102, pp.91-115.

Joshi P.K., *et al.* (2015) 'Directional dominance on stature and cognition in diverse human populations', *Nature* 523, pp.459-462.

Kerr S.M., *et al.* (2019) 'An actionable KCNH2 Long QT Syndrome variant detected by sequence and haplotype analysis in a population research cohort', *Scientific Reports* 9, p.10964.

Kerr S.M., *et al.* (2023) 'Clinical case study meets population cohort: identification of a BRCA1 pathogenic founder variant in Orcadians' *European Journal of Human Genetics* 31, pp.588-595.

Rohde D.L.T., *et al.* (2004) 'Modelling the recent common ancestry of all living humans', *Nature* 431, pp.562-566.

Wilson J.F. (1994) *The Genealogy of Fair Isle*. Kirkwall: Orkney Library & Archive, Orkney Room shelf mark: 929 Z.

14

A Shetland witchcraft case: historical documents and oral tradition

Liv Helene Willumsen
(Arctic University of Norway)

On 22 April 2016, I was sitting together with 89 year-old Peter Garrick in the living-room in his house in Tingwall. We talked about the witchcraft trial of Katie Ratter from Sandness, which he had heard about when he was growing up there. This was the first of several conversations I had with Peter, and these conversations show how Katie Ratter's story has been passed on orally for over 300 years.

Peter Garrick and Liv Helene Willumsen. *Copyright: Liv Helene Willumsen*

I had managed to get in contact with Peter Garrick with the help of Shetland Archivist Brian Smith. Since I started on my PhD at the University of Edinburgh about witchcraft trials in Scotland and Finnmark, Northern Norway, I have received much support from Brian. I met him the first time in 2003, when I came to Lerwick to work in the archives with witchcraft documents. He has always been helpful, meeting all my questions with his comprehensive historical knowledge, and I am very grateful for this. This time, when I needed some help to find out whether there was anybody who knew about the Ratter family in Sandness and the accusations of witchcraft against this family, Brian was an obvious person to approach. Thus, I came in contact with Peter Garrick, his son John Garrick and Andrea Jeromson. They were all good informants on the oral tradition of a Sandness witchcraft case.

The historical records

In the original presbytery records of the questioning of the Ratter family, three family members are mentioned (Presbytery of Shetland records, Shetland Archives CH2/1071/1). On 9 June 1708, two sisters and one brother of the Ratter family from Collaster (written as Colvaseter in the original text) in Sandness – Andrew, Kathren, and Elspeth Ratter – were questioned before the Presbytery. The three were accused of witchcraft, sorcery and deluding the people. They were examined by the brethren of the presbytery and the moderator, James Milne (for Milne see Scott, 1928, p.285). A series of witnesses, mainly neighbouring men and women, were called forth. The witnesses said that the Ratter family had come begging for food, and when they were refused, they cursed. Shortly after the visit, sickness and death occurred, allegedly as a result of the curse. The minutes from the Presbytery give us a good insight into the way neighbours reacted against people in local society who they feared might cause bad luck. The testimonies of the witnesses show that they were convinced of a strong cause-and-effect relation between the cursing of the Ratter family and sudden sickness in the village.

The only written historical records that survive are the presbytery minutes. The case of Kathren Ratter was passed on to the sheriff court, and she was prosecuted in a criminal trial. Unfortunately, we do not have the court records that would tell us what happened to her.

The first entry in the presbytery minutes is dated Sandness 9 June 1708. The kirk session consisted of six members, including the clerk. The moderator said that he had cause to cite Andrew, Kathren and Elspeth Ratter as persons suspected of witchcraft. He also submitted a list of witnesses, who declared that they were terrified by the Ratter family's cursing. These people claimed that if the Ratters were refused what they desired, malicious events followed.

The witnesses testified that Elspeth Ratter went to houses, begging for food and threatening people when she was refused, and that she had received a warning to move out of Colvaseter. Kathren Ratter had been heard cursing a man who died shortly afterwards. She was also suspected of having caused the death of a young woman in connection with blood letting. Kathren Ratter denied this, and witnesses were called. Kathren Ratter was also reported to have been begging for alms, and threatened adults and children if she was denied. Andrew Ratter was suspected of casting spells on cows and humans, with the result of sickness and death. He was interrogated and denied the accusation.

On 11 June 1708, there was another kirk session at Brebuster in Walls. Andrew Ratter was suspected of the death of lambs and sheep, as well as the death of cows and oxen because of curses he allegedly made when he was refused alms. In addition, he was suspected of the death of a child. It was decided that the whole process should be sent to the sheriff, John Mitchell.

The presbytery records thus give an image of the Ratter family as poor people who went among their neighbours asking for aid, and cursing and threatening when they were refused. Their cursing is related to sickness and death of humans as well as animals. Several witnesses testified that they were afraid of the Ratter family. The first kirk session entry from Sandness includes the three siblings Elspeth, Kathren and Andrew Ratter. The last kirk session entry from Walls deals with Andrew Ratter only. The kirk session passed on the case to the sheriff, thus instigating a criminal trial.

The oral tradition

In addition to the Presbytery minutes, the story of Kathren Ratter is known today thanks to oral tradition. The story about her fate has lived on in Sandness for more than 300 years. The historical documents do not tell us the final fate of Kathren, John and Elsbeth Ratter. I wanted to find out whether oral tradition could tell what had happened with the family members so I went to Shetland. It was very exciting for me to come to Lerwick to meet Peter Garrick. Peter, who grew up in Sandness, was 89 at the time of our interview. He remembered well hearing the story about one member of the Ratter family, Kitty Ratter. My other informants were John Garrick, son of Peter Garrick, and Andrea Jeromson from Sandness, who I spoke to the day after I visited Peter. John Garrick had learned the story about Kitty Ratter from his father.

The conversation I had with Peter Garrick on 22 April 2016, with the support of John Garrick, showed me how the main elements in an interesting story may continue to live on orally for generations. When the conversation started, Peter Garrick welcomed me and said he was pleased 'to discuss the pieces we know'. All quotations in the following are Peter Garrick's own words from our recorded conversation. He made clear that personally he did not believe in witchcraft: 'The time when I grew up, they said it was rubbish'. This comment led the conversation into reflections about different ways of thinking today compared with the 1700s.

When we moved on, Peter said that he could not remember who told him the story of Kathren Ratter, or Kitty, which was the short form of her Christian name used orally in Sandness. He did not think it was from his mother or father: 'It could not have come from my mother's side. She was a great believer in Christianity'. The teacher never mentioned it in school, so it had been told to him from people in Sandness: 'I was a rather young man (...) I just heard about it'. The sister and brother of Kitty Ratter, mentioned in the Presbytery minutes, are not mentioned in the story which has lived on.

Told and retold in the local community, a very dramatic story emerges. Kitty Ratter and members of her family went to neighbours to beg for food, and if they were refused, they cursed. Kitty was accused of witchcraft because she had cursed several persons who became sick and died. Peter believed that there was a connection between Kitty Ratter's cursing and her being reported to the authorities, the kirk session. The reason was a growing fear among the villagers: 'After two or three times they would have been feared by the whole community (...) 'The whole parish was terrified of her (...) They were afraid of her (...) They certainly believed she was a witch'.

The type of witchcraft that Kitty Ratter allegedly performed was the old, harmful witchcraft, *maleficium*, the idea that some people had an inherent power to cast spells causing sickness and death. It was not the learned concept of witchcraft which came to the fore in Europe 1450-1750, demonology, with the core ideas of a person entering into a pact with the Devil to get evil power, and taking part in witches' gatherings. In the Kitty Ratter story, she was feared because she cursed, the old-fashioned type of witchcraft. Peter had never heard about the Devil being involved in the story – she was not feared because she was the Devil's ally. In addition: 'You never heard much of the Devil in Shetland at my time, unless "May the Devil take you!"'.

During our conversation, Peter emphasized several times the kirk session's responsibility for persecution of alleged witches and that they handled witchcraft cases in the wrong way: 'That they [the judges] were so stupid to believe in this rubbish (...) It is just unbelievable that such things could go on (...) As the Ratters were concerned, it was terrible things they were going through (...) The community of Sandness was very different at this time'. When the witchcraft trials ended: 'The kirk must have been thinking it had gone too far (...) people were as scared for the kirk as they were for the Ratters'.

Peter Garrick knew that Kitty Ratter was taken away from Sandness by the authorities, but he did not know that her case was sent on from the presbytery to the sheriff court. As the historical documents show, the first session of the presbytery dealing with Kitty Ratter's case, was held in Sandness, then there was a session in Walls. Further, there must have been a trial held in Scalloway, as it was necessary to send the case from the kirk to the sheriff court in order to have a sentence passed in witchcraft trials. Although we do not have the written records to prove it, we can perhaps assume that she was accused of witchcraft in a criminal trial in Scalloway but not sentenced to death.

In the oral tradition, the story goes that Kitty Ratter perished in a snow storm in the hills outside Sandness on her way home. She was buried in the hill where she was found, and, subsequently, the hill was named 'Kitty Ratter's hill'. Peter Garrick: 'We all knew Kitty Ratter's hill (...) It set a scare to speak about it'.

Then, 'her dog found the bones afterwards and brought the bones to Sandness' (...) Kitty Ratter was brought back to Sandness and buried at Sandness, near a stone.' She was not buried in the kirk-yard (...) there was 'a deep respect for the dead.'

It is not known whether any of the Ratters were married: 'I don't think there was any marriage involved. They would not ask a witch to marry you.' It might also be that the accusations of witchcraft had effect on demographic conditions: 'The fact that there are no Ratters on the west coast of Shetland – the family disappeared maybe because there was no marriage.' If there had been any children in the Ratter family, Peter's opinion was that 'they would have had a poor life'.

Several times during the conversation, Peter commented on the missing information about Kitty Ratter's brother and sister, who were brought before the kirk session at the same time as her: 'Very funny. What happened to the brother and the sister? (...) You could not say that Kitty was worse than the other two (...) She was the one that was most spoken about. The other two could not have been burnt'.

With regard to belief in witchcraft, a new age was coming, 'because nobody believed in that any more'.

Additional oral features of the story

On 23 April 2016, John Garrick and Andrea Jeromson took Peter Garrick and I on a drive to Sandness, and also showed me the place in the hills where Kitty Ratter was said to have been buried. Peter Garrick was sitting in the car while Andrea and John and I went up into the hills to look for this place. Andrea Jeromson learned from her grand-uncle in Collaster the story of Kitty Ratter and her burial place. Andrea found the place in the hill where she had been told Kitty Ratter had been laid to rest. It was on a slope, on the back side of the hill when you looked at it from Sandness.

According to oral transference of the story to Andrea, Kitty Ratter was tried before the court in Scalloway and sentenced to be branded on her forehead. She also was fined: she owned many sheep which she had to give away. Kitty perished in the hills in a snowstorm on her way back to Collaster. Her body was found and buried in the hills, at a place known by local people. Years later, her dog found the bones of her skeleton and brought some to her home farm, where they were buried near the houses. The fates of Andrew and Elspeth Ratter were not mentioned to Andrea Jeromson.

The fact that Andrea Jeromson had been told the story of Kitty Ratter from her grand-uncle shows that the story was still alive in Sandness one generation after Peter Garrick. There is something about the tale which makes it interesting – it is a story to be told and retold. Also, the fact that Andrea's grand-uncle had shown her the place in the hills where Kitty Ratter was buried points to the emphasis put on landscape and markers in landscape in the passing on of oral tradition.

A document in private hands

Andrea Jeromson also showed me a hand-written document in her possession which contains historical information about Sandness. The author of this document is unknown, however it might have been written by folklorist Christina Jamieson (1864–1942), who was born at Cruisdale, Sandness (for more about Jamieson see Smith, 2004), and who interviewed a number of people from the district for her literary and historical work. The document mentions Collaster and Katie Rattray.[1] It tells us that she owned the farm Collaster in Sandness and that she was well off, having 'so many sheep that when they came from the hill to the shore to eat *waar* [i.e. kelp] the last sheep was coming in over Swirtifield when the first one was at the Banks of Garth'. On account of this wealth she was called to Scalloway to answer a charge of witchcraft. According to this document, the charge was not proven, or was waived after she agreed to the forfeiture of her sheep. But to ensure against any future chance of practicing witchcraft, she was 'cuttit abüne the headh – that is, cut deeply across the forehead and allowed to go'. On her way home from Scalloway, she was caught in a snowstorm, and died on the back of 'Katie Rattray's Hill'. When her body was at last found, it could not be moved, and was buried where it lay.

This document is interesting, as it records in a written form that Kitty Ratter was tried and sentenced. It also shows how new information can be added to what the Presbytery minutes tell us and give us a new perspective. In the document owned by Andrea Jeromson, it is said that Kitty Ratter had many sheep, and that she managed to pay the fines in court. This stands in contradiction to information in the presbytery minutes, where it is said that the members of the Ratter family were poor and had to go begging for food.

Orality features

In the story of Kitty Ratter, as it comes to us today via a combination of historical records and oral traditions, features of orality are prevalent. Orality plays a threefold role in this article. First, people's voices are found in the original presbytery document reporting suspicions of witchcraft against the Ratter family. Second, orality plays an important role in the transfer of the story of Katie Ratter in Sandness, a transfer taking place from 1708 and continuing today as told to me by Peter Garrick and Andrea Jeromson. Third, orality markers surface in the story told in the document in Andrea Jeromson's possession.

Orality markers in written documents are identified by Walter J. Ong in his book *Orality and Literacy*, where he points to features such additive sentence structures, aggregative language elements, redundancy, closeness to the human lifeworld, and an agonistical tone (Ong, 1982, pp.37-45).

---

1   In the document, it is mentioned that Rattray is said to be a Dutch name, and that the Rattrays may have come to Collaster through the Dutch fishing at Bousta.

When looking for orality features in the Presbytery minutes, we see the use of additive sentence structures. The testimonies of the witnesses are structured by one sentence combined with the next, often using 'and' as the combining conjunction. The accusations are compiled by one witness after the other bringing forth their suspicions against the Ratter family, a long flow of accusations, wherein both the addition of new accusations and repetition of already presented accusations, play a part.

Aggregative language elements are seen in the witnesses' testimonies and in the court session discourse, often where two nouns with the same meaning are combined, for instance 'horrid curses and imprecations'.

Linguistic redundancy is seen in the detailed portraying of the animals and persons allegedly attacked by witchcraft, where also the time is also central: first some angry words are uttered, then sickness and death follow shortly afterwards. In fact, the seriousness of the accusation is based on this cause-and-effect connection.

Closeness to the human lifeworld is seen in all the testimonies, as the threat of the Ratter family comes as a result of walking around to the houses in the village, begging for food, and what happened when they were refused what they asked for.

The agonistical tone is found throughout the documents, as the words used in the discourse of the kirk session members, as well as the rendered oral speech from the witnesses, are harsh and negative in tone. This terminology bears witness to fear and hatred, and tells us about the distress of the peasants in the local community of Sandness when they faced accidents and tragedies that they believed took place because of witchcraft.

The historic reliability of oral tradition always has to be questioned. In the story of Kathren Ratter, as it has been transmitted through many generations, there are elements which are not documented in the Presbytery minutes. But we have to bear in mind the way stories change over time, and the fact that we do not have the Court records from Scalloway. It is difficult to make reliable judgements about some of the story elements brought forth in oral versions of the story.

However, even if oral tradition may have added elements to the story of Kathren Ratter, there is reason to believe that she in fact was tried in Scalloway by the Sheriff John Mitchell, and sentenced to be branded and fined. Since the Presbytery session in Sandness was in June and Kathren Ratter died in winter, the trial in Scalloway could have taken place about half a year after the Presbytery session.

In the story told by Peter Garrick, orality markers are seen in the way particular elements are emphasized. He was well aware of the dramatic elements of the story, and of the ways memory can reshape oral tradition. Even so, strong elements of Kitty's life story have survived. For example, the highly emotional element of her dog finding her skeleton is part of the oral tradition, and this is strengthened by the knowledge of the place in the hills where she was buried and the dog bringing her bones back home. Yes, it is possible that it happened, and it has added an element to the story. In oral transmission, a story always becomes more interesting if the narrator can add a new element to the existing story.

The question why information about Elspeth and Andrew Ratter are missing in the orally transferred story is interesting. Peter Garrick returned to this several times, and his opinion was: 'The case that she [Kitty] perished in a snow storm and the bones were found, makes it outstanding'. Kitty's tragic fate certainly makes an impression, which is perhaps the reason the story has survived for so long in the oral tradition.

In the story passed to Andrea Jeromson by her grand-uncle, Kitty Ratter was branded after a trial, perished in the hills on her way home and was buried there. Finally free from the conviction in Scalloway, she could not wait to come home to her beloved village and her dear dog. After the branding, however, she would always have to live with a very visible stigma. This was the fate of those who were marked by the legal authorities, as it was thought right that it should never be forgotten when a person was convicted. The story becomes stronger by the fact that the narrator knew the burial place in the hills – the orality-marker of proximity to the human life-world is activated. The narrator points to a place in the landscape, making the story absolutely reliable.

In the written document owned by Andrea Jeromson, there are interesting differences to note. The description of Kathren Ratter mainly deviates from the Presbytery minutes in depicting her as a rich woman. Also, it is said that it was due to her wealth she was called to Scalloway to answer a charge of witchcraft. The poor, begging woman has disappeared. On the contrary, she used her wealth to pay the fine. And the branding is explained as a means of ensuring that there would be no future performance of witchcraft. This does not take into account all the witnesses giving testimonies against Kitty Ratter, who clearly feared witchcraft. The informant has tried to give another explanation than that which appears in the presbytery minutes about why she was brought to Scalloway. She is portrayed like an innocent victim, and the wrong-doing of the authorities is underlined. Orality markers are used, for instance the wonderful image of the sheep coming to eat 'waar'. However, the main content of the story has changed: she is not portrayed as a witch that angry neighbours wanted to get rid of.

The oral passing on of Kitty Ratter's story is alive today, and it will hopefully be alive for new generations taking an interest in the fascinating fate of this woman. It is interesting to give the story a continued life also because it tells us something about people's attitudes to one another in a small community in a bygone time, and shows us something about how power operated in their society.

I am very grateful to Peter Garrick, John Garrick and Andrea Jeromson, who have shared their knowledge with me. It has been wonderful to hear the story about Kitty Ratter in oral transference, a testimony of oral culture and its way of travelling.

Bibliography

Ong, Walter J. (1982) *Orality and Literacy. The Technologizing of the Word.* London: Routledge.

Presbytery of Shetland minute book (1700-1719), Shetland Archives CH2/1071/1

Scott, Hew (ed.) (1928) *Fasti Ecclessiæ Scotticanæ: The Succession of Ministers in The Church of Scotland from the Reformation.* Edinburgh: Oliver and Boyd.

Smith, Brian (2004) 'Jamieson, Christina (1864–1942)', Oxford Dictionary of National Biography. Oxford University Press. Available at: https://www.oxforddnb.com/display/10.1093/ref:odnb/9780198614128.001.0001/odnb-9780198614128-e-63872 (accessed: 26 May 2021).

15

James Loutit and Shetland Methodism

David Bebbington
(University of Stirling)

Methodism was the Christian movement led by John Wesley in the eighteenth century that concentrated on saving souls. It spread into Scotland before the end of the century but reached the Shetland Islands only in 1819 or 1820, when a Shetlander, John Nicolson, who had been converted in London while serving in the army, returned to preach in the islands. Nicolson requested help from the Methodist authorities, who despatched regular preachers to Shetland. The movement enjoyed remarkable early growth, so that by 1831 there were over 1,400 members. Although numbers rose and fell during subsequent years, there were more than 1,500 members and twenty-four chapels at the end of the century. Methodism did not take root in most parts of Scotland, but in Shetland it became a sturdy presence (Bebbington, 2021).

James Loutit was a Shetlander who in 1825 was the first from the islands to enter the Methodist ministry. He did not serve in Shetland, instead preaching in a variety of towns and cities up and down England, and he played a major role in fostering the welfare of Methodism there. He was born in Lerwick on 6 October 1801, the second son of another James who had married Janet James in 1798 (Old Parish Registers). His father may well have come from Scalloway, where a young James Loutit was living in 1785 and where the minister still had relatives in 1869 (Grant, 2011, p.12; Caley, 1869). The father entered the Royal Navy as an ordinary seaman in 1803, apparently as a volunteer rather than as a pressed man, serving on H.M.S. *Carysfort* until he died two years later in an accident while his ship was at Antigua in the West Indies (Beattie, 2017). His son, the future minister, was described many years later as 'a ragged, shoeless boy', or at least hatless (Dunn, 1850), the family having fallen on hard times. The small sum of compensation money paid by the Admiralty to Loutit's mother was channelled through the parish minister, John Menzies, who set up a Sunday school attended by the young James (Beattie, 2017; Loutit, 1869a). Menzies also supported foreign missions, an indication that he was an Evangelical, one of the ministers of the Church of Scotland who believed in vigorous Christian efforts to seek conversions (Clausen and Manson, 1979,

James Loutit

p.2). Sitting under Menzies' preaching, Loutit would have been instilled with biblical expertise. He became, according to his own recollection, one of the 'earnest Churchmen' of Lerwick (Memoranda, 1870).

In 1822, however, the first regular Methodist preacher came to Shetland. He was Daniel M'Allum, a physician as well as a minister, who was charged with investigating whether John Nicolson's plea for a Methodist mission to Shetland was warranted. On the evening of Sunday 30 June, Loutit heard M'Allum lecture on the parable of the prodigal son. The lecture led him 'directly to the Personal Ch[ris]t in whom he found the peace of [God]' (Loutit, 1872c). The outcome of this conversion was a theological revolution in Loutit's mind. He turned 'from the earnest pursuit of justification by works to that of justification by faith in Ch[ris]t – a faith, nevertheless, productive of good works' (Loutit, 1869b). That was a formula typical of Methodism. Loutit identified himself wholly with the new movement in the islands. He became the first leader of a class, one of the small groups for discussion of spiritual experience in which Methodists were organised, and the first local preacher. His sermons were not initially distinguished. John Lewis, the third minister stationed in Shetland, commented that when Loutit preached in Gruting in May 1825 it was 'not well', though he did 'a little better' in the nearby Bayhall the following day (Bowes, 2005, p.115). Despite these mediocre prentice efforts, Lewis recommended him for full-time

Methodist ministry in that year and Loutit left the islands for work in England (Loutit, 1855b).

Already Loutit had turned his professional skills to account in the service of the movement. For over seven years he was a clerk in the office of James Greig, the leading Lerwick solicitor who acted as procurator fiscal for the islands from 1806 onwards and an elder in the parish church (Loutit, 1873b; Robertson, 1991, p.64; Clausen and Manson, 1979, p.26). Starting a career there was a natural step because Greig was married to the sister of Loutit's uncle (Beattie, 2017). Greig's daughter joined the Methodists in 1824, probably under Loutit's influence (Bowes, 2005, p.61). While serving in Greig's office, Loutit drew up the deeds for the earliest Methodist chapels in Shetland, a task to which he would return in later years (Loutit, 1854). After entering the ministry, Loutit married a woman five years his senior, probably in 1831-33 while stationed in Witney, Oxfordshire, the birthplace of his wife Martha. Childlessness allowed him to give free rein to his energies (England and Wales, 1851). He sustained his interest in his homeland, to which he always gave its official title, 'Zetland', by joining Adam Clarke, the most scholarly and urbane of the denomination's preachers, on a visit to Shetland in 1828 (Clarke, 1833, p.173). Clarke took the mission to the islands under his wing in the years before his death in 1832. Loutit subsequently revered the memory of Clarke, whose patronage, in his eyes, ensured the initial rapid advance of Methodism in Shetland. Loutit cast himself in the same mould. He organised the despatch of Bibles and Testaments for distribution in Shetland in 1840, advised (with Greig's help) on securing chapel sites over the next few years and raised money in his own circuit – the Methodist term for a group of chapels – at Louth in Lincolnshire for the erection of buildings in 1844 (Loutit, 1840; Baylis, 1841; Loutit, 1844c). In a copious correspondence he showed a healthy appetite for news of anything bearing on the progress of Methodism in Shetland, whether revivals, preaching tours or negotiations with landowners. 'God sent Methodism to Z[etland]', he wrote – 'Z[etland] embraced it' (Loutit, 1844a). Loutit was dedicated to furthering what he conceived to be the work of God in the islands.

During the 1850s Loutit's role expanded. From 1853 he was a member of the denomination's Zetland committee, travelling to the islands again in 1853 and 1856 to promote the cause (Loutit, 1853; Loutit, 1856a). At first his chief task, as a legal expert, was the settlement of the Methodists' title to their chapels, and in 1855 he prepared a lengthy report on the subject which impressed the committee (Minutes, 1855, pp.3-5). Loutit, however, believed that he held a much wider remit. He maintained that, after the original guidance given to the Shetland mission by Adam Clarke, the cause had prospered far less than it might have done. The men sent to Shetland were generally young and inexperienced, requiring guidance, but there had been an 'absence of an active supervision & intelligent counsel to direct the staff of preachers in the Islands'. Matters improved, Loutit held, when from 1850 to 1853 John Stephenson, a senior Methodist who had earlier travelled in Shetland, was appointed to attend the annual district meetings, but he had done little more. 'I at last interposed', wrote Loutit (who rarely minimised his role in affairs), wielding the authority of the Zetland committee (Loutit, 1859). From 1853 onwards Loutit was the chief figure on the mainland promoting the interests of Shetland Methodism.

A large part of his time was spent on money raising. Loutit pressed the Methodist authorities to give financial support to Shetland. In 1856 he drew up a plan for church extension entailing erecting a chapel at Aith, reroofing the Sand chapel, transferring the Westerskeld chapel to a new site and rebuilding the chapel and manse in Unst. He applied to John Mason, the secretary of the denomination's chapel committee, for a grant. The reply was a sharp rejection. 'I now then tell you once for all', wrote Mason, 'I have no fund whatever in my hands for building <u>or for assisting in the building of Chapels or Ministers [sic] houses in Zetland, therefore no help must be calculated upon from me</u>'. There might, he conceded, be merely a little for repairs (Mason, 1856a). Loutit, however, was not discouraged, sending a further plea with a breakdown of expenses. Mason now offered £10 each for repairs at Aith, Sand and Unst chapels, warning that it would be some time before Loutit could expect any more from him (Mason, 1856b). But Loutit returned to the fray, requesting a further £10 each for the Westerskeld chapel and the Unst house (Loutit, 1856b). This type of perseverance did bring results. Most money was raised from prosperous Methodists to whom Loutit despatched appeals for help. In 1868, for instance, Loutit asked William Mewburn, a Manchester businessman who had just bought a country estate in Oxfordshire, to make a gift to a destitute local preacher in Shetland and was rewarded with £5. On that occasion the minister called himself 'the beggar general for Methodism in the Zetland Islands' (Loutit, 1868a). It was a fair self-description.

Loutit, however, was not only a collector of funds from others. He was repeatedly generous with his own money. When, at the start of the 1870s, subscriptions were being solicited for a new chapel and manse at Walls, William Mewburn, though an immensely wealthy man, contributed only £2:10 shillings, but Loutit himself gave £50, the same sum as the earl of Zetland, the islands' largest landowner (Donations, 1872). Moreover Loutit made this contribution anonymously, hiding under the soubriquet 'Thule'. The source of his financial assets is unclear since Methodist ministers were not generously paid, though perhaps he had accumulated some money during his time in Greig's solicitor's office. He had certainly acquired some dwellings in Hangcliff Lane, Lerwick, from which he drew a small income, sometimes resorting to law to secure an eviction or unpaid rent (Summons, 1854; Summons, 1856). In 1857, however, he told a correspondent that he had sold all the houses to raise money for his church extension scheme (Loutit, 1857). He especially exerted himself in assembling the funds for the Adam Clarke Memorial Church, designed to add to the respectability of Lerwick Methodism, that was opened in 1872. According to the accounts, Loutit gave as much as £100, four times as much as Arthur James Hay, the most prosperous seatholder in the new building, who was factor for the earl of Zetland and a partner in the largest employers in the islands (Account Book, 1868-74; Robertson, 1991, p.71). Loutit was still energetically channelling resources into Shetland in his final years. In 1878 he canvassed the richer Methodists in the town to which he had retired, Halifax, for donations to the home mission in the islands. Of the thirty contributions received from all over the country, eighteen were from Halifax (Zetland Home Mission, 1880). Loutit devoted himself to the financial needs of the cause.

He was equally persistent in supplying advice to the ministers in Shetland. In 1856, for instance, George Hester, a junior minister stationed in Unst, was finding it difficult to persuade islanders to meet in weekly classes, the way in which attenders at Sunday services became Methodist members. They would not give up their formal allegiance to the Free Church of Scotland, which was particularly strong in Unst (Hester, 1856). In reply, Loutit encouraged him to persevere. 'Depend upon it', he wrote: 'those who taste remission of sins by <u>your</u> ministry, will <u>join you</u>' (Loutit, 1856d). Loutit could also champion the ministers of the islands. In 1858 Robert Howarth, the chair of the Shetland Methodist district, sought permission from the president of the Conference, the highest authority in the denomination, to allow William Sellers, the probationer preacher in the Northmavine and Delting circuit, to preside at communion services. Permission was refused because it was against denominational law for a probationer to dispense the sacraments (Bowers, 1858a). That policy was unsuited to Shetland, however, because, unlike elsewhere, a single preacher served a circuit and so there was nobody else to conduct communion. It had been customary in Shetland to allow such probationers to baptise and give communion (Foster, 1858). Loutit took up the cudgel. He extracted from the president a modification of the official line: the president would not authorise the practice but neither would he prohibit it if that was the established custom in Shetland (Bowers, 1858b). Loutit delighted to report to Howarth that Sellers could still administer the sacraments (Loutit, 1858). Loutit functioned as a perennial source of support for the ministers in Shetland.

Sometimes the issues that Loutit addressed in his correspondence were immensely important to the individuals concerned. Methodist preachers were required to go wherever they were sent by the Conference stationing committee. When, in 1855, Loutit was the Shetland representative on that committee, he received a pained letter from a young minister, George Hester, who strongly objected to going to the North Isles circuit of Unst and Yell (Hester, 1855). Loutit, however, told him that the committee declined to revise his appointment because he had given no reason for his objection (Loutit, 1855c). Hester duly went and, as we have seen, consulted Loutit during his ministry in Unst. When Loutit was again representing Shetland on the stationing committee in the following year, he received a letter from the preacher stationed at Walls marked '<u>Strictly private & confidential</u>' strongly recommending that John Duncan should not be transferred to that circuit for the following year. Duncan had married a woman from Walls who, as the daughter of a Church of Scotland minister who showed no inclination to Methodism, appeared 'a very improper person for <u>a Minister's Wife</u>' (Dent, 1856). Duncan was not transferred to Walls. Loutit was given to taking decisive action, something that frequently aroused resentment.

That can be illustrated from his later dealings with Duncan. In 1862 when Loutit reprimanded him over the expense of building the Scalloway chapel, Duncan's abrupt reply was that 'I do not like the style of your note' (Duncan, 1862). Duncan was thoroughly alienated by Loutit's manner. His oversight of Shetland could be distinctly overbearing.

Yet Loutit's contribution to the development of Shetland Methodism was in one respect pivotal. Normally Methodists were known for their fostering of lay participation in church affairs with much preaching, leadership and administrative responsibility placed in the hands of men in secular employment (and occasionally women). In Shetland that was not initially the case. Although there were a few local preachers who were laymen, there were no lay trustees of chapels and manses at all (Loutit, 1855a). In mainland Methodism there were chapel stewards who looked after the premises on a day-to-day basis, society stewards who organised the affairs of individual congregations and circuit stewards who did the same for the groups of congregations in a circuit, but not in Shetland. All these duties were performed by the ministers, whom Loutit described as the 'factotums of the Concern' (Loutit, 1868b). 'All other denominations in Zetland', he declared in 1870, 'have lay officials. Methodism is pointed to as a ministerial oligarcy – the Christian people ignored!' (Loutit, 1870). The principal reason why was set out in the same year by George Hobson, the minister in Lerwick. 'With very few exceptions', he wrote, 'our members are poor men and ignorant men as to affairs' (Hobson, 1870). Loutit would have none of that. Suitable persons were available. 'The Zetland intellect', he insisted to Hobson, 'whether Scandinavian, Scotch, or both, did not use [sic] to be inferior to any portion of Great Britain – only give it fair play' (Loutit, 1871a). With a strong dose of Shetland patriotism, Loutit demanded change.

His opportunity came when, in 1870, the Shetland Islands were taken out of the Edinburgh and Aberdeen District of Methodism to become a separate district under the auspices of the Home Mission Department. Loutit primed Alexander M'Aulay, the representative of the department who visited Shetland in 1870, with his views on the imperative need for greater lay involvement (Loutit, 1870). M'Aulay duly reported that laymen should be appointed as chapel, society and circuit stewards 'with all convenient speed' and Conference accepted his recommendations (Suggestions, 1870). Furthermore he embraced a parallel idea for the deployment of laymen that Loutit had long canvassed. It was a scheme for what Loutit had called as long ago as 1844 'native agency' (Loutit, 1844b). The term, normally used of the foreign mission field, meant employing local folk as paid lay preachers. Loutit had suggested in 1866 that if £50 were distributed among eight or ten men, the effect would be better than the acquisition of two additional ministers (Loutit, 1860). In 1870 M'Aulay took up the scheme, though proposing only two such appointments, for Walls and Burravoe on Yell (Suggestions, 1870). As a result of Loutit's pressure there were not only voluntary lay officials but also paid lay agents. By 1898 there were four such agents in post (Shetland Methodist District Synod, 1898). In the later Victorian years Methodism in Shetland appointed a full panoply of laymen to local positions, so becoming more like other districts in the denomination, and at the same time was served by a flow of dedicated young men, which made Shetland unusual. Both were Loutit's achievements.

The minister's other major role was, surprisingly, political. After the death of Loutit's wife in 1866 and his retirement from active ministry in the following year, he had time to expend on wider causes. He had long been acutely aware that the endemic poverty of the people of Shetland was largely a result of the relationship between landlord and tenant (Loutit, 1856c). The system of fishing tenure and truck, giving landlords or their lessees control of the catch and a monopoly of supplies, made life precarious. Bamford Burrows, the preacher at Dunrossness, reported to Loutit in 1868 that the harvest was poor and the fish scarce so that hardship threatened. 'I much wish English Public Opinion could be awakened', he remarked, 'as to the horrible serfdom of your fellow Islanders' (Burrows, 1868). Loutit marked this sentence with a double line in the margin and replied that public exposure would indeed have some effect, typically adding his regret that the preachers had done nothing about it for forty-six years (Loutit, 1868c). In September 1870 he was stirred into efforts of his own. Alexander M'Aulay, who had seen conditions in Shetland earlier in the year, drew Loutit's attention to the commencement of a royal commission to investigate the truck system in Scotland (M'Aulay, 1870). Loutit sprang into action, writing to urge the commissioners to take evidence on the islands, and, when they replied that they might not have time, requesting that at least they should include in their report the need for a government enquiry into the case of Shetland (Loutit, 1870a, 1870b). The Liberal government had just passed the Irish Land Act, extending greater rights to tenants, and Loutit considered the claims of Shetlanders far superior. 'The people have not, like the Irish, taken the law into their own hand', he told the commissioners, 'but their docility & good order will surely no longer lead to their neglect' (Loutit, 1870b). He turned his campaigning talents into secular channels.

The commissioners did take evidence in Shetland in Edinburgh in the following year, and Loutit made the most of their findings including the recommendation of a further enquiry into Shetland. When the report appeared, he called on H. A. Bruce, the Home Secretary, to appoint a special commission to investigate Shetland on the spot. 'For God's sake', he declared in his letter, 'let not this foul blot any longer remain upon the escutcheon of the Kingdom' (Loutit, 1871b). He obtained permission to reproduce much of the evidence from the Truck Commission report in a penny pamphlet of his own (Liddell, 1871). Completed in July 1871 and called *Truck: Or, Semi-Serfdom in the Shetland (Zetland) Isles*, it rehearsed the history of the islands, claiming that the original transfer of the islands from Norway to Scotland in 1470 included the proviso that the inhabitants should retain their laws and customs. The freehold properties of the people, however, had subsequently fallen into the hands of 'Scotchmen' and the British period had been 'one of oppression' (Loutit, 1871g, p.3). The report showed that a thorough government investigation into the islands was imperative. A second edition of the pamphlet, finished in November 1871, added a clarion call to Shetlanders to petition the Home Secretary for that outcome and stressed the need for a Shetland equivalent of the Irish Land Act (Loutit, 1871h, VII, VI). Meanwhile Loutit had sent out a flurry of letters with the same purpose to eminent figures including W. E. Gladstone, the Prime Minister, and Lord Shaftesbury, the Evangelical philanthropist (Loutit, 1871c, 1871d). In November Loutit heard from Whitehall that a special commission was to address the specific problems of the islands (Winterbotham, 1871). The government might well have acted on the recommendation of the Truck Commission in any case, but there can be no doubt that Loutit's crusade helped ensure that it happened.

When the name of the commissioner, William Guthrie, was announced, Loutit hastened to supply him with details of a recent episode in which a mass eviction in Bressay was threatened (Loutit, 1871f). The commissioner corresponded courteously with Loutit, twice asking him for names of suitable people to examine (Guthrie, 1871; Guthrie, 1872), but in the end Guthrie's report proved a huge disappointment because, as Loutit complained to him, he did not make any recommendations about the land question (Loutit, 1872a). Loutit concentrated on demanding a measure going beyond the truck issue to deal with the relations of landlord and tenant. In March 1872, while Guthrie was still conducting his enquiry, Loutit prompted MPs to mention the specific needs of Shetland in the House of Commons (Powell, 1872). In September he despatched a letter of over ten foolscap pages to the Home Secretary calling for parliamentary action (Loutit, 1872b). Later in the year he composed another pamphlet, *Semi-Serfdom in the Zetland (or Shetland) Islands*, which in January 1873 he sent to 450 MPs (Loutit, 1873a). 'For generations', he trumpeted, 'the Scandinavian inhabitants have been down-trodden by the Scot, who has acquired possession of their lands' (Loutit, 1873d, pp.13-14). In February 1873 he even travelled to London to lobby the Home Secretary, subsequently sending him a printed memorandum on a 'Tenant-right, Land and Truck Act' that he had drawn up (Loutit, 1873c). But the campaign came to nothing. In June he was informed that the Home Secretary could not consider a special law relating to Shetland alone and that there would be no bill on the truck question that session (Winterbotham, 1873). Early in the following year the Conservatives replaced the Liberals in office and there was no further possibility of legislation. At the time Loutit's political – almost Shetland nationalist – agitation proved a failure, but it was one of the stepping stones towards the Crofters' Act of 1886 that gave security of tenure to the people of the Highlands and Islands.

James Loutit died on 18 January 1885. Although pursuing his career in England, he had been a doughty Shetlander. Born in Lerwick, he became a Methodist preacher, devoting his legal skills to the service of the denomination. He advocated the interests of Shetland within Methodism and enjoyed success in raising money on behalf of Methodist developments in the islands. Loutit gave advice freely, if sometimes acerbically, to ministers stationed there. His most marked achievement lay in encouraging the selection of lay officials and masterminding the appointment of lay agents, both strategies that long sustained the strength of Methodism in the islands. Exceptionally among the

Methodist ministers of his day, Loutit launched a campaign in public life. His effort to end the truck system and to assert tenants' rights in Shetland may have failed, but it helped place the need for reform on the political agenda. His agitation was founded on a powerful sense of identification with the mass of the Shetland people against the alien elite. 'As to myself', he told the secretary of the Methodist home mission committee in 1871, 'being a native of Lerwick & of Norse descent I care for none of them neither Lairds nor Shopkeepers, but will do what little is in my power to ameliorate the serfdom of my countrymen' (Loutit, 1871e). Loutit was a champion of Shetland as much as of Methodism.

Abbreviations

HMR – Home Mission Records

Bibliography

Account Book (1868-74) Of the Adam Clarke Methodist Memorial Chapel. Shetland Archives, CH11/79/2/52.

Baylis, Edward (1841) Letter to James Loutit, 11 October. HMR.

Beattie, Alan (2017) Letters to author (for which he is grateful).

Bebbington, David (2021) 'Methodism in Victorian Shetland', *Scottish Church History* 50 (2), pp.75-97.

Bowers, John (1858a) Letter to Robert Haworth, 11 September. HMR.

Bowers, John (1858b) Letter to James Loutit, 6 October. HMR.

Bowes, Harold R. (2005) *Two Calves in the House: Being the Shetland Journal of the Reverend John Lewis, 1823-1825*. Lerwick: Shetland Amenity Trust.

Burrows, Bamford (1868) Letter to James Loutit, 23 November. HMR.

Caley, Joseph (1869) Letter to James Loutit, 16 August. HMR.

Clarke, J. B. B. (1833) *An Account of the Religious and Literary Life of Adam Clarke, LL.D., F.A.S., &c., &c., &c.*, vol.3. London: T. S. Clarke.

Clausen, E. J. F., and T. M. Y. Manson (1979) *150th Anniversary of Lerwick Parish Church*. Lerwick: Lerwick and Bressay Parish Church.

Dent, Jonathan (1856) Letter to James Loutit, [before 14 July]. HMR.

Donations (1872) In Aid of the Re-erection of the Chapel with School & Manse, Walls, Zetland. HMR.

Duncan, John T. (1862) Letter to James Loutit, 27 January. HMR.

Dunn, Samuel (1850) quoted in *John O'Groat Journal*, 14 June.

England and Wales (1851) Census, Nottingham.

Foster, William (1858) Letter to James Loutit, 6 October. HMR.

Grant, Eric (2011) 'Where have all the Louttits gone?', *Coontin Kin* 80, pp.8-13.

Guthrie, William (1871) Letter to James Loutit, 25 December. HMR.

Guthrie, William (1872) Letter to James Loutit, 23 March. HMR.

Hester, George P. (1855) Letter to James Loutit, 10 August. HMR.

Hester, George P. (1856) Letter to James Loutit, 3 September. HMR.

Hobson, George (1870) Letter to Alexander M'Aulay, 22 September. HMR.

Home Mission Records. Methodist Archives, John Rylands Library, Manchester.

Liddell, J. F. O. (1871) Letter to James Loutit, 6 July. HMR.

Loutit, James (1840) Letter to Edward Baylis, 2 March. HMR.

Loutit, James (1844a) Letter to Joseph Watson, 20 July. HMR.

Loutit, James (1844b) Letter to Joseph Watson, 29 October. HMR.
Loutit, James (1844c) Letter to Joseph Watson, 9 December. HMR.
Loutit, James (1853) Letter to James Findlay, 25 July. HMR.
Loutit, James (1854) Letter to William Barton, 18 November. HMR.
Loutit, James (1855a) Letter to Secretary of the Wesleyan Chapel Committee, 25 February. HMR.
Loutit, James (1855b) Letter to John Lewis, 14 March. HMR.
Loutit, James (1855c) Letter to George Hester, 15 August. HMR.
Loutit, James (1856a) Expenses to and from Zetland. HMR.
Loutit, James (1856b) Letter to John Mason, 17 May. HMR.
Loutit, James (1856c) Letter to Charles Prest, 17 June. HMR.
Loutit, James (1856d) Letter to George Hester, 17 September. HMR.
Loutit, James (1857) Letter to William Parsonson, 30 January. HMR.
Loutit, James (1858) Letter to Robert Howarth, 9 October. HMR.
Loutit, James (1859) Letter to John Scott, 27 October. HMR.
Loutit, James (1860) Memorial of Methodism in the Zetland Islands, 5 June. HMR.
Loutit, James (1868a) Letter to William Mewburn, 18 January [misdescribed as 1867]. HMR.
Loutit, James (1868b) Letter to Charles Prest, 16 October. HMR.
Loutit, James (1868c) Letter to Bamford Burrows, 21 December. HMR.
Loutit, James (1869a) Letter to Peter Peterson, 6 February. HMR.
Loutit, James (1869b) Letter to Sir Francis Crossley, 15 June. HMR.
Loutit, James (1870a) Letter to the Commissioners on the Truck System in Scotland, 5 September. HMR.
Loutit, James (1870b) Letter to the Commissioners on the Truck System in Scotland, 20 September. HMR.
Loutit, James (1871a) Letter to George Hobson, 30 May. HMR.
Loutit, James (1871b) Letter to H. A. Bruce, 30 June. HMR.
Loutit, James (1871c) Letter to W. E. Gladstone, 31 August. HMR.
Loutit, James (1871d) Letter to the earl of Shaftesbury, 31 August. HMR.
Loutit, James (1871e) Letter to Charles Prest, 2 November. HMR.
Loutit, James (1871f) Letter to William Guthrie, 15 December. HMR.
Loutit, James (1871g) *Truck: Or, Semi-Serfdom in the Shetland (Zetland) Isles*. Leeds: H. W. Walker.
Loutit, James (1871h) *Truck: Or, Semi-Serfdom in the Shetland (Zetland) Isles*, 2nd edition. London.
Loutit, James (1872a) Letter to William Guthrie, 20 August. HMR.
Loutit, James (1872b) Letter to H. A. Bruce, 19 September. HMR.
Loutit, James (1872c) Letter to Peter Peterson, 7 November. HMR.
Loutit, James (1873a) Letter to R. S. Wright, 24 January. HMR.
Loutit, James (1873b) Letter to Sir Peter Tait, 30 January. HMR.
Loutit, James (1873c) Letter to William McArthur, 27 February. HMR.
Loutit, James (1873d) *Semi-Serfdom in the Zetland (or Shetland) Isles, in a Letter to a M.P., by a Zetlander*. London: Elliot Stock.
Mason, John (1856a) Letter to James Loutit, 3 April. HMR.
Mason, John (1856b) Letter to James Loutit, 9 April. HMR.
M'Aulay, Alexander (1870) Letter to James Loutit, 31 August. HMR.
Memoranda (1870) For the Use of the Zetland Deputation, 11 March.
Minutes (1855) Of the Committee of Conference on the Affairs of the Zetland District, 1855-60. Methodist Archives, John Rylands Library, Manchester, MAM P7b.
Old Parish Registers, Lerwick. Scotlands People. Available at: https://www.scotlandspeople.gov.uk (Accessed: 3 April 2023).

Powell, Francis S. (1872) Letter to James Loutit, 19 March. HMR.

Robertson, Margaret Stuart (1991) *Sons and Daughters of Shetland, 1800-1900*. Lerwick: Shetland Publishing Company.

Shetland Methodist District Synod (1898) Minute Book, 10 May. Shetland Archives, CH11/79/1/3.

Suggestions (1870) Submitted to Conference by the Rev. Alexr. McAulay. HMR.

Summons (1854) Of Removing, 21 March. Shetland Archives, SC12/6/1854/35 and SC12/6/1854/36.

Summons (1856) Of Sequestration and Sale, 10 November. Shetland Archives, SC12/6/1856/153.

Winterbotham, Henry (1871) Letter to James Loutit, 21 November. HMR.

Winterbotham, Henry (1873) Letter to James Loutit, 21 June. HMR.

Zetland Home Mission (1880) Annual Subscriptions [hardbound booklet]. HMR.

16

'Is du da man?'
– male violence and ritual in Shetland

Lynn Abrams and Callum G. Brown
(University of Glasgow)

On New Year's Eve Old Style (11 January) 1805, a riot erupted in Greenmoe in the parish of Cunningsburgh in which a man was attacked with a weapon, one was badly hurt and the mother of one of the participants was knocked into a ditch. While some of the events of that evening are confused, the petition of the complainants (including Andrew Duncan who was struck) summarised the grounds upon which five of their alleged assailants, all neighbours in the parish, were to be prosecuted for assault. It read:

> That whereas the crimes of mobbing, bearing offensive weapons, rioting, quarrelling and fighting [and] exciting others to do the same, calumniating and defaming our neighbours good name & reputation threatening to beat & wound & actually beating and wounding to the effusion of blood and danger of people's lives, blaspheming the blessed name of God and breaking his holy Sabbath are crimes of an atrocious nature and highly punishable by the laws of this and every other well governed realm. (Shetland Archives, Papers of Lerwick Sheriff Court: SC12/6/1805/8: Complaint and petition [assault] 16 January 1805)

One of the central characters in the events of that night was Oliver (Olla) Smith, a distant relative of our Festschrifter. He was described as a 'disputatious individual' whose troublesome disposition was well known to the inhabitants of Cunningsburgh. Indeed it was said that Smith bore 'the character of a riotous person threatening to fight those with [...] whom he has any quarrel.' He certainly had a history that supported this assertion. Twice in the previous three years Smith had been bound over to keep the peace following threats of violence to his neighbours. In 1802 it was claimed Smith had challenged Erick Laurenson to what looked like a duel, to meet him 'Man for man at fear [fair] play over a rop over a stick or any yow pleas' (SC12/6/1802/8: Petition for Lawburrows, 15 March 1802). And two years later he was back in court accused, along with three of his brothers and two uncles, of threatening two of his neighbours, stripping off his clothes with the intention to 'beat and bruise', returning the next evening 'with manifest intention of rioting and picking a quarrel' and refusing to 'quit the spot he was then on should he remain there all night untill he had the petitioners knocked down' (SC12/6/1804/2: Petition for Lawburrows, 21 January 1804). Whilst on both occasions the petitions for lawburrows (a legal restraining order) by the complainants were granted, less than a year later Smith, at the age of 34, was found guilty of a 'gross breach of His Majesty's peace' for his role in the Cunningsburgh Yuletide riot and in the light of his previous misdemeanours. His punishment was banishment from Shetland for seven years and to be impressed (press-ganged) into the Royal Navy.

It is owing to Brian Smith's stewardship of Olla's place in these archives that we are able to reconstruct the disturbance through the voluminous legal papers produced for the trial of Smith and his fellow rioters. Shetland Archives has one of the best collections of legal records in Scotland, comprising not only the trial depositions in cases heard in the sheriff court, but the witness statements, or precognitions, taken by the procurator fiscal's officers prior to a court case proceeding. And it is these statements, from defendants, pursuers and witnesses, that provide the grist for the historian's mill, offering a rich description of events that provide an insight into the social and economic relationships of Shetland inhabitants. Although we must bear in mind that the verbatim accounts in the written documents have been 'translated' by the various law officers from the Shetland dialect into acceptable court English, requiring the historian to 'translate back' to hear the more authentic voices of the protagonists, nonetheless these surviving documents are an entry point into the world of ordinary men and women. In this chapter we use the 1805 Yuletide riot as a window onto Shetland society at this time and in particular onto the ways in which labouring men used violence or the threat of violence to assert power in an environment in which they possessed very little. Our focus on an incident discovered amongst the many hundreds of sheriff court records dealing with everything from defamation and assault to theft speaks to the richness of this archive for two social historians who have spent many happy hours in both the original Shetland Archives building, cramped but always welcoming and a good way of immersing oneself in Shetland past and present, and in its new location at Hay's Dock. Moreover, as historians who have been interested in ritual and gender in Shetland in the nineteenth and twentieth centuries, this case throws up some intriguing questions about the ways in which men performed masculinity and regulated social relations in an unequal society.

On the face of it the Cunningsburgh riot was nothing more than a drunken brawl involving men from neighbouring families who already had a tempestuous history. The circumstance from which the riot developed was a gathering of men in the house of Gilbert Duncan at Greenmoe, ostensibly 'to drink a few choppins of Ale which he had prepared for them and to spend the evening in hilarity and friendship'. There was also card playing and dancing. This was Old New Year, a time when Shetlanders, like many Scots, traditionally celebrated with drinking, dances and, on the next day, games of various kinds – most often 'ba' games of the sort we now associate with Kirkwall, Jedburgh and a few places in England like Ashbourne. And it reminds us of the sprees or informal gatherings of men on Whalsay described by the anthropologist Anthony Cohen in the 1980s (Cohen, 1987). These gatherings, especially at Yule, were occasions of semi-organised activities engaged in by men, though most often involving some levels of chaos amidst extreme drunkenness. We can see this in the uninvited arrival of Olla Smith at the house of Duncan along with a band of friends and relatives, already inebriated, immediately disturbing the gathering. One witness, Erick Laurenson, a man who, as we have seen, had already had cause to petition the sheriff court for lawburrows against Smith a few years earlier, stated that 'He heard Olla challenge James [Halcrow] to a fight if he said another word.' Halcrow and his friends 'kept the defenders out of the house by shutting the door and 'by keeping their backs to the door'. Another witness, Hugh Duncan, heard Olla 'vociferously declare that he would take up or fight one half of the company and his cousin Peter Adamson would take up or fight the other half.' Olla Smith was said to have taken 'his handkerchief from his neck and seemed in the act of preparing himself for fighting' with a ritual stripping to the waist ready to wrestle in a way found in many cultures. At the same time, at the other end of the room, there was a dispute about dancing which escalated into a bad-tempered confrontation; the party spilled out of the door and were 'gone out upon the fields in a state of rioting' whereupon men were struck with weapons and Olla Smith's mother was knocked into a ditch. While there is no definitive account of what happened that night, the statement on behalf of the pursuers, Andrew Duncan, James Halcrow and other residents of Aith, offers a vivid portrayal of the encounter:

> Peter Adamson first attacked the petitioner Andrew Duncan with his fists with which he made several blows at him and while he was defending himself from him Charles Adamson the father of Peter came up behind the said Andrew Duncan unknown to him & with a prodigious large club which he brought there with him, he struck him a blow over the forehead which brought him to the ground & deprived him of his senses for a little, but on recovering so much that he could enquire at those around him who it was that had struck him & being informed that it was the said Charles Adamson he took an opportunity soon after enquiring at him if it was he that did it, to which he answered that it was, adding that if he wished any more of the same sort he should get it. That after the said Andrew Duncan had been assisted into the house again the said Peter Adamson followed him there, renewed his threats against him, calling him a scoundrel, rascal & other approbrious [sic] epithets saying that he would beat his soapy head about because he had assisted to take up his father who had been but a few weeks before

committed to Jail at Mr. James Ross Instance to stand trial for an assault committed upon him, and in his way going home that same evening he threatened Laurence Bain for the same thing.

Men formed the overwhelming majority of participants, as perpetrators and victims, in violent acts here as elsewhere in Scotland. Between 1771 and 1882, 542 cases of assault were prosecuted in the Lerwick sheriff court. Men made up the majority of pursuers (400 men to 203 women) and outnumbered female defendants by five to one (582 men to 105 women). Male assaults on women and individual male-on-male acts of violence or threats of violence dominate the cases heard in the sheriff court. An even greater imbalance is to be seen in cases of lawburrows brought before the same court: men constituted 183 of pursuers and 301 defendants while the equivalent numbers of women were 44 and 72. Lawburrows cases are perhaps more indicative than cases of actual assault of the levels of threat of potential violence in society and of the degree to which individuals would resort to legal means to protect themselves.

Moreover, men had a far greater propensity to become involved in collective disturbances in this period, the exception being women's participation in grain riots and other subsistence protests (Logue, 1979). In the Highland context this has been termed 'social banditry' – a resort to collective retribution with few or no rules and far less regulated than traditional feuding (Dodgson, 1989). These kinds of encounters, in which a group of men wreak vengeance on another group of men in a violent confrontation which serves to maintain the honour of the avenging party, were often planned and operated according to an agreed set of rules manifested in ritualised behaviour (Wilson, 2003). The Cunningsburgh riot is one of those occasions. There are many elements contained in the accounts of both sides of the story that conform to patterns of recreational violence seen elsewhere in Scotland amongst men: ritualistic confrontation, concepts of fair play, a sense of grievance or retribution, family or kin loyalty, all lubricated by alcohol, exacerbated by the availability of weapons which may have been tools or items in everyday use such as the 'hand spikes, Kempston Barrs [i.e. capstan bars], Flails & knives' referred to by Smith in his evidence, and played out in a recreational context (Abrams, 2013).

Interpersonal violence and the threat of violence between men in Shetland in the late eighteenth and early nineteenth centuries was not uncommon. The use of the law of lawburrows, essentially a restraining order to prevent a threat (usually of violence) being carried out, whereby the defendant was required to pay a caution if found guilty by the sheriff, peaked in 1799 in Shetland – though increasingly this law seems to have been used by spouses and servants presumably as a means of protection against a violent partner or employer. Cases of actual assault which came before the sheriff, on the other hand, rose exponentially from the 1840s, possibly to be explained by a trend towards prosecution in order to effect punishment in the courts rather than on the streets and hills of Shetland. The Cunningsburgh riot, however, took place at a time when only a handful of assault cases were prosecuted each year prior to the imposition of civic and religious control in Shetland (Brown, 1998, pp.126-129). It contains many elements of violent confrontation that conform to what historians have described as a 'rough-and ready seventeenth-century manhood' in contrast with a 'a polite and civil eighteenth century masculinity' that began to emerge amongst the middling classes and gentry in Scotland from mid-century. (Harvey, 2005; Abrams, 2013, pp.103-104). This was a masculinity that used violence as a legitimate means of avenging a slight or grievance, and to protect or affirm status. This kind of interpersonal violence has been described as customary amongst certain groups of men whereby they acted out codes of manhood in a public display of physical power and status. The high level of ritual signified the importance of the occasion, and was quite apparent from the law's obliviousness to these rules of fighting. For the participants it was maintaining well-grounded custom into the modern era.

One thing to note is that fighting and rioting at New Year seems to have been common throughout Scotland in the eighteenth and early nineteenth centuries. The Cunningsburgh riot was unusual in being so minutely recorded by the legal officers of the sheriff court. This was probably because one of the participants was quite badly hurt but also, in a stroke of serendipity, one of those present in the house was himself a sheriff's officer, Laurenson Jaimeson, leading more readily to court proceedings. But the context for this riot was likely no different to similar events taking place on such a night in many parishes. Clearly the time of year, the taking of drink and the presence of longstanding rivalries and grievances amongst the parties, all played a part in fuelling the incident, turning it from a bad-tempered encounter into a full-blown case of violent assault involving weapons and causing bodily harm.

In this particular case, the careful code governing the build-up, conduct and end to fighting spoke to the rules each participant knew and had to negotiate with care: the challenge to fight, the move to the pitch dark outdoors for more room, and, most notably, a highly ritualised invitation by a beaten or scared participant to a more powerful opponent to dance – thereby being submissive and ending their bout of violence. We have already seen how Olla Smith was reported to have challenged the other men to a fight, removing his neckerchief 'and seemed in the act of preparing himself for fighting.' But another piece of evidence provided by one of the defendants, Peter Adamson, contains multiple elements of this kind of customary violence: challenges to another's manhood, stripping to the waist to prepare for a fist fight, and the use of weaponry. Adamson asserted that Malcolm Halcrow attempted to defuse the confrontation between Smith and Andrew Duncan outside the house:

> Malcolm Halcrow coming to him [Smith] at the same instant, advised him to put on his clothes and come away with him which he accordingly did – and thereafter coming to the door, they both got admittance again into the house when Andrew Duncan ran up with a flail in his hand, & asked him if he was for fighting now to which he replied are you the man, which he said he was if he had not received a wound by a stroke

from the Respondent's father, when he replied Andrew you are not the man & better drop it. - upon which words Malcolm Halcrow called a reel, & took the Respondent as a party in it, and all disputes were dropped and thereafter the respondent went home.

The description of Duncan's challenge 'are you the man' – 'Is du da man?' in Shetland dialect – and Smith's counter 'you are not the man' – 'du is not da man' - suggests that being willing to fight was part and parcel of a model of manhood cleaved to by at least some of the men involved in this riot and is a feature seen elsewhere in violent encounters. Similar challenges can be found elsewhere such as that by John Williamson to George MacLennan in the county of Moray in 1844 when the former provoked MacLennan by saying 'he was a tailor and not a man' gave rise to a violent response from MacLennan: 'Answered him that if he would not be quiet I would show to him what I was.' MacLennan then struck Williamson in the face with a spade (National Records of Scotland, SC25/56/1: Dingwall Sheriff Court: Criminal Court Indictments). This is an incident which, on the face of it, is about George MacLennan's sense of manhood and his belief that he was being insulted by a manual worker who questioned his manliness by casting aspersions on his occupation as a tailor. Fuelled by alcohol, MacLennan challenged his detractor with the implication that he would demonstrate his manliness in a physical way. When Williamson refused to retract his remarks or to give way to MacLennan's authority, the incident descended into a struggle. This was a random violent spat sparked by a comment on MacLennan's manliness which he interpreted as an insult and which required he take steps to redeem his honour. An apology from Williamson might have sufficed to satisfy MacLennan's wounded pride but when this was not forthcoming MacLennan, with a few drams inside him, believed a physical assault was justified. And having been quite seriously wounded, Williamson sought his satisfaction through the courts.

But more intriguing here, and possibly distinctive to Shetland, is Halcrow's calling of a reel or dance to defuse the tensions. Did Halcrow represent a mood of modernity ill-disposed to sustained atavistic fighting? There had been dancing in the house before Smith had arrived to disrupt proceedings.

Robert McPherson was dancing on the floor, and Robert McPherson said that no persons should dance upon the floor, so long as he pleased to keep the floor, when the Respondent [Smith] answered it was a pity that no person should dance but him. Then Hugh Duncan rising from the fire, menacing his fist in the Respondent's face, said you damn'd Villain if you speak one more word more I have as many men here as can tye you hand & foot and carry you to the Tolbooth of Lerwick, and called the Respondent twice a theiff [sic], which Laurence Halcrow in Blasta & Francis Johnson in Fladabister can witness they heard him say. - Then Gilbert Duncan in Grunmor desired him to walk out of his house, calling him a dog.

Here we have challenge, hesitancy, name-calling, and the calling of a reel for man-on-man dancing to defuse the occasion. There may be other levels of ritual to be dissected here, but there is enough to appreciate the social complexity of such an event. We should be careful to not assume that because this event was called a 'riot' for legal purposes, that it lacked structure, meanings and agreed forms of ritual communication. This was men speaking a long-understood language of behaviour designed to regulate relations amongst themselves.

We might interpret the Cunningsburgh riot and other incidents involving male interpersonal violence in Shetland as rooted in the distinctiveness of Shetland society. As Brian Smith has argued, the Shetland economy from the seventeenth century enmeshed rural peasantry in a system of debt bondage whereby tenants were bound by fishing contracts to sell their fish to their landlords for a poor return. Smith terms this peasant bondage (Smith, 2000). Whilst the absence of rebellion against the system of fishing tenure might suggest an acceptance of the situation, evidence of interpersonal and intercommunal conflict suggests that economic powerlessness found alternative forms of expression.

Conflict over sparse resources was commonplace and Cunningsburgh had its fair share. Just thirty years previous to the Yuletide riot, a pitched battle had taken place on the west side of Cunningsburgh parish, ostensibly over the right to gather *floss* (rushes) from the common land or *scattald*. Access to the resources on this land was critical to tenants' livelihoods in a place where most of the land was poor and these privileges were protected by Shetland's laws (Smith, 2000, p.42). However, whilst the dispute over resources was the spark for this particular conflict, in the case for lawburrows heard by the sheriff the defendants claimed that 'the dispute did not arise originally about Floss, but about some private concerns betwixt [Jerom] Umphray the Pursuer and some of the defenders; and now that the pursuer has found a matter upon a dispute about floss, that he might have the better appearance in wreaking his vengeance upon the defenders and intimidating them hereafter from craving him for his just debts' (Shetland Archives, SC12/6/1771/3). Indeed, the confrontation on the common land or grazings between Umphray and the Cunningsburgh men was underpinned by a grievance over the alleged non-payment of a debt:

> Some of them particularly Laurence Halcrow in Bloberg said ... you are surely come to pay me for what you are owing my father so long for selling horses to you on which Jerome burst most bloodily and said he should pay him well enough then he called to his son (a stout young man) to give him his floss knife and ... [waved it at Bloberg].' Bloberg grabbed a cassie of floss --- 'Jerom again began his cursing and called powerfully for his knives, which luckily had fallen to the ground upon their being first drawn as above, and finding he could not fall upon his

knives, for if he had a Bloody massacre would in all likely hood have ensured. He beat the above Laurence Smith in the face with his fists to the very great effusion of his blood. Here the battle began...

This was not an isolated incident. Just a month or so later to this 'battle' the parishioners of the west side of Cunningsburgh were once again the subject of a lawburrows petition, this time from the landowner, James Scott of Scalloway, who accused 43 men and women of 'having conceived hatred malice and ill will causelessly against the Petitioner, dayly and continually trouble molest and oppress him, by pasturing their horses [Illegible] ... and sheep upon his pasture grounds in the Clift Hills of Cunningsburgh, and within other known bounds, limits and marshes thereof' (Shetland Archives, SC12/6/1772/4: Petition for Lawburrows, 16 January 1772).

These incidents do not conform to the kind of behaviour associated with the prank playing of younger men in Lerwick during Yule in the eighteenth and early nineteenth centuries and which the invented festival of Up-Helly-Aa was designed to contain and ritualise peaceably (Brown, 1998). The majority involved in the 1805 riot were almost all married men in their 30s and 40s, not the youngsters who may have been expected to have engaged in high jinks at new year. These middle-aged men were likely fishermen-crofters, with a precarious living as tenants of landowning merchants, and this gave rise to grievances and antagonisms rather than collective protest. This situation only changed following confiscation of the scattald in the 1870s when crofters on the Sumburgh estate lands revolted, taking the law into their own hands. (Renwanz, 1980; Smith, 2000, p.56).

Oliver Smith was the only participant in the 1805 riot to be significantly hurt by the law – to be imprisoned and banished for seven years on being found 'guilty of a gross breach of His Majesty's peace' 'in respect of the crimes committed by him, and of his public bad character as a riotous and mischievous person, having been more than once laid under Caution of Lawburrow, and among others by Gilbert Duncan, in whose house he excited the riot upon the day above mentioned'. The other assailants were given cautions to 'keep the peace. It seems that Smith's reputation had caught up with him. Smith was imprisoned in the Tolbooth in Lerwick until he was pressed in October 1805 to service on the Royal Navy ship the *Mary*. This was not the end of Olla Smith's story however. Transferred to H.M.S. *Resistance* he deserted in Portsmouth in 1806. On being recaptured some 18 months later, Smith was court martialled and sentenced to 100 lashes though only received 43 because of his 'ill state of health'. In 1808 he was discharged and made his way back to Shetland. Our last sight of Smith in the records is in 1810 when he was once again a prisoner in the Tolbooth and in poor health when he petitioned the sheriff for a surgeon to attend to him.

What does the 1805 riot tell us about the nature of Shetland society and men's place within it? Firstly it suggests that the propensity of men to use violence to settle scores was as much a feature of men's social relationships here in this period as it was elsewhere in Scotland. But secondly, mass brawls like this one suggest the relative weakness of social control in Shetland in the form of religious influence over behaviour and codes of respectability in comparison with the rest of Scotland where enlightenment understandings of public behaviour were already beginning to make inroads into the acceptability of communal violence. Thirdly, Shetland men performed their masculinity in ways that would have been familiar outwith the islands yet, at the same time, they were not afraid of resolving conflict in less conventional ways such as on the dancefloor. And finally, paying close attention to this one event reminds the historian what riches of social interpretation can be gleaned from a relatively minor episode, with tribute to Brian Smith for preserving legal processes that in most of Scotland have been – very sadly – consigned to the pulping machine by late twentieth-century record keepers wanting to prioritise shelf space for more 'serious' crime.

Bibliography

Abrams, Lynn (2013) 'The Taming of Highland Masculinity: Inter-personal Violence and Shifting Codes of Manhood c.1760-1840', *Scottish Historical Review* 92 (1), pp.100-122.

Brown, Callum (1998) *Up-Helly-Aa: Custom, Culture and Community in Shetland*. Manchester, Manchester University Press.

Cohen, Anthony (1987) *Whalsay: Symbol, Segment and Boundary in a Shetland Island Community*. Manchester, Manchester University Press.

Dodgshon, Robert A. (1989) '"Pretense of blude" and "place of thair dwelling": the nature of highland clans, 1500-1745', in R. A. Houston and I. D. Whyte (eds.), *Scottish Society 1500-1800*. Cambridge, Cambridge University Press.

Harvey, Karen (2005) 'The history of masculinity c.1650-1850', *Journal of British Studies* 44, pp.296-311.

Logue, K.J. (1979) *Popular Disturbances in Scotland 1780-1815*. Edinburgh, Edinburgh University Press.

Renwanz, Marsha (1980) 'From Crofters to Shetlanders: the Social History of a Shetland Island Community's Self-Image 1872-1978', PhD thesis, Stanford University, Stanford CA.

Smith, Brian (2000) *Toons and Tenants: Settlement and Society in Shetland, 1299-1899*. Lerwick, The Shetland Times Ltd.

Wilson, Stephen (2003) *Feuding, Conflict and Banditry in Nineteenth-Century Corsica*. Cambridge, Cambridge University Press.

Appendix:
Works by Brian Smith (to date)

1972
'From bourgeois island', *Scottish International*, 5

1976
(editor) Thomas Gifford, *Historical Description of the Zetland Islands* (reprint), Sandwick 1976
'Introduction' in *ibid*.

1977
'Shetland archives and sources of Shetland history', *History Workshop Journal*, 4

1978
'Click-em-in – an explanation of its derivation', *New Shetlander*, 124
'The Shetland question', *Scotia Review*, 20, 1978

1979
'"Lairds" and "improvement" in Shetland in the seventeenth and eighteenth centuries', in T.M. Devine, ed., *Lairds and Improvement in the Scotland of the Enlightenment*, Glasgow
Introduction in Robert L. Johnson, *A Shetland Country Merchant*, Lerwick
Obituary of Prophet Smith, *New Shetlander*, 128

1980
'Stock-stove houses', *Shetland Folk Book*, 7

1981
'Sam Anderson of the Croegreen', *Nortaboot*, 7

1982
'William Moffat and theories of social change in Shetland', *New Shetlander*, 141

1983
'Shetland and the Napier Commission 1883-1983', *New Shetlander*, 145
Review of Withrington, ed., *Shetland and the Outside World, 1469-1969*, *The Shetland Times*, 29 July

1984

'What is a scattald? rural communities in Shetland, 1400-1900', in Barbara E. Crawford, ed., *Essays in Shetland History*, Lerwick

'James Robertson 1873-1911', parts 1-2, *New Shetlander*, 149-50

Review of Smith, *Shetland Life and Trade*, *The Shetland Times*, 13 July

1985

(editor) *Shetland Archaeology, new work in Shetland in the 1970s*, Lerwick

1986

'The Kebister stone, a theory', *New Shetlander*, 157

Review of Hunter, ed., *For the People's Cause*, and Cameron, *Go Listen to the Crofters*, *The Shetland Times*, 20 June

Review of Scott, *The True Romance of Busta*, *The Shetland Times*, 28 November

1987

(editor) John Stewart, *Shetland Place-names*, Lerwick

'Introduction' in *ibid*.

'Shetland and the Crofters Act', in L. Graham, ed., *Shetland Crofters*, Lerwick

Review of Goldman, *Lister Ward*, *The Shetland Times*, 6 February 1987

Review of Crawford, *Scandinavian Scotland*, 7 August

'The tarry kirk' (career of William Alexander Grant), *The Shetland Times*, 24 December

'The archdeacon of Kebister', *New Shetlander*, 160

Review of Thomson, *History of Orkney*, *New Shetlander*, 162

1988

'Shetland in saga time: re-reading Orkneyinga saga', *Northern Studies*, 25

With Olwyn Owen, 'Kebister, Shetland: an armorial stone and an archdeacon's teind-barn', *Post-medieval Archaeology*, 22

'Kirstie Caddel's Christmas: "National prosperity" and mid-Victorian Shetland', *Shetland Folk Book*, 8

'The humble cuttell', *New Shetlander*, 165

'Bismars and pundars', *New Shetlander* 166

Review of Wylie, *The Faroe Islands*, *The Shetland Times*, 28 January

1989

'In the tracks of Bishop Andrew Pictoris of Orkney, and Henry Phankouth, archdeacon of Shetland', *Innes Review*, 40

Review of Crawford, ed., *St Magnus Cathedral*, *The Shetland Times*, 20 January 1989

Review of Fenton, *The Turra Coo*, *The Shetland Times*, 15 December

1990

'Shetland, Scotland and Scandinavia, 1400-1700: the changing nature of contact', in Grant G. Simpson, ed., *Scotland and Scandinavia 800-1800*, Edinburgh

'The development of literature in Shetland', parts 1-2, *New Shetlander*, 174-5

Review of Renaud, tr., *La Saga des Orcadiens*, *The Shetland Times*, 12 October

Brian Smith at Houlland, Unst.

Copyright: Ian Tait

1991

'Shetland, Christianity in', in Nigel M. de S. Cameron et al., eds., *Dictionary of Scottish Church History*, Edinburgh

Review of Armit, ed., *Beyond the Brochs*, *The Shetland Times*, 19 July

1992

(editor) with Laurence Graham, *MacDiarmid in Shetland*, Lerwick

'Stony limits: the Grieves in Whalsay', in *ibid*.

'Adam Smith's rents from the sea', in T.C. Smout, ed., *Scotland and the Sea*, Edinburgh

'Up-helly-a'', *Up-Helly-A' Programme*, and subsequent years

'Kebister—a short history', *Shetland Life*, 135

'Handigert and Kebister', *Shetland Life*, 137

'Who was Luggie?' *New Shetlander*, 179.

'The dreadful death of Jean Moffat', *The Shetland Times*, 10 January

Report concerning Viking Congress, *The Shetland Times*, 22 May

Review of Anderson, *Black Patie*, *The Shetland Times*, 9 October 1992

1993

'Up-Helly-A'—separating the facts from the fiction', *The Shetland Times*, 22 January

Obituary of Gordon Donaldson, *The Shetland Times*, 26 March

Review of Fojut and Pringle, *The Ancient Monuments of Shetland*, *The Shetland Times*, 23 April

'The vanishing toonmel', in Hugh Cheape, ed., *Tools and Tradition*, Edinburgh

'Shetland', in Philip Pulsiano and Kirsten Wolf, eds., *Medieval Scandinavia: an encyclopedia*, New York and London

1994

(editor) with John H. Ballantyne, *Shetland Documents 1580-1611*, Lerwick

Review of Donaldson, *Isles of Home* and Sandilands, *Whit? dee a nurse? The Shetland Times*, 16 December 1994

1995

(editor) with John Graham, *Shetland Folk Book*, 9

'Waithing and waith in Shetland, with a note on waifs', in *ibid*.

'The last of the Shetland aristocrats', in Barbara E. Crawford, ed., *Northern Isles Connections: essays from Orkney and Shetland presented to Per Sveaas Andersen*, Kirkwall

'Scandinavian place-names in Shetland, with a study of the district of Whiteness', in Barbara E. Crawford, ed., *Scandinavian settlement in Northern Britain*, Leicester

Obituary of Alan Bruford, *The Shetland Times*, 26 May

1996

'The development of the spoken and written Shetland dialect: a historian's view", in Doreen Waugh, ed., *Shetland's Northern Links: language and history*, Edinburgh

Obituary of George Gear, *The Shetland Times*, 5 January

Obituary of T.M.Y. Manson, *The Shetland Times*, 26 January

Review of Thomson, ed., *Lord Henry Sinclair's Rental*, *The Shetland Times*, 14 June, and *Orcadian*, 20 June

1998

'Camphor, cabbage leaves and vaccination: the career of Johnie "Notions" Williamson of Hamnavoe, Eshaness, Shetland', *Proceedings of the Royal College of Physicians of Edinburgh*, 28

Appreciation of George Mackay Brown, *New Shetlander*, 204

Review of Barnes, *The Norn Language of Orkney and Shetland*, *The Shetland Times*, 13 March

Review of Kendall, *With Naught but Kin behind Them*, *The Shetland Times*, 8 May

Review of Graham, *A Vehement Thirst after Knowledge*, *The Shetland Times*, 14 August

'Tracking down what's in a name ...', *The Shetland Times*, 14 August

Review of Forsyth, *Language in Pictland*, *The Shetland Times*, 25 September

Review of John J. Graham and Laurence I. Graham, eds., *A Shetland Anthology*, The Shetland Times Ltd, 24 December

1999

(editor) with John H. Ballantyne, *Shetland Documents 1195-1579*, Lerwick

'18th and 19th-century Shetland: the historical background', *Vernacular Building*, 23

'Earl Robert and Earl Patrick in Shetland: good, bad or indifferent?' *New Orkney Antiquarian Journal*, 1

Chapters in Olwyn Owen and Christopher Lowe, eds., *Kebister, the four-thousand-year-old story of one Shetland township*, Edinburgh

Obituary of Grace Halcrow, *The Shetland Times*, 22 January

Review of Cox, *The Language of the Ogam Inscriptions of Scotland*, *The Shetland Times*, 30 April

2000

Toons and Tenants: settlement and society in Shetland, 1299-1899, Lerwick

'Writing about MacDiarmid in Shetland', *New Shetlander*, 212

Obituary of Ronald Cant, *The Shetland Times*, 14 January

2001

'The Picts and the martyrs: did vikings kill the native population of Orkney and Shetland?' *Northern Studies*, 36; http://www.orkneyjar.com/history/ vikingorkney/warpeace/index.html

'The not-so-secret scroll: priceless relic or floorcloth?' *Orcadian*, 29 March; http://www.orkneyjar.com/history/historicalfigures/henrysinclair/kirkwallscroll2.htm

Review of Fereday, ed., *The Diary of Samuel Laing*, *The Shetland Times*, 16 March

Review of novels of Freeman Wills Croft, *The Shetland Times*, 29 June

Review of *New Selected Letters* of Hugh MacDiarmid, *The Shetland Times*, 7 September

Review of MacKie, *The roundhouses, brochs and wheelhouses of Atlantic Scotland*, *Scottish Archaeological Journal*, 24

Review of McManus, *Jo Grimond*, *The Shetland Times*, 16 November

Review of Thomson, *New History of Orkney*, *The Shetland Times*, 14 December

'At last - the collected Lollie Graham', *Shetland Post*, 4

2002

With Kristina Soderpalm, 'Captain Gustav Ekeberg's sojourn in Shetland, 1745', *Review of Scottish Culture*, 14

'The 1299 letter about Papa Stour: a note', in Barbara E. Crawford, ed., *Papa Stour and 1299: commemorating the 700th anniversary of Shetland's first document*, Lerwick

'Earl Henry Sinclair's fictitious voyage to America', *New Orkney Antiquarian Journal*, 2; revised version at http://www.alastairhamilton.com/sinclair.htm

'Dialect in the novels of John Graham: a note and a tribute', *New Shetlander*, 221

Contribution in Allan I. Macinnes et al., eds., *Scotland and the Americas, c.1650 - c.1939*, Edinburgh

'Thinking about Shetland brochs', *Hentins*, 2

Review of Crawford, ed., *The Papar in the North Atlantic*, *The Shetland Times*, 11 October

2003

'Martin, Brand and Shetland', in *Martin Martin - 300 years on*, Ness

'Not welcome at all: vikings and the native population in Orkney and Shetland', in Jane Downes and Anna Ritchie, eds., *Sea Change: Orkney and Northern Europe in the later Iron Age AD300-800*, Balgavies

'Archdeacons of Shetland 1195-1567', in Steinar Imsen, ed., *Ecclesia Nidrosiensis 1153-1537*, Trondheim

'Pilot whales, udal law and custom in Shetland', *Northern Studies*, 23

'Whale driving in Shetland and the Faroes', *Shetland Sea Mammal Report*, 2003

'Holy Moses! Orkney historians on medieval Orkney', *New Orkney Antiquarian Journal*, 3

Review of Ekrem and Mortensen, eds., *Historia Norwegie*, *The Shetland Times*, 9 May

Review of Morton, *The Further North you go*, *The Shetland Times*, 19 September

'Udal law: salvation or romantic fiction?' *The Shetland Times*, 3 October

'Taxing German merchants in 17th century Shetland', *Hentins*, 6

2004

'The clearances in Shetland', parts 1-2, *Coontin Kin*, 52-3

'Anderson, Thomas James (1910–1991)', *Oxford Dictionary of National Biography*, Oxford

'Burgess, (James John) Haldane (1862–1927)', *Oxford Dictionary of National Biography*, Oxford

'Manson, (Thomas) Mortimer Yule (1904–1996)', *Oxford Dictionary of National Biography*, Oxford

'Jamieson, Christina (1864–1942)', *Oxford Dictionary of National Biography*, Oxford

'Saxby, Jessie Margaret Edmondston (1842–1940)', *Oxford Dictionary of National Biography*, Oxford

'Williamson, John (c.1730–c.1796)', *Oxford Dictionary of National Biography*, Oxford

'Williamson, Laurence (1855–1936)', *Oxford Dictionary of National Biography*, Oxford

Review of Wallace-Murphy and Hopkins, *Templars in America*, *The Shetland Times*, 24 December

Review of Manson et al., 'The revolutionary art of the future: rediscovered poems by Hugh McDiarmid', *New Shetlander*, 227

'"Eels": strange masterpiece', *New Shetlander*, 230

2005

'Something more romantic: origins of Up Helly Aa revisited', *New Shetlander*, 231

'"Wir ain auld language" - attitudes to Shetland dialect since the nineteenth century', in Shetland Arts Trust, *Dialect 04*, Lerwick

Review of Housley et al., eds., *Atlantic Connections and Adaptations*, *The Shetland Times*, 12 March

Review of Abrams, *Myth and Materiality in a Woman's World: Shetland 1800-2000*, *The Shetland Times*, 11 November

Review of Gear, *John Walker's Shetland*, *The Shetland Times*, 23 December

Review of Turner et al., eds., *Tall Stories*, *New Shetlander*, 233

Foreword in John Stewart, *Folklore from Whalsay and Shetland*, Lerwick

2006

'The Halcrow family of the South Mainland of Shetland', parts 1-2, *Coontin Kin*, 59-60

'Gibbets and gallows: local rough justice in Shetland, 800-1700', http://normblog.typepad.com/normblog/2006/09/gibbets_and_gal.html

'Bulter, Rhoda', and 'Spence, Catherine Stafford', in Ewan et al., eds., *Biographical Dictionary of Scottish Women*, Edinburgh

Review of Gammeltoft et al., eds., *Cultural Contacts in the North Atlantic*, *The Shetland Times*, 10 February

Review of Waite, *Peter Tait*, *The Shetland Times*, 17 March

Review of Fojut, *Prehistoric and Viking Shetland*, *The Shetland Times*, 16 June
'Laurence Williamson of Mid Yell', *New Shetlander*, 237

2007

'Stobister, Sinnabist and Starrapund: three wilderness settlements in Shetland', in Beverley Ballin Smith et al., eds., *West over Sea: studies in Scandinavian sea-borne expansion and settlement before 1300*, Leiden
'An intriguing monument', *Unkans*, 1
'The mysterious Black's Castle', *Unkans*, 2
Article about conference and Festschrift in honour of Barbara Crawford, *The Shetland Times*, 23 February
'Opinion divided on the big question over Shetland's historical origins', *The Shetland Times*, 30 November
Introduction in *Da Book o Trows*, Lerwick

2008

Review of Charlton, *Travels in Shetland, 1832-1852*, *The Shetland Times*, 1 February
Obituary of John Graham, *The Shetland Times*, 22 February
Review of Thomson, *Orkney Land and People*, *The Shetland Times*, 11 April
Review of Scott, *Gardie*, *New Shetlander*, 243
Review of Jamieson, *Nort Atlantic Drift*, *New Shetlander*, 243
Review of Davis, *The Early English Settlement of Orkney and Shetland*, *The Shetland Times*, 9 May
'How German merchants ran local trade', *The Shetland Times*, 13 June
Review of Wolfson, *Tacitus, Thule and Caledonia*, *New Shetlander*, 246

2009

'Andrew Wawn, shrieks and Radio Moscow', in Cook at al., eds., *Wawnarstræti (allar leið til Íslands)*, Reykjavík
'Bagheera, bad boys and Bulldog: problematical reminiscences', *New Shetlander*, 249
'On the nature of tings: Shetland's law courts from the middle ages until 1611', *New Shetlander*, 250
'A tribute to Lollie Graham', *The Shetland Times*, 13 November
'Rough justice' (about Gallow Hill, Fetlar), *Unkans*, 16

2010

'When did Orkney and Shetland become part of Scotland? a contribution to the debate', *New Orkney Antiquarian Journal*, 5
'The facts in the case of Arentsburg', *New Shetlander*, 252
'"Not a gate but a grind!" Gilbert Goudie: an exiled banker-antiquarian in Edinburgh', *New Shetlander*, 253
Review of Harding, *The Iron Age Round-house*, *New Shetlander*, 253
'Who was Gregory "Keeker"?', *Unkans*, 21
Obituary of Tommy Watt, *Museums Journal*, August
(editor) with Turið Sigurðardottir, *Jakob Jakobsen in Shetland and the Faroes*, Lerwick

2011

'A racist in Bressay: James Hunt's anthropological expedition to Shetland in 1865', *New Shetlander*, 256
'Earl Rognvald, Shetland and other problems', *New Shetlander*, 257
'Some Shetland heiresses, 1360-1660', *New Shetlander*, 258
'John Paul Jones and the Mousa men', *Unkans*, 29
Thomas Woore: an artist-surveyor in Shetland, 1828 (exhibition leaflet)

'Hákon Magnusson's root-and-branch reform of public institutions in Shetland, c.1300', in Steinar Imsen, ed., *Taxes, Tributes and Tributary Lands in the Making of the Scandinavian Realm in the Middle Ages*, Trondheim 2011

'Violent vikings and squeamish scholars' (paper given at St Magnus Conference, Kirkwall, 2011)

2012

Review of Hobbs and Thompson, *Out of the Burning House*, New Shetlander, 259

Review of Manson ed., *Dear Grieve*, New Shetlander, 259

Review article, Tait, *Shetlander Vernacular Buildings*, New Shetlander, 260

'The Nidaros church and "Norgesveldet": Shetland, 1320-1470', in Steinar Imsen, ed., *Ecclesia Nidrosiensis and 'Noregs veldi': the role of the church in the making of Norwegian domination in the Norse world*, Trondheim 2012

'Shetland's tings', in Olwyn Owen, ed., *Things in the Viking World*, Lerwick 2012

'Zetland zombies', *Shetland Life*, 278

Foreword in Stewart, *Shetland Fireside Tales*, Lerwick

Obituary of Mary Prior, *The Shetland Times*, 13 January

2013

Review of Anderson, *The Stewart Earls*, New Shetlander, 263

Review of Sutherland, *Morton Lodge*, New Shetlander, 263

Review of Crawford, *The Northern Earldoms*, New Shetlander, 266

'Dull as ditch water or crazily romantic: Scottish historians on Norwegian law in Shetland and Orkney', in Steinar Imsen, ed., *Legislation and State Formation. Norway and its neighbours in the middle ages*, Trondheim

'Did Henry Mayhew come to Shetland?', *Unkans*, 38

'Goings-on at Grevavoe', *Unkans*, 41

'Wadmal'; 'Stockings and mittens, 1580-1851'; 'The truck system'; in Laurenson, ed., *Shetland Textiles*, Lerwick

2014

Review of Sutherland, *Mirth, Madness & St Magnus*, New Shetlander, 268

Review article, Smith, *The Literature of Shetland*, New Shetlander, 269

Foreword in *Hairst is Coosed. The Rhoda Bulter collection*, Lerwick

With Eileen Brooke-Freeman, '"Butter" names in Shetland', *Unkans* 43

'Furious radical: John Sands in Shetland 1883-1893', *Unkans*, 44

'600 years of incoming in Shetland', in *Incoming, some Shetland Voices*, Lerwick

2015

'The campaign for a Town Hall in Lerwick, 1880-1887', *New Shetlander*, 272

Review of Thompson, *Work, Sex & Power*, New Shetlander, 274

'How not to reconstruct the Iron Age in Shetland: modern interpretations of Clickhimin Broch' (tenth Hermann Pálsson lecture [2014]), *Northern Studies*, 47

'Totally dumbfounded' in *Gamanleikir Terentíusar, settir upp fyrir Terry Gunnell, sextugan 7 Júlí 2015*, Reykjavik

'Doreen Waugh 1944-2015', in *Journal of Scottish Name Studies*, 9

'Poetry in the languages and dialects of Northern Scotland; Shetland', in Sassi, ed., *The International Companion to Scottish Poetry*, Glasgow

'John Murdoch - friend of crofters', *Unkans*, 50

'Mapping Shetland' (about Ordnance Survey), *Unkans*, 52

'Gifford Laurenson's brochs', *Unkans*, 53

2016

'Did the broch of Mousa have a roof? – and why not!' *New Shetlander*, 276

'Doreen Waugh: an appreciation', in *Shetland and the Viking World, papers from the proceedings of the seventeenth Viking Congress*, Lerwick

'"An idea original and sympathetic": Viking Congresses and their transformations, 1950-2013', in *Shetland and the Viking World, papers from the proceedings of the seventeenth Viking Congress*, Lerwick

Obituary of William P.L. Thomson, *The Shetland Times,* 15 July

Biographical essay about Hugh Marwick in reprint of *Orkney Farm-Names*, Kirkwall

'Swinburgh or Soundburgh!' *Unkans*, 55

'Charles Forret - "a superb calligrapher"' *Unkans*, 56

'The fall of the house of Vaila', *Unkans*, 57

'Placenames man [Bill Nicolaisen] sparkled with wit', *The Shetland Times*, 26 February

2017

'David Sanderson Scott of Reafirth and his family', *Coontin Kin*, 105

'Viking genocide: the enigma and fate of the Picts in Shetland during the Viking Age', *Hugin and Munin*, 1

2018

'Surly Cunningsburgh: a lingering reputation', *New Shetlander*, 284

With John Ballantyne, 'The collection of falcons and "hawk hens" in Shetland and Orkney, 1472-1840', in Grimm, ed., *Raptor and Human*, Hamburg

'Willie Thomson: historian of Orkney and Shetland', *New Orkney Antiquarian Journal*, 8

'Viking genocide', *60 North*, 22-3

2019

'The historical evidence' in S. Dockill, ed., *Excavations at Old Scatness, Shetland: the post-medieval township*, Lerwick

'Horse Holm or Swine Holm?', *Shetland Life*, 461

'Shetland and her German merchants, c.1450-1710', in Natascha Mehler et al., eds, *German Trade in the North Atlantic c.1400-1700. Interdisciplinary perspectives*, Stavanger

'The Unst lay: ancient verse, or the earliest Shetland dialect poem?', *Northern Studies*, 50

'Stumps and stations: stoo-names in Orkney and Shetland', *Orcadian*, 18 and 25 July

Review of *At the Bridge: James Teit and the anthropology of belonging*, *New Shetlander*, 290

2020

Article about Kirsty Caddell junior, *The Shetland Times*, 10 April

Demonstrations in Lerwick, *The Shetland Times*, 17 April

Up Helly Aa, *The Shetland Times*, 1 May

'*Dispecta est Thule* …' *The Shetland Times*, 22 May

Career of Ninian Neven, *The Shetland Times*, 29 May

Profile of James Teit, *The Shetland Times*, 12 June

Careers of Peter Adamson and Olla Smith, *The Shetland Times*, 3 July

'Stone Age scholar Calder', *The Shetland Times*, 17 July

With Alan Beattie, Dutch sources, *The Shetland Times*, 31 July

Amiable Vikings, *The Shetland Times*, 7 August

Church choir strike, *The Shetland Times*, 21 August

Obituary of Raymond Lamb, *The Shetland Times*, 30 October

Obituary of Euan MacKie, *The Shetland Times*, 13 November

Paper about Lochend, *The Shetland Times*, 24 December

2021

Introduction in Jamieson, *Letters on Shetland*, Melby

Obituary of John Hedges, *The Shetland Times*, 5 February

Obituary of Jim Irvine, *The Shetland Times*, 1 October

Books of my life, *The Shetland Times*, June

2022

'Þursasker - a note', in Christian Cooijmans, ed., *Islands of Place and Space. A Festschrift in honour of Arne Kruse*, Edinburgh

With Danny Jamieson, 'Steelnaheelenagro and Skuldigert: rough justice in medieval Shetland', *New Shetlander*, 298

Review of Sutherland, *Shapansay Square-Dance*, *New Shetlander*, 298

Lecture (UHI) on Shetland in Sagas, April

2023

'"As he came, so, mysteriously, did he vanish": John George Glass, teacher in Lerwick, 1842-54', *Northern Scotland*, 14

Obituary of Willie Thompson, *The Shetland Times*, 30 June

'No mystery about whodunnit: the Fox Lane murders of 1858', *New Shetlander*, 301

Forthcoming, '"God knowis my sleipis ar short and unsound": Andro Smyth's collection of rent, tax and tithe in Shetland, c.1640', in Harriet Cornell, et al., eds., *Agriculture, Economy and Society in Early Modern Scotland*, Woodbridge

Lecture at REMRA event, Kirkwall

Obituary of Douglas Sinclair, *Shetland News*, 8 September

Lecture on Shetland-Faroe links, UHI symposium, 22 September

2024

Lecture 'Shetland and the north boats', Shetland Maritime Heritage Society, 22 February

Lecture 'The last days of the German trade in Shetland and the origins of a Shetland merchant class', Shetland Museum and Archives, 7 March

Lecture 'In da nips: "W.H." on the *Sarah and Elizabeth* in 1857', UHI St Magnus Conference, 18 April

Index

A

Aberdeen, 171
Adam Clarke Memorial Church, 186
Adam of Bremen, 16
Adamson, Charles, 196
Adamson, Peter, 196, 198
Aith, Cunningsburgh, 196
Aith Methodist Chapel, 186
Aithsting, 90, 163, 172
Alexander of Clapham, 21
Almqvist, Bo, 151
Althing of Shetland *see* Lawting of Shetland
Amsterdam, 98
Ancesti, 53
Anderson, Peter, 108
Anderson, Tom, 157
Antigua, 183
Asbjørnsen, P.C., 155ff
Ashbourne, Derbyshire, 196
Ashipattle, 158
Asker, Viken, 53
Asta, 51
Ása, 62-63, 66

B

ba games, 196
Bailasta, 40, 44, 88ff
Bailister, 50-51
Bain, Laurence, 197
Baller, Johan, 100
Balta, 9
Baltasound, 91
Banks of Garth, 179

Barber, John, 3
Bardister, 51
Barkland, 164
Barnes, Michael, 138
Basta, 45
Battle of Summerdale, 117
Bayhall, 184
Beaker folk, 164
Benston, 49
Beowulf, 153
Bergen, 20-25, 97-100, 102-104
Bergen court book 1592-1594, 107n
Bibre, Paul, 68
Bigton, 117
Birsay, 3, 19-20, 163
Bishop's Palace, 127
Black Death, 111, 170
Bloberg, 200
Blosta, 199
Bokn, Rogaland, 71
Bøyg legend, 153ff
Braby, Alan, 12
Breibister, 176
Bremen, 98, 100
Brindister, 53-54
British Columbia, 171
British Isles, 39
brochs, 1ff, 92
Broch of Channerwick, 5
Bronze Age, 29
Broo *see* Brow
Brough, 46
Brough of Birsay, 3

Brough of Deerness, 3, 34
Brow, 54-55, 116ff
Bruce, H.A., 189
Bruce, Laurence, 108ff
Bruce of Cultmalindie *see* Bruce, Laurence
Bruse Sigurdsson, 16, 17
Bu, Orkney, 4
Bull, Edvard, 19
burials, 29, 32-34
Burravoe, 100, 188
Burrows, Bamford, 189
Busta, Delting, 47
Busta, Fair Isle, 162, 163, 167, 168

C

Cairns, South Ronaldsay, 6, 8
Caithness, 3, 11, 18, 20, 39, 73-74
Calback, 21
Caldback, 94
Calf of Daaey, 72
Calf of Grunay, 72
Calf of Linga, 72
Calf of Score Holm, 72
Calmar Union, 109, 111
Calsta, 46
Cant, Ronald, 22
Cecilia Sverresdotter, 20
Channel Islands, 71
Channerwick, 5, 8, 81
Christian IV, 107n, 109n
Christian V, 107
Christianity, 17, 19, 32-34, 83-84
Church of Scotland, 167, 183
Clachtoll, Sutherland, 5, 6, 10
Clarke, Adam, 185
Clickimin, 4
Clift Hills, Cunningsburgh, 201
Clousta, 49-50
Cohen, Anthony, 196
Collaster 175ff
Cologne, 31
Cooper, Davy, 151
Corsies of Orkney, 163

Court Book of Shetland, 1602-1604 (Donaldson), 107, 108
Carysfort (H.M.S), 183
Crawford, Barbara, 15, 16, 68
Crofters' Act (1886), 190
Crosskirk, Caithness, 6
Cruisdale, 179
Culbin, Fife, 118
Cumbrae, 73
Cunningsburgh, 165, 194ff
cystic fibrosis, 172

D

Dales Voe, 28
David Haraldsson, 20
Deerness, 3
Delting, 90, 163, 165, 187
Denmark, 16, 38
Die Hard movies, 153
Domra, 109ff
Donaldson, Gordon, 107
Dorset, 171
Duncan, Andrew, 194, 196, 198-199
Duncan, Gilbert, 195, 199, 201
Duncan, Hugh, 196, 199
Duncan, John, 187-188
Dunrossness, 113, 117, 162, 165, 171, 189
Dun Vulan, South Uist, 5
Durham, county of, 171

E

Eadgar the Peaceful, 34
Earl Patrick *see* Stewart, Patrick
Earl Robert *see* Stewart, Robert
Earl's Palace, 127
Earls' Saga see Orkneyinga Saga
Edinburgh, 166, 171
Egilsay, 71
Eigersund, Rogaland, 52
Einar Ragnvaldsson, 14
Einar Sigurdsson, 16
Einarr of Gulberwick, 66-67
El Gran Grifón, 161, 163

Elizabeth II, 165
Elvister, 52
Erasmus Manisoun, 112
Erik II, 22
Erik III, 21
Erik XII, 22
Erik Magnusson *see* Erik II
Erik Magnusson *see* Erik XII
Erik of Pomerania *see* Erik III
Erlend Thorfinnsson, 17
Erling Vidkunsson, 21
Eunsons of Fair Isle 161ff
Eyrbyggja saga, 153
Eysturoy, Faroe, 94

F

Fair Isle, 41, 75, 125, 161ff
Fairhurst, Horace, 5-6
Farne Islands, Northumberland, 82-83
Faroe, 15, 16, 19, 22, 24, 25, 33, 39, 75, 77, 79, 97-98, 100
Faroe, bishopric of, 20, 22
Faroese language, 139ff
Farsund, Agder, 53
Færøsk Anthologi (Hammershaimb), 145
Fetlar, 74
Fife, 165
Finland, 38
Finnmark, Norway, 175
Fishing tenure, 188, 200
Fífa, 60-61
Fjaler, Vestland, 47, 53
Fladdabister, 199
Flamister, 48
Flateyjarbók, 62, 66
Flotta, 82
Forvie, Aberdeenshire, 118
Foud, 21, 22, 92, 98, 109ff, 117
Foula, 41
Free Church of Scotland, 187

G

Gaelic, 140, 142
Gaila, 168

Gallow Hill, 94-95
Gardiestaing, 90-93
Garrick, John 175ff
Garrick, Peter, 174ff
Gausdal, Innlandet, 47
Geirhildarvatn, 50
Geirhildr Flókisdotter, 50
German merchants, 25, 97ff, 117-118
Gigha, 84-85
Gille, Harald, 17
Giltarump, 77
Girlsta, 50
Gjemnes, Møre og Romsdal, 51
Gjesdal, Rogaland, 44
Gladstone, W.E., 190
Godøya, Møre og Romsdal, 76-79, 84-85
Gosforth stone, 158
Great Quantity Shift, 144ff
Greenland, 16, 19, 39, 71
Greenmow, 194ff
Greig, James, 185
Gremista, Lerwick, 28, 53
Gremista, Quarff, 54
Griesta, 51
Grettis saga, 153
gripstair, 111
Gruting, 184
Grutness, 117
Gudbandsdal, Norway, 154, 156
Gulberwick, 60
Gunnista, 52
Gurness, Orkney, 8
Guthrie, William, 190
Guttorm Sigurdsson, 14

H

haaf fishery, 118
Haggersta, 52
Håkon IV, 85
Håkon V, 20, 22, 110-111
Håkon VI, 22
Håkon Håkonsson (Håkon the Old) *see* Håkon IV
Håkon Magnusson *see* Håkon V

Håkon Magnusson *see* Håkon VI
Halcrow, James, 196
Halcrow, Laurence, 199, 200
Halcrow, Malcolm, 198-199
Halifax, 187
Hamarøy, Nordland, 47
Hamburg, 25, 98
Hamilton, John, 6
Handigert, 35-36
Hangcliff Lane, 186
Hans, 97
Hanseatic trade *see* German merchants
Harald I, 14-16
Harald III, 17, 19
Harald Halfdansson (Harald Fairhair) *see* Harald I
Harald Maddadsson, 18, 20, 61
Harald Sigurdsson *see* Harald III
Hascosay, 99
Hay, Arthur James, 186
Hebrides, 14, 15, 17-18, 39, 56, 71-72, 75
Henderson, Brucie, 151ff
Herdis Torvaldsdotter, 20-21
Hergilsey, Iceland, 71
Hertzberg, Ebbe, 110
Hester, George, 187
Heughe, 116, 120
Hildina ballad, 141
Hildisay, 70
Historia Norwegie, 14
Hjálp, 60-61
Hjeltefjorden, 25
Hobson, George, 188
Holy Land, 60, 66
Home Mission Department, 188
Horse Island *see* Hundholm
Hoversta, Bressay, 52-53
Hoversta, Unst, 44
Howarth, Robert, 187
Howe, 4-6
Hoy, 72, 162
huinzska, 111
Hundholm, 63-64
Husabroo, 116, 133

I

Iceland, 16, 19, 22, 24, 33, 38-39, 71-72, 81, 97, 100
Icelandic language, 139ff
ichthyosis, 172
Indre Østfold, Viken, 46
Inge I, 60
Inge II, 20
Inge Bårdsson *see* Inge II
Inge Haraldsson (Inge the Hunchback) *see* Inge I
Ireland, 33, 84
Irish Land Act, 190
Iron Age, 1ff, 29-30, 36
Irvines of Fair Isle 161ff
Isle of Man, 38-40, 72

J

Jakobsen, Jakob, 41, 56, 139ff
Jæren and Dalane, Norway, 107ff
James III, 139
James, Janet, 183
Jamieson, Christina, 179
Jamieson, Laurenson, 198
Jarlshof, 5-8, 16, 103
Jedburgh, 196
Jesch, Judith, 16
Jews, 169
Johnson, Francis, 199
Jon Haraldsson, 20
Jondal, Norway, 35
Jones, Michael E., 120
Jørmungandr, 158

K

Kale Kolsson *see* Ragnvald Kale Kolsson
Kebister, 28ff, 100-101, 104
Kennemerland, 131
Kik, Gregorius, 20
kings of Norway, 15
Kirkwall, 24, 166, 171, 196
Kitty Ratter's Hill, 177ff
Kolbeinsay, Iceland, 71
Kragerø, Telemark, 47
Kristiansand, Agder, 49, 50

Kristiansson, Reidar Th., 153
Kummertho, Hinrik, 100
Kvitsøy, Rogaland, 74

L

Lamb, H.H., 119, 131, 134
Lamb, Raymond, 3
Langfjelli, Norway, 156
Larvik, Vestfold, 51
laryct aith, 111, 112
Laurenson, Erick, 194, 196
law, 14ff, 107ff, 194ff
lawburrows, 195
Lawman of Shetland, 22-24, 92, 110
Lawrightman, 24, 94
Lawting of Shetland, 18-19, 24
Laxfirth, 99
Leith, 171
Leogh, 168
Lerwick, 139, 183
Lerwick Tolbooth, 199, 201
Leslie, Harald (Lord Birsay), 164
Leslies of Fair Isle 161ff
Lewis, 39, 117
Lewis, John, 184
Liestøl, Knut, 156, 158
Life of Findan, 33-34
lindorm, 157
Linga, 82
Linga Holm, 82
Litla Skalda, 72
Little Ice Age, 120, 131-132, 134
Loch of Cliff, 91
Loch of Houlland, 9
Loch of Huesbreck, 120
Lofoten, Norway, 16
Logmaðr see Lawman of Shetland
London, 183
Longer Magnus saga, 43
Lords of Norway, 21
Lord's Prayer in Norn, 141
Louth, Lincolnshire, 185
Loutit, James 183ff

Low, George, 90, 133, 140-141
Lørja, Arne, 20
Luggie's Knowe, 28, 35
Lumbister, 44
Lund, archbishopric of, 19
Lunnasting, 24, 90
Lübeck, 100, 103
lyritar eið see laryct aith

M

MacCrimmon, Donald, 170
MacKie, Euan, 4
MacLennan, George, 199
Magnus III, 17, 40
Magnus VI, 18, 22, 24
Magnus VII, 21, 22
Magnus Code, 107ff
Magnus Eriksson *see* Magnus VII
Magnus Erlendsson, 17, 68
Magnus Gilbertson, 20
Magnus Håkonsson (Magnus Law-mender) *see* Magnus VI
Magnus Jónsson, 21
Magnus Olafsson, 62-63, 65
Magnus Olavsson (Magnus Bareleg) *see* Magnus III
Mainland, Shetland, 21, 165
Malise II, Earl of Strathearn, 21
M'Allum, Daniel, 184
Margaret, princess, 139
Marwick, Ernest, 158
Marwick, Hugh, 39, 41
Mary (H.M.S.), 201
Mason, John, 186
Mathewson, Andrew Dishington, 152
M'Aulay, Alexander, 188-189
McPherson, Robert, 199
McVities, 171
Meadow Burn, 167
Melchers, Gunnel, 138
Meldal, Trøndelag, 47
Menzies, John, 183
Mester Stoorworm, 157
Methodism, 167, 183ff

Mewburn, William, 186
Mid Yell, 151, 157
Milne, James, 175
Mitchell, John, 180
Moray, 199
Møre, Norway, 16
Morrison, Agnes, 36
Mousa, 4, 7, 12, 29
Muckle Heog, 91
Muness, 103, 117, 127
Munkeliv, Norway, 99

N

Neipnating, 23
Ness of Burgi, 4
Ness of Hamar, 46
Nesting, 24
Netherlands, 163
Newark, 34
New Brunswick, 166, 171
New York, 171
New Zealand, 162, 171
Nicolaisen, W.F.H., 39-40, 82
Nicolson, John, 183-184
Nidaros, archbishopric of, 19, 99
Nikolas, archdeacon of Shetland, 20
Nora, Pierre, 157
Nordal, Sigurður, 68
Nordfjord, Norway, 155
Norn, 138ff
Norske Huldreeventyr og Folkesagn (Asbjørnsen), 155-156
Northmavine, 187
Norway, 14-16, 18, 22, 24-25, 38, 41, 57, 60, 70ff, 100
Norwegian language, 139

O

oaths, 111-113
Oddsta, 45-46
Odin (Óðinn), 67
Ogmund Finnson, 21
Olav I, 15, 17
Olav II, 17, 19

Olav Haraldsson (St Olav) *see* Olav II
Olav Nilsson, 22
Olav Tryggvasson *see* Olav I
Olaw Mansoun, 112
Old Norse, 139ff
Old Scatness Broch, 5, 123
Old Statistical Account, 168
Ong, Walter J., 179-180
Orkney, 3, 7, 14-16, 18, 39-41, 60, 66, 117, 122, 125, 165
Orkney, bishopric of, 19, 24-25, 31-33, 99
Orkney, earldom of, 14-27ff
Orkney, seal of, 24
Orkneyinga saga, 14, 15, 17, 18, 20, 33, 60ff, 75
Orphir, 162
ounceland, 17-18, 23
Out Skerries, 131
Oxensta, 55
Østre Toten, Innlandet, 50

P

Papa Stour, 100, 103, 111
Papa Stour document (1299), 109
Paul Thorfinnsson, 17
Peer Gynt (Ibsen) 153ff
pennyland, 17-18, 23
Pentland Firth, 15, 71-73, 77
Phankouth, Henry, 31-32, 36, 100, 102
Philip, prince, 165
Pictoris, Andrew, 31
Picts, 14-15, 33-34, 73, 162, 163
placenames, 38ff, 70ff
Pool of Virkie, 117
Portsmouth, 201
pottery, 102-104
Presbytery of Shetland, 175
press gang, 195
Ptolemy, 75
Pytheas, 73

Q

Quendale, 117, 122, 132-133, 163
Quendista, 54-55, 116

R

Raefirth, 93
Ragnvald Brusesson, 15
Ragnvald Kale Kolsson (St Ragnvald), 17, 18, 20, 60ff
Ragnvald Øysteinsson (Mørejarl), 14
Ratter, Andrew, 175ff
Ratter, Elspeth, 175ff
Ratter, Kathren, 174ff
Rauðarþing, 23, 93
Reformation, 114
Resistance (H.M.S.), 201
Ringasta, 54
Ritchie, Anna, 16
Romsdal, Norway, 155-156
Ross, James, 197
Rousay, 71
Royal Navy, 183, 195, 201
Rubh an Dunain, 4
Rygh, Oluf, 57

S

Sagnagrunnur database, 151
Samphrey, 71
Sand Methodist Chapel, 185
Sanday, 162
Sandness, 174ff
Sands of Breckon, 103
Sandsting, 112
Sandwick, Orkney, 163
Sandwick, Shetland, 80, 164
Scalloway, 177, 179-180
Scalloway Castle, 6, 103, 127
Scatness, 4, 5, 103, 117
scat, 17, 21
Scatsta, 47
scattald, 200
School of Scottish Studies, 151
Scotland, 38-40, 70ff, 100, 102
Scott, James, 201
Scottish Vowel Length Rule (SVLR), 144ff
Scottish Wars of Independence, 170
Scousburgh, 117
Selbu, Trøndelag, 44
Sella Ness, 47
Sellers, William, 187
settar eið see Sixter aith
Shaftesbury (Lord), 190
Shapinsay, 163
Shetland, archdeaconry of, 31-32, 36, 102
Shetland, lordship of, 21
Shetland Court Book 1602-1604, 108ff
Shetland dialect, 171
Shetland Life under Earl Patrick (Donaldson), 108
Shirva, 162-164
Sigurd Hlodvirsson (Sigurd the Stout), 16, 17, 33
Sigurd Øysteinsson, 14
Sigurðr a Kallbak, 94
Sinclair, Charles, 126
Sinclair, Henry, 21
Sinclair, James, 162
Sinclair, John, 21, 22
Sinclair, Ola, 117
Sinclairs of Broo, 117, 130
sixter aith, 112
Skagafjörður, 46
Skåne, Sweden, 156-157
Skáldskaparmál, 72
Skellister, 48
Smith, Laurence, 201
Smith, Olla, 194ff
Sogndal, Vestland, 48
Sokndal, Rogaland, 51
Solund, Vestland, 71, 81
Solund Sea, 14, 74, 77
Soost, Henrik, 99-100
South Ronaldsay, 71
South Uist, 118
Sør-Fron, Innlandet, 44
Södermanland, Sweden, 89
Spanish Armada, 165
Spences of Windhouse, 152, 158
Sperra, Malise, 21
Springar, Kenert, 100
Springfield, 162, 169, 170

St Andrews, 32, 162
St Kilda, 161, 170, 172
St Magnus Cathedral, 20, 32
St Mary's, 32
St Ninian's Isle, 33
St Sunniva, 19
Stavanger, bishopric of, 19
Stembelshoull, 88ff
Steansgarth, Jean, 163
Steinkjer, Trøndelag, 45
Stephenson, John, 185
Stevenson, Thomas, 170
Stewart, Edward, 32
Stewart, James, 171
Stewart, John, 41, 55-56
Stewart, Patrick, 107ff, 163
Stewart, Robert, 108ff
Stout, Robert, 162
Stouts of Fair Isle 161ff
Strong, James, 167
Stronsay, 163, 171
Sumarlide Sigurdsson, 16
Sumburgh, 63
Sumburgh estate, 201
Sunnfjord, Norway, 155
Sutherland, 39, 74
Sverre, 18, 20, 22
Sverre Sigurdsson *see* Sverre
Sweden, 16, 38
Swirtifield, 179
Sysselmann, 20-22, 109-111
Syslumaðr see Sysselmann

T

taboo language of fishermen, 140
Taft, 167
taxation in the Earldom of Orkney, 17-18, 21, 23
Telemark, Norway, 156
Terence, 32
Thomas Håkonsson, 21
thing see tings
Thor (Þórr), 65, 84, 90, 158
Thorvald Toresson, 109, 111

Thrumster, Caithness, 5, 6
Thvæitaþing (Þvæitaþing), 23
tings, 23, 88ff, 110
Tingaholm, 23, 51, 94
Tingwall, 36, 90, 93, 95, 100, 163
Tobar an Dualchais / Kist o Riches website, 151
Torfinn Sigurdsson (Torfinn the Mighty), 15-18
Torosay, Mull, 84
Tønsberg, Vestfold, 52
Tresta, Aithsting, 50
Tresta, Fetlar, 46
Trondheim, archbishopric of *see* Nidaros, archbishopric of
Trondra, 71
trows, 156-157
Trøndelag, 24, 71
Truck Commission, 189-190
Tulloch, Laurence, 151ff
Tulloch, Tom, 151ff
Tumblin, 9
Tustna, Møre og Romsdal, 71
tylptar eið, 112

U

Ugasta, 46, 56
Ulsta, 45
Umbot, 94-95
Umphray, Jerom, 200
Ungirsta, 43
Unst, 74, 88ff, 102-104, 165, 187
Unst Methodist Chapel, 186
Up-Helly-Aa, 139, 201
Uppsala, 62
Uppsala, archbishopric of, 19
Upper Scalloway, 6
Uyeasound, 95

V

Valdres, Norway, 156
Vatsland, 36
Vementry, 70
Vestre Slidre, Innlandet, 54
Vikings, 33, 38-40, 70ff, 88, 92-93

Viking Genes study, 171
Vinland, 16
Visligarth, 116
Voe of Spiggie, 117
Vollister, 44-45
Voss, Vestland, 53

W

Wales, 71
Walls, 177, 187-188
Walls Methodist Chapel, 186
Weisdale, 112
Wesley, John, 183
West Indies, 183
West Voe of Sumburgh, 117, 122
Westerskeld Methodist Chapel, 186
Westray, 163, 164, 170-172
Westshore, 162
Wethersta, 48

Whale Firth, 45
Whalsay, 163, 165, 196
Whiteness, 99, 112
Wiitstok, Hermen, 100
William the Old, 20
Williamson, John, 199
Williamson, Laurence, 152ff
Williamsons of Fair Isle 161ff
Willom Monssøn, 94
Wilsons of Fair Isle 161ff
Windhouse, 151ff
witchcraft, 111, 114, 174ff
Witney, Oxfordshire, 185

Y

Yell, 41, 74, 157, 165, 170, 187
York, archbishopric of, 19
Yorkshire, 84, 163